OPERA IN THE BRITISH I

To Sue
In Memoriam

Opera in the British Isles, 1875–1918

PAUL RODMELL
University of Birmingham, UK

Routledge
Taylor & Francis Group
LONDON AND NEW YORK

First Published 2013 by Ashgate Publisher

Published 2016 by Routledge
2 Park Square, Milton Park, Abingdon, Oxfordshire OX14 4RN
711 Third Avenue, New York, NY 10017, USA

First issued in paperback 2016

Routledge is an imprint of the Taylor & Francis Group, an informa business

British Library Cataloguing in Publication Data
A catalogue record for this book is available from the British Library

The Library of Congress has cataloged the printed edition as follows:
Rodmell, Paul, author.
Opera in the British Isles, 1875–1918/by Paul Rodmell.
pages cm. — (Music in Nineteenth-century Britain)
Includes bibliographical references and index.
ISBN 978-1-4094-4162-5 (hardcover : alk. paper)
1. Opera—Great Britain—19th century. 2. Opera—
Great Britain—20th century. I. Title.
ML1731.4.R63 2013
782.10941—dc23

2013006007

ISBN 13: 978-1-138-25204-2 (pbk)
ISBN 13: 978-1-4094-4162-5 (hbk)

Contents

List of Figures

List of Tables

Acknowledgements

I should like to thank all the friends who have supported me during the writing and production of this book. In particular I should like to give grateful thanks to the following: all my colleagues at the University of Birmingham; the staff of the various libraries and archives I have used, especially those at my own university, the British Library, the Royal Academy of Music, and the Royal College of Music (especially Paul Collen at the Centre for Performance History). Andrew Tilly and Ian Richards graciously allowed me to retire to the south of France on several occasions to write uninterrupted in a civilised and warm environment, and Duncan Campbell and Duncan Atkinson entertained and accommodated me on countless visits to London; I am very lucky to have such helpful friends!

Finally, I should particularly like to thank John Whenham, my recently retired colleague at Birmingham, who has given me support and encouragement with neither end nor stint, and the Arts and Humanities Research Council, whose decision to award me a Research Fellowship gave me the last essential period of extended research and writing that enabled me – finally – to complete this book.

Paul Rodmell
Birmingham, November 2012

List of Abbreviations

Journals and Newspapers

Published in London unless otherwise stated

BDP	*Birmingham Daily Post* (Birmingham)
DN	*Daily News*
DT	*Daily Telegraph*
FJ	*Freeman's Journal* (Dublin)
HC	*Huddersfield Chronicle* (Huddersfield)
IT	*Irish Times* (Dublin)
MG	*Manchester Guardian* (Manchester)
MH	*Musical Herald*
MoM	*Magazine of Music*
MMR	*Monthly Musical Record*
MN	*Musical News*
MOMTR	*Musical Opinion and Music Trade Review*
MP	*Morning Post*
MS	*Musical Standard*
MT	*Musical Times* [*and Singing-Class Circular*]
MW	*Musical World*
OMR	*Orchestral Music Review*
PMG	*Pall Mall Gazette*
SR	*Saturday Review*
WM	*Western Mail* (Cardiff)

Libraries and Archives

BL	British Library, London
NLI	National Library of Ireland, Dublin, Ireland
NLW	National Library of Wales, Aberystwyth, Wales
RAM	Royal Academy of Music, London
RCM	Royal College of Music, London
ROHA	Royal Opera House Archive, Covent Garden, London
WYAS	West Yorkshire Archive Service (Kirklees), Huddersfield

General Editor's Series Preface

Music in nineteenth-century Britain has been studied as a topic of musicology for over two hundred years. It was explored widely in the nineteenth century itself, and in the twentieth century grew into research with strong methodological and theoretical import. Today, the topic has burgeoned into a broad, yet incisive, cultural study with critical potential for scholars in a wide range of disciplines. Indeed, it is largely because of its interdisciplinary qualities that music in nineteenth-century Britain has become such a prominent part of the modern musicological landscape.

This series aims to explore the wealth of music and musical culture of Britain in the nineteenth century and surrounding years. It does this by covering an extensive array of music-related topics and situating them within the most up-to-date interpretative frameworks. All books provide relevant contextual background and detailed source investigations, as well as considerable bibliographical material of use for further study. Areas included in the series reflect its widely interdisciplinary aims and, although principally designed for musicologists, the series is also intended to be accessible to scholars working outside of music, in areas such as history, literature, science, philosophy, poetry and performing arts. Topics include criticism and aesthetics; musical genres; music and the church; music education; composers and performers; analysis; concert venues, promoters and organizations; the reception of foreign music in Britain; instrumental repertoire, manufacture and pedagogy; music hall and dance; gender studies; and music in literature, poetry and letters.

Although the nineteenth century has often been viewed as a fallow period in British musical culture, it is clear from the vast extent of current scholarship that this view is entirely erroneous. Far from being a 'land without music', nineteenth-century Britain abounded with musical activity. All society was affected by it, and everyone in that society recognized its importance in some way or other. It remains for us today to trace the significance of music and musical culture in that period, and to bring it alive for scholars to study and interpret. This is the principal aim of the Music in Nineteenth-Century Britain series – to advance scholarship in the area and expand our understanding of its importance in the wider cultural context of the time.

Bennett Zon
Durham University, UK

Introduction

While the music and musical culture of the British Isles in the 'long nineteenth-century' has been a subject of greatly increased academic interest in the last 30 years, opera and operatic culture in the latter part of the period remains largely neglected. Even those determined to rebut the concept that nineteenth-century Britain was 'das Land ohne Musik' have been reticent about celebrating the nation's operatic life, acknowledging certain flurries of activity (for example, the undertakings of the Pyne-Harrison Company around 1860, or the curious case of Sullivan's *Ivanhoe*) but sadly conceding that, all in all, these are but brief flashes of light in the darkness. Activities up to about 1870 have recently attracted more attention, for example in the work of Rachel Cowgill, George Biddlecombe, Gabrielle Dideriksen, Jennifer Hall-Witt and Roberta Marvin, but the era of the so-called 'British Musical Renaissance' has, ironically, been largely ignored. Perceptions of a 'Renaissance' have, indeed, been a part of the problem: in the conventional view, Britain's operatic achievements after 1880 inconveniently failed to equal the improvements and expansion seen in other genres. The domination of London by foreign opera (repertory, conductors, and singers), an elitist audience more interested in protecting its own exclusivity than in culture itself, the rise of operetta and musical comedy, and the lack of trained native musicians who could create and promote an original product have all been cited as reasons for the failure to establish a nation of opera-lovers and canon of British operas.

It is not my intention to debunk all of that narrative, for there is certainly truth within it, but I hope to show two things in particular. Firstly, that British operatic culture in the late nineteenth century was not so forlorn as has often been believed. There was, in fact, a great deal going on, with more opportunities for composers, performers and audiences than ever before, exemplified by the fact that more than 100 serious operas by British composers were premiered between 1875 and 1918. Secondly, and conversely, I want to explore the undoubted challenges faced by participants in this period, and to explain why Britain's operatic culture failed to develop as much as many observers hoped. The aim of this book is, therefore, to examine the nature of operatic culture in the British Isles between 1875 and 1918, looking at the way in which opera was produced and 'consumed' by companies and audiences, social and intellectual attitudes to the genre, the repertory performed, and the position of British composers and their work within this area of activity.

Previous published work in this area has been patchy in coverage. There exists no overarching survey beyond those by White and Burton, both of which are contained within larger studies.[1] Other, specific, research has included studies of individual composers, performers (especially singers) and the dominant venue, the Royal Opera House, Covent Garden. I do not aim in this volume to add to the research of recent scholars on their specific subjects, but rather to put their work into the wider context.

Sources of information are diverse and plentiful though far from comprehensive. I have made extensive use of press coverage throughout this volume: newspapers and periodicals were the primary conveyors of information and public arbiters of taste at this time and the richness of the information contained and the influence they wielded is a central part of the 'story'. The rapid increase in recent years of on-line availability of these sources has been a huge boon. The content has to be treated with caution; rumours and speculation inevitably form a significant part of the material and performance reviews are naturally subjective. Frequently, though, newspaper reviews are the sole records of the performances of new operas, the music itself having been lost, although, perhaps surprisingly, a large number of the native operas premiered were published. Other primary sources are less plentiful: the business records of the opera companies have generally not survived, nor has the personal correspondence of most participants.

It is important to explain and delimit parameters. Firstly, this book is about 'opera in the British Isles' rather than 'British opera': it aspires to examine the broad sweep of public and professional (as opposed to private and/or amateur) operatic activity with a particular focus on organisations and repertories and their reception.[2] Foreign works dominated and native composers were profoundly influenced by continental operatic culture. The United Kingdom of the time included the whole of the island of Ireland, and it is included here, as are the works of Irish composers; I have frequently used the words 'Britain' and 'British' when referring to the whole of the United Kingdom, but only as a short-hand, and no political implications are intended. References to 'English Opera' in the text generally refer to opera performed in the English language, although Victorian and Edwardian commentators frequently used 'English' as a catch-all term for the United Kingdom's entire population. Regarding the operas in Chapter 6, the essential criteria for inclusion were that the composer was British and that the work was premiered between 1875 and 1918. Contrary to popular myth, relatively few British operas were premiered abroad and most of these were performed in the United Kingdom subsequently; all of these have been included, as have, for completeness, the small number of works performed overseas only. A few composers are problematic in terms of nationality; as far as possible I

1 Eric Walter White, *A History of English Opera* (London, 1983); pp. 303–82; Nigel Burton, in Nicholas Temperley (ed.), *Music in Britain: The Romantic Age 1800–1914* (London, 1981), pp. 330–57.

2 Given the exclusively commercial nature of Britain's opera companies, I have made many references to their finances; rather than translating these into immediately obsolete modern equivalents, readers are referred to www.measuringworth.com, which converts historic monetary amounts to present-day values.

have used citizenship and contemporary perceptions as the decisive factor and thus Clutsam, D'Erlanger, De Lara, Esposito and Delius are all included, but D'Albert and Emil Bach are not.

My choice of start and end dates requires explanation. While 1815 and 1914 have become 'canonic' in the study of nineteenth-century history, the selection of 1875 and 1918 for this study is not so immediately obvious. Within musicology 1880 became equally canonic as the commencement of the 'British Musical Renaissance', symbolised by the first performance of Hubert Parry's *Prometheus Unbound* at Gloucester. Just as this choice would have been questioned at the time,[3] so recently musicologists have been concerned to view 1880 within a greater continuum.[4] It is, nevertheless, difficult to reject completely emblematic events and in choosing 1875 for my start date I have the advantage of not one, but three such happenings: the first appearance in London by the Carl Rosa company, the inauguration of the project to build a new 'national opera house' on the Victoria Embankment, and the definitive establishment of Wagner's operas in the British operatic repertory (see Chapter 1). In terms of native composition, 1875 is further thrown into relief by the collapse, in 1864, of the Pyne-Harrison Company, which effectively ended the opera-composing activities of a generation of British composers, including Balfe, Wallace, Benedict and Macfarren; the post-1875 period saw the arrival of the new group of 'Renaissance' writers, Cowen, Stanford, Mackenzie and Goring Thomas.

The choice of 1918 arises for different reasons. While 1914 has canonic status as an end date, for Britain's opera companies the outbreak of war represented anything but an end as they determined to carry on 'business as usual', with only Covent Garden suspending activities for the duration of the Great War. New operas appeared every year with the exception of 1917. Consequently I have chosen the end of the Great War as my finishing point.

As regards a definition of 'opera', I draw a distinction between 'grand' or 'serious' opera, and 'operetta' and 'musical comedy', allowing for some flexibility, and examine the former. While a postmodernist view may be wary of such dividing lines, in Victorian and Edwardian Britain there was little uncertainty about them and so, as far as possible, I have embraced the contemporaneous distinctions. The arrival of French *opéra bouffe* in Britain in the late 1860s delineated the division between comic and serious opera more clearly than before, and initiated an audience desire for 'light' or 'comic' opera that Cellier, Clay and the 'Savoy Operas' aimed at developing and satiating. The most useful guide to distinguishing between 'comic' and 'serious' genres as late nineteenth-century audiences perceived them is neither the subject matter nor the musical structure, but the mode of production: in general 'comic'

---

3 See Nicholas Temperley, 'Xenophilia in British Musical History', in Bennett Zon (ed.), *Nineteenth-Century British Music Studies, Volume 1* (Aldershot, 1999), pp. 3–19.

4 Stradling and Hughes's seminal study takes 1840 as its starting point: Robert Stradling and Meirion Hughes, *The British Musical Renaissance: Construction and Deconstruction* (2nd ed. Manchester, 2001).

works were usually produced in 'runs' (performed in the same theatre on successive nights or by single-work touring companies), while 'serious' operas were produced on a 'repertory' basis. Exceptions were relatively few, notable examples being the productions of Sullivan's *Ivanhoe* and Stanford's *Shamus O'Brien*. Consequently, it is on the 'repertory' companies and the works they performed (including 'comedies' such as *Le nozze di Figaro*) that this study focuses.

Given the diverse issues and subjects, the layout of chapters is not strictly linear. Chapter 1 summarises the state of opera in Britain in 1875. Chapters 2 and 3 focus on London's West End between 1876 and 1918, using Augustus Harris's death in 1896 as a dividing line; this area was distinctive in organisation and practice, and the participants – executants and consumers – generally preferred it to be so. Britain's notoriously capital-centric culture has tended to emphasise the difference – and metaphorical distance – between central London and everywhere else and it would be counter-productive to ignore that distinction here. The West End was the focus of critical comment, composer aspiration, and influenced – for good and ill – operatic culture and practice in the rest of the country. Chapter 4 focuses on opera outside the West End and endeavours to give a summative survey of opera performances in the provinces. Chapters 5 and 6 focus on 'British opera'; in the former I consider contemporaneous perceptions that there was an 'operatic problem' and the solutions proposed, in particular the foundation of a 'national opera house', while Chapter 6 is a 'gazetteer' providing information on all the traced operas by British composers premiered between 1875 and 1918.

Even a book focused on this relatively short period will, in many respects, only skim the surface of the subject. The British Isles were a hive of operatic activity and London was one of Europe's main operatic centres; whilst contemporaneous commentators and later advocates of British music may have felt that the country's operatic life did not measure up to their aspirations or ambitions, there was no shortage of activity and, even if this was not necessarily that which was considered desirable, it had a significant and lasting impact on the nation's musical culture. Given this, I hope that this volume will prove a source of information and stimulus for future scholars.

Chapter 1
Prologue: Opera in the British Isles in 1875

> That the richest and most productive period in the history of opera coincided in date and length with what is known as the Victorian Era is a fact that must be generally conceded … [D]uring no period … did there ever occur such an amazing concatenation of great works and great performances in the domain of the lyric drama attended with such widespread support from an ever-growing and increasingly responsive public.[1]

Herman Klein's view, expressed in 1933, has often been debunked in more recent years, but serves as a useful reminder that, for many observers of the time, the late Victorian and Edwardian decades, at least so far as the truly 'Grand Operas' of Covent Garden and its West End rivals were concerned, did indeed represent a golden age: a period of high performance standards, innumerable and unrivalled star singers, and unsurpassed social opulence.

A contrary view, that might be termed the 'Land ohne Musik' perspective, would argue that opera in Victorian Britain was in the doldrums. In central London, opera performed in Italian dominated, characterised by a restricted non-native repertory and frequently slack performance standards, while indigenous music was performed in second-rate theatres by itinerant companies, characterised by an equally stagnant repertory and still lower standards of performance. Outside London things were worse still, with only a few of the largest towns enjoying even occasional glimpses of the operas or singers that appeared in the capital, and the remainder of the country resting content with even more paltry fare.

Over a century later, it is easy to regard Klein's view as rose-tinted nostalgia but, equally, the derogatory perspective that prevailed subsequently would be a description unrecognised by many Victorians other than advocates for specific causes or with personal agendas. Inevitably, the truth lies somewhere between these two extremes. This was a period of great diversity: from the elitist and expensive Italian operas in the West End of London to modest touring troupes playing in towns from Penzance to Aberdeen and Limerick to Norwich, opera came within reach of a greater proportion of the population than either before or since, and the culture and practices prevailing in this period have had an influence on Britain's operatic culture which can, in some respects, still be felt.

---

1 Herman Klein, *The Golden Age of Opera* (London, 1933), p. xiii.

'Grand Opera' in Central London

In 1875, in London's West End, activity was dominated by Italian opera, which was, in turn, dominated by two men, Frederick Gye and James Mapleson. English opera, since the collapse of the Pyne-Harrison Company in 1864, had had only an intermittent presence and was wholly without momentum and consistent support.[2] Mapleson and Gye each managed Italian opera companies that attracted audiences of superior social status (including royalty and nobility), and which gave the performances of the highest – albeit sometimes compromised – standard available at the time.

Gye[3] had been a lessee of the Covent Garden Theatre and manager of the Royal Italian Opera since 1850.[4] He was a meticulous, sometimes ruthless and single-minded businessman who confined his operatic activity to London during the annual 'grand season' of late spring and early summer.[5] On retiring in 1877, he handed the business to his sons (see Chapter 2). His long, unbroken period of management secured Covent Garden's status as the leading opera house in London, a perception which has endured to this day.

James Mapleson's circumstances were more precarious.[6] He ran his first opera season at Her Majesty's Theatre, Haymarket, in 1861, although he had been manager in all but name since 1858 of companies nominally run first by Benjamin Lumley and then Edward Tyrrell Smith. Mapleson's marginal but distinctly secondary status arose for several reasons. His interests in opera were more diverse than Gye's, resulting in a periodic lack of focus; Mapleson took companies around the provinces throughout the 1860s and '70s[7] and, from the late 1870s,

---

2 The terms 'Italian opera' and 'English opera', were used at the time to refer to the language of performance rather than the origin of the repertory (discussed below).

3 For further information on Gye, most of whose career lies outside the scope of this book, see his obituary in *MW* (7 December 1878, p. 790); Gabrielle Dideriksen and Matthew Ringel, 'Frederick Gye and "The dreadful business of opera management"', *Nineteenth Century Music*, 19 (1995–96), pp. 3–30; and Harold Rosenthal, *Two Centuries of Opera at Covent Garden* (London, 1958). Gye's diaries are held at the Royal Opera House Archives.

4 In 1858 Gye opened a new theatre, the third on the site, after fire destroyed its predecessor; this building (with many extensions and modifications) is still in use today.

5 During the remainder of the year he sublet the theatre. The London 'grand season' was much shorter than those in other European capitals, which tended to run from early Autumn to March, but these dovetailed together since singers across Europe were disengaged as London opened; Gye and Mapleson were able to obtain good singers as they paid well and London engagements were highly valued by performers as status symbols.

6 See James Mapleson, *The Mapleson Memoirs* (2 vols, London, 1888) for his own anecdotal account. See also his obituary in *The Times*, 15 November 1901, p. 4.

7 Gye did this only in 1857 when Covent Garden was being rebuilt; his regular singers did undertake provincial tours, often as a company, but Gye himself did not take an active part.

produced opera in the United States (see Chapter 2), as well as sometimes giving short runs of Italian opera in London in late autumn. Most important, however, was the itinerancy forced upon Mapleson after Her Majesty's Theatre burnt down on 7 December 1867. While Gye had been able to secure the lease and swift rebuilding of Covent Garden, Mapleson was less lucky as the leaseholder of Her Majesty's, the Earl of Dudley, proved to be obstructive and stubborn. Mapleson decamped to Drury Lane in 1868 but, although Her Majesty's was rebuilt within a year it remained empty, allegedly due to Dudley's high rental demand.[8] Mapleson continued to look elsewhere and the next three years saw a series of plots and scheming almost worthy of the works he and Gye put on stage.

Both men had felt the financial impact of running rival opera seasons for seven years and, by the end of 1867, a plan was afoot by which Gye would retire from Covent Garden with Mapleson taking his place, but as a salaried manager, not an independent impresario. This idea fell through following the exposure of a rogue investor,[9] and the two men instead joined forces at Covent Garden for the 'coalition' seasons of 1869 and 1870. Their characters, however, were scarcely complementary and the working relationship was never an easy one. In contrast to Gye, Mapleson was raffish and charming, an instinctive rather than methodical businessman who frequently survived by the skin of his teeth and sheer luck rather than by careful planning. This joint endeavour was destabilised in 1870 by the actions of George Wood and Henry Jarrett.[10] After many shenanigans,[11] Wood ran a financially disastrous season of Italian opera at Drury Lane (which did, however, include the first London performance of a Wagner opera (*Der fliegende Holländer*, given as *L'Olandese dannato*, and starring Charles Santley and Ilma di Murska, on 23 July 1870)) while, after teetering on the edge of legal action, Gye and Mapleson agreed to separate their interests.[12] Gye bought Mapleson out, thanks to a loan of £105,000 from Andrew Montagu,[13] and the two impresarios again mounted competing seasons, Gye still at Covent Garden, and Mapleson at Drury Lane, where he remained until 1876.[14] The impression of Mapleson as an

8 Frederick Leader quoted in *MW*, 7 March 1874, p. 154. When the Royal Italian Opera company was formed in 1881, the annual ground rent of Covent Garden was £1,216 12s, whereas for Her Majesty's it was £1,934 6s (*MW*, 15 April 1882, p. 232, and Chapter 2, note 9).

9 Rosenthal, p. 151.

10 Respectively, employees of the music publishers Cramer and Co., and of Mapleson and also a disaffected former member of the Covent Garden orchestra employed by Gye.

11 See Mapleson, vol. 1, pp. 129–33, and Rosenthal pp. 167–8.

12 The original agreement between Gye and Mapleson had been for three years, but it was dissolved, trust between the two men having broken down. See Mapleson, vol. 1, pp. 136–9, and Rosenthal, pp. 172–3.

13 A wealthy landowner, of High Melton, near Doncaster.

14 Mapleson secured the services of Sir Michael Costa as conductor at Drury Lane in 1871; Costa had been Gye's conductor from 1847 to 1868 and only departed from Covent

itinerant remained as he gave pre-Christmas seasons at Covent Garden in 1870 and 1871, and his company throughout retained the name 'Her Majesty's Italian Opera', creating the impression that a return to the empty theatre on the Haymarket remained Mapleson's objective.[15]

In 1875, therefore, Gye was at Covent Garden with a season lasting from 30 March to 17 July (83 performances) while Mapleson was once more at Drury Lane from 10 April to 24 July (64 performances). While both companies performed exclusively in the Italian style and language, the repertory was mixed. Works from Italy dominated, but French operas were also given, especially those of Meyerbeer, and Gounod's *Faust*. German opera featured rather less frequently, with only *Fidelio*, *Der Freischütz*, *Die Zauberflöte*, and *Lohengrin* (discussed below) appearing at Covent Garden in 1875. Non-Italian works were translated and, as spoken dialogue was deemed unacceptable, *secco* recitatives were introduced if needed.[16] The presence of any sort of indigenous culture was largely frowned upon: a fundamental part of the ethos of Covent Garden and its rivals throughout this period was that everything was seen to be the best that money could buy, wherever in the world it came from. Consequently, the overt incorporation of either native repertory or performers was typically viewed as parochial and a lowering of standards to be avoided, even to the extent that in the 1870s British singers often took Italian aliases.[17] Another facet of this cosmopolitan culture of

---

Garden when the coalition seasons started (Rosenthal, p. 163), as did the orchestra leader, Prosper Sainton, who was also employed by Mapleson in 1871.

15 Mapleson claimed that he was prevented by Gye from returning to Her Majesty's in 1870 (Mapleson, vol. 1, p. 139); although Gye later fell out with Dudley, Mapleson did not regain possession of Her Majesty's. In 1874 Mapleson made another attempt to access the theatre but Dudley still required an excessive rent (*MW*, 7 March 1874, p. 154, and Mapleson's prospectus for that year, refers to him occupying Drury Lane 'pending more definite arrangements' (ibid, p. 156)). In its own commentary, *MW* declared that 'unquestionably the legitimate home of Her Majesty's Opera is Her Majesty's Theatre; and it is a matter of regret that [Mapleson's] efforts to secure the building which rose out of the ruins of the well-remembered old house have failed' (ibid, p. 149). Although Mapleson wanted to use the new theatre, the retention of the company name had as much to do with claiming an implicit seal of royal approval (as Gye did in the title 'Royal Italian Opera'). Although Queen Victoria had ceased to attend the opera after the death of Prince Albert in 1861, several of her children attended regularly.

16 For example, those written for *Fidelio* by Balfe for its 1851 production at Her Majesty's were still in use in the 1870s (see *The Times*, 30 March 1874, p. 14); a certain Gelli supplied the recitatives for the performances of Auber's *Les Diamants de la Couronne* (*MW*, 16 May 1874, p. 314).

17 The companies comprised performers of all European nationalities and, from the 1860s, singers from North America. Aliases were employed especially by British singers (for example Henry Maclean Martin took the stage name Enrico Campobello, and the Irishman Allan James Foley was known as Signor Foli). *The Times* noted that the singers billed as Mdlle Perdi and Signor Talbo in the autumn 1877 season at Her Majesty's had reverted to

'conspicuous consumption' was the employment of 'star' singers which, although regularly derided in the press throughout this period, was an essential part of both companies' fortunes.[18] In 1875 both Italian companies could claim the possession of highly regarded leading ladies: Gye retained the services of both Adelina Patti (since 1861) and the up-and-coming Canadian Emma Albani (since 1872),[19] while Mapleson had the long-serving German Therèse Tietjens, who had first worked for Benjamin Lumley in 1858, and the Swede, Christine Nilsson. Both companies lacked a man of equal status (Gye's best were the tenor Ernest Nicolini and baritone Victor Maurel, while Mapleson had the tenor Italo Campanini) but, while the presence of a *bel canto* tenor who could produce the magical 'ut in poitrine' (a chest voice high C) was a great asset to any opera company, it was the presence of the *prime donne* that was the true essential.

Gye's seasons between 1871 and 1874 indicate the state of his repertory immediately preceding the period under consideration.[20] He gave 316 performances in total, in seasons varying in length between 77 and 82 nights, typically starting just after Easter and lasting into July.[21] The earlier performances were put on by secondary members of the company and provided opportunities for debutantes, while stars were kept in reserve for about a month, in order that momentum was built up gradually. A typical week in both houses comprised four performances (Monday, Tuesday, Thursday and Saturday), although extra performances were often added, especially as the season progressed. Subscriptions, which formed about half of the box office income,[22] were sold for 40 nights, with a limited choice

---

their own names of Lisa Purdy and Talbot Brennan for the winter English season at the same theatre in 1878 (quoted in *MW*, 9 February 1878, p. 101). Singers of other nationalities were less likely to use aliases: North Americans, such as Minnie Hauk, often performed under their own names and, by introducing a growing proportion of non-Italian names, they initiated a trend amongst British singers also to appear without foreign disguise.

[18] For a frank acknowledgement of the importance of the 'star system' see Walter Maynard [alias of Thomas Willert Beale], *The Entertaining Impresario* (London, 1867), pp. 86–7.

[19] Real name Marie Louise Cécile Lajeunesse; she took 'Albani' as her stage name in 1870. Mapleson claimed that he heard of Albani first, but through a mixture of confusion and sleight of hand, Gye secured her services (Mapleson, vol. 1, pp. 141–4). Albani married Gye's son Ernest in 1878.

[20] That is, excluding the second of the 'coalition' seasons in 1870 so as to consider Gye independent of Mapleson.

[21] Performances during an 'ante-season', typically starting in Lent, died off gradually in the 1850s.

[22] For the first of the 'coalition' seasons, Mapleson stated that £41,000 was received in subscription income with a further £29,000 coming from one-off ticket sales and £10,000 from other sources (Mapleson, vol. 1, p. 127). Although the amounts are doubtless unrepresentative of the usual competitive seasons, it seems probable that the relative proportions of income were not unusual. Subscription income does not mean, however, that the same individuals occupied their boxes for 40 nights: many subscriptions were sold to

Table 1.1 Most frequently performed operas at Covent Garden under Frederick Gye, 1871–74

Composer	Opera	Performances
Gounod	*Faust*	22
Rossini	*Il barbiere di Siviglia*	22
Mozart	*Don Giovanni*	21
Donizetti	*Lucia di Lammermoor*	16
Rossini	*Guillaume Tell*	16
Meyerbeer	*Les Huguenots*	15
Bellini	*La Sonnambula*	15
Meyerbeer	*L'africaine*	13
Meyerbeer	*L'étoile du nord*	13

of dates offered to the subscriber, and it was on subscription nights, when 'society' (see below) was present in its greatest numbers, often with royalty as an added attraction, that the star singers generally appeared. In 1875 the subscription prices ranged from 100 to 240 guineas for boxes, with orchestra and amphitheatre stalls costing 35 and 18 guineas respectively.[23] Gye's diaries usually record the amount of non-subscription box office receipts for each evening: in 1875 his best nights were for *Roméo et Juliette* (£700 on 18 June), *L'étoile du nord* (£644 on 5 July), and *Dinorah* (£632 on 11 May). The British première of *Lohengrin* on 8 May netted on-the-night receipts of £553; 4 June was one of the worst nights, when a performance of *L'Africaine* brought in only £80.[24] Over the five seasons 1871–74

agencies at a discount, which then sold on the subscriptions to individuals or sold tickets for individual performances; this provided Gye and Mapleson with an 'up-front' though reduced income whilst transferring to the agencies the risk of seats remaining unsold.

23 Assuming four people in a box, an individual seat cost between 13s 2d and £1 11s 6d, orchestra stalls 18s 4d and amphitheatre stalls 9s 5d. Mapleson's subscription rates in 1875 were the same as Gye's.

24 As detailed accounts for Covent Garden no longer exist it is difficult to place these figures in a larger context. In 1876, however, Gye referred to the total nightly income capacity of Covent Garden as being somewhere between £1,200 and £1,400 (see Gye's diary, 11 and 23 June 1876, ROHA). On 11 May, when the Prince of Wales attended the opera on the day he arrived back from a State Visit to India, his attendance, having been trailed by Gye in the press, resulted in £1,150 in total receipts. When the Royal Italian Opera became a limited company in 1881, the prospectus stated that the average annual profits in Gye's last six seasons (1873–78) were 'upwards of £15,500' (see Chapter 2, note 10, and *The Times*, 21 July 1881, p. 12). Assuming a season of 80 performances, this is an average profit of just under £195 per night.

Table 1.2 Performances at Covent Garden under Frederick Gye by composer, 1871–74

Composer	Number of works	Total performances	Average number of performances per work	% of total performances
Meyerbeer	5	55	11.0	17.4
Verdi	7	46	6.6	14.6
Rossini	3	43	14.3	13.6
Donizetti	6	42	7.0	13.3
Mozart	3	39	13.0	12.3
Bellini	3	25	8.3	7.9
Gounod	1	22	22.0	7.0

Gye mounted 40 different operas, the most frequently performed of which are shown in Table 1.1.

The obvious omission is Verdi but, although no work of his appears among the most frequently performed at Covent Garden, more of his works (seven) were performed than those of any other composer (see Table 1.2).

Mapleson's seasons tended to be slightly shorter than those of Gye; in the four years under consideration, Mapleson gave 252 performances in seasons varying between 57 and 73 nights.[25] His repertory was more restricted as he gave only 30 operas over this four-year period; the most frequently performed are shown in Table 1.3 and again *Faust* tops the list. Beyond this there are relatively few duplications; the explanation for this is unclear but is most likely influenced by the audience associating certain singers with specific roles and the singers' own preferences – the strong appearance, for example, of *Fidelio* in Mapleson's list is due solely to Therèse Tietjens's interest in it and her portrayal of Leonora.[26]

A comparison of the composers most frequently performed shows few surprises and here the concordances between Gye and Mapleson are much stronger (see Table 1.4) – Mozart at Covent Garden is exchanged for Beethoven at Drury Lane. The order in which the composers are ranked, however, is significantly different and overall suggests a more conservative audience at Drury Lane which preferred the more 'traditional' *bel canto* style of Donizetti and Bellini to composers such as Verdi and Meyerbeer. In both houses, however, it seems likely that had Gounod been able to provide more than one successful opera, he would have held sway.

---

25 For the purposes of direct comparison Mapleson's short autumn seasons are excluded from this analysis.

26 Leading singers may have avoided duplicating the roles of their competitors for fear of adverse comparison.

Table 1.3 Most frequently performed operas under James Mapleson, 1871–74

Composer	Opera	Performances
Gounod	*Faust*	25
Rossini	*Semiramide*	23
Bellini	*La Sonnambula*	20
Donizetti	*Lucia di Lammermoor*	19
Meyerbeer	*Les Huguenots*	18
Donizetti	*Lucrezia Borgia*	17
Verdi	*Rigoletto*	12
Verdi	*Il Trovatore*	11
Beethoven	*Fidelio*	10
Donizetti	*La fille du Régiment*	10

Table 1.4 Performances by James Mapleson by composer, 1871–74

Composer	Number of works	Total performances	Average number of performances per work	% of total performances
Donizetti	7	63	9.0	25.0
Verdi	3	29	9.7	11.5
Bellini	3	28	9.3	11.1
Rossini	2	25	12.5	9.9
Gounod	1	25	25.0	9.9
Meyerbeer	3	22	7.3	8.7
Beethoven	1	10	10.0	4.0

A significant point not shown by these figures is that neither Gye nor Mapleson were at all interested in commissioning or premiering new works. At best, they gave first British performances of (usually) recently composed operas but typically only after these works had made a successful début elsewhere in Europe; such were the financial risks involved that both men were inclined to caution.[27] During the period 1871–74, Gye gave first British performances of just three operas, none of which

27 There was the simple commercial risk of producing an unknown work, exacerbated by the various fees that had to be paid to secure the right of representation in Britain, plus the additional costs incurred through extra rehearsals, new scenery etc. Even the risk of producing a new work well-established elsewhere was considerable.

secured regular appearances: Cimarosa's *Le Astuzie Femminili* (composed 1794, performed 15 July 1871), Gomes's *Il Guarany* (13 July 1872) and Poniatowski's *Gelmina* (4 June 1872).[28] Mapleson, meanwhile, gave Cherubini's *Les Deux Journées* (composed 1799, performed 20 May 1872) and, exceptionally, a British work, Balfe's *Il Talismano* (11 June 1874).[29] Thus London's two Italian companies were essentially reactive in their policies to music: the tried and tested dominated (although this was no guarantee of a London success) and it was a central part of the business philosophies of both men to follow rather than innovate. The danger inherent in this policy, which became increasingly a reality in the 1880s, was that, while some parts of the repertory became moribund, popular new works did not appear to replace them (see Chapter 2).

It is very difficult to gain a sense of exactly what operatic performances at this time were like; although contemporaneous press reviews are sometimes critical, they start from an unstated baseline, and very often notices are lengthy but replete with platitudes and generalities. If, however, less complimentary press comments are considered in conjunction with what is known about working practices, it seems certain standards were, at the very least, mixed. Performance schedules were rarely announced by either Mapleson or Gye more than a week in advance, and 'stock' operas (by far the greater part of the repertory) were put on stage with little rehearsal beforehand.[30] The first performance of a new work might be given more notice, but was often postponed if more rehearsals were needed and precise dates of premières were never given more than two weeks in advance.[31] Once announced, the schedule was adhered to as far as possible but, if a leading singer was ill, it could be superseded or the advertised opera played with cuts;[32] there was

---

28 Poniatowski's opera was originally given in Paris, 28 April 1868, as *La Contessina*.

29 Based on Walter Scott's novel *The Talisman* but entitled *The Knight of the Leopard* by Balfe and unfinished when he died in 1870. The opera was completed by Costa for Her Majesty's and was promised for, but not performed during, the 1873 season, due to the visits to London of the Shah of Persia and the Tsarevich and Tsarevna of Russia; Mapleson stated that, 'the present time is most inopportune for the production of a work of such magnitude and of such historical interest as *Il Talismano* especially recalling the fact that it is the last composition of our countryman Balfe' (*Era*, 13 July 1873, p. 11).

30 Gye noted that Victor Maurel, Joseph Tagliafico, Clarice Sinico and Sofia Scalchi all failed to attend a rehearsal of *Guillaume Tell* (Gye's diary, 26 March 1875, ROHA), but the performance, on opening night, four days later, was reviewed positively in *The Times* (31 March 1875, p. 8). Performers did not get paid for pre-season rehearsals so some reluctance to participate is understandable; see Maynard, p. 83.

31 Season prospectuses often announced new works conditionally, that is, in the terms that at least two out of the four works promised would appear; subscribers and critics were expected to accept that the impresario had fulfilled his obligation by producing the minimum rather than maximum number. Thus, although Gye promised *Lohengrin* in 1872 (Rosenthal, p. 179), it was not performed at Covent Garden until 1875 (see below).

32 For example, a mutilated performance of *Guillaume Tell* was given at Covent Garden on 28 March 1876 (the opening night of the season) due to the illness of Ignazio Marini,

no systematic organisation of understudies and the billed opera could only go on if another member of the company was able to step into the breach.[33] Some singers, such as Mathilde Bauermeister and Anna d'Angeri were especially valued due to their ability to be of service in this way.[34] The American soprano Minnie Hauk recalled the lack of preparation:

> [*Le nozze di Figaro*] was produced at short notice, giving me no time to get a costume as Cherubino. So I had to borrow a bit here and a bit there. Madame Therese Tietjens … offered me a pair of long boots for the last act … She sang the Comtesse, and as I had never even heard the opera, she obligingly showed me some stage business, and helped at the only stage rehearsal we had. Although I had to learn the part in two days, the performance was praised in the papers.[35]

Although this was apparently an exceptional event rather than a commonplace, it illustrates the priority to keep the theatre open at all costs: closure for any reason led to losses of both money and reputation (nor did any performers get paid if the theatre was closed, hence the appreciation of the flexibility noted above[36]) and consequently almost any step might be taken in order to ensure that the show (any show!) did indeed go on.

---

who was playing Arnold; the duet with Mathilde in Act II was omitted, as was the whole of Act IV, and a premature curtain was brought down on Act III (*MW*, 1 April, p. 235). In the same season the promised performance of *Lucrezia Borgia* by Her Majesty's on 15 May was replaced with *La Sonnambula* due to the illness of Therèse Tietjens (*MW*, 20 May, p. 351).

33 Elena Varesi, for example, successfully played Rosina in *Il barbiere di Siviglia* on 3 June 1876 for Her Majesty's when substituting at short notice for Mlle Chapuy (*The Times*, 5 June 1876, p. 10); Varesi replaced her in several other roles during this season.

34 For example, 'In consequence of the indisposition of Mdme Pezotta, Mdlle d'Angeri, who was cast for Donna Anna [in *Don Giovanni*], undertook … to represent Donna Elvira instead, Mdme Saar assuming the character of Donna Anna. There is no more generally useful member of Mr Gye's company than Mdlle d'Angeri. She can play, at the shortest notice, almost any part in the repertory that comes within her line, or near to it; and, what is more, plays whatever she agrees to accept right well' (*MW*, 8 April 1876, p. 251, of the performance on 1 April; the role of Don Giovanni was played by Antonio Cotogni despite Victor Maurel having been billed to take the part). Similarly, Mathilde Bauermeister took the role of Oscar in *Un ballo in maschera* in place of an indisposed Mila Rodani at Her Majesty's on 7 November 1877; *MW* much later commented that 'Mdlle Bauermeister has often rendered service of this kind to her manager for, no matter what the opera, she seems to have it somewhere in her memory, ready for production on the instant' (*MW*, 23 Oct 1880, p. 673, of a performance of *Faust* on 18 October).

35 Minnie Hauk [Baroness de Wartegg], *Memories of a Singer* (London, 1925), p. 54, probably of the performance by Mapleson's company at Covent Garden on 24 November 1868.

36 Maynard, p. 82.

According to Emma Albani, these and all manner of other alterations or mishaps did not compromise the standard of performance:

> Naturally in Italy … I had been associated with artistes who were either beginners or whose talents or voices had not enabled them to rise to the first rank; but [in London] I found opera given with such a combination of the highest artistic talent as probably had never existed before … The orchestra was the finest in Europe, and the chorus and ensemble generally far beyond anything I had ever known.[37]

Notwithstanding these comments, both Gye and Mapleson often put singers on stage who had little experience. Sometimes this paid off – Gye's diaries show the progress of sixteen-year-old Zaré Thalberg:

> [8 April 1875] Zaré Thalberg rehearsed for the first time with the other artistes. Zerlina in *Don Giovanni* … all the artistes were pleased with her and prophesied a great career for her.
> [9 April] Band rehearsal of *Don Giovanni*; Zaré Thalberg sang with an orchestra for the first time in her life. She sang and acted well and did not appear the least nervous or frightened.
> [10 April] It was *Don Giovanni* with little Zaré Thalberg as Zerlina her first appearance on any stage; she had a great success. The Prince and Princess of Wales were there, Lord and Lady Dudley, the Duchess of Sutherland … everyone very pleased … Zaré was encored in the Duet 'Là ci darem', 'Batti, batti' and 'Vedrai carino'.
> [12 April] All the newspapers of today are most enthusiastic about Zaré's performance on Saturday, as well as that of the opera in general.
> [13 April] Zaré Thalberg's second appearance; she sang and acted even better than on Saturday … I thought the house would have been crammed seeing the unanimous favourable report of all the papers, but the public seem to have no reliance on their musical reports for there was only £240 in the house.[38]

---

37 Emma Albani, *Forty Years of Song* (London, 1911), p. 56; as Albani was Ernest Gye's wife an unbiased view is unlikely.

38 Gye's diary, ROHA. *The Times* commented that, 'it was scarcely credible that a girl in her 17th year, who had never trod the boards and never sung with the accompaniment of an orchestra until now, could be so entirely at ease, exercise so unrestricted a control over her voice, round off her phrases with such apparent art, and preserve an intonation so irreproachable' (12 April 1875, p. 12). Her next roles were another Zerlina, in Auber's *Fra Diavolo* (*The Times* 17 May, p. 7), and Cherubino in *Le nozze di Figaro* (*The Times*, 29 June, p. 8). For further information on Thalberg, whose real name was Ethel Western and who was not, contrary to contemporaneous belief, the daughter of the famous pianist, see Rosenthal, p. 189.

Gye was also successful with Gilbert Campbell (stage name Gilberto Ghilberti) who first appeared as Sarastro in *Die Zauberflöte*, and whose voice was praised in *The Times* as being 'of genuine quality and ample compass, only wanting just now more depth and solidity of tone in the lower notes to be unexceptional. He uses it too, with judgment, his phrasing being well-balanced and his style devoid of exaggeration'.[39]

On other occasions, debutantes experienced severe attacks of nerves, but placing untested singers on the stage was clearly part of the operatic ritual and nerves were, indeed, expected: audiences were indulgent on a first appearance and critics generally held back, giving the benefit of the doubt until having heard a singer in two or three different roles. For example, the first appearance of a Mr Perkins (an American, who took the stage name Costa) at Her Majesty's attracted the comments 'his appearance is manly and dignified and his voice of considerable power and sonority. As an actor, also, Signor Costa displays real power. On Tuesday night, however, [as Oroveso in *Norma*] the vocalist evinced a tendency to flatness which was apparently unconquerable'.[40] The performance was sufficiently convincing, however, to secure Perkins sub-principal roles in *Rigoletto*, *La Favorita*, and *Die Zauberflöte* during the course of the season and opinions improved.[41] Most of these debutantes, however, disappeared after one or two performances; very few managed to establish themselves in either of the London companies.[42]

From a modern perspective it is hard to avoid concluding that performances were often slapdash, and it is notable that adverse press comment on all aspects of operatic performances became much more common in the 1880s, due to some real crises in the Italian companies, and to seasons given by both Carl Rosa and some German companies undoubtedly being of a much higher standard (see Chapter 2).

As far as audiences of the 1870s were concerned, such shortcomings were often of relatively little consequence other than when a severe alteration took place, or when a star singer was prevented from appearing. Rather, critical and audience attention focused on the nuances of the abilities and interpretations of the leading singers, in particular vocal quality. This is reflected in reviews, with many references to tone, intonation, flexibility, dynamic range and tessitura:

---

39 *The Times*, 24 April 1876, p. 7, of the performance on 22 April. Gye's diaries show that Campbell had auditioned for him on 7 April and accepted an engagement three days later.

40 *MW*, 4 April 1874, p. 216 (see also p. 209).

41 See *MW* 11 April 1874, p. 233; 18 April, p. 250; 18 July, p. 471.

42 Another American, appearing under the stage name Imogene Orelli, did not receive universal acclaim as Violetta in *La Traviata*: 'The part was decidedly ill-chosen for this lady's debut, and we do not think the mistake will be repeated' (*MW*, 9 May 1874, p. 296, of the performance on 5 May). Although *The Times* was more charitable (11 May, p. 14) it does not appear that Orelli appeared in any further solo roles during the season.

> Once more *La Sonnambula*! This time, however, with a new Amina, our only excuse for dwelling upon it again, however briefly. Mdlle Sarda … might … have selected a less ambitious [role] for her first appearance on the stage of such a theatre as the Royal Italian Opera … [She has] a voice which, by aid of persevering application, may achieve good things, the tones of which, moreover, in level passages, are nearly always sympathetic, and the range [is] extensive. Her command of *mezza voce*, the liquid and penetrating quality of her higher notes, and her power of sustaining and fining [*sic*] them off gradually from loud to soft, while persevering [*sic*] strict tonality, were on several occasions remarked and appreciated … She did quite enough, unequal as was her performance regarded as a whole, to show decided promise.[43]

The primary focus was upon the skills of the *prima donna* to such an extent that faults in other singers were easily forgiven or sidelined; established singers such as Patti or Albani could carry an audience with them almost regardless of the actions of those surrounding them (although audiences greeted good sub-principals enthusiastically) and reviews tend to contain little more than padding.[44] For some, this intense concentration on leading ladies proved frustrating. Henry Lunn wrote:

> The recent performances of works new to this country, and the excellent revivals of almost forgotten old ones, seem looked upon as quite secondary matters in comparison with the announcement that Madame Patti or Madame Nilsson appeared in a character her assumption of which is known to be one of the regular occurrences of the season. Should it happen that one of our petted Queens of Song has not been heard in a part for some time, an additional excitement is manufactured, and the exact date of her last performance of it is hunted up was as much care as it were a matter of vast artistic importance.[45]

Lunn's prose reflects the resentment felt by a growing portion of the musical establishment and a perception that London's operatic scene was stale, monotonous and averse to innovation. A more general shift in aesthetic norms underlies this attitude, notably an increasing value placed on the musical score as the artwork, rather than the performance as presented by its executants.[46] As Susan Rutherford

---

43 *The Times*, 29 April 1878, quoted in *MW*, 4 May, p. 293, of the performance on 23 April.

44 See, for example, reviews in *MW*, 22 May 1875, p. 342 (Patti in *Il barbiere di Siviglia* on 20 May), 29 May, p. 361 (Albani's first performance as Marguerite in *Faust* on 22 May), and 31 July, pp. 524–5 (Nilsson in *Les Huguenots* (19 July) and Tietjens in *Lucrezia Borgia* (20 July)).

45 Henry Lunn, 'The London Musical Season', *MT*, 1 September 1873, pp. 203–5 (p. 203).

46 It is impossible here to do other than note the gradual shift in the views of British critics demonstrable in the nineteenth century which, in broad terms, placed increasing weight

outlines, the concept of theatrical direction was only just taking root in the 1870s; audiences did not expect, for example, subtle interactions between characters, complex stage business or a 'naturalistic' style of acting.[47] Rather, interaction was between the singer and the audience and the former's success in communicating directly with the latter (rather than with other members of the cast) was prized.

Reviews frequently mentioned acting skills, but in coded terms. For contemporaneous audiences and critics only the exceptional needed to be mentioned as the archetypal was taken as given. This review of Christine Nilsson in *Les Huguenots* is typical:

> From a dramatic point of view her impersonation was admirable. Her command of pathos … was never more powerfully manifested than in her rendering of Valentine; and her ability to depict the highest tragic emotions was no less conspicuous. In the great scene with Raoul her acting was so terrible in its reality that the illusion was complete, and the breathless attention paid by the audience showed how entirely she had enlisted her sympathies. Her attitudes and gestures in the closing passages of this scene were sometimes statuesque, sometimes impetuous – always spontaneous and graceful.[48]

Notably, 'reality' was regarded as shocking, but Nilsson's good judgment in her acting is complimented in the final sentence; for *prime donne* this was a particularly difficult task as they negotiated a compromise between the increasing need to be 'realistic' and the requirement to preserve a Victorian sense of idealised femininity.[49] The art of operatic acting was, however, entering a period of change and while many similarly laudatory reviews may be found the anecdotes contained in some singers'

---

on the works of German-speaking composers and the genres most frequently associated with them. Italian opera, with the exception of the mature compositions of Verdi, was more frequently viewed as a lesser art form. For further discussion see Chapters 2 and 3.

47 See Susan Rutherford, *The Prima Donna and Opera* (Cambridge, 2006), pp. 205–13. In the 1870s principal singers arranged their own costumes, and most gestures and stage business; the role of Director largely did not exist. With this degree of freedom and the absence of a unified conceptual view of how an opera should appear on stage, the need for rehearsal of stock operas was considerably reduced. In the second half of the nineteenth century interest in this aspect of opera production increased greatly: Wagner had already taken on some aspects of the role of Director and Verdi did likewise. Closer to home, W.S. Gilbert took on the same responsibilities in the production of the 'Savoy' operas of the 1880s, the military precision of his organisation being almost revolutionary in Victorian theatre.

48 *Observer*, quoted in *MW*, 31 July 1875, p. 525, of the performance by Mapleson's company on 19 July.

49 Rutherford, pp. 266–70. For further discussion see Rachel Cowgill and Hilary Poriss (eds), *The Arts of the Prima Donna in the Long Nineteenth Century* (Oxford, 2012), especially Chapter 2 (Roberta Montemorra-Marvin, 'Idealizing the Prima Donna in mid-Victorian London', pp. 21–40).

memoirs make it clear that the old practices were increasingly disparaged.[50] Minnie Hauk, who played a much-lauded Carmen in 1878 (see Chapter 2), wrote:

> The real reason for [the refusal of some Italian singers to sing at the London premiere] was that they had been singing mostly purely Italian music in front of the footlights, without making any effort to act the parts. To deviate from the traditional windmill acting, to the average Italian singer, would surely mean disaster … They looked as though they were being drilled for optic telegraphy or railroad switching. They stood, to all appearances, nailed to the boards, the soloists in a straight line right in front, the choristers in two or more lines behind, the men on one side, the women on the other, and every high note was accomplished by the raising of their right arms![51]

An anecdote related in an account of Zelia Trebelli reinforces the lack of concern for consistent acting among performers:

> When Ambroise Thomas's *Hamlet* was first brought out at Covent Garden [19 June 1869], with Christine Nilsson and Santley in the leading parts, the English baritone took a great interest in the production, and at rehearsal he would share the work of stage-management with Augustus Harris (the elder). He noticed that Signor Bagagiolo (the king) during the performance of the murder of Gonzago, remained perfectly calm and indifferent.
> 'Why don't you look frightened?' said the Englishman.
> 'Frightened,' answered the Italian, 'surely it would be most undignified for a king to be afraid of anything.'
> 'But don't you know this represents the murder you have committed on your own brother?'
> 'How should I know?'
> 'Perhaps you have not read the play?' (This ironically.)
> 'Certainly not. Do you think I bother myself about such things? I learn my part and read my cues, and that is quite sufficient *I* think!'[52]

This indifference was of relatively little concern to audiences of the 1870s, who placed the greatest stress on vocal ability; while there was interest in individual character (and, especially in the case of female singers, appropriate physical appearance), dramatic pacing and overall *mise-en-scène* were considered relatively insignificant. The prolonged applause given to the *prima donna*'s first entrance and to appreciated musical items, when singers were expected to step out of character and acknowledge the approbation, exemplify this. Requests for

---

50 See also comments made by Francis Neilson quoted in Chapter 3.

51 Hauk, pp. 160–61.

52 Marie de Mensiaux, *Trebelli: A Biographical Sketch and Reminiscences of Her Life* (London, 1890), pp. 16–17.

encores were still frequent (though falling) and often complied with, despite the inevitable disruption of dramatic narrative; one of the changes wrought by the establishment of Wagner's work in London was a decline in these habits (see below and Chapter 2). Similarly, the insertion of arias from other operas (especially as encores) was also increasingly rare, as were transpositions and cuts.[53]

At the commencement of this period the London opera season was of significant social consequence and undoubtedly, in the case of a great many habitués of the two theatres, the social function was of as great an importance as the musical one. Klein gave a neat account of the situation at Covent Garden in 1872:

> As high up as the amphitheatre stalls every tier contained, on the old continental plan, only private boxes … [The theatre] was illuminated, of course, by gas, this being some twenty years before electricity for lighting theatres came into use … Young as we were, my sister and I could fully appreciate the rare elegance of the ladies' gowns, the profusion and beauty of their glittering jewels, and the glint of their gorgeous tiaras. Neither in boxes or [*sic*] stalls did these dignified dames stir from their places during the entire evening. During the *entr'acte* scarcely a single lady was seen in the foyer … Thus the whole attraction of the opera house as a centre of social intercourse for the highest folk in the land was concentrated in and around the auditorium. If the ladies did not move, the gentlemen made up for it by visiting box after box whilst the curtain was down or gathering in groups to chat in the corridors. Nor did they constitute an altogether silent assemblage when the curtain was up. One could hear them chatting freely and passing critical comments even whilst the music was in progress. Their noisy 'bravos' would rattle out like a *feu de joie* even before the Rosina had finished her ultimate note or Violetta had run off trilling her final shake. In these respects they were certainly not the restrained, well-behaved audience that listens to good music nowadays. But they did, on the other hand, go regularly and constantly to the opera; and in their way they loved it with a profound, sincere and genuine affection.[54]

It is important to be clear about what Klein meant by 'the highest folk in the land': extensive research by Jennifer Hall-Witt has shown that, by the 1870s, the Italian opera seasons were no longer the exclusive preserve of the aristocracy or

---

[53] Transpositions are difficult to document as they were rarely commented upon in reviews, but the move away from the strict separation of numbers by secco recitative made transposition less practical than hitherto. In the case of both transpositions and cuts the trend towards valuing the score as a document to which performers remained faithful reduced incidences although, as Costa's performances of *Lohengrin* demonstrate, extensive alterations might still be made (see below) and cut versions of operas were still in use by all companies beyond the Great War.

[54] Klein, pp. 20–22. His comment regarding lighting is slightly misleading: electricity was installed at Her Majesty's in 1881 (*MW*, 14 May 1881, p. 308) but not at Covent Garden until 1892.

the landed gentry, whose members frequently took boxes for the whole season and attended most of the performances.[55] Compared to 50 years previously, the audience base had broadened but, as a percentage of the population, it remained minute; 'standards' were maintained by the requirement for evening dress at all performances in the grand season,[56] high prices, and a late starting time (8.30 pm) which made the journey home impossible without private transport.[57] In the second half of the nineteenth century, in order to reinforce the perception that they were socially respectable institutions, most West End theatres overtly sought to attract audiences from the middle classes and above; the opera houses were at the apex of this pyramid.[58]

Despite this slight broadening of the audience base, the social dimension was always important (and grew in the Edwardian years): Gye's diaries contain frequent references to the royalty and record their attendances. The Prince of Wales sometimes exploited his position by asking for certain operas on specific days, often putting Gye to considerable inconvenience.[59] Interest in royalty extended to the press and audience; when the Prince of Wales and his party appeared unexpectedly at Her Majesty's part-way through *La Traviata*:

---

55 See Jennifer Hall-Witt, *Fashionable Acts: Opera and élite culture in London 1780–1880* (Durham (New Hampshire), 2007).

56 Mapleson in particular relaxed this requirement after the official end of the grand season when additional performances at 'popular prices' were often given; nor was evening dress required at his autumn and winter seasons.

57 This starting time was standard until 1914. Performances frequently ended after midnight which led George Bernard Shaw to complain that this was unfair on anyone needing to catch last trains to the suburbs; at the same time many members of the affluent section of the audience still arrived late and Shaw regretted that they 'also insist on long waits between the acts, in order to get through the rounds of visits to one another's boxes, conversations in the crushrooms, promenades round the corridors, and cigarettes on the balcony over the portico' (see George Bernard Shaw, *London Music in 1888–89 as heard by Corno di Bassetto* (New York, 1973), pp. 141–3, first published in *The Star*, 7 June 1889).

58 For further discussion see Michael Booth, *Theatre in the Victorian Age* (Cambridge, 1991), especially pp. 21–6.

59 Gye wrote: 'The Prince of Wales came. Francis Knollys [the Prince's Private Secretary] had written to me to change the opera next Friday and Saturday and the Prince asked me to do it. *Lucrezia* is announced for Friday [23rd] and *Fra Diavolo* for Saturday the 24th and he wanted me to change the days to give *Fra Diavolo*, which he wanted to see, on Friday as he was engaged on Saturday. I pointed out to him that the whole week's operas had already been announced every day for 10 days, that country people had taken their tickets and that great disappointment … would be caused by a change … [but] HRH would not take "no" for an answer and he pressed me to make the change!! At last I said I would do what I could' (Gye's diary, 16 April 1875, ROHA). The Prince made a similar request a few weeks later (see Gye's diary, 20 May, ROHA). See also note 24 above.

> Sir Michael Costa immediately stopped the performance; the whole audience rose and cheered the Royal visitors with unanimous and genuine enthusiasm; the National Anthem was played; renewed cheering followed; and Madame Christine Nilsson, who was on the stage alone, went on with her part, and the opera was allowed to proceed without further interruption.[60]

Silent reverence of the performance was still to come; as Hall-Witt shows, there had been a gradual change over preceding decades and audiences were considerably quieter than hitherto, but universal rapt and undivided attention had not been achieved.[61] The practice of dimming the lights aided this change.[62] Notwithstanding the comments on singers above, there was also a gradual shift in attitudes (emphatically encouraged by many critics and later aided by the establishment of Wagner in the repertory) which placed a greater emphasis on the importance of the work performed; the expanded and more changeable audience helped this process. Complaints about audience behaviour were still made in the 1900s,[63] however, and the social function of the 'grand' seasons remained a central feature until the Great War.

Other Opera in London

Studies of British operatic culture in the late nineteenth century have usually focused on Covent Garden, not least because it was the only house with an unbroken run of seasons. Mapleson's itinerant company (Her Majesty's) has received less attention, although his rivalry with Gye, his entertaining memoirs, his employment of many leading singers, and his attempt to build the country's first 'national opera house' (see below) have ensured a recurring interest and, at the time, he stood almost on a par with Gye in terms of achievement and recognition. But while, in social terms, the two Italian companies certainly dominated London's operatic world, other troupes also appeared. In addition to the Carl Rosa Company's first London appearance (see below), there were also two other seasons of English opera and also a run of French operas, together comprising some 80 further performances.

60 *MW*, 20 May 1876, p. 351, of the performance on 13 May.

61 Heckling and loud conversations were frowned upon but whispering was frequent, as were late arrivals and early departures.

62 Placing the auditorium in near darkness was a practice only adopted in the 1890s but, from the 1850s, auditorium lighting was reduced during performances. Occasionally, in the winter, the weather reduced visibility: '[*The*] *Lily of Killarney* … would probably have been enjoyed by a larger audience as well as better appreciated by those actually present had not a dense fog darkened the streets and obscured the stage … everybody, on the stage and off it, agreed to "make the best of a bad job"' (*MW*, 31 January 1880, p. 67, of the Carl Rosa performance at Her Majesty's on 27 January).

63 See, for example, Violet Markham's letter to *MOMTR*, 1 July 1905, p. 743.

The French season took place at the Gaiety Theatre[64] between 5 June and 24 July and included performances of several works rarely performed in Britain; as well as the well-known *Fra Diavolo* (Auber) and *Zampa* (Hérold), there was also Auber's *Haydée*, Maillart's *Les Dragons de Villars*, Massé's *Galathée*, and Adam's *Le Postillon de Longjumeau*. Although attendance was variable there were good reviews in the *Era*, which commented of the opening night:

> All the brightest and best comic operas written for the French stage are produced one after another with a completeness which reflects the highest credit upon the company ... A theatre crowded in every part awaited with eagerness the first performance of *Zampa* last Saturday, and the audience present were well rewarded for the attendance, for the general representation of the opera was one of the best we can remember.[65]

The two English seasons trod rather more familiar ground. The first of these took place at Islington's Philharmonic Theatre.[66] It commenced on 30 January with Balfe's *Bohemian Girl*, with *Maritana* and *Fra Diavolo* subsequently added to the programme, and the season ended on 24 March. Despite the limited repertory the performances were praised and the length of the season suggests that attendances were buoyant. By early March, however, the *Era* was sufficiently encouraged to question the narrowness of the repertory:

> English Opera appears already to have taken deep root at Islington. Year after year we have been grumbling that nobody found a home for it. Year after year we have been saying 'Where are the native composers – where the English opera singers?' To these queries the management of the Philharmonic may now give an answer of the most emphatic kind in their success which has attended the representation of native composers at merrie [*sic*] Islington ... We have a host of really good operas, some of recent date, some now almost forgotten by the rising generation ... [W]hat of Barnett's delightful *Mountain Sylph*, Loder's *Night Dancers*, Sir Julius Benedict's *Lily of Killarney*, and several others by the same accomplished musicians, such for instance, as *The Crusaders*, [and] *Brides of Venice* etc.? What of Macfarren's *Robin Hood* ... What of the same composer's *Charles the Second*?[67]

---

64 The Gaiety Theatre was located on Aldwych; opened in 1868, it later became a major venue for musical comedy. It closed in 1939 and was demolished in 1956.

65 *Era*, 13 June 1875, p. 12.

66 Theatres outside the West End are best regarded as 'provincial' in this period (see Chapter 4), but Islington was within fairly easy reach of the metropolitan area and this season is included here for completeness.

67 *Era*, 7 March 1875, p. 14.

The Era was over-optimistic; the repertory of the English seasons was essentially moribund, relying on three or four native works and a greater number of foreign operas in translation. The second English season demonstrates the point; this commenced at the Gaiety on 31 July, just one week after the French operas had ended. Hopes were high; Wallace's lesser-known *Lurline* launched the enterprise, with the promise of Balfe's *Satanella* and *Geraldine* to come. The repertory was to be dominated by foreign works though: *Faust, Le nozze di Figaro* and Auber's *Crown Diamonds*, *Le Domino Noir*, and *Fra Diavolo* were all also promised. The timing of the season – high summer – was probably disadvantageous and it closed on 28 August, although *Satanella* was performed as promised and attracted a good review:

> The revival of *Satanella* ... attracted a wonderfully large house, remembering that it was August. The opera was as good as new to a great many who were present, since it has not been heard in London for years. If not the strongest of Balfe's work, the opera has many catching and also some elegant melodies, and the instrumentation is in many portions more careful and effective than is customary with Balfe, who was apt to trust more to the tender tenor and principal soprano than to the ensemble ... [Blanche Cole] never looked more fascinating, was never in better voice, and her acting has a charm such as is not always associated with English prima donnas ... The chorus was moderately good and the band excellent, and an additional attraction upon the stage was the ballet.[68]

As these three seasons and that of Carl Rosa show (see below), it would be erroneous to assume that there was little opera in London in 1875 or that it was exclusively Italian. In terms of social status though there can be no doubt that the two Italian companies held sway; the other seasons aimed firmly at a more 'middle-brow' audience. A common disability affected all participants, however: that of a restricted and static repertory. Within a few years this failure to renew, together with an avalanche of Wagner, brought Italian opera in London to the verge of collapse. For the present, however, singers, managers, audiences, and press colluded in maintaining the *status quo* and, as Klein's memoirs show, created an illusion of brilliance in all departments which remained totemic for decades to come.

Opera Outside London

Opera performances outside the metropolis in the nineteenth century have attracted scant academic attention, but, by the 1870s, there was plenty of activity, even if it was of variable quality. Touring opera companies had become an established feature of provincial life, first becoming a regular if infrequent occurrence at leading provincial theatres in the 1830s. The expansion of the railways invigorated

68 *Era*, 29 August 1875, p. 4, of the performance on 20 August.

operatic culture outside the metropolis, especially as this encouraged London's Italian companies to undertake tours from the 1850s onwards. In many larger cities (Dublin, Glasgow, Liverpool, Manchester, Birmingham, Newcastle, Edinburgh) brief operatic seasons could pay handsomely and, by the early 1870s, several leading singers eschewed long continental seasons in favour of the relatively short (though very intense) provincial tours run by men such as Mapleson and Willert Beale.[69] These Italian seasons came in addition to the performances mounted by smaller touring English companies. Taking all the activity together, most British towns of any size experienced at least one week of opera per year (albeit often of a very basic standard) and the biggest cities might enjoy several weeks of performances, some of which almost equalled those in the metropolis in standard. The nature of opera outside London is discussed in detail in Chapter 4.

1875: A Seminal Year

Three events make 1875 an important year in Britain's operatic history. It is symptomatic of the times that none of them was the performance of a new work by a British composer, still less one of landmark quality, and that all three took place in London. Two, at least, instigated significant shifts in Britain's operatic culture.

The first, most heralded, but ultimately least important of the three, was James Mapleson's proposal to build a new opera house on the Victoria Embankment, close to the Houses of Parliament.[70] Mapleson was frustrated by his failure to regain occupancy of Her Majesty's after it had been rebuilt (see above) and there were mixed feelings about Drury Lane: in 1874 the *Musical World* stated that 'having in view the experience of four or five seasons, much may be said in favour of Drury Lane – so much, indeed, that no great amount of philosophy is requisite for satisfaction with things as they are'[71] yet the following year the same theatre 'left much to be desired in many respects'.[72]

---

69 For further information on the activities of these companies see, for example, Maynard; Luigi Arditi, *My Reminiscences* (London, 1896); Thomas Willert Beale, *The Light of Other Days Seen Through the Wrong End of an Opera Glass* (London, 1890); Frederic Cowen, *My Art and My Friends* (London, 1913); and Paul Rodmell, '"The Italians are coming": Opera in mid-Victorian Dublin', in Rachel Cowgill and Julian Rushton (eds) *Europe, Empire and Spectacle* (Aldershot, 2006) pp. 97–112.

70 For a full discussion see Paul Rodmell, 'James Mapleson and the National Opera House' in Paul Rodmell (ed.), *Music and Institutions in Nineteenth-Century Britain* (Aldershot, 2012), pp. 99–117. See also Chapter 5.

71 *MW*, 7 March 1874, p. 149.

72 *MW*, 6 February 1875, p. 100. Mapleson commented that the rebuilt Her Majesty's was lacking as far as opera was concerned (Mapleson, vol. 1, pp. 173–4); his comments were vague but seemingly directed at the specifications of the auditorium and the circulation

The construction of the Victoria Embankment made land available at a newly desirable location. Mapleson submitted a proposal to the Metropolitan Board of Works in January 1875 and received considerable backing in the press:

> The scheme in which Mr Mapleson and Sir Michael Costa are associated may therefore be expected to give to London an Opera House on a site almost unrivalled among great cities. The new Opera of Paris looks, indeed, upon gleaming white streets and brilliant crowds, but an Opera House with a river front, or with the Victoria Embankment for its river terrace, will be something almost unique … [W]e cannot see how the spirit of aestheticism itself could suggest anything more harmonious and delightful than a lounge between the acts of an opera on a balcony looking on a moonlit river … with floating swans.[73]

Not only was there approval for the site and scheme itself, but it led many musicians to hope that Britain was on the way to acquiring a truly national opera, in which native works performed in English rubbed shoulders with high class performances of foreign works in both local and foreign tongues.

As details of the proposed building emerged, optimism increased: it would be large and comfortable, there would be direct access to the District Railway's station at Westminster, and also to the Houses of Parliament. Work commenced on the building in late spring, but delays were encountered almost immediately; the proximity of the Thames meant that the foundations had to be laid more deeply than expected which, together with recurrent flooding, increased the cost of this initial stage from an estimated £5,000 to an actual £33,000.[74] The first brick was laid by Therèse Tietjens on 7 September and, at the lunch which followed this small ceremony, Mapleson declared that 'whilst giving his usual attention to Italian opera, and endeavouring to produce all the available talent in Europe, three or four months in the year would be devoted to the English opera, executed, as far as possible, by English singers'.[75] Work continued, and the foundation stone was laid by the Duke of Edinburgh on 16 December. According to Mapleson's 1876 prospectus, however, his hope of holding that year's season in his new building had fallen through, due to the extra time needed to construct the foundations, and a severe winter.[76] Work ground to a halt. In June 1877 Mapleson asked the

---

areas; his pursuit of reoccupation, though, demonstrates that he placed great value on regaining the premises.

73 *DN*, quoted in *MW*, 30 January 1875, p. 79. The construction in Paris of an opulent new opera house just four years after its defeat in the Franco-Prussian War and the upheavals of the Commune highlighted for many London's lack of a purpose-built opera house.

74 Mapleson, vol. 1, p. 176. The estimate had been provided by W. Webster, the engineer responsible for building the Victoria Embankment.

75 *MP*, 8 September, quoted in *MW*, 11 September 1875, p. 100.

76 Prospectus of Her Majesty's Opera, Theatre Royal, Drury Lane, in *MW*, 15 April 1876, p. 284.

Metropolitan Board of Works to give him until September 1878 to complete the building,[77] but there was insufficient capital available.[78] Despite several further extensions, no physical progress was made and, in November 1882, the uncompleted building was sold for £29,000.[79] A scheme to build a hotel on the site also fell through and, subsequently, the above-ground parts of the building were demolished and the site used for the headquarters of the Metropolitan Police – New Scotland Yard – which opened in 1890.

In retrospect, the failure of the scheme seems inevitable: it required huge capital expenditure to be repaid by the erratic profits generated by grand opera. After regaining access to Her Majesty's Theatre, Mapleson's interest dwindled and he was further distracted by the enticing commercial possibilities of giving Italian opera in the United States. When he went bankrupt, in 1888, he claimed the chief cause was the failure of the national opera house (see Chapter 2). Although abortive, however, the scheme is of significance in terms of its scope and ambition, and because so much money (though not enough) was forthcoming to support it.

The second significant 'happening' of 1875, for it was a series of events, was the first appearance of Wagner's *Lohengrin* in London, the first stage production of one of his works in Britain apart from the solitary appearance of *Der fliegende Holländer* in 1870 (see above). Klein stated that this early exposure to Wagner aroused little enthusiasm and that tickets were easy to obtain,[80] and its cold reception in the press may have dampened any enthusiasm there was for Wagner other than among fervent supporters.[81] Gye promised *Lohengrin* in 1872 on the grounds that 'Wagner's grandest work has lately been produced at Bologna, and also at Florence, and has been received by the purely Italian audiences with the utmost enthusiasm'.[82] This may seem a strange justification for performing Wagner in London, but Gye probably made a shrewd judgment in promoting the idea that an opera well-received in Italy should merit the attention of the Covent Garden audience. He prefaced this declaration with comments to the effect that there had previously been too much division among London's opera audience as to the merits of Wagner's works to make the risk of mounting a production worthwhile. It was not, however, until 8 May 1875 that *Lohengrin* finally appeared

77 *Minutes of the Metropolitan Board of Works January-June 1877* (London, 1877), p. 746, of the meeting on 1 June.

78 Mapleson to *The Times*, 4 August 1877, p. 10; see also *MW*, 11 August 1877, p. 540. In view of Mapleson's letters, it seems that his application to the Board of Works for more time was opportunistic rather than a manifestation of deliberate intent.

79 *Minutes of the Metropolitan Board of Works July-December 1882* (London, 1882), p. 1015, of the meeting on 22 November 1882, and Mapleson, vol. 1, p. 183.

80 Klein, p. 14.

81 Mapleson stated that he had secured an Italian version of *Tannhäuser* in 1864, but had been dissuaded from producing it by cautious friends, it being only three years since the opera had been booed off the stage in Paris (Mapleson, vol. 1, p. 144).

82 Quoted in Rosenthal, p. 179.

at Covent Garden. This event would have been less important had not Mapleson also been determined to produce *Lohengrin* in the same season, thus creating a race to secure the first performance.[83] Gye won easily; Mapleson's production did not appear until 12 June, but the competition served to spur the curiosity of London's opera-going public and the appearance of *Lohengrin* was declared the 'great event of the season, and, should it turn out successful, we may dismiss the other promised novelties from consideration'.[84] Between them, the two companies gave 17 performances. Klein recalled that he only secured a seat for the first performance at Covent Garden after queuing for four hours and that he had 'never sat among a more excited crowd'.[85]

Press reaction was qualified; the divisions Gye referred to (see above) applied as much to the capital's music critics as to the mass audiences. *The Times* was largely positive:

> The English public has at length heard *Lohengrin*, and, if outward appearances may be trusted, heard it with satisfaction ... This singularly interesting drama in feeling so poetical, in simplicity of design, in purity of conception and logical symmetry of form, [is] so beautiful that, from a certain point of view, it seems incredible how Wagner the poet should also be Wagner the composer. Whatever may be said, and from whatever point of view, about the music of Wagner, and the theory upon which he constructs it ... [w]hat cannot fail to enlist sympathy is an earnestness which carries him with more or less artistic self-contentment through every task he undertakes.[86]

The *Musical World* grudgingly conceded that, 'we have never advocated the peculiar theories the application of which Herr Wagner thinks indispensable to ideal perfection ... But to deny the stern consistency with which he has endeavoured, and still endeavours, to enforce and carry them out is manifestly unjust'.[87]

Noting that the performance did not end until after 1 am, the *Daily Telegraph* remained largely unmoved:

---

83 Mapleson claimed that Gye had underhandedly acquired Marchesi's translation of *Lohengrin* for which Mapleson had paid Marchesi £150. Unfortunately, under British copyright laws, Mapleson had not secured legal possession of the right of representation of Marchesi's version because he had not mounted a 'mock performance before a sham public' and could not, therefore, prevent Gye from producing the opera. See Mapleson, vol. 1, p. 145.

84 *MW*, 3 April 1875, p. 228.

85 Klein, p. 36. Gye's diary states that on-the-night ticket sales were very healthy: the first four performances brought in £553 (8 May), £503 (10 May), £530 (19 May) and £436 (5 June).

86 *The Times*, 10 May 1875, quoted in *MW*, 15 May 1875, p. 316.

87 *MW*, 22 May 1875, p. 342.

Nearing Covent Garden we are sensible of a special occasion … The Teutonic element is [in the amphitheatre and gallery] in strong force, signalized by round, florid faces, a profusion of straw-coloured beards, many spectacles, and a prevailing expression of that solemn thoroughness which characterizes the worshipping German mind … Even royalty basks in the dawning light of the day of future opera. First to enter the Royal box are the Duchess of Cambridge and the Duke and Duchess of Teck, after whom come the Prince and Princess of Wales and the Duke of Connaught, with their respective suites. But much more conspicuous to discerning eyes than these 'dignities' is the gathering of men and women famous in the worlds of literature and art …

A minute's pause and then the prelude begins. We do not like the manner of its beginning. Liszt describes the opening bars as a 'vaporous ether' but we find them neither vaporous nor ethereal, but simply a commonplace sequence of chords for violins, in eight parts, played much too loudly … [Of Elsa's Act I monologue] The music here is full of tenderness and beauty. It is melodious besides and the ear rejoices in it … [At Lohengrin's arrival] a wonderful double chorus expresses the astonishment of the on-lookers – such a chorus as only genius could have written … Here, not the Germans up aloft merely, but everybody is delighted, and, in response to loud applause, Signor Vianesi repeats the chorus … [At the end of Act I] are we satisfied as well as excited? Some of us, at least, must answer 'no'. Weary of blazing tone-colour, endless surprises, unmelodious declamation, and the constant strain at which the composer works, we doubt … if this be the only true dramatic music …

[End of Act II] We are now within half-an-hour of midnight, and numerous departures from boxes and stalls take place. But the enthusiasts up above hold out, and, in scarcely diminished numbers, address themselves to what yet remains of the work …

Will *Lohengrin* commend itself to the taste of English opera-goers, and establish Wagner amongst us? Of its present success we have no doubt. It will be the feature of the season. But how as to future seasons … Can our amateurs transfer their allegiance to music without form; to music as the slave of poetry, to music which is melodious only by snatches, and is charming only in the degree in which it is a violation of Wagner's advanced opinions … Music is not an affair of declamation, tremolos, trumpets, chromatics, and general swimming about in the vast ocean of tone. Music is tune, form, key-relationship, and adherence to those contrapuntal laws which can never be violated with impunity because they spring from a natural necessity. Wagner may triumph awhile, but the masters will return to their old place, and, after all, temporary good fortune means little.[88]

88 *MW*, 22 May 1875, pp. 344–5 and 29 May 1875, pp. 359–60.

Mapleson's production at Drury Lane, was, Klein argued, the better of the two.[89] *The Times* was full of admiration for the production but its interest in the work seemed to have waned:

> Until the fall of the curtain at the termination of each act, [no] marked approval of [the singers' efforts was] tolerated … On principle, we by no means complain of this new custom; any more than we complain of Sir Michael Costa's stern and persistent refusal to comply with certain 'encores' … He, in addition to other by no means unwelcome curtailments, omitted at least one half of the finale to Act I, [of] which, if we may be allowed to judge by the uproarious applause from the upper regions … [they] did not seem to be aware … [T]he curtailments in the score of *Lohengrin* made by Sir Michael are decidedly to the advantage of the work, which, if unabridged, consisting as it does almost exclusively of declamatory recitative, more or less elaborately accompanied by the orchestra, would wear out the patience of any audience … Airs, duets, trios, concerted pieces, choruses &c., with a beginning, middle and end, according to generally received ideas of music, even in a dramatic shape, are scarcely anywhere to be found. Nevertheless, there is a certain attraction about the whole not fairly to be questioned.[90]

It remained for the critic of the *Globe* to come up with a sentence which suggests a degree of foresight: 'The opera of Wagner may not take the place of the opera of Mozart, of Rossini, of Meyerbeer, or of Verdi, but the opera of the next musician of genius will be very different from what it would have been had Wagner never lived'.[91]

The common threads from these reviews are that, while Wagner could be admired for his self-belief and talent, the results were too far distant from the accepted norms of what constituted opera in the British mind. Diffuse form, convoluted tonality, aimless melody and excessive length were all cited as weaknesses, and it took time for critics and audiences alike to adjust to this new musical language. Crucially, however, as the event of the season in both houses, a momentum was initiated which, when added to by events of the next two years, assured Wagner's place in British operatic practice. In the following year no-one reading any musical journal could escape coverage of *Der Ring* at Bayreuth, and Wagner's own visit (albeit financially disastrous) to London in 1877 maintained this trend. *Tannhäuser* was premiered at Covent Garden in 1876 and *Der fliegende Holländer* in 1877; Carl Rosa gave the first performances of Wagner in English (*The Flying Dutchman*) at the Lyceum in 1876. All three operas appeared at Covent Garden in each season from 1878 to 1880, although, in 1881 and 1882 only *Lohengrin* appeared – but by then German Opera Seasons had started and Italian opera's dominance of the London stage was under threat.

---

89 Klein, p. 38.

90 *The Times*, 14 June 1875, p. 10.

91 *Globe*, 14 June 1875, quoted in *MW*, 26 June 1875, p. 421.

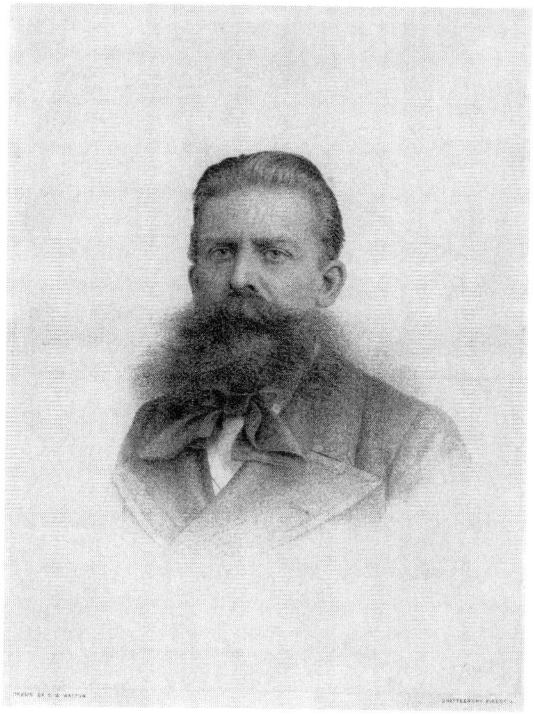

Figure 1.1 Carl Rosa, engraving by C.W. Walton

The last of the three happenings in 1875 was the first appearance in London of the Carl Rosa Opera Company. English opera, meaning here both the language of performance and an established native repertory, was in a rather desultory state in 1875 (see above). What was lacking, crucially, was the finance to facilitate the activity and an individual or small group with the charisma and determination to maintain a company once established. Rosa was fortunate in possessing money, presence, and resolution, as well as being a practising musician. He had had a thorough grounding in European operatic culture and had married the singer Euphrosyne Parepa, who had appeared with British opera companies since the late 1850s. Their collaborative activities started in the United States in 1867 but Euphrosyne's indifferent health precluded the creation of a regular operation. In 1873, however, the Parepa-Rosa Opera Company embarked upon a British tour, taking in Manchester, Dublin, Cork and Liverpool, and arranged to take Drury Lane for a season of English opera (including an English language version of *Lohengrin*) in March 1874. Euphrosyne, however, died unexpectedly on 22 January 1874 while Carl was abroad; the company completed its engagement in Liverpool, ending on 7 February, and it was stated that it would be disbanded.[92] The Drury Lane season was cancelled. A year later, though, Rosa returned to

[92] *Liverpool Daily Albion*, 3 February 1874, quoted in *MW*, 14 February 1874, p. 100.

Britain, reformed his company, and started on another provincial tour, in Dublin on 29 March 1875.

Rosa made a canny decision in not launching his opera company in London, where critical scrutiny was at its most extensive and forensic. After Dublin he went to Liverpool, Birmingham, and Leeds, and took a summer break before opening a six-week season in the capital on 11 September at the Royal Princess's Theatre.[93] Rosa also made the wise decision to engage some first-rate singers; he induced Charles Santley, the leading British baritone, to return to the London operatic stage after an absence of several years, and also recruited Ostava Torriani, who had sung for Mapleson in 1873. Both choices were good ones: although there were many British singers in the Italian companies, Santley had a well-established reputation and was the only one who could take a leading role in an Italian company and hold his own; the engagement of Torriani demonstrated that Rosa was more interested in getting the best singers he could afford than in taking British singers for the sake of it.

Rosa also chose his repertory astutely, including a judicious mixture of established classics, native works, and a couple of novelties. He did not try to compete with the Italian companies in this first London season by giving Meyerbeer, Donizetti or Bellini, and his only direct challenges were performances of *Faust* and *Il Trovatore*. He supported this with two other perennial favourites, *Le nozze di Figaro* and Flotow's *Martha*, and added *Zampa*, and the native works *The Bohemian Girl*, *The Siege of Rochelle*, *The Rose of Castile* (all Balfe) and Wallace's *Maritana*. Finally there was the British premiere of Cagnoni's *The Porter of Havre* and the English language premiere of Cherubini's *The Water Carrier*. That Rosa's season was socially less exalted and aimed at a more middle class audience than those of the Italian companies is reflected by his playing six nights every week (instead of the traditional four), selling no subscriptions, playing outside the social season, and charging considerably less for single performances: boxes ranged from 1 to 3 guineas, stall seats were 7s 6d, Dress Circle 5s, upper boxes 3s, pit seats 2s 6d, and gallery seats 1s.

The absence of 'society' led to a far greater interest on the part of the press in the performances themselves and artistically the season was proclaimed a success. In addition to the quality of the singers, Rosa's production values were praised with few qualifications; the proficient orchestra of 40 was especially welcomed.[94] Cagnoni's music was felt to be too slight,[95] but *The Water Carrier* was well-received; of the revival of *The Siege of Rochelle* the *Musical World* declared 'the work has been carefully put on the stage and has evidently been well rehearsed, while the case of the *dramatis personae* is about as strong a one as could now be easily obtained'.[96] One of the few notes of criticism was that Rosa had not been

93 A seventh week was added and the season finished on 30 October.

94 *The Times*, 14 September 1875, p. 6.

95 *Era*, 19 September 1875, p. 14.

96 *MW*, 16 October 1875, p. 694.

able to premiere a new British opera.[97] The financial results of the season are unknown, although Charles Santley stated:

> For some reason which I could not understand the performances being so good, the receipts were not what they ought to have been. In order to attempt to increase them, Rosa begged of me to waive my stipulation and play di Luna in *Il Trovatore* ... I believe the opera was successful in replenishing the exchequer.[98]

Whatever the financial results, it was essential for Rosa's reputation as a producer of superior opera to appear in London annually; this demonstrated both that his company was truly national, and that provincial audiences could be sure that they were being treated to something which would satisfy their metropolitan counterparts and was a cut above the other touring troupes. The company returned to London in subsequent years (see Chapter 2), building up a consistent reputation for careful and successful productions, later strengthened by the introduction of new British works.

Conclusion

For the contemporaneous observer there was much to praise and some grounds for encouragement in the nation's operatic activity in 1875. Shortcomings could easily be identified and adverse comparisons made with other European countries, most obviously France, Germany, Austria-Hungary and Italy, but London was still running two rival Italian companies, plus at least four other seasons, comprising over 200 performances. The provinces were served by at least two touring companies, plus the West End troupes themselves (see Chapter 4). Performance standards that now seem poor would have drawn far less censure (reflected in contemporaneous press reviews) and the presence of so many 'star' singers in London was a source of pride and enthusiasm. There was also a new company making a great impression, a scheme to build a new, dedicated opera house, and Britain was slowly opening its mind to Wagner. Although native opera was in a much less satisfactory state, the presence of the Rosa company signalled a real possibility that a corner might soon be turned and British composers might once more find an outlet for their work. With the advantage of hindsight it is easy to see weaknesses, foibles, and faults; for those contemporaneous observers looking for the start of a renaissance, however, the events of 1875 must have been a cause of optimism.

---

97 *Graphic*, quoted in *MW*, 23 October 1875, p. 711.

98 Charles Santley, *Reminiscences of my Life* (London, 1909), pp. 108–9. Santley had agreed to work for Rosa on condition that he would not appear in either *Il Trovatore* or *The Bohemian Girl*; see Chapter 4.

Chapter 2
Opera in London 1876–96

Stagnation: Italian Opera 1876–81

The 1860s and early '70s represented the high-watermark of Italian opera in central London. From the mid-1870s onwards, however, the environment in which the Italian companies operated became less receptive as tastes, repertories, rivalries and other circumstances changed. Initially, there was a 'business as usual' attitude; this itself contributed to later difficulties, which became acute in the mid-1880s. Only with the emergence of Augustus Harris as an impresario in 1887 did the situation stabilise.

From 1876 to 1881, the Italian seasons of Gye and Mapleson operated in a manner similar to that of the previous 15 years. Mapleson regained access to Her Majesty's Theatre in 1877 and remained there until 1881, but was increasingly distracted by American tours that proved more lucrative than performances in London; Frederick Gye retired in the same year and was succeeded by his son Ernest.[1] The musical policies of both companies continued unchanged and focused on leading singers at the expense of repertory. 'Novelties' were produced but their receptions varied. The success of *Lohengrin* in 1875 encouraged Gye to produce *Tannhäuser* the following year, along with *Aïda*; Mapleson's greatest success was with *Carmen* in 1878 and he also gave the British premiere of Boïto's *Mefistofele* in 1880, but his track record was otherwise desultory.[2] Most of the remaining premieres (see Table 2.1) proved of little interest to audiences, although Gye's presentation of Massenet's *Le Roi de Lahore* was a further contribution to the steadily increasing vogue for French opera created by *Faust* and *Carmen*, which persisted for the rest of the century.

Patti and Albani remained the leading *prime donne* at Covent Garden. For Mapleson circumstances were more complex; Tietjens managed only a few performances in the 1877 season due to cancer, and died on 3 October that year.[3] Her place was taken in most roles by either Christine Nilsson or Ethelka Gerster. Both companies lacked a true tenor; Jean de Reszke later embodied this ideal,

[1] Frederick was accidentally shot on 27 November 1878 at a shooting party at Dytchley Park, Oxfordshire, and died on 4 December.

[2] Mapleson brought Hans Richter to London as an operatic conductor for the first time for four performances of *Lohengrin* in 1880. Richter's conducting was praised; see *MW*, 5 June 1880, p. 351 and *MS*, 5 June 1880, pp. 355–6.

[3] Her last performance was in *Lucrezia Borgia* on 19 May; an emotional account is given in Herman Klein, *Thirty Years of Musical Life in London* (London, 1903), pp. 20–21.

Table 2.1 Italian Company opera premieres 1876–81

Composer	Opera	Company	Date
Wagner	*Tannhäuser*	CG	6 May 1876
Verdi	*Aïda*	CG	22 June 1876
Ernest, Duke of Saxe-Coburg	*Santa Chiara*	CG	30 June 1877
Massé	*Paul et Virginie*	CG	1 June 1878
Bizet	*Carmen*	HM	22 June 1878
Flotow	*Alma l'incantatrice*	CG	9 July 1878
D'Ivry	*Les Amants de Vérone*	CG	24 May 1879
Massenet	*Le Roi de Lahore*	CG	28 June 1879
Hérold	*Le Pré aux Clercs*	CG	26 June 1880
Cohen	*Estella (Les Bluets)*	CG	3 July 1880
Boïto	*Mefistofele*	HM	6 July 1880
Rubinstein	*The Demon*	CG	21 June 1881
Baron Bódog 'Felix' Orczy*	*Il Rinnegato*	HM	9 July 1881

CG: Royal Italian Opera (Gye)

HM: Her Majesty's Italian Opera (Mapleson)

* Orczy (1835–92) was formerly director of the National Opera of Budapest and came to England in 1880; he also composed *Sisyphus*, to a libretto by Frederick and Henrietta Corder (1882).

but another decade was to pass before he established himself in London.[4] The appearance of Minnie Hauk as Carmen created the sort of excitement about a new singer previously enjoyed by Patti, Albani and Marietta Piccolomini, and she had considerable success in other roles. The 'star system' remained dominant; most press reviews continued to show a greater interest in established singers and debutantes than in any other aspect of the opera, but new stars were rare.

Considering the pre- and post-season reviews of these years, there is little sign of discontent: 'the prospectus issued by Mr Gye to his subscribers and the public for the 31st season of the Royal Italian Opera, is likely to afford almost unqualified satisfaction,'[5] stated *The Times* in respect of Covent Garden's 1877 season. The writer highlighted proposed productions of *Der fliegende Holländer*, *Les Vêpres Siciliennes*, Nicolai's *Die Lustigen Weiber von Windsor*, Rubinstein's *Nero* and

[4] His younger brother, Edouard, a bass, sang in London from 1880 onwards; Jean appeared briefly as a baritone in 1875 to little acclaim but as a tenor only from 1887.

[5] *The Times*, 30 March 1877, p. 6.

the Duke of Saxe-Coburg's *Santa Chiara*, although only the last two were new to Britain. Nevertheless, the *Pall Mall Gazette* described the prospectus as 'even more interesting than usual'.[6]

Seasons, however, were shortening: Gye's longest, in 1875, comprised 83 performances; by 1881 his son had reduced this to 63. Mapleson's seasons varied much more, reaching 77 performances in 1878 (aided by 11 renditions of *Aïda* and 12 of *Carmen*) but reducing to only 44 the following year. Of Mapleson's 1878 season, the *Musical World* commented:

> The production of *Carmen* alone would have sufficed to make … [it] memorable … How much of this is due to the exceptional merits of the work, how much to the thoroughly efficient cast, and how much to the unique assumption of the gipsy heroine by Miss Minnie Hauk, we leave the amateurs to decide.[7]

Italian opera as practised in London for three decades was starting to wane in popularity.[8] At the end of the 1881 grand season, Ernest Gye and Mapleson announced that they were joining forces in a move reminiscent of the 'coalition' seasons of 1869 and 1870. The Royal Italian Opera was converted into a limited company, with Gye as managing director and Mapleson the manager of the American tours.[9] With Mapleson in the United States, Gye became the sole provider of Italian opera in London in the grand season. A *Musical World* retrospective of activities in 1881 stated:

> Recent events clearly show that we are going through a time of transition. Practically, Italian opera no longer exists in this country. The production of Verdi's *Aïda* made it flicker for a while, but the composer of *Rigoletto* is growing

6 *PMG*, 21 March 1877, p. 11.

7 *MW*, 3 August 1878, p. 493.

8 Mapleson also gave some autumn seasons at Her Majesty's; the repertory was confined to repeats. The only other traced Italian season in London was mounted by Samuel Hayes at the Lyceum (1 October to 12 November 1881); no new works were presented but the performances were quite well received. He returned in 1884; see note 23.

9 *The Times* stated that 'the average annual profit for the six years immediately preceding the death of the late Mr [Frederick] Gye was upwards of £15,500. Mr Gye's sudden death … and other exceptional causes in the years 1879 and 1880 occasioned a falling off in the revenue for those two years, but during the present year (1881) the subscriptions are largely in excess of any previous season' (21 July 1881, p. 12). As well as Ernest Gye, the directors of the new company included former Conservative minister Lord Lathom (Edward Wilbraham-Bootle), Count Gleichen (Prince Viktor of Hohenlohe-Langenburg), and Baron Ferdinand de Rothschild (banker and later Liberal MP). A more detailed prospectus appeared in *MW* (15 April 1882, p. 232). The total value of the Covent Garden building and its contents was estimated at £332,000, the likely annual profits of the American seasons at £20,000, and it was noted that during the previous 'coalition' seasons annual profits had exceeded £22,000. The company also acquired the lease of Her Majesty's Theatre.

old, and has no successor, the genius of Boïto possessing little in common with that of his country. Our so-called Italian opera has for years been mainly supported by French works, and last season its chief hope rested upon the *Il Demonio* of the Russian, Rubinstein. Whither does all this tend? … [M]ay we expect the advent of a lyric drama under new forms? To the first query we tender a decided negative, the experience of 1881 having shown that opera in Italian has a very scanty public outside the limits of 'society' and apart from the famous artists whom 'popular prices' cannot attract … Meanwhile, we are at liberty to contemplate the threatened invasion of German opera next season. As to this there is no cause for alarm. The mellifluous tongue of Italy will not be succeeded by the gutterals of the Teuton, not the melodious phrases of Rossini and his compeers by the harsh progressions of the full-blown Wagner.[10]

A Wagnerian Deluge: Grand Opera in 1882

The impact of the German opera seasons of 1882, together with the consistent advance over several years of Carl Rosa and an increasing interest in light opera, combined to end the domination of London by Italian troupes. By 1884 Gye's company had been wound up and Italian opera appeared close to disappearing altogether. But in 1882 commercial speculation led to German opera overplaying its hand. Two companies appeared in London in the late spring, partly concurrently, one managed by Angelo Neumann at Her Majesty's and the other by Hermann Franke at Drury Lane. Both, in effect, mounted Wagner seasons, resulting in an over-supply that undermined the achievement and both were encompassed by the grand season at Covent Garden, which ran from 18 April to 20 July. Taking all three seasons together seven British premieres occurred within two months (see Table 2.2).

Neumann's season, conducted by Anton Seidl, opened on 5 May and comprised three complete performances of *Der Ring*, one per week; a fourth cycle was announced but only *Die Walküre* and *Götterdämmerung* were given. Press reaction was mixed both in respect of the works themselves, and the performances: the ambivalence of many of London's critics to Wagner's music is well-documented.[11] At the positive end *The Times* stated:

---

10 'Music in 1881', *MW*, 7 January 1882, p. 3.

11 See, for example, Meirion Hughes, *The English Musical Renaissance and the Press 1850–1914: Watchmen of Music* (Aldershot, 2002); R.T. Bledsoe, *Henry Fothergill Chorley: Victorian Journalist* (Aldershot, 1998); C. Reid, *The Music Monster: A Biography of James William Davison, Music Critic of 'The Times' of London* (London, 1984).

Table 2.2 Opera premieres in London in 1882

Date	Theatre	Work
5 May	HM	Wagner *Das Rheingold*
6 May	HM	Wagner *Die Walküre*
8 May	HM	Wagner *Siegfried*
9 May	HM	Wagner *Götterdämmerung*
30 May	DL	Wagner *Die Meistersinger*
20 June	DL	Wagner *Tristan und Isolde*
4 July	CG	Lenepveu *Velléda* (world premiere)

> There has been no falling off in the interest of the public … Looking back at the four performances we have witnessed, it is impossible to overstate their importance for the development of dramatic music in this country.[12]

The *Musical World* remained hostile, and reported (with *Schadenfreude*) that the second and third cycles had drawn smaller audiences than the first, and that the two final performances were given at 'cheap prices':

> Wagner's trilogy [*sic*] has not proved a success amongst us. Our public saw its approach without enthusiasm, and will witness its departure with indifference … We affect no regret at the artistic failure of the trilogy [*sic*] in London. The result was hoped for, and is now rejoiced over, not out of passion or prejudice, nor because of any sectarian feeling, but from an honest conviction that its principles are the reverse of those which make for the good of the lyric stage.[13]

Franke's season, conducted by Hans Richter, opened on 18 May and closed on 30 June. Fortunately he duplicated none of Neumann's repertory: at Drury Lane audiences could see *Lohengrin*, *Der fliegende Holländer*, *Tannhäuser*, *Die Meistersinger*, *Tristan und Isolde*, *Euryanthe* and *Fidelio*.[14] Unsurprisingly it was the performances of the two new operas which drew the greatest interest; opinion was much more favourable towards *Die Meistersinger* (performed 10 times) than *Tristan* (given twice). On the latter the contrast between *The Times* and the *Musical World* was stark:

[12] 'Wagner's *Ring of the Nibelung IV*', *The Times*, 11 May 1882, p. 6; reviews of the first three operas were published on 6 May, p. 12; 8 May, p. 12; 9 May, p. 10. These were almost certainly written by Francis Hueffer, an enthusiastic Wagnerian.

[13] *MW*, 3 June 1882, pp. 330–32.

[14] *Così fan tutte* was also promised but not produced (*MS*, 18 March 1882, p. 166). See also Christopher Fifield, *True Artist and True Friend: A Biography of Hans Richter* (Oxford, 1993), pp. 187–93.

> No other work of Wagner is so thoroughly his own and so entirely unlike what any other composer has ever done or is likely to do. The unity of feeling and expression, the continuity of unremitting passion here displayed, are probably unprecedented in the history of music … Perhaps nowhere else has Wagner shown greater boldness than in the continued strain of passion which he sustains throughout this opera.[15]

> Vocal melody had hardly a place on the lyric stage. Save for a few passages wherein the voice is permitted to drift, as by accident, into the 'infinite melos' of the orchestra, *Tristan and Isolde* is one long bout of declamation … If marriage be illustrated at all in *Tristan und Isolde*, it is marriage in which the woman, Music, has no rights, but becomes a slave to the man, Poetry … Music so treated loses its dignity, and, which is of greater practical consequence, stands forth deprived of its essential charm.[16]

Even before the German seasons, the stagnant nature of Gye's operation was apparent from the reliance in his advertisements on the attractiveness of the *prime donne*.[17] The only new work (and a rare London world premiere), Lenepveu's *Velléda*,[18] failed, it being unable to withstand the Wagnerian onslaught in any respect, despite Patti being cast in the title role. By the end of July London, which had also hosted Carl Rosa at the beginning of the year (see below) was overwhelmed, and it was unsurprising that none of the companies had done well financially. Had the Wagner seasons taken place at different times they would almost certainly have done better. It was particularly unfortunate for Richter, who received widespread praise for the consistency of his cast, the quality of his conducting, and his orchestra. A lengthy retrospective by Joseph Bennett summed up the position:

> It is depressing to hear on all hands stories of evil fortune rather than good. Far from flourishing circumstances at Covent Garden, loss at Her Majesty's, and absolute disaster at Drury Lane … The lesson to be learned is this – the supporters of opera, Italian and German, are few, and appear to be getting fewer as, on the one hand, love for the higher forms of music is gratified by innumerable concerts, and, on the other, comic opera increasingly ministers to a public that craves amusement at the least possible trouble to itself …

---

15 *The Times*, 22 June 1882, p. 4.

16 *MW*, 24 June 1882, p. 380.

17 See weekly advertisements in *MW*; until 6 May the entry for each day starts with the opera, but, from 13 May, the names of the *prime donne* come first, in bold type on individual lines.

18 Massenet's *Hérodiade* was included in the prospectus 'if time should permit, towards the end of the season' but not produced (*MW,* 8 April 1882, p. 220).

> Against [Wagner] Italian opera, with its staler charms, could do little. The musical world talked of nothing but the Nibelung's Ring, the *Meistersinger*, *Tristan und Isolde*, Richter and his orchestra, the German ensemble and the German artists. *La Traviata* and *Il Trovatore, et hoc genus omne*, even with the renowned *prime donne* singing their best and loudest over the footlights, were for once deposed, thrust into a corner, and forgotten. We certainly do not complain of the result. It was inevitable, and from many points of view it was just ... Who can tell what great things rivalry of German discipline, thoroughness, and devotion might do for slipshod Italian opera? It might give new life and new charm to an entertainment which loose and inartistic habits have made vapid and profitless.[19]

To the Brink and Back: Italian Opera 1883–87

After the intense and varied activities of 1882, Grand Opera in London reverted to type. Despite Gye's monopoly, the 1883 season at Covent Garden comprised only 62 performances, the shortest for over 20 years; London premieres over the next five years reduced to a trickle (Table 2.3).

Table 2.3 Opera premieres in London, 1883–87 (all at Covent Garden)

Date	Work
31 May 1883	Ponchielli *La Gioconda*
9 July 1884	Stanford *Savonarola*
15 July 1884	Reyer *Sigurd*
22 April 1887	Bizet *Les pêcheurs de perles* (given as *Leila*)
12 July 1887	Glinka *A life for the Tsar*

The 1884 season was slightly better: in addition to the Italian company, a German troupe conducted by Richter was engaged and gave 15 performances. The German repertory included, as in 1882, *Tristan* and *Die Meistersinger* but reviews were generally poor: although Richter, his orchestra, and some of the singers were praised, the performances overall were judged unsatisfactory and Stanford's *Savonarola* was criticised on all fronts (see Chapter 6).[20] The Italian company gave only 53 performances, the fewest since 1858;[21] Reyer's *Sigurd*

19 Joseph Bennett, 'The Opera Season' in *DT*, quoted in *MW*, 29 July 1882, p. 463.

20 See also Fifield, pp. 205–10.

21 The 1858 season was atypical; its opening was later than usual due to the theatre being rebuilt after the fire of 1856.

attracted mixed reviews, suffering principally from comparisons with Wagner.[22] The *Magazine of Music* lamented:

> The opera season … has turned out thoroughly disappointing … [T]he failure … has not been confined to the financial side of the campaign. In an artistic sense the results have been equally unsatisfactory … The very first performance given by the Germans proved the troupe to be of third-rate quality … Two or three good artists came to the front during the season: the orchestra was generally excellent and the chorus tolerably good, while Herr Richter executed marvels with the baton. But in all other respects the undertaking was, from first to last, unworthy … With regard to the Italian season it must be candidly confessed that results have hardly been of a nature to reassure those who claim that Italian opera is not 'on its last legs'. Never has the attitude of the aristocracy towards their whilom favourite amusement been more clearly demonstrated … Save on three or four of the Patti nights … there has been a conspicuous absence of the brilliant gatherings which in the palmy times used to be a feature of the ordinary subscription night. But even on such exceptional occasions the glitter of the crowd has emanated from *les nouveaux riches* rather than the personages whose names fill the pages of Debrett.[23]

At the end of the season the Royal Italian Opera Company, formed only two years earlier, went into voluntary receivership. While the immediate cause was given as the failure of the company's tenant at Her Majesty's and costs imposed by the Metropolitan Board of Works for new safety measures, the *Musical Standard* argued that, 'Public opinion would have been better satisfied by a few frank confessions as to the evil effects on the company's finances of the extortionate star system'.[24] While the *Standard*'s claims cannot be substantiated, it appears that Patti and Nilsson, like Mapleson, had discovered how much money could be made in America and were demanding similar sums in London; Patti was rumoured to be receiving £450 per night.[25] If this is true it confirms the company's vulnerability: stars could demand huge fees in the knowledge that, without them, there was little left with which to attract an audience. The reasons for society's desertion of the opera are unclear; the trend had been noted previously, but in the mid-1880s the decline was much more marked and provoked a crisis; Joseph Bennett's statement

22 *Sigurd* (1862–67), is based on part of the *Nibelungenlied* and unfavourable comparisons arose from this coincidence; see *The Times* 16 July 1884, p. 8, and *MT*, 1 August, pp. 455–6.

23 *MoM*, 1 August 1884, p. 8. Samuel Hayes presented Italian operas in November but gave no new works and his season was indifferently received; there was also a concert performance of *Parsifal* on 10 November (*MW*, 15 November 1884, p. 717).

24 *MS*, 16 August 1884, p. 78.

25 If a very well-populated house brought in £1,150 (see Chapter 1, note 24), Patti's fee represented 40 per cent of box office income.

above seems reasonable, but the explanations given by Félix Remo relating to the death of Prince Leopold and the military setbacks in Africa and central Asia are persuasive as they would explain the temporary nature of the crisis.[26]

In the light of these events and trends, it is unsurprising that 1885 and 1886 represent the nadir of Italian opera in London. No performances in the 1885 social season were expected at all until early April, when Mapleson announced a short run of 14 nights at Covent Garden fronted by Patti,[27] who cancelled two appearances, including the opening night (20 June), due to illness; her début as Carmen was generally deemed a failure. Despite this she received £500 per performance, and this season vividly demonstrates the impossible position in which Italian companies found themselves: total reliance on a *prima donna* who demanded huge fees resulting in a highly truncated season comprising only standard repertory.[28] The financial results are unknown; it is unlikely that Mapleson made any money.

In the view of the *Musical Standard*, Italian opera was in a desperate state:

> The *Figaro* informs us that Mr Gye will probably retake [Covent Garden] next year, and that the Wednesdays will be reserved as a sort of exclusive night for the Royal Family and the 'Upper Ten': the *profanum vulgus* to be excluded; … We are to return then to the good old times of stiff collars, footmen's trousers, shoe buckles, powdered hair and paste diamonds. The Directors of Italian opera seem to be leading a forlorn hope. The star system has been their ruin and the outlook shews that when existing stars disappear no Lucifer is likely to rise in the east.[29]

If true, this rumour would show why Italian opera had steadily become less attractive over the years, that is, the very social exclusivity of previous decades was a principal reason that the richest part of the audience attended. Beyond the

---

26 Félix Remo, *Music in the Land of Fogs*, trans. A.J. Robertson (London, 1887), p. 16. A Frenchman living in London, Remo suggested that the social seasons of 1884 and '85 were dampened by the death of Prince Leopold, Queen Victoria's youngest son (28 March 1884), the Mahdist War in Sudan (which included the Siege of Khartoum and death of General Charles Gordon in early 1885), and the 'Panjdeh Incident' (30 March 1885), a military skirmish between Britain and Russia in Afghanistan.

27 *MS*, 4 April 1885, p. 216.

28 After the last performance on 25 July, Patti was presented with a diamond-studded bracelet to commemorate her 25 consecutive seasons at Covent Garden and her carriage was escorted by individuals carrying torches and accompanied by a large crowd to the Midland Hotel, St Pancras. See *MS*, which commented that 'it is supposed that this kind of enthusiasm, whether real or artificial, spontaneous or paid for, is now and then necessary for the support of the star system' (1 August 1885, p. 66).

29 *MS*, 8 August 1885, p. 81. The term 'upper ten [thousand]' originated in the United States; in Britain it was used to refer to the ruling elite, incorporating the aristocracy, gentry, and the most influential politicians, financiers and industrialists. *Kelly's Handbook to the Upper Ten Thousand*, first published in 1875, exemplifies its use; in 1878 the title was revised to *Kelly's Handbook to the titled, landed and official classes*.

external reasons suggested by Remo, it is not clear why the collapse of Italian opera came precisely when it did: the moribund repertoire, the lack of new *prime donne*, the lack of a tenor to match them, the growth of alternative attractions (light opera, concerts, and non-musical events), the often poor standards of performance (thrown into relief by the continuing presence of Rosa, and the German seasons of 1882), and the gradual desertion by the audience members the opera needed to survive financially, are all relevant factors. Seemingly there was a cumulative effect and in 1885 and 1886 the force became overwhelming. The *Musical Standard*'s comments above are illuminating, though, because of the emphasis they place on the social function of the opera season – a function of which the press in general was increasingly contemptuous – and the crucial economic role of the occupants of the boxes and stalls. Frederick Gye had been assiduous in courting members of society – possibly Ernest lacked his father's ability or willingness and, without particular individuals promoting the opera behind the scenes as a social occasion, society in general found other things to do. Subsequently, Augustus Harris and his supporters charmed these people back and, by 1890, it was almost as if the crisis had never happened.

The year 1886 was equally disastrous: a short 'pre-season' opened at Her Majesty's on 27 February but commenced so badly that after a week it had 'not yet reached the level of efficiency where serious criticism becomes possible. The opening performance of *Il Trovatore* [was] one of the worst ever seen in London'.[30] Within days the season had collapsed completely; at the final farcical rendition of *Faust* most of the orchestra left after Act II and the performance came to a complete halt after the third act as the scene-shifters struck. It transpired that none of the staff had been paid in full and several of them appeared on the stage appealing for help; in response some audience members threw coins at them and a riot almost ensued.[31]

Gye mounted no opera season in London in either 1885 or 1886 and only in April 1886 did rumours of Italian seasons emerge.[32] That given by Joseph Lago, a former prompter at Covent Garden, was moderately successful: comprising 27 performances, there were no novelties, despite early rumours of an Italian version of Mackenzie's *Colomba*, previously promised at Covent Garden in 1884.[33] Lago

30 *MW*, 6 March 1886, p. 157.

31 *The Times* pronounced the events as heralding the 'ignominious end of an institution for two centuries the most fashionable in England' (8 March 1886, p. 7). This season was mounted by 'Monsieur Carillon' who was rumoured to be a chemist and money-lender named Cargill (*MW*, 20 March 1886, p. 189).

32 *MW*, 17 April 1886, p. 247, and 1 May, p. 279.

33 *MW*, 15 May 1886, p. 313. *MW* had previously stated 'that Signor Lago is more than the figurehead of the enterprise few persons will believe' (1 May, p. 279). According to *MoM* (1 May, p. 37) the financial backer of Lago's season was a Mr Montagu (almost certainly the Andrew Montagu referred to in Chapter 1; he retained financial interests in the Covent Garden theatre until his death in 1896 (see Klein, *Thirty Years*, pp. 291–2)).

engaged Albani and ticket prices were reduced by between 20 and 25 per cent.[34] Initially positive press reaction waned, and the general conclusion was that the season had been pleasant but dull.[35] Mapleson's rumoured season did not materialise, although a benefit performance was given for him at Her Majesty's on 15 June.

Almost as equivocal were the productions of French operas by L. Mayer.[36] There had been no dedicated French seasons in the West End since 1875 (see Chapter 1) until Mayer, who had mounted French dramas for several years, included operas in his 1885 run at the Gaiety. Only three works were given but they included the British premiere of Delibes's *Lakmé* (6 June).[37] Mayer reappeared in November 1886 at Her Majesty's, with a diffuse mixture of plays, Grand Opera and *opéra bouffe* (*Les Cloches de Cornville* and *La Grande Duchesse*) but largely without success. French versions of *Rigoletto* and *La Traviata* were of little interest to London audiences; *Faust*, *Carmen* and *Mignon* were also given. Performances were often poor – on one night the chorus 'played their part so badly ... that they were soundly hissed for their pains'.[38] Mayer appears to have confined his subsequent seasons to drama and *opéra bouffe*. There were no further French opera seasons in London for the remainder of this period but, once he was established, Harris increasingly promoted this repertory at Covent Garden (see below).

Had 1887 not been the year of Victoria's Golden Jubilee, it is possible that Italian opera would have remained in as forlorn a state as ever, but the desire to celebrate supplied an inadvertent boost as society flocked to London. Both Mapleson and Lago returned, and Augustus Harris also stepped into the fray; after the dearth of performances in the previous two years, London was offered three separate seasons of Italian opera between March and July, plus six-weeks of English opera by Carl Rosa. Press reaction was at first cynical: *Orchestral Musical Review* declared that '[Mapleson's Covent Garden] season will no doubt be a short run – probably shorter even than that of [Lago] last year – and the old repertoire, the old scenery, and doubtless the old familiar performers will be utilised again ... Italian opera is at death's door'.[39] This season ran from 12 March to 7 May in order to avoid the climax of the jubilee celebrations; with a company almost bereft of familiar 'stars', Mapleson introduced the Wagnerian soprano Lillian Nordica and Bizet's *Les pêcheurs de perles* to London. Press reviews were quite good and Mapleson transferred to Her Majesty's, (re-)opening on 4 June. His season closed

34 *OMR*, 29 May 1886, pp. 78–9.

35 See, for example, *SR*, 26 June 1886, p. 887, and *MW*, 24 July, p. 472.

36 Mayer was a long-standing London theatre manager and had been in charge of the Princess's Theatre during Rosa's season in 1875.

37 Marie van Zandt, for whom Delibes had created the role, played Lakmé.

38 *Era*, 13 November 1886, p. 9, of the performance of *Faust* on 6 November; the orchestra was also heavily criticised.

39 *OMR*, 1 March 1887, p. 4; see also *SR*, 5 March, p. 329, and 12 March, p. 356; the latter was more positive.

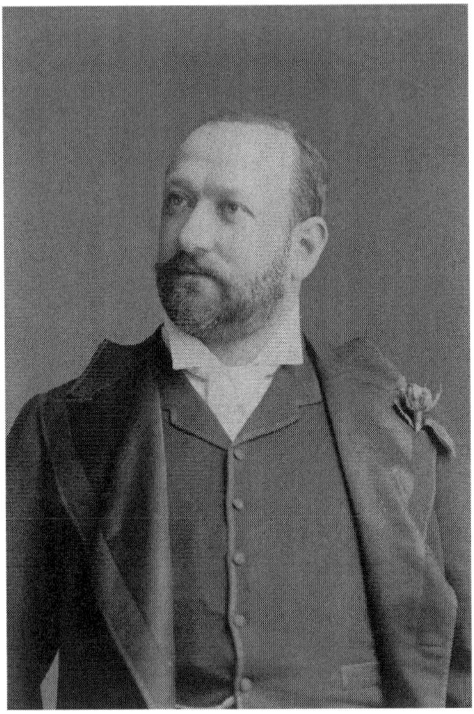

Figure 2.1 Augustus Harris, cabinet photo by Walery

on 13 June after poor audiences, reviews, and alleged financial difficulties,[40] only to reopen again 12 days later. Patti was promised (this time at a fee of £650 per night) but only sang once and failed to appear as billed on the last night (9 July). Humiliated, Mapleson managed to put on *Carmen* and give refunds to those that wanted them. Lago's troupe, which included Albani and one of the few really good tenors of the time, Julián Gayarre, appeared at Covent Garden (24 May to 16 July); the premiere of Glinka's *A Life for the Tsar* received mixed reviews.[41]

Finally, Harris opened at Drury Lane on 13 June and closed on 30 July (and, like Lago, called his company the 'Royal Italian Opera'). Although new to opera management, Harris had been his entire life a member of London's theatrical community: his father had been Frederick Gye's stage manager at Covent Garden and his mother ran a theatrical costumier's business. Harris himself had acted briefly, and been Mapleson's stage manager in the mid-1870s. In 1879, aged 27, he became the manager of Drury Lane (and soon acquired the nickname 'Druriolanus') and was renowned for his spectacular Christmas pantomimes. In

40 Mapleson, vol. 2, pp. 250–57, and Rosenthal, pp. 220–21.

41 For a summary of critical opinion see *MS*, 23 July 1887, p. 50.

1883 he collaborated with Carl Rosa, and Rosa's company consequently used Drury Lane for its West End performances for the next few years.[42]

A crucial factor in the success of Harris's Italian opera season was that he managed to secure the backing of certain members of society; the sponsors of the 1887 campaign are not known, but it is likely that several of the members of his 1888 committee were involved (see below) and they brought excellent social links. According to Rosenthal, the support of Ladies Jeromina Beresford and Constance de Grey was crucial.[43] The latter remained a central behind-the-scenes figure at Covent Garden until 1914 (see Chapter 3). Harris did not give any new works but gained Nordica from Mapleson, and re-introduced Jean de Reszke to London audiences.[44] For the first time in many years the leading men (the de Reszke brothers and Victor Maurel) balanced the *prime donne* in concerted strength.

Critical reaction to all seasons was fairly consistent: Mapleson was mostly judged to have been disastrous, Lago non-descript, and Harris a great artistic success. All three, to varying extents, tried to put aside the 'star' system, but Harris took this furthest and also took a leaf out of Rosa's book by trying to ensure that production values were consistent across the board; Harris's casts were much more even, ensemble was better and, as might be expected from a producer of spectacular pantomimes, his operas looked splendid: costumes, scenery, and overall *mise-en-scène* all drew praise. Ebenezer Prout's retrospective review of the season fairly sums up both the achievement and critical view:

> Some of [Mapleson's] performances … were fairly good, others mediocre and others again about the worst I have ever seen … I am told that the subscription [for Lago's season] was the worst ever known at Covent Garden … The performances varied considerably in quality … From an artistic point of view [Harris's] performances were the greatest possible success. Whether they were the same financially speaking I cannot say … [but he] has shown that he can mount Italian opera to perfection, and that he is able to delight critics as well as the general public … The dresses and sceneries were in striking contrast to what was offered at Covent Garden at nearly double the prices of admission.[45]

---

42 For further biographical and anecdotal information see Rosenthal, p. 223; W.J. MacQueen Pope, *Theatre Royal Drury Lane* (London, 1945), pp. 283–90; James Glover, *Jimmy Glover His Book* (London, 1911), pp. 105–45; Klein, *Thirty Years*, pp. 135–40.

43 Rosenthal, p. 223.

44 Klein suggested de Reszke to Harris and he was insisted upon by Ladies Beresford and de Grey (see Herman Klein, *The Golden Age of Opera* (London, 1933), pp. 131–2 and Rosenthal, p. 223; for an account of the assembly of Harris's company see Klein, *Thirty Years*, pp. 207–29). De Reszke appeared on the first night of Harris's season as Radames in *Aïda*. See also note 4.

45 *MS*, 30 July 1887, p. 67.

In fact, Harris lost between £14,000 and £16,000 and was set to give up, but was promised substantial support by his backers and persuaded to carry on.[46] It was through his agency that the rejuvenation of Italian opera in London, and its transformation into multi-language Grand Opera in the succeeding years was achieved (see Chapter 3). Lago also remained active for some years, but Mapleson's career was almost at an end, he being seemingly unable to conceive of Italian opera without a star singer. While the star system was far from dead, Mapleson had neither the singers nor the money to carry on; he attempted one more season at Her Majesty's in 1889 which ended, as his 1887 season had, in ignominy.

In the five years 1883 to 1887 Italian opera in London reached the brink of extinction but, against all expectations, bounced back. In 1885 and 1886 the situation looked hopeless as audiences, from top to bottom, chose other amusements. By accident and good fortune, the coincidence, in 1887, of Victoria's jubilee, and the enthusiasm for social events that came with it, plus the entry of Harris into the field, gave Italian opera a fillip, and set it on the road to recovery: the terminal decline anticipated for several years turned out only to be a temporary hiatus.

Carl Rosa in London 1876–96

After his successful first London season in 1875, Rosa worked to establish his troupe in the capital as a serious rival to the Italian companies. His success was brief; the company was not immune from the turbulence of the mid-1880s and, just when it appeared that it had survived these unstable times, Rosa himself died in 1889. After this, the company lost direction and was absent from central London for much of the 1890s.

Rosa had always conceived of his company as a touring troupe and his acquisition of Liverpool's Royal Court Theatre as its permanent base in 1881 created a very different management dynamic to that of the London-based companies. For Rosa, although establishing a London reputation was important (not least to enhance his standing in the provinces), it was not the sole aspect of his operation. Consequently, the length and timing of his seasons in the capital varied over the years; only from 1883 to 1887 did he attempt to put his London performances on during the 'social season' (see Table 2.4).

Critical reception of Rosa's seasons was generally very positive; the *Musical World* and *Saturday Review* are representative:

> The great charm of Mr Rosa's representations lies in the artistic spirit that dominates them … As to the enterprise of the past season, it is enough to mention the words *Aïda*, *Lohengrin*, *Mignon*, and *The Taming of the Shrew*. The production of the first three operas in English and of the last for the first time

---

[46] Augustus Harris, 'The Opera in England: Some Notes and Reminiscences', *New Review*, 9 (1893): pp. 257–67.

Table 2.4 Carl Rosa opera seasons in London and premieres, 1876–96[47]

Year	Dates	Theatre	British or World Premieres
1876	9 Sept – 30 Nov	Lyceum	(B) Adam *Giralda* (22 Sept) (B) Isouard *Joconde* (25 Oct) (W) Cowen *Pauline* (22 Nov)
1877	No season		
1878	11 Feb – 6 Apr	Adelphi[1]	(B) Brüll *Goldene Kreuz* (2 Mar)
1879	27 Jan – 22 Mar	Her Majesty's	(B) Guirard *Piccolino* (4 Jan, Dublin) (B) Goetz *Der widerspänstigen Zähmung* (27 Nov, Birmingham)[2]
1880	10 Jan – 6 Mar	Her Majesty's	(B) Wagner *Rienzi* (27 Jan)
1881	No season		
1882	14 Jan – 11 Mar	Her Majesty's	(B) Balfe *Pittore e Duca* (28 Jan)
1883	26 Mar – 21 Apr	Drury Lane	(W) Goring Thomas *Esmeralda* (26 Mar) (W) Mackenzie *Colomba* (9 Apr)
1884	14 Apr – 10 May	Drury Lane	(W) Stanford *Canterbury Pilgrims* (28 Apr)
1885	6 Apr – 30 May	Drury Lane	(W) Goring Thomas *Nadeshda* (26 Apr)
1886	30 May – 26 June	Drury Lane	(W) Mackenzie *Troubadour* (8 Jun)
1887	30 Apr – 11 June	Drury Lane	(W) Corder *Nordisa* (26 Jan, Liverpool)
1888–89	No seasons		
1890	6 Apr – 10 May	Drury Lane	(W) Cowen *Thorgrim* (22 Apr)
1891–95	No seasons (see below)		(W) Goring Thomas *The Golden Web* (15 Feb 1893, Liverpool) (W) MacCunn *Jeanie Deans* (15 Nov 1894, Edinburgh)
1896	20 Jan – 14 Feb	Daly's[3]	

Notes to table: [1] Located on the Strand and opened originally in 1806; rebuilt in 1858, 1901 and 1930, it is still in operation. [2] This was the first performance of a professional standard (advertised in *BDP*, 24 November 1879, p. 1); the London premiere was on 20 January 1880 (*MW*, 24 January 1880, p. 52). The opera was performed at Drury Lane on 12 October 1878 by Carl Meyder but the standard of the performance was lamented (see *The Times*, 14 October 1878, p. 8, and *Academy*, 19 October, p. 393). [3] Located on Cranbourn Street, Leicester Square, it opened in 1893 and was demolished in 1937. Warner Brothers built a cinema on the site, which is still in operation as the Vue West End.

in this country [but see note 47] are achievements of which all concerned have reason to be proud … In the great and undoubted success of Mr Rosa's season,

[47] Although there was no season in 1877 there was effectively a consistent 'winter' presence between 1875 and 1880.

> together with the conditions of its management, a way is suggested out of the maze in which opera in England seems every year to be more involved.[48]

> On looking back at the [1880] season we find but little to regret. Mr Randegger has evidently spared no pains in superintending the musical part of the undertaking and, with but few exceptions, Mr Betjemann has been equally careful with stage arrangements ... [*Maritana*, *The Bohemian Girl*, and *The Lily of Killarney*] have, we regret to say, not been produced with the same care as the more important works ... On the whole, however, this season has been one of great artistic success and has done much for spreading the taste for operatic music.[49]

Most London critics had an ideological interest in encouraging both 'English Opera' and opera in English, and Rosa's was then the best vehicle for this activity (see Chapter 5). It was not, however, just ideology that encouraged the positive reception. Rosa's conception of opera may not have been radically different from that of the Italian companies but he presented a more consistent standard across all aspects of production: *mise-en-scène*, stage business, the cast *in toto*, orchestra, and conductor were praised in equal measure and there is a sense that every aspect was given attention. This contrasted directly with the Italian companies' emphasis on 'stars', and praising Rosa was another means by which famous singers, managers and society supporters could be chastised for getting in the way of fidelity to the musical work itself. Rosa's approach must have been principally ideological; it does not seem that he lacked the financial resources to employ 'star singers' but, seemingly, a combination of canny financial sense, the knowledge that he had to offer something different to the Italian companies, and a genuine belief that things were better done differently, led him to present opera in the form of an all-round 'package'.[50] Although he was a shrewd businessman he was also a practising musician, giving him a perspective different from that of either Mapleson or the Gyes.

Rosa's 1883 London season marked a shift in direction. It was the first in which he collaborated with Augustus Harris, who at first greatly helped but later hindered the company's progress in London. Until 1887 Harris and Rosa's joint efforts took the company to new heights of achievement; previously chastised

48 *MW*, 13 March 1880, p. 166.

49 *SR*, 13 March 1880, p. 346. Rosa was ill during the 1880 season and conducted only the final performance.

50 Rosa did employ some 'star' singers, for example, Charles Santley and Minnie Hauk, but the all-round strength of the troupe was a greater priority. His approach was supported in the press: 'Experience has taught us to expect from [Rosa's] company performances remarkable alike for individual merit and excellence of ensemble – features that will ... contrast strangely enough with the utter inefficiency and wretched arrangements that characterized the immediately-preceding season [by Mapleson] at Her Majesty's' (*Examiner*, 10 January 1880, p. 45). For notes on the financial situation of Rosa and his company see note 54 below, and Chapter 4, note 2.

by the press for providing 'opera in English' rather than 'English opera', Rosa supplied his riposte, giving the premieres of six works commissioned from the new generation of British composers between 1883 and 1887.[51] Additionally, the London seasons were now given after Easter, aiming firmly to capture a part of the 'society' audience and endeavouring to claim not only musical parity with the Italian companies (which, for many critics, it had already achieved or surpassed) but social parity too.

In part the difficulties of the Italian companies aided this aspiration. In 1885, for the first time, Rosa offered a subscription package, again trying to create the impression that he was operating in a manner comparable to his Italian rivals.[52] This ambition achieved variable results: while the 1885 and 1887 seasons were both eight weeks long, the 1886 season lasted only four. The reception of the three new English works introduced in these seasons became progressively less enthusiastic; Corder's *Nordisa* was roundly condemned by the metropolitan press in 1887 and Rosa did not perform in London in 1888. Definite reasons for this decision are not known, although it was rumoured that no suitable theatre was available.[53] Rosa may also have been influenced by the organisation's conversion to a limited company in April 1887.[54] At the same time, he also formed a 'Light Opera' company, doubtless hoping to capture a part of a lucrative market.[55] To what extent the failing fortunes

---

51 See, for example, Charles Salaman's critique of the company, quoted in Chapter 5.

52 *MW*, 14 March 1885, p. 172.

53 *Graphic* reported that 'Mr Carl Rosa finds that he cannot give his projected London opera season in August at the new Grand Theatre as the house will not then be finished. Meanwhile he has secured a site for his new theatre near Piccadilly Circus and is now engaged in the task of selecting an architect' (28 April 1888, p. 455). The 'new theatre' was never built.

54 Shares to the value of £100,000 were issued; the company's main assets were given as the lease on the Royal Court Theatre, Liverpool (£45,490), its materials (scenery, props, music library etc., £20,000), and the exclusive rights of representation, mostly of English language translations, of 25 operas. Directors of the company included Viscount Folkestone (William Pleydell-Bourverie, Conservative MP and later 5th Earl of Radnor), Lord Arthur Hill (Conservative MP and younger son of 4th Marquess of Downshire), the 5th Earl of Wilton (Seymour John Grey Egerton) and George Grove (*MW*, 16 April 1887, p. 304). In its first year of public trading dividends of 8 per cent were paid, somewhat short of the anticipated 12 per cent (*The Times*, 13 February 1888, p. 11, and 14 June, p. 14). Augustus Harris joined the Board of Directors in April 1889 (*PMG*, 20 April 1889, p. 4).

55 This frustrated *The Times*: 'During [1888] not a single performance of serious opera in English has taken place in [London] ... Mr Carl Rosa ... seems to have given up all hope for the present of extending his sphere of action to the metropolis and he has emphasized the hopefulness [sic] by embarking in an enterprise of operetta, which will commence at the Prince of Wales's Theatre early in January. Operetta and the rapidly growing taste for it among the public are, as everyone knows, the bane of serious music drama ... A manager cannot be blamed for giving the public what the public desires to see, and it follows then, that in the matter of operatic music, London audiences are as wanting in taste and culture as ever' (31 December 1888, p. 13).

of Italian opera affected Rosa is not clear but its subsequent rejuvenation did not help him. It does not appear that Rosa planned to visit London in 1889 (see note 55) and any plans that might have existed were overturned by his premature death, at the age of 47, on 30 April. The musical world was shocked and praised Rosa for his work in promoting both opera in English and British opera.[56] Rosa had continued to encourage British composers: Klein claimed that both Goring Thomas and Hamish MacCunn had commissions from the company, and Cowen's *Thorgrim* was also half completed.[57] Stanford was also writing an opera which he hoped Rosa would produce but abandoned it after Rosa's death.[58]

The company, now managed by Harris, returned to London in 1890 in a season that included *Thorgrim*. Harris's interests were strongly drawn elsewhere, however: his Covent Garden seasons were increasingly successful both artistically and financially, and he resigned from the Rosa board towards the end of 1890,[59] reportedly binding the company to appear only in the provinces 'for some years'.[60] From this point the Rosa troupe lost managerial and artistic direction. Klein claimed that its London seasons had never paid financially but had continued in order to maintain its reputation and public profile as 'naturally it was essential that the company should from time to time visit the metropolis that it might receive the cachet of London approval that so strongly influences the mind of the provincial opera-goer'.[61] If Harris did force the Rosa Company out of London, it was an immensely damaging act from which the company found it difficult to recover. A rumoured season at Drury Lane commencing on 28 March 1891 failed to materialise[62] and, other than furnishing Harris with a troupe to perform a run of Humperdinck's *Hänsel und Gretel* in 1894–95,[63] the company did not appear in central London again until 1896 when it gave a four-week season of matinees

---

56 For an extensive but hagiographical account of Rosa's London seasons, see Herman Klein, 'The revival and progress of English opera under Carl Rosa', *MW*, 29 June 1889, pp. 410–11, 6 July, p. 428, 13 July, pp. 453–4, and 20 July pp. 473–4. See also Harold Rosenthal, *'The Carl Rosa Story' Opera*, 18 (1967), pp. 272–8; 460–4; 547–50; and 719–26.

57 *MW*, 20 July 1889, p. 474; see also Frederic Cowen, *My Art and My Friends* (London, 1913), pp. 227 and 243.

58 Stanford completed the first act of *The Miner of Falun* in March 1888, and showed it to Rosa; see Paul Rodmell, *Charles Villiers Stanford* (Aldershot, 2002), p. 137.

59 Klein, *Thirty Years*, p. 295.

60 *BDP*, 11 November 1890, p. 7.

61 Klein, 'Revival and Progress', *MW*, 20 July 1889, p. 474.

62 *Era* stated that the company's presence at Drury Lane would be subject to Harris's convenience, implying that he later withdrew his offer without leaving the company enough time to secure another venue (15 November 1890, p. 10).

63 This production opened on 26 December 1894 and transferred to the Princess's Theatre on 4 March 1895; the 'main' Rosa company commenced a 10-week season in Liverpool on 31 December 1894 which also included Humperdinck's opera (*MS*, 29 December 1894, p. 505, and *Athenaeum*, 9 March 1895, p. 321).

only at Daly's Theatre, which included the first metropolitan performance of MacCunn's *Jeanie Deans* on 22 January.[64]

Stability Regained: Harris and Grand Opera in London 1888–96

Following his well-received season at Drury Lane in 1887, Harris, with the help of his supporters, turned his attention to Covent Garden. For the next eight years his domination of Grand Opera in London was complete; no other impresario managed to achieve any sort of momentum or sustainability. Harris's success can be attributed both to his personal qualities and the influence of his backers. He was well-liked, a man with a genuine love of the theatre and opera, and a very good although sometimes ruthless businessman with interests in many venues, not all in London, and his operatic activities, although focused principally on Covent Garden from 1888, were by no means confined to it. Crucially, Harris managed, like Frederick Gye before him, to court members of society; his success can be seen in the rejuvenation of interest in opera amongst the 'upper ten thousand' that lasted well beyond his death. The committee formed to promote Harris's 1888 Covent Garden season contained men with significant social connections and influence and, as noted above, the work of at least two of their wives, Ladies Beresford and de Grey, were just as significant in promoting the presence of society at the opera; the frequent presence of the Prince and Princess of Wales provided further invaluable support.[65] After the instability of the 1880s, Harris created a sense of security that was sustained until the Great War.

Given this stability, a narrative account of his seasons is unnecessary.[66] This section comprises an overview of Harris's achievements and failures during his tenure. In many respects, Harris managed to restore the fortunes of Grand Opera to their 1860s and '70s heyday, through subtle rather than radical changes. The social importance of the opera was restored, the element of exclusivity continued

---

64 Daly's was described as 'by no means large enough for Grand Opera, but Covent Garden being out of the question and no other suitable theatre being available, it had to serve, the sacrifice of the first row of stalls to the gentlemen of the orchestra being, perhaps, the most conspicuous sign of cramped conditions.' (*MT*, 1 February 1896, p. 94). *Era* stated that the company was negotiating an autumn season at Drury Lane (15 August 1896, p. 15), but this came to nothing (*Minim*, 1 October, 1896, p. 6).

65 Rosenthal, *Two Centuries of Opera*, pp. 223–5, and *Era*, 5 May 1888, p. 12, give the committee as Lord Charles Beresford (Conservative MP, friend of the Prince of Wales); Earl de Grey (Frederick Robinson, Liberal MP, later Marquess of Ripon); Oliver Montagu (younger son of 7th Earl of Sandwich and Equerry to the Prince of Wales); Henry Chaplin (cabinet minister under Lord Salisbury, later Viscount Chaplin); Henry Oppenheim (banker and part-proprietor of the *Daily News*); and Adriano de Murietta (banker and younger son of a Spanish noble, the Marquis de Santurce). For the opening night of the 1889 season, MS printed a substantial list of society figures who attended; see Appendix 2.1.

66 For this, see Rosenthal, *Two Centuries of Opera*, pp. 222–73.

and the star system maintained, albeit without Patti-like excesses. New stars, most notably Jean de Reszke,[67] Nellie Melba, Emma Eames, Pol Plançon, and Emma Calvé were all introduced to London, and enjoyed substantial success. Harris also employed the conductors Luigi Mancinelli, Landon Ronald, and, for the 1892 German season, Gustav Mahler,[68] in addition to the established figures of Bevignani, Arditi and Randegger.

Harris continued to pay great attention to the appearance of the opera on stage and the standard of his performances in this respect was significantly higher than previously seen at Covent Garden (although apparently still capable of much improvement; see Chapter 3). For example, the *Musical World* wrote of the opening night of the 1889 season (Bizet's *Les pêcheurs de perles*), that 'it is pleasant to be able to say with what worthy care the opera was presented and played. The *mise-en-scène* was as superb as the most exacting … could desire'.[69] Not all reviews were complimentary: the *Saturday Review* declared that the production of Gluck's *Orfeo* was, 'deplorable. The Elysian fields are represented by a scene used in a Drury Lane pantomime some years ago; the dresses and appearance of the chorus occasioned general mirth and the stage management of the scene with the Furies was so bad that its effect was entirely lost'.[70] George Bernard Shaw's reviews of the 1889 season make it clear that there was still considerable room for improvement: acting, orchestral playing, cuts, and infidelity to the score are all mentioned.[71]

Harris's most notable achievements are a shift in language policy and a substantial change in repertory, although in both respects he was responding in part to outside pressure and not pursuing a one-man crusade for change. From 1889, Harris gradually started presenting operas in their original languages; as a result, in 1892, the word 'Italian' was dropped from the company name and it became the 'Royal Opera' (hence also the change from 'Italian Opera' to 'Grand Opera' in the subheadings of this chapter). His first venture along this road was the production of Gounod's *Roméo et Juliette* (15 June 1889). Other French-language operas followed and by 1896 most of the Italian translations of French

---

67 De Reszke sang for Harris at Drury Lane: see above and note 4.

68 Mahler's performances of *Der Ring* and *Tristan* were almost uniformly praised in the press; his readings of the more familiar *Tannhäuser* and *Fidelio* gained more variable reviews.

69 *MW*, 25 May 1889, p. 333, of the performance on 18 May.

70 *SR*, 28 May 1892, p. 626, of the performance on 21 May. Of the same performance, *MT* commented 'the mounting of the piece, though still erring on the side of garishness, was improved by the toning down of some of the details introduced in last year's production' (1 June, p. 342).

71 See George Bernard Shaw, *Music in London 1888–89 as heard by Corno di Bassetto* (New York, 1973); of a performance of *Les Huguenots* Shaw noted that 'The performance began about twelve minutes past eight. At the end of the fourth act it only wanted five minutes of twelve. The band accordingly cut the entertainment short by going home. Signor Mancinelli, after a moment's hesitation, followed their example. I left several of the audience waiting for the fifth act' (p. 153).

works had been abandoned. Performing German operas in their original language proved more challenging not least because, with the exception of Wagner, German repertory barely featured in Harris's seasons. His first solution, in 1892, was to organise a 'season within a season', when a separate German troupe, mainly from Hamburg, was engaged and its schedule integrated into that of the Italian/French company; German language performances of *Der Ring*, *Tristan*, *Tannhäuser*, and *Fidelio* were given.[72] In the following years Harris pursued a mixed policy: in 1893, for example, *Tristan*, *Die Walküre* and *Siegfried* were given in German but *Tannhäuser*, *Der fliegende Holländer* and *Die Meistersinger* in Italian.[73] Harris did not, however, extend his policy to performance in English; operas by British composers form only a small fraction of the works he produced (see below) and these were mainly given in translation: English remained *infra dig*.[74]

Harris's approach to repertory was, like that of Gye and Mapleson, more re-active than pro-active, although in the promotion of new works his record (see Table 2.5) is a good one compared to either of his predecessors. Harris only started to give first performances after he had established himself with five Grand Opera seasons, suggesting a great deal of initial caution; from autumn 1891, however, perhaps nettled by the fact that he had failed to give the British premieres of either *Otello* or *Cavalleria Rusticana*, his support for new works increased dramatically.

Given Harris's rather good record, it is a shame that he failed to pick more 'winners'; few of the works he premiered secured either short- or long-term success. In part this was because of the paucity of established composers who were a guaranteed 'draw': Wagner was dead, Verdi had almost ceased composing, and Puccini's career was still in its infancy, but it was also in part because Harris rarely ventured beyond two or three performances of new works and so they failed to establish themselves. Also of significance is that Harris gave no operas at all by Russian or Eastern European composers, despite the massive growth in popularity of their music in concert halls in the 1890s.[75]

---

[72] These were the first performances of *Der Ring* and *Tristan* in Britain since 1882. *Der fliegende Holländer* and *Lohengrin* were given by the 'original' company in Italian; the German troupe's success was such that Harris transferred them to Drury Lane during late June and most of July for further performances, where it also gave Nessler's *Der Trompeter von Säkingen*. Harris tried a further experiment in 1895 when the Ducal Court Company of Saxe-Coburg appeared at Drury Lane from 17 June to 13 July, performing a mixture of comic opera and drama including first British performances of Zeller's *Der Vogelhändler* (17 June), *Die Fledermaus* (22 June), *The Bartered Bride* (27 June), and Lortzing's *Der Wildschütz* (3 July).

[73] In 1896 *Die Walküre* was uniquely given in French.

[74] Of the operas given by Harris with original libretti in English, only Cowen's *Harold* was performed in that language, all others being given in either Italian or French. Harris gave *Hänsel und Gretel* in English, but this may have been because he first purchased the rights of the English translation.

[75] Harris did not take up *Eugene Onegin*, which Lago gave in 1892, nor any of the Russian operas performed in Britain in the 1880s.

Table 2.5 British and world premieres given by Augustus Harris 1888–96

Date	**Theatre**	**Work; (B) = British premiere; (W) = world premiere**
24 Oct 1891	CG	(B) Gounod *Philémon et Baucis*
29 Oct 1891	CG	(B) Bruneau *Le Rêve*
23 May 1892	CG	(B) Mascagni *L'amico Fritz*
8 July 1892	DL	(B) Nessler *Der Trompeter von Säkingen*
11 June 1892	CG	(W) De Lara *The Light of Asia*
5 July 1892	CG	(W) Bemberg *Elaine*
8 Dec 1892	CG	(W) Emil Bach *Irmengarda*
19 May 1893	CG	(B) Leoncavallo *Pagliacci*
13 June 1893	CG	(B) Bizet *Djamileh*
7 July 1893	CG	(B) Mascagni *I Rantzau*
20 July 1893	CG	(W) De Lara *Amy Robsart*
26 July 1893	CG	(B) Stanford *The Veiled Prophet*
11 June 1894	CG	(B) Massenet *Werther*
30 June 1894	CG	(B) Cowen *Signa*
4 July 1894	CG	(B) Bruneau *L'attaque du moulin*
21 July 1894	CG	(W) Emil Bach *The Lady of Longford*
20 June 1894	CG	(W) Massenet *La Navarraise*
14 May 1894	CG	(B) Puccini *Manon Lescaut*
19 May 1894	CG	(B) Verdi *Falstaff*
8 June 1895	CG	(W) Cowen *Harold*
29 June 1895	CG	(W) Maclean *Petruccio*

Partly in response to changing tastes, Harris's repertory shifted significantly towards French opera. A comparison of Table 2.6 and Tables 1.1 and 1.3 (Gye's and Mapleson's seasons 1871–74) shows that only *Faust*, *Les Huguenots* and *Don Giovanni* are common to both periods; *Orfeo* had hardly ever appeared in London before Harris produced it,[76] and the remaining six operas in Harris's 'top ten' were all introduced to London from 1875 onwards; Harris himself was responsible for *Philémon et Baucis* and *Pagliacci* (see Table 2.5).[77]

[76] The popularity of this opera was largely due to the portrayal of the two leading parts by the sisters Sofia and Giulia Ravogli (*Speaker*, 21 May 1892, p. 618).

[77] As well as the 'main' seasons, Harris gave autumn seasons at Covent Garden in 1891 and 1892 and a 'pre-season' at Drury Lane in April 1893; Drury Lane was also used as an 'overspill' theatre during the grand seasons for additional, mainly German, performances

Table 2.6 Operas most frequently performed by Augustus Harris, 1888–96

Composer	Opera	Performances
Mascagni	*Cavalleria Rusticana*	76
Gounod	*Faust*	70
Bizet	*Carmen*	58
Wagner	*Lohengrin*	56
Gounod	*Roméo et Juliette*	55
Gounod	*Philémon et Baucis*	32
Gluck	*Orfeo*	30
Meyerbeer	*Les Huguenots*	30
Leoncavallo	*Pagliacci*	28
Mozart	*Don Giovanni*	25

Sources: Rosenthal; statistical summaries in contemporary journals; advertisements in *The Times*

The relative popularity of different composers is, unsurprisingly, more stable: comparing Table 2.7 with an aggregate of Tables 1.2 and 1.4, Gounod had risen to the top of the table (previously 11.5 per cent), Verdi had slipped from third to fourth place (previously 16.3 per cent) and Meyerbeer had dropped from second to sixth (previously 16.7 per cent). The other Italian composers (Donizetti, Bellini and Rossini) had all dropped out of contention, to be replaced by Wagner, Bizet and Mascagni. Mozart is placed last in both periods (8.5 per cent previously).

The success that Harris achieved is demonstrated by the lengths of his seasons; from a modest 48 performances in 1888 (and 36 in 1887) he moved to 94 at Covent Garden in 1891 and averaged 76 in the subsequent five grand seasons there, almost comparable to Gye 20 years earlier. In all Harris gave 806 performances (and 842 if the 1887 season at Drury Lane is added).[78] While his repertory totalled 67 operas, renditions of the top 10 comprised almost exactly half of his total performances and half of the works in his repertory were performed four times or fewer. Ticket prices also remained broadly similar to those of 1875 although, as Britain experienced deflation during this period, in real terms they increased.[79]

in 1892–94 (in 1894 all German operas except *Lohengrin* were given at Drury Lane). Performances in all of these seasons are included in Tables 2.5 to 2.7.

[78] 806 performances does not equal 806 'nights' as shorter operas were played in double bills; this total includes the autumn seasons and all performances at Drury Lane.

[79] Harris's 1888 subscription was for 32 nights with prices from £80 to £192 for boxes, £32 for stalls, and £16 for the amphitheatre (*Era*, 5 May 1888, p. 12). These produce per performance prices of 12s 6d to £1 10s; £1, and 10s respectively. Real-terms adjustments

Table 2.7 Performances by Augustus Harris by composer, 1888–96

Composer	Number of works	Total performances	% of total performances
Gounod	4	160	19.9
Wagner	9	134	16.6
Mascagni	3	93	11.5
Verdi	8	90	11.2
Bizet	3	64	7.9
Meyerbeer	4	47	5.8
Mozart	3	37	4.6

Sources: as Table 2.6

Harris's death on 22 June 1896 at the age of 45 came as a shock; the Covent Garden season proceeded as normal in accordance with his wishes.[80] Press tributes were generous – *The Times* and *Musical Times* commented:

> Though very little of a musician himself, Sir Augustus Harris succeeded not only financially but artistically in operatic management, which, for a great many years, had spelt ruin to all who meddled with it. Not his musical or dramatic tastes alone, but his general discernment, borne of wide experience, led him to use his influence largely in the cause of Wagner, but his convictions were not as strong as to blind him to the demands of a different class of amateurs. A spirit of eclecticism may have been deplored by purists of various schools but this was one of the secrets of success which made opera a living thing in London once more, and the eight or nine years of his management have done more to destroy the baleful 'star system' and place London on an artistic level with continental centres of operatic life than all the years that have elapsed since the advent of Handel in London society.[81]
>
> His success as an operatic manager may be attributed to lavish *mise-en-scène* and the engagement of the most celebrated artists, combined with an intuitive sympathy with the spirit of the day. No manager ever felt the pulse of the public with more sagacity than Sir Augustus Harris. We owe to him the removal of many of the absurd customs of Italian opera … May the seeds he has sown in this field bear abundant fruit.[82]

from 1875 to 1888 show rises of between 11 per cent and 29 per cent. For the 'popular' seasons tickets cost less; Drury Lane 'pre-season' tickets cost between 1s and 10s 6d.

80 There was no performance on the day of his funeral, 27 June.

81 *The Times*, 23 June 1896, p. 12. Harris was knighted in 1891 when he served as Sheriff of London (an honour bestowed automatically).

82 *MT*, 1 July 1896, p. 461.

Harris's achievement was hugely significant: without his mounting of the Italian opera seasons in 1887 and 1888 it is difficult to see how Grand Opera in London would have recovered after the near collapse of the preceding years, although it would, doubtless, have arisen in some form or other. His promotion of Wagner – and French opera – changed operatic culture in central London substantially.

In some respects, however, the tributes above are excessive: the behaviour of audiences was, for example, already changing before Harris's time (see Chapter 1). The introduction of electric light to Covent Garden in 1892, though, and the decision to the play Wagner's operas in a wholly darkened theatre certainly forced a further change in audience behaviour.[83] Harris did not abolish the 'star system' as the popularity of Nellie Melba and Jean de Reszke demonstrates, but, almost certainly, he reduced its ruinous financial impact. He was undoubtedly subject to the whims of his subscribers, some of whom demanded that he perform operas that he might have otherwise avoided. He did not (and probably could not) take any steps to free himself of them and, in the Edwardian years, the influence of 'society' at Covent Garden became an increasing source of tension with the press.

Harris took some years to 'get into his stride' and he achieved some of his success by ruthlessly choking off opposition: he controlled the best three theatres in London for opera (Covent Garden, Her Majesty's and Drury Lane), forcing any opposition into less suitable venues. In October 1891 he deliberately tried to undermine Lago's company by unexpectedly announcing his own season of Italian opera to run almost concurrently,[84] and in the following year employed the same tactics:

> It has pleased [Harris] however to look upon Signor Lago's attempt to establish a new opera house as an audacious interference in his prescriptive rights as manager of the Royal Italian Opera; and by regarding each step taken by his would-be rival as a challenge, he has made up his mind to show that, whatever work Signor Lago may bring out at the Olympic, he can give a better representation of that same work at Covent Garden … When Signor Lago ventured to present *Lohengrin* with Madame Albani in the part of Elsa, Sir Augustus Harris hastened to give the same work with Madame Melba as the heroine. The manager of the Olympic having dared to announce *The Magic Flute*, the manager of Covent

---

83 Shaw wrote, 'For many long hours the audience sat in darkness, the attention being fixed upon the stage, simply because nothing else could be seen … It was all most oppressive to old opera-goers who in the lively days of the past used to vacate their seats when dull choruses or monotonous recitatives were coming. But there was no escape for the dandies at the *Nibelungen Ring*, no chat with a fair lady in a neighbouring box, no cigar with a chum, no glance at the evening paper. The Wagnerites have changed all that' (*Era*, 30 July 1892, p. 13). Shaw, however, still complained of late arrivals and an attitude in which 'the act is the interval and the interval is the act' (see Shaw, *London Music in 1888–89 as heard by Corno di Bassetto*, p. 141; see also pp. 134–5, 142 and 179–80).

84 *MS*, 10 October 1891, p. 289.

Garden lost no time in promising, on his side, the production of Mozart's great German opera.[85]

Harris was not without his critics and an excoriating passage from the *Saturday Review* in 1891 provides an alternative view of his management:

> Surely no impresario was ever so beslavered with adulation as the enterprising tradesman who deals in opera at Bow Street. First, he is credited with a mixture of genius and philanthropy in running the opera at all. He is supposed to have rescued or revived a moribund art by the sheer exertion of his own brilliant talents, and we are to be vastly grateful. Then, he does things so splendidly. Never were so many 'unprecedented casts', such 'magnificent mounting', such 'ideal stage management' as his … [I]t is time all this nonsense was dropped. In the first place, to talk of reviving the most popular of all arts … is rubbish. It had fallen into disfavour simply because it was badly done … And, in the second place, no-one who really understands what opera ought to be can pretend to be satisfied with Sir A Harris's management …
>
> The reigning idea in Covent Garden seems to be that staging means furbishing up old scenery, crowding up the stage with extra choruses, horses, and supers, or getting costumes from Milan … The fact is that with a performance every day, and constant changes of operas and casts, there is no time in Covent Garden for the work that a serious *mise-en-scène* necessitates, and, consequently, nothing ever approaching it has even been seen, or even attempted there …
>
> The lack of rehearsal is patent to all opera-goers in every detail of any performance: the din in the orchestra, the absence of nuances, the coarseness of the choruses, the cues missed, the prompter audible in the gallery, the long waits [between the acts] and what not. The lack of discipline is shocking: it is enough to draw attention to the constant hubbub behind the wings, to the unshaven faces and dirty hands of the chorus singers.
>
> However serious these grievances may be, they fade into insignificance before one [other] – the poverty of the repertory … Sir A Harris has been with us five years, and he has not given us a single novelty.[86]

In respect of production values the *Saturday Review* was ahead of its time: within a few years Harris's productions were remembered as inadequate (see Chapter 3).

Perhaps Harris's greatest failure was that he did little for British opera: although he gave some premieres, few new works were given more than one performance and none had a real opportunity to establish itself. Similarly, he did almost nothing for the performance of opera in English in the grand seasons, with even native

---

[85] *Speaker*, 5 November 1892, p. 558. *Die Zauberflöte* had only been given at Covent Garden once since 1877; Harris did not give it in 1892, but his tactics are obvious. For further discussion of Lago's seasons in the early 1890s, see below.

[86] *SR*, 25 July 1891, p. 111.

works translated into Italian or French (but see below for details of his English-language seasons). Doubtless this was in part because of the feelings of the leading subscribers and the issue became an ever greater bone of contention in the Edwardian years. More seriously, his alleged banishment of the Rosa Company from London after 1890 caused significant damage to that company.

Harris's legacy lived on for decades: in essence he established the basic pattern of opera-giving at Covent Garden that pertained until well after the Second World War. The Grand Opera Syndicate, which ran the main Covent Garden seasons until 1914, comprised principally Harris's friends and supporters from his first season at the theatre, and viewed its role as to carry on Harris's work.

Other Opera Companies in London 1887–96

In these years Italian/Grand Opera in the West End was almost entirely monopolised by the activities of the companies discussed above. The cost of mounting a foreign-language season with an international company of artists was such that, without significant patronage from the well-off, any enterprise was financially very risky, and this discouraged all but the bravest and foolhardy.

Despite having been declared bankrupt in 1888, attributing his failure to the large loss sustained on the uncompleted National Opera House,[87] Mapleson bounced back and gave one more, disastrous, season, at Her Majesty's in 1889. Inviting 'his many old supporters to place renewed confidence in his experience and judgment by affording to him their immediate presence',[88] he promised a repertory drawn from a selection of 21 standard operas plus the British premiere of Bizet's *La jolie fille de Perth*. The opening night (1 June, postponed from 25 May) was not auspicious: half the chorus had missed their train in Turin and were yet to arrive in London and the role of the Count in *Il barbiere di Siviglia* was recast. Furthermore, amongst the audience 'the only well-known faces to be seen were those of various musical celebrities, and "rank and fashion" in its most concentrated form was conspicuous by its absence'.[89] Due both to the lack of society's support and his over-reliance on Donizetti, Rossini and Bellini, by then largely unfashionable, Mapleson was quickly in deep trouble, and on 15 June the operation was taken over by a syndicate of financial backers and prices reduced

---

[87] Mapleson was found to have liabilities of over £40,000 and no assets whatever (*Era*, 28 April 1888, p. 16, and 19 May, p. 10).

[88] *MS*, 1 June 1889, p. 442.

[89] *PMG*, 3 June 1889, p. 4, which further commented: 'Mr Mapleson is a wonderful man. The disasters which have fallen upon him … seem only to increase his buoyancy, and he rises once more to the surface as if nothing has happened.' *SR* had already predicted doom for Mapleson's enterprise (1 June, p. 665).

by half, although three days later Mapleson claimed to be back in command.[90] On 29 June, allegedly due to the illness of Marcella Sembrich, the theatre closed and failed to reopen: Mapleson had run out of money and supporters. His luck had finally expired and he did not produce any more opera in London.

More significantly, a year later, Verdi's *Otello* was introduced to Britain in a series of 12 performances mounted by L. Mayer at the Lyceum between 5 and 27 July 1889. These were well attended; the performances were well executed by a company largely brought from Milan, including Victor Maurel as Iago, the role's original representative. The *Saturday Review* fairly summed up press reception:

> [T]he band is throughout kept in its proper place as the accompanist of the voice, emphasising and illustrating the dramatic situations ... but never, as with Wagner, leaving its proper place ... [T]he set Aria and suchlike conventionalities have been abandoned, and what concerted pieces are retained arise naturally out of the situations ... Signor Verdi's phrases and themes are cast in the same mould which has been used by every Italian composer for the last fifty years, and yet in *Otello* he has managed to turn them to so novel a purpose that they appear with all the charm of freshness.[91]

With Mapleson vanquished, only Joseph Lago provided London with an alternative to Harris in the field of Grand Opera. He gave autumn seasons at Covent Garden in October and November 1890 (notable only for his revival of *Orfeo*, which was taken over by Harris with great success, see above), and then at the Shaftesbury Theatre in 1891. This season opened on 20 October with the British premiere, albeit poorly rendered, of *Cavalleria Rusticana*,[92] and a revival of Cimarosa's *Il matrimonio segreto*, not heard in London since 1849.[93] The former proved particularly successful, being given 45 times before the season ended on 12 December.[94] Lago returned once more in autumn 1892, this time at the new Olympic Theatre, Drury Lane,[95] opening on 17 October with the British premiere of *Eugene Onegin* (performed in English). Given the lack of familiarity with Russian opera (only *A Life for the Tsar* and *The Demon* had previously been

---

90 See *DN*, 17 June 1889, p. 3; *Graphic*, 22 June, p. 686; and *Era*, same date, p. 7. Even popular works such as *Faust* failed to draw a sizeable audience (*PMG*, 18 June 1889, p. 6, of the performance on the previous night, during which 'a modest debut was made during the 'Salve dimora' by a fine tortoise-shell cat, which executed a rapid pirouette across the stage, just behind the singer's back').

91 *SR*, 13 July 1889, p. 40.

92 *MN*, 23 October 1891, p. 679, and *SR*, 24 October, p. 473.

93 *SR*, 21 November 1891, p. 585, and *MT*, 1 December, p. 722.

94 *MN*, 11 December 1891, p. 819.

95 The original Olympic opened in 1806 but was completely rebuilt in 1889 with a capacity of 2,150; it closed 10 years later and was demolished in 1904 during the Aldwych/Kingsway development.

heard in London), it is unsurprising that critical reaction varied, but Lago was praised for his enterprise:

> [The] first two acts fall a little flat, if the truth must be told; but the pent-up fire and passion of [the] last scene are enough to make the audience forget the tameness of what has gone before … The most striking passage in the earlier part of the work is a *scena* in which the heroine writes to Onegin, confessing her love for him; it is beautifully written and its main theme is brought back with altogether excellent effect at the point when the tables are turned and Onegin discovers too late that love has conquered him.[96]

Lago's repertory was mixed; in addition to *Die Zauberflöte* and *Maritana*, a second novelty was Bantock's *Caedmar* (see Chapter 6). On 3 November, however, the season collapsed: Lago blamed the non-availability of some of his regular singers, bad weather, unexpected competition from Harris, and poor attendances.[97] The press noted that some performances had been of dubious quality, but there was sympathy for Lago nevertheless, especially given Harris's behaviour (see above). Lago did not mount an opera season in London again, and there were no subsequent attempts to rival Harris before his death.

A unique, naively enterprising, and poignant undertaking was the visit of the Russian National Opera Company in 1888. This troupe had toured Europe, ending in Britain, and, unable to find a theatre in London,[98] played in the first provinces, visiting Manchester (twice, where they gave the British premiere of Tchaikovsky's *Mazeppa* on 27 August[99]), Liverpool, Huddersfield, Birmingham (twice) and Cardiff before returning to London in October to give selection concerts at the Royal Albert Hall.[100] Finally the company secured the Jodrell Theatre[101] for staged performances of *A Life for the Tsar*, *The Demon*, and *Mazeppa*, commencing on 22 October. Within two weeks, however, the season collapsed, *The Demon* only having been given, and the company was stranded. The *Pall Mall Gazette* reported:

> We call the attention of all … to the great distress and trouble of the Russian Opera Company, the misfortunes of the company at the Albert Hall having culminated in the disappearance of the director, Mr Alexandroff, who left nothing

96 *SR*, 22 October 1892, p. 478.

97 Lago to *The Times*, 4 November 1892, p. 7.

98 *PMG*, 25 April 1888, p. 6.

99 For enthusiastic critical reaction to the Manchester performances, see *MG*, 4 July 1888, p. 8 (*The Demon*); 11 July, p. 8 (*A Life for the Czar*); 30 August, p. 5 (*Mazeppa*).

100 These were not well reviewed; the inclusion of a piece played by 48 pianists at 24 pianos was ridiculed (*Graphic*, 13 October 1888, p. 386).

101 Great Queen Street, Kingsway; the theatre opened in 1882 and operated under a variety of names until it closed in 1941. It was damaged in the London Blitz and demolished in 1959.

> behind but his debts and obligations. They were engaged for four months at the Jodrell Theatre … With difficulty an orchestra was induced to play; the star singer, being refused an advance, deserted them; another [Mikhail Vinogradov] succumbed to Mr Harris's tempting offer of an engagement for three years; and then Mrs Jodrell … broke off the engagement in the middle, and refused to pay the company the £185 which the remainder of the engagement should have brought them. Mr Austin Brereton, Mrs Jodrell's stage manager, considering that the Russians have a claim upon her, resigned, and strongly commended the matter to our attention. These poor people are absolutely, as Mr Brereton assures us, starving. One of them came up to him, in desperation: 'I hungry. I have a wife. She starve. Please give me shilling.' 'His words of thanks,' added Mr Brereton, 'were choked by tears as he kissed my hand'.[102]

The naivety and irresponsibility of the absconding director were chiefly to blame for the failure; in an earlier interview with the *Pall Mall Gazette* he was asked:

> 'How do you manage to put your large [company] up, Mr Alexandroff? I suppose you want a whole hotel to stow them away with all their goods' … 'They all have to find quarters for themselves, which is much easier, and we have nothing further to do with them than to see that they are in their places for the performances.'
>
> 'And is it not difficult to get along in England without knowing the language? Or are some of your artists acquainted with it?' 'No, none of us understand a word. We had one gentleman with us who knew some English, but he had to go back to fulfil an engagement in Russia, so now we don't know a single word and we have to transact business by interpreters, or make ourselves understood by gesticulations. Yes,' with a sigh and a mournful smile, 'it is … very hard and very difficult to accustom ourselves to the English way of living. We are not used to the food and it does not suit us, and we do not like it. But I myself do not feel it as much as the others, as my wife is with me, and who tries to prepare food in the Russian way, and who has even taught our landlady to make real Russian *shtshi*.'
>
> 'But otherwise I suppose you like life in England?' 'Well, no,' reluctantly, 'I cannot say that I do. I liked Germany much better because that is much more like our own life at home. More lively and more cheerful, and not such much grey air and foggy weather.'[103]

Given London's size, it would appear surprising that there was not more opera in English in this period. In fact, there were many English-language performances, but by touring companies in the suburbs rather than in the West End; English

---

[102] *PMG*, 8 November 1888, p. 9. An appeal was launched to fund the return of the company to Russia; see *PMG*, 24 November, p. 13; also *Bristol Mercury*, same date, p. 6.

[103] *PMG*, 8 November 1888, p.9. 'Shtshi' is cabbage soup.

opera performances were also a recurring feature of the musical programmes at the Crystal and Alexandra Palaces. Troupes such as those managed by James Turner, Arthur Rousbey and Valentine Smith aimed at a less affluent audience than that targeted by the Grand Opera troupes or the Carl Rosa; their suburban residencies were identical to their seasons in the provinces (see Chapter 4). These visits were generally met with enthusiasm but rarely lasted more than a week: standard practice was to keep moving, even if it meant shifting only from Camden to Kennington. Coverage of these performances in the West End-focused musical and metropolitan press is relatively sparse. Shaw's review of the Turner Company's production of Macfarren's *Robin Hood* at the National Standard Theatre, Shoreditch, is therefore illuminating:

> With the singers at the Standard I have no serious fault to find, although I may remark that Mr Turner has probably no idea of how unsatisfactory his intonation is when he is not bringing down the house with stentorian high notes. For the chorus I have nothing but praise: the men deserved the thundering encore they got for the unaccompanied chorus in the second act. The scenery, though of the old-fashioned sort, was sufficiently plausible. But the orchestra should not have been inflicted on Shoreditch ... The economies in the woodwind I pass over: the sufficiency of the brass I acknowledge. But imagine the effect, in a theatre of the largest size, of a string band consisting of five violins, one tenor, and two cellos ... [and] for the conductor to wield his baton with one hand and play the harmonium with the other ... more and better strings would have made an enormous difference for the better, and ought to have been provided.[104]

While the touring companies were the biggest providers of English opera in greater London, four other ventures should be noted here. Firstly, the Royal English Opera Company (not to be confused with Carte's enterprise discussed below), active in the West End from 1883 to 1886, briefly attempted to rival Carl Rosa in status, and gave a short season at Covent Garden in January and February 1884, which included the London premiere of Nessler's *Pied Piper of Hamelin* (January 7).[105]

Secondly, Harris gave English-language seasons of increasing length at Drury Lane from 1893 to 1896; his repertory comprised mainly the most popular works of his Grand Opera seasons in translation. The seasons started on or shortly after Easter Monday and reached five weeks in length by 1895 and were frequently well reviewed; Fanny Moody and Charles Manners were recurring members of the ensemble. Additionally, Harris allowed the Canadian tenor Charles Hedmondt to give a season of opera in English for four weeks at Covent Garden from 12 October

[104] Shaw, *London Music in 1888–89*, pp. 112–13 (first published in *The Star*, 4 May 1889).

[105] The British premiere was also given by the company (Queen's Theatre, Manchester, 16 November 1882).

1895, which included the first English-language performances of *Die Walküre*.[106] The occurrence of these seasons makes Harris's apparent banishment of the Carl Rosa from London all the more curious; perhaps the most likely explanation is that he thought that running his own troupe would be more profitable than renting out one of this theatres to his erstwhile colleagues.

The other two ventures, the occasional opera performances given by the London music colleges, and Carte's Royal English Opera House, are atypical of London operatic life, but nevertheless significant. The Royal College's roughly annual productions started in 1885 and were conducted by Stanford until 1914. Several less frequently performed operas were given and singers who later achieved great success were introduced to audiences. The most notable productions in terms of repertory are Goetz's *Der Widerspänstigen Zähmung* (10 July 1889), Cornelius's *The Barber of Bagdad* (9 and 16 December 1891), Delibes's *Le Roi l'a dit* (13 December 1894) and Purcell's *Dido and Aeneas* (20 November 1895).[107] The Guildhall School operated on a similar basis, with its first production in 1890; its most significant performances were of *Esmeralda* (18 June 1896) and Mendelssohn's *Son and Stranger* (23 December 1896).

The story of Richard D'Oyly Carte's Royal English Opera House and its production of Sullivan's *Ivanhoe* in 1891 has been extensively related elsewhere so a summary is appropriate here.[108] Carte had originally conceived of the new theatre as a new venue for Gilbert and Sullivan in which more serious works by them would be played; unfortunately Gilbert refused to leave either the comic opera genre or the Savoy Theatre, and Carte soon found himself saddled with a large theatre and nothing to put in it. Sullivan was, however, amenable to Carte, not least in order to prove that he was capable of writing a Grand Opera and to break free from what he felt was Gilbert's restrictive nature. Over two years elapsed between the laying of the foundation stone (15 December 1888) and the opening of the theatre, at Cambridge Circus, for the premiere of *Ivanhoe* on 31 January 1891 (see Chapter 6). Carte adopted the strategy used for comic opera and the light dramatic stage, and produced the opera in a 'run' (which required two sets of principal singers), a practice almost unheard of in Grand Opera seasons which nearly always operated on the repertory principle. Consequently, the run of *Ivanhoe* of over 150

106 See *MS*, 5 October 1895, pp. 215–16; *Academy*, 19 October, pp. 322–3; *SR*, 19 October, pp. 502–3; and *MT*, 1 November, pp. 743–4. The repertory also included *The Bohemian Girl*, *Carmen*, *Faust*, *Der fliegende Holländer*, *Lohengrin* and *Tannhäuser*. Hedmondt (1857–1940) made his reputation in Leipzig and joined the Carl Rosa company in 1891; he also appeared in the 'English Ring' cycles of 1908 at Covent Garden and was still active during the Great War.

107 For a complete list see Henry Colles and John Cruft, *Royal College of Music: A Centenary Record*, (Portsmouth, 1982), pp. 99–100.

108 See Arthur Jacobs, *Arthur Sullivan, A Victorian Musician* (Oxford, 1984), pp. 320–33; Jeff S. Dailey, *Sir Arthur Sullivan's Grand Opera Ivanhoe and its Theatrical and Musical Precursors* (New York, 2008).

performances is quite astounding. The question of a successor work soon arose; in early March it became known that Carte had obtained the rights to Messager's *La Basoche*, and Bemberg's *Elaine*.[109] New operas by MacCunn, Cowen and Goring Thomas were also rumoured but, despite these possibilities, it was already being suggested that the theatre would close after one season.[110] Interest rallied when *Ivanhoe* was given its 100th performance on 23 May,[111] but insufficiently to sustain it and the theatre closed on 1 August, reopening on 4 November with *La Basoche*, alternating with *Ivanhoe*, and *Elaine* promised for future production. Interest in Sullivan's work had diminished, however, and *Ivanhoe* was withdrawn after two weeks with rumours that Carte had lost £25,000 on the venture. 'There is no good end served,' remarked the *Pall Mall Gazette*, 'by shutting our eyes to the fact that English Grand Opera in Cambridge Circus has been a failure and the reputation of the Royal English Opera House has been saved by a French *opéra comique*.'[112] A brief closure of the theatre followed and it reopened with *La Basoche* the sole work on the bill, which itself closed on 16 January 1892. Despite hopes that Carte might reopen the theatre for opera once again, he soon sold it, and it later reopened as the Palace Theatre of Varieties.[113]

With hindsight it is clear that Carte made a fundamental misjudgement in his conception of the project: he hoped that Grand Opera could be produced in a 'run' and to charge Covent-Garden-level prices for it, but a run depended on a far larger audience base than could afford (or was inclined to pay) the prices that Carte was charging, and the proportion of the population interested in Grand Opera was far smaller than that interested in the comic operas he had previously produced. 'Society', if it attended the theatre two or three times each week during the season, also expected a varied bill of fare, and not to see the same work more than three or four times unless it was a great favourite (this distinction between runs and repertory still pertains today, even in an age of state subsidy, as a perusal of British theatre listings demonstrates). Even with Sullivan as his composer (and even if *Ivanhoe* had been a stronger work), Carte could not draw in audiences at sufficient a level to make his venture pay and, such was the elaborateness of the production that, when he tried to alternate *Ivanhoe* with *La Basoche*, he found that the time and manpower needed to change all the sets and props on an almost nightly basis was itself a huge drain on his resources.[114]

---

[109] *PMG*, 13 March 1891, p. 3, and *Era*, 14 March, p. 10.

[110] *PMG*, 20 March 1891, p. 3, and *Graphic*, 21 March, p. 319.

[111] Not on 25 May as frequently stated; Sullivan was unable to conduct the 100th performance and the 102nd performance was celebrated instead (*Graphic*, 30 May 1891, p. 616).

[112] *PMG*, 21 November 1891, p. 1.

[113] The Palace Theatre continues in operation.

[114] *PMG*, 5 December 1891, pp. 1–2.

Conclusion

Although the period 1876–96 was a somewhat chequered one in the annals of opera in London, performances were still plentiful and there were probably more British premieres of works in this 20-year span than any other previously. Attention hitherto has tended to focus on the brief success of Carl Rosa and the near collapse of Italian opera in the mid-1880s and, while this is certainly significant, it should not obscure the many other operatic ventures of the period, especially impressive given the increasing availability of alternative entertainments and the absence of state support (see Chapter 5). The general press consensus was that standards of performance gradually improved in parallel with changing working practices, technology, and audience and press tastes. The failure, however, of the most up-market opera companies to take any interest in native opera played a major role in its lack of growth. It is difficult, in particular, to avoid scrutinising the career of Augustus Harris; while he was praised at the time for resuscitating Grand Opera when it had all but collapsed, his very success in this endeavour can, from a longer perspective, be seen to have reinvigorated many practices and attitudes which inhibited innovation and the development of Britain's operatic culture in general long after his death.

Appendix 2.1 – 'Society' Members Noted at the Opening Night of Augustus Harris's Covent Garden Opera Season, 19 May 1889, as listed in *MS* (25 May 1889, p. 414).

Summaries of personal backgrounds are taken from *Kelly's Handbook of the Titled, Landed and Official Classes* (1880 and 1891 editions). Many names are too imprecise to be traced but are included for completeness. Many attendees had addresses in Mayfair (the area bounded by Park Lane, Oxford Street, Regent Street and Piccadilly), St James's (between Piccadilly and Victoria Street), Belgravia (between Grosvenor Place and Sloane Street), and just north of Oxford Street (between Portland Place and Edgware Road); these are given where known. Political offices and roles in the Royal Household, where noted, were not necessarily current in 1889, but may have been held at some point previously.

	Personal details	**London address where known**
Royal Box		
Princess (Alexandra) of Wales and three daughters (Princesses Louise, Victoria and Maud)		*Marlborough House, Pall Mall*
Maria, Duchess of Edinburgh		*Clarence House, The Mall*
Grand Tier Boxes		
Hon Frederick Ernest Allsop	Son of 1st Baron Hindlip (see also Lady Hindlip below)	*12 New Cavendish Street*
Mr Cavendish-Bentinck	Presumed related to Duke of Portland below	
Lord Charles Beresford	See note 65	*100 Eaton Square*
Hon Algernon Bourke	Son of 6th Earl of Mayo	*33 Cadogan Terrace*
Lady Roberta Dashwood	Widow of Sir Edwin Dashwood, Bt	
Sir Julian Goldsmid, MP, Bt		*105 Piccadilly*
Countess of Gosford	Louisa Acheson, wife of 4th Earl (Lord of the Bedchamber to Prince of Wales)	*22 Mansfield St, Cavendish Square*
Earl de Grey	See note 65	
Lord Herschell	Farrer Herschell; Lord High Chancellor (self-made lawyer of Polish Jewish origin).	*46 Grosvenor Gardens*

	Personal details	**London address where known**
E. Lawson	? Edward (HM Lieutenant for the City of London)	*? 42 Grosvenor Square*
Harry L. Webster Levy-Lawson MP		*37 Grosvenor Square*
Sir Thomas Lucas, Bt		
Henry ('Harry') Stacy Marks		
Duchess of Marlborough	Frances Spencer-Churchill, widow of 7th Duke	*50 Grosvenor Square*
Duke of Portland	William Cavendish-Bentinck, 6th Duke	*3 Grosvenor Square*
Lord Revelstoke	Edward Baring, 1st Baron (banker; Director of Bank of England)	*37–38 Charles Street, Berkeley Square*
Mrs Edward (Aline) Sassoon	*née* Rothschild; husband MP	
Sir Charles Tennant, MP, Bt		*40 Grosvenor Square*
Lady Alberta Windsor	wife of Lord Robert Windsor	*53 Grosvenor Street*
Lord Wolverton	Frederick Glyn, 4th Baron (banker)	*32 Eaton Place*
Llewellyn Malcolm Wynne MP		
Lord Zetland	Lawrence Dundas, 3rd Earl, 1st Marquess (Lord Lieutenant of Ireland)	*19 Arlington Street*
Mentioned but not traced: Mme von André; Baroness de Brienen; Frederic Hartmann; Mrs Lawrence; Mr Lucas; Mr Montague; Hon George Paget; Hon Gerald Paget; Mrs Parkinson Sharpe; Mrs Vanderbilt; Gwgnydd Williams; Mrs Wilson		
Pit Tier Boxes		
Lord Arlington	Augustus Fitzroy; also 7th Duke of Grafton	
Mrs Ernest (Lucy) Beckett	*née* Lee, of New York; husband partner of Beckett's Bank, Leeds, and MP	
Henry L Bischoffsheim		*75 South Audley Street*
Lady Alice Borthwick	wife of Algernon Borthwick, later 1st Baron Glenesk (owner of *Morning Post*)	*139 Piccadilly*

	Personal details	**London address where known**
Col William Carington MP	Groom in waiting to the Queen	
Sir Philip Currie	Assistant Under Secretary, Foreign Office	*1 Connaught Place*
Lady Georgina Dudley	widow of 1st Earl (see also Lord Dudley below)	*Dudley House, Park Lane*
Mme Eleanor de Falbe	wife of Christian Frederick de Falbe (Danish Minister to England)	*19 Grosvenor Square*
Lady Georgiana Hindlip	wife of 2nd Baron	*33 Hill Street, Berkeley Square*
Duchess of Montrose	Violet Hermione Graham, wife of 5th Duke	
Dowager Duchess of Newcastle	Henrietta Pelham-Clinton, widow of 6th Duke	*15 Hill Street, Berkeley Square*
Mrs Isabel Oppenheim		*16 Bruton Street*
Lady Hannah Rosebery	*née* Rothschild; wife of 5th Earl (later Prime Minister)	*38 Berkeley Street*
Lord Rothschild	Nathaniel Rothschild (first ennobled Jew)	*148 Piccadilly*
Alfred de Rothschild	brother of preceding (banker, director of Bank of England)	*1 Seamore Place, Curzon Street*
Baron Ferdinand de Rothschild	See note 9	*143 Piccadilly*
Marquis de Santurce	HE Señor don C de Murrieta (Spanish aristocrat)	
Albert and Rueben Sassoon	British Indian Jewish Bankers	
Hon Mrs Anna Tatton Egerton	wife of Alan Egerton (MP; later 3rd Baron)	*9 Seamore Place, Curzon Street*
Mentioned but not traced: Mrs Arthur Paget; Mrs Mills; Mrs S Lewis; Y C Hanbury; Mrs Adair; J Morgan; Mrs Hwfa Williams; James Sterne; Mrs McEwen		
Stalls		
Capt Henry Chetwynd	son of 6th Viscount Chetwynd	
Arthur Cohen QC MP		
Hon F G Curzon	? member of Curzon family of Kedleston Hall, Derbys.	

	Personal details	**London address where known**
Lord Dudley	William Ward, 2nd Earl; (later Lord Lieutenant of Ireland (see also Lady Dudley above))	*Dudley House, Park Lane*
Seager Hunt MP	distiller (head of Seager, Evans & Co)	
Adriano de Murietta	son of Marquise of Santurce (above); banker	*Carlton House Terrace*
Major Gen Sim	One of two brothers: Charles Alexander or Edward Coysgarne	*? 8 James Street, Buckingham Gate*
Augustus Spalding		*3 Morpeth Terrace, Victoria St*
Lady Waterford	? Blanche, wife of 5th Marquis of Waterford	*30 Charles Street, St James's Square*
Mentioned but not traced: the Spanish Ambassador; the Portuguese Ambassador; Col Boyle; Henry Randal Burroughes; Mr Cooper; Mme Haarbleicher; Lt Col Thomas Heywood; Mrs Mahlon Sands; Mr Sharp; Mr Travers Smith; Mr Spiers; Mr Campbell Wilkinson;		
Other Boxes		
Mrs Bishoffsheim	? wife of Henry Bishoffsheim (above)	*? 75 South Audley Street*
Lady Adora Brougham	wife of 3rd Baron Brougham & Vaux	*36 Chesham Place*
Lady Randolph (Jenny) Churchill	*née* Lee (American); wife of Lord Randolph Churchill	*2 Connaught Place*
Lady Martha Crossley	widow of Sir F Crossley, Bt.	
Lady Louisa Goldsmid	widow of Sir Francis Goldsmid, Bt	*13 Portman Square*
Lady Emily Hart Dyke	wife of Sir William Hart Dyke, MP, Bt	
Lord Lathom	Edward Bootle-Wilbraham, 1st Earl (Conservative peer; Lord Chamberlain of Queen's household)	*41 Portland Place*
Mrs Henry Lawson	? wife of H.L.W. Lawson (above)	*? 37 Grosvenor Square*
Duchess of Leinster	Hermione Fitzgerald, wife of 5th Duke.	

	Personal details	**London address where known**
Lord William Nevill	son of 1st Marquess of Abergavenny; husband of Luisa de Murrieta, eldest daughter of Marquise de Santurce (above)	
Lady Flo Sturt	wife of 1st Baron Alington	*8 South Audley Street*
Lord Sudeley	Charles Hanbury-Tracy, 4th Baron	*7 Buckingham Gate*
Lady Candida Tweeddale	*née* Bartolucci (Italian); wife 10th Marquis of Tweeddale	
Mentioned but not traced: Miss Cadogan; Lady Esther Gore		

Chapter 3
Opera in London 1897–1918

In the years preceding the Great War, London's operatic life was dominated more than ever by Covent Garden. For the part of 'society' for whom the opera was an essential part of the social season, for the press, for artists who hoped to forge successful careers, for composers who hoped to their works would appear on its stage, and for the wider musical establishment which frequently resented its financial and social clout, the opera house or, more accurately, the Grand Opera Syndicate which leased it, was both the pinnacle and the nucleus of the whole country's operatic life. While vastly greater numbers saw opera in provincial and suburban theatres, with their knowledge and interests shaped accordingly, and despite the fact that the cumulative total of opera performances in London's suburbs between 1897 and 1914 far outnumbered those given at Covent Garden, the power and centrality of what was Britain's national opera house in all but name is undeniable and in the Edwardian decade it reached its zenith. Only between 1910 and 1914 did any serious opposition to Covent Garden emerge and such was the house's unquestioned supremacy that all but one of the alternative providers were reluctant to challenge its dominance directly. Inevitably, therefore, the greater part of this chapter focuses on the theatre in Bow Street and most material detailing other activity in the capital is conceived in relation to it. Only during the Great War, when the theatre closed and the Syndicate suspended its activities, does the narrative alter.

The Grand Opera Syndicate

Harris's death could have thrown the West End opera scene into chaos, rather as the death of Carl Rosa seven years earlier had robbed his company of its dynamo. In London, however, social interest in the annual 'grand' season at Covent Garden, and the long-standing involvement of several leading society figures led to this scenario being avoided: within barely a month of Harris's death, the Grand Opera Syndicate had been formed as a limited liability company with the intention of carrying on at Covent Garden in Harris's manner. For its first season, in 1897, the Syndicate was boosted, as Harris had been 10 years previously, by a royal jubilee. Once again, the 'upper ten' were determined to celebrate with gusto.[1]

---

[1] *MMR* stated: 'Already every box is subscribed for; the stalls are being bought up ... [O]wing to the celebration of the sixtieth year of the Queen's reign the society season is likely to be exceptionally brilliant' (1 May 1897, p. 102).

The Syndicate's membership[2] comprised Harry Higgins (Chairman),[3] Earl de Grey,[4] George Faber,[5] Montague Guest, Neil Forsyth (Secretary, Business Manager, later General Manager),[6] George Causton, and Maurice Grau (Managing Director).[7] Certain differences characterised the Syndicate's regime compared to that of Harris, who had interests in many London theatres and forms of entertainment while the Syndicate focused solely on opera at Covent Garden. After purchasing the building's lease in 1899 it also became concerned with the theatre building and its fabric, and in sub-letting the theatre to other companies, but always with a mind to maintaining the primacy of the annual May-July grand season. In practice most of the day-to-day management was undertaken by Forsyth and Higgins, with Lady de Grey, unofficial voice of the subscribers, exerting a powerful influence, as she had done previously (see Chapter 2). Unlike Harris, but like Frederick Gye, none of these individuals had any theatrical or operatic experience. The dominance of this triumvirate was augmented by Grau's commitments at the Metropolitan Opera, which reduced his involvement in London. His successor, André Messager (1901–06), was in a similar position with respect to the Grand Opéra, Paris. After Messager's resignation Forsyth took on greater managerial responsibility while Percy Pitt became Musical Director.[8] In certain respects this different management structure was an advantage for artists as neither Higgins nor Forsyth interfered with practical aspects of production other than to maintain financial probity, but the lack of artistic direction proved problematic in the Syndicate's early years. As Francis Neilson, stage manager from 1900, commented, 'I soon gathered sufficient evidence to convince myself that not one person connected with the management of the Royal [*sic*] Opera Syndicate had

---

2 *Minim*, 1 September 1896, p. 179. Rosenthal and Chamier's lists vary slightly; Lord Esher is included, but Causton and Guest are omitted (Harold Rosenthal, *Two Centuries of Opera at Covent Garden* (London, 1958), p. 277; Jacques Chamier, *Percy Pitt of Covent Garden and the BBC* (London, 1938), p. 93. *Era* stated that the company's capital was £15,100 (15 August, p. 15).

3 Henry Vincent Higgins was a solicitor with aristocratic connections through both of his marriages; for further information see his obituary (*The Times*, 22 November 1928, p. 16). Rosenthal's claim (p. 277) that he was Lady de Grey's brother-in-law appears to be incorrect.

4 See Chapter 2, note 65.

5 Incorrectly identified by Rosenthal and Chamier as 'Fisher'; Faber became a Conservative MP, and ennobled as Baron Wittenham. He inherited the lease of Covent Garden from Andrew Montagu and sold it to the Syndicate for £80,000 in 1899 (see F. Sheppard (ed.), *Survey of London: volume XXXV: The Theatre Royal, Drury Lane, and the Royal Opera House, Covent Garden* (London, 1970), pp. 71–85).

6 Forsyth was associated with Covent Garden through most of Harris's tenure; Frank Rendle was a mutual brother-in-law, who was later lessee of the theatre.

7 Grau was General Manager of the Metropolitan Opera, New York (1893–1903). At Covent Garden his role was to oversee the practical aspects of production.

8 Grau and Messager's lack of involvement meant that neither man created a distinct ethos at Covent Garden. Although Messager, unusually, was an active composer and conductor, he appeared only rarely in either role during his tenure.

the faintest idea of what was necessary for the production of an opera, old or new. A greater set of amateurs I had never met in my life!'[9]

Little information about the personalities of either Higgins or Forsyth survives; both were regarded as affable and gentlemanly, but wholly focused on the business aspect of the theatre. Lady de Grey's position is more complex; she exercised significant influence behind the scenes but eschewed entirely a public profile. Herman Klein published revealing comments in 1900:

> Her ladyship never for an instant relaxed the hold which her initial efforts had given her in the control and working of the organisation … [T]he wishes of this indefatigable lady have grown to be the commands – nay, the absolute law – of the most independent opera-house in Europe …
>
> During the early years of the renaissance [the Harris seasons] much diplomacy was used by all parties. Mr Higgins would convey suggestions to Mr Harris, who would thereupon have a chat with Lady de Grey and promise to do his best to meet her wishes … A new *prima donna* had to be engaged, a new opera to be commissioned, a Continental success to be mounted, a new box subscriber to be passed and admitted. Ere any of these things could be done it was essential that Lady de Grey should be consulted. So by degrees her word became law; and law it remains to this day.[10]

As Klein implied, this influence derived from social position: as well as her own family connections[11] she was also a member of the Prince of Wales's 'Marlborough House set'. A later, waspish, portrait by E.F. Benson suggested that her involvement in opera did not arise from love of music but rather from the need of a role:

> [S]he regarded everything connected with politics with a sort of weary repulsion … [and] she neither had nor wished to have a great London house for stately and magnificent entertaining …

---

9 Francis Neilson, *My Life in Two Worlds*, (2 vols, Appleton (Wisconsin), 1952–53), vol. 1, p. 174. Neilson stated that Forsyth 'had not a musical nerve in his body' (p. 183). An Englishman, Neilson lived in the United States for several years, where his interest in opera was encouraged by the conductor Anton Seidl. Returning to England in 1897, Neilson worked for E.C. Hedmondt and the Rosa Company prior to Covent Garden. He served as a Liberal MP (1910–16) but later returned to the United States. See also *Era*, 8 December 1900, p. 13.

10 Herman Klein, *Thirty Years of Musical Life in London 1870–1900* (New York, 1900), pp. 266–70.

11 Constance Gladys Herbert was a member of the Pembroke family of Wilton House, Salisbury. Her father had been a cabinet minister; one brother was an MP (later Earl of Pembroke), another became Ambassador to the United States, and her sisters Maud and Mary married Hubert Parry and the theologian Friedrich von Hügel respectively. Constance married twice; her first husband, George Lowther, Earl of Lonsdale, died unexpectedly in 1882. She had one child by her first marriage.

> She wanted a definite 'stunt' to occupy her and … she had found it in the opera …
>
> Opera must be made the fashion: boxes must gleam with the jewels of beautiful women, and the stage must resound with glorious voices singing noble music. About music technically Lady de Grey knew nothing, nor was she musical in the sense that it was a need of her nature … But now when in this regeneration of the opera, which was mainly due to her, great artists flocked to London, Edouard and Jean de Reszke and Ternina and Melba, her friendship with them gave her stunt a living interest which mere music did not possess for her …
>
> She had no sort of sympathy with the indigent music lover (not being a music lover herself) who wanted his opera cheap … her opera at Covent Garden was not for such, it was an expensive piece of luxury for the wealthy. For English composers and English singers, similarly she had no sympathy at all: she thought of them vaguely as people who wrote and performed oratorios in cathedral towns.[12]

Although a force to be reckoned with, Lady de Grey was not unconquerable:

> We had been rehearsing [Smyth's *Der Wald*] for about a week when Lady de Grey came to me [Francis Neilson] and asked about the production of two new French works. I told her frankly that, as the season was drawing to a close and as *Der Wald* was in rehearsal, I did not see how it was possible to put on two other new operas. She seemed disappointed and went off to find Mr Higgins. Later in the day he told me that the French works must be done and … suggested that *Der Wald* might be done the next season …
>
> A date had been fixed for the production, but paragraphs appeared in the newspapers stating that it had been postponed … [Smyth] came to me and told me to put on my hat and go with her to see Lady Warwick … I sat in the cab while she went in to see [her]. In about twenty minutes [Smyth] joined me. 'It's all right,' she said, 'there will be a message tomorrow at Covent Garden, asking the date of the first performance of *Der Wald*, as the King will wish to send a representative to it'.[13]

Given the discretion with which Lady de Grey exercised her power, there is no primary source evidence to corroborate the assertions of Klein, Rosenthal, Neilson and Benson. Clearly, though, she was one of the individuals most responsible for the rejuvenation and maintenance of the social aspect of the Covent Garden opera seasons from 1887 to 1914.

---

12 E.F. Benson, *As We Were: a Victorian peep-show* (London, 1930), pp. 182–8.

13 Neilson, pp. 208–9. Daisy Greville, Countess of Warwick, was another member of the 'Marlborough House set'. Smyth told a similar story but in her version the Duchess of Connaught, Edward VII's sister-in-law, was Smyth's intercessor (see Ethel Smyth, *What Happened Next* (London, 1940), pp. 231–3).

While the social function of the opera season is undoubted, and was used by music critics as an easy explanation for aspects of the Syndicate's management they disliked,[14] it is not the whole story. The social elite did not form the majority of the audience, though they constituted a greater proportion than in any other theatre. Nevertheless, the importance of keeping the wealthiest subscribers 'on side' – whatever their reason for attending the opera – is clear. The Syndicate's financial model depended significantly on season-long subscriptions, especially for the most expensive seats, facilitating the influence of well-off subscribers, with Lady de Grey acting as conduit. The presence of royalty was continued to be important – although Prince Edward and Princess Alexandra had been regular visitors, Edward's accession in 1901 brought a reigning British monarch to the opera the first time in over 40 years. Social cachet augmented Covent Garden's importance over the next 14 years. George V and Queen Mary subscribed annually and attended regularly; tickets for the gala performance after their coronations in 1911 were sold at unprecedented prices.[15] A further indication of the heightened social function is the publication in newspapers of lists of box subscribers for grand seasons from 1909 to 1914. These lists typically contain between 250 and 300 names. Those who subscribed for at least three of these seasons included the ambassadors of Germany, Austria-Hungary, Portugal, and the United States; one duke; one marquess; 11 earls or countesses; four viscounts; 19 barons or baronesses; 17 knights, baronets, or spouses; and at least 24 present or former members of the House of Commons (see also Appendix 2.1).

Although the greater part of the audience was not drawn from the 'upper ten', Covent Garden attendees continued to come from higher income brackets than at any other theatre, the Beecham audiences possibly excepted.[16] Evening dress remained compulsory (often relaxed for the performances of *Der Ring* which had to start much earlier than the normal 8.30 pm).[17]

---

[14] *MS* commented: 'It is this fashionable and wealthy [society] element that is at once the support and the hindrance of opera in London, for the tastes of the fashionable patron have to be considered and, unfortunately, their tastes do not make for progress in music' (20 March 1897, p. 181).

[15] Box prices for this performance (26 June 1911), were raised to 100 guineas; the Syndicate made a profit of £11,558 on one night. Other command performances given for visiting heads of state typically produced profits of between £3,000 and £4,000 (handwritten accounts sheet, Programmes Box (Covent Garden 1793–1905), RCM, Centre for Performance History).

[16] In 1914 box prices ranged from 2½ to 8 guineas (between 10s 7d, and 2 guineas for an individual seat); orchestral stalls cost 1 guinea, and remaining seats ranged from 2s 6d to 15s. These prices are similar in real terms to those charged by Gye in 1875 except that the most expensive boxes had increased. Beecham's prices in 1914 were almost identical.

[17] Rosenthal, p. 287. The earlier start times and relaxation of dress regulations for *Der Ring* caused annoyance; some men went home during the dinner interval to change from morning to evening dress (*MN*, 18 June 1898, pp. 591–2).

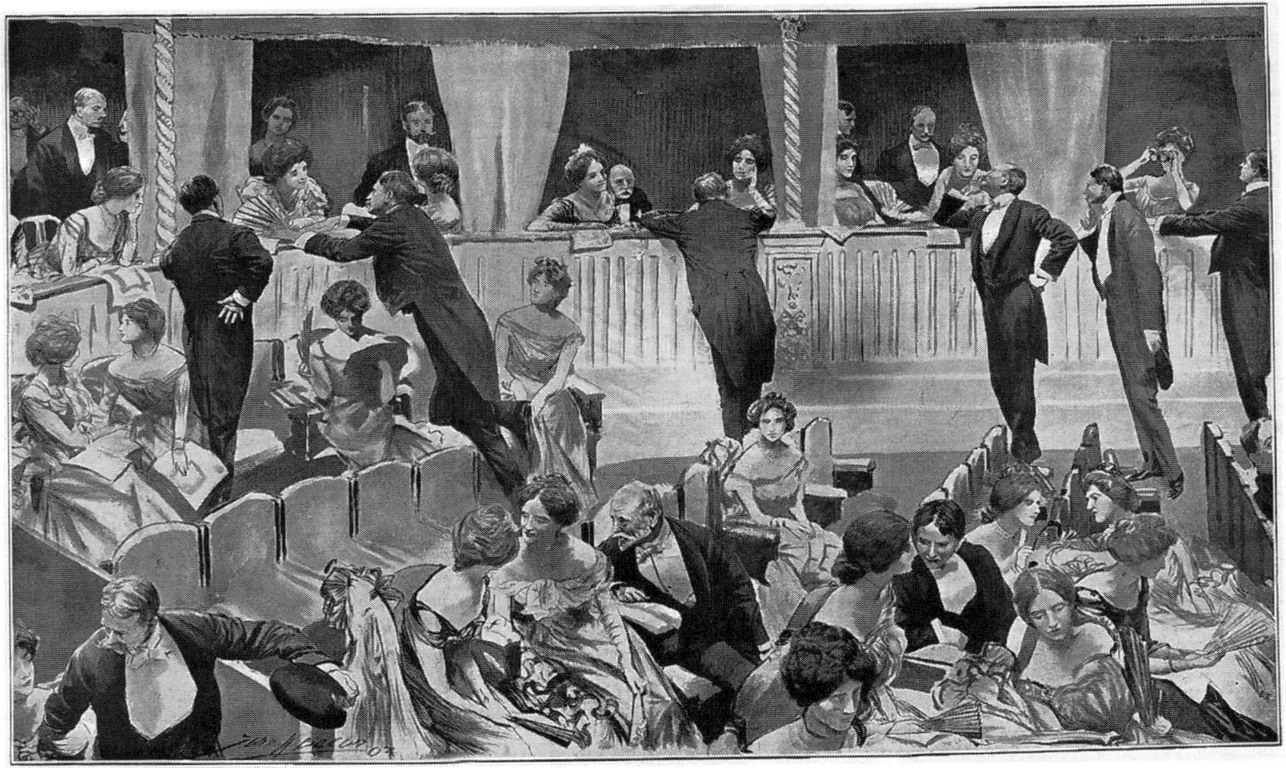

Figure 3.1 'The Last Night of the Opera' (*Black and White*, 2 August 1902)

The Syndicate's primary objective being to maintain the established 'grand' season, it placed heavy emphasis on recruiting the 'best' singers and bringing new operas to London, especially those that had been successful elsewhere. Seasons averaged 76 performances[18] and there was a steady stream of 'novelties' although at a slower rate than during Harris's later seasons, and few new works were given the opportunity to establish themselves (see Table 3.1; operas marked † appeared in three or more seasons up to 1914). Many received their first performances late in the season and were soon discarded. World premieres (marked *) remained extremely rare. In some important instances the Syndicate lost out to other companies (see below).

The popularity of individual works and composers varied during the Syndicate's pre-War operation (see Table 3.2).[19] There are no natural dividing points so a division chronologically halfway through the period has been selected.

In the early years a marked shift towards Wagner is observable although *Faust*, *Roméo et Juliette* and *Carmen* all maintained their established popularity. After a decline in the Harris years, Verdi returned via *Aïda* and *Rigoletto*; the vogue for *Cavalleria Rusticana* evaporated, while Mozart and Meyerbeer both declined significantly. From 1906, however, Italian opera, represented by Puccini and an ever-resurgent Verdi made significant gains. *Madama Butterfly*, *La Bohème* and *Tosca* were all extremely popular, while *La Traviata* was rejuvenated after years of sporadic performances. *Faust*, *Tannhäuser*, *Lohengrin*, and *Roméo et Juliette* all declined significantly, although the first three of these remained in the top 10 operas performed across the whole period.

An examination of the most popular composers over the same time span shows slightly different trends, with Wagner performing more strongly (Table 3.3). The surge in the popularity of Wagner compared to the Harris years is striking despite the later decline;[20] although the number of works in the repertory remained the same until the addition of *Parsifal* in 1914, they account for a far greater proportion of the total (up from 16.9 per cent). This was achieved by more performances of the complete *Ring* cycle. Harris had mounted this only in 1892, but under the Syndicate performances were roughly biennial until 1906 and almost annual thereafter. When performed, two or three complete cycles were given, and *Die Walküre* and *Siegfried* were given still more frequently. The resistance to Wagner observable in the early 1880s had dissolved and the

---

18 The shortest season took place in 1912 (61 performances due to the integration of appearances by the Russian Imperial Ballet) and the longest in 1909 (89).

19 Tables 3.2 and 3.3 include consideration of all performances managed by the Syndicate, not just those in the grand season; from 1904 onwards the Syndicate sometimes mounted additional seasons so the total number of performances is rather greater in the later period: 916 in 1906–14 against 747 in 1897–1905.

20 These statistical summaries obscure some wide variations; in the main season of 1909 Wagner was represented only by two performances of *Die Walküre* and, in 1911, there were no Wagner nights in the grand season at all.

Table 3.1 Opera premieres produced by the Grand Opera Syndicate at Covent Garden, 1897–1914

Composer	**Opera**	**Date**
Kienzl	*Der Evangelimann*	2 July 1897
D'Erlanger	*Inèz Mendo*	10 July 1897
Mancinelli[1]	*Ero e Leandro*	11 July 1898
Saint-Saëns	*Henri VIII*	14 July 1898
Adam	*Le Châlet*	8 July 1899
De Lara	*Messaline*	13 July 1899
Puccini	† *Tosca*	12 July 1900
Stanford	* *Much Ado About Nothing*	30 May 1901
Lalo	*Le Roi d'Ys*	17 July 1901
Bunning	* *La Princesse Osra*	14 July 1902
Smyth	*Der Wald*	18 July 1902
Missa	*Maguelone*	20 July 1903
Saint-Saëns	*Hélène*	20 June 1904
Massenet	*Hérodiade*[2]	6 July 1904
Cilea	*Adriana Lecouvreur*	8 November 1904[3]
Puccini	† *Madama Butterfly*	10 July 1905
Leoni	* *L'Oracolo*	3 July 1905
Poldini	*Der Vagabund und die Prinzessin*	11 May 1906
Massenet	*Le jongleur de Notre Dame*	15 June 1906
Gluck	† *Armide*	6 July 1906
Giordano	† *Fedora*	5 November 1906
Catalani	*Loreley*	12 July 1907
Franchetti	*Germania*	13 November 1907
Naylor	* *The Angelus*	27 January 1909
Saint-Saëns	† *Samson et Dalila*	26 April 1909
Debussy	† *Pelléas et Mélisande*	21 May 1909
Charpentier	† *Louise*	18 June 1909
D'Erlanger	* *Tess*	14 July 1909
Laparra	*La Habanera*	18 July 1910
Puccini	† *La fanciulla del West*	29 May 1911
Massenet	*Thaïs*	18 July 1911

Composer	Opera	Date
Humperdinck	*Königskinder*	27 November 1911
Wolf-Ferrari	† *Il segreto di Susanna*	11 July 1911
Wolf-Ferrari	*I gioielli della Madonna*	30 May 1912
Zandonai	*Conchita*	3 July 1912
Waltershausen	*Oberst Chabert*	24 April 1913
Camussi	*La Du Barry*	3 July 1913
Wagner	*Parsifal*	2 February 1914
Méhul	*Joseph*	3 February 1914
Montemezzi	*L'amore dei tre re*	27 May 1914
Zandonai	*Francesca da Rimini*	16 July 1914

Notes to table: [1] Luigi Mancinelli was a regular conductor at Covent Garden; *Ero e Leandro* received its world premiere in a concert version at the Norwich Festival in 1896 and was first staged in Madrid in 1897. [2] Given under the name *Salome* with the names of other characters changed and relocated to Ethiopia, in order to conform to the impermissibility of representing biblical characters on stage. [3] The Syndicate mounted autumn seasons from 1904 to 1907; see below.
Sources: Rosenthal;[21] contemporary periodicals.

Covent Garden audiences had become, in Shaw's words, 'perfect Wagnerites' barely 20 years later. The surge in the popularity of Puccini was spurred by the runaway success of *Madama Butterfly*.[22] The presence of Verdi and Gounod was due to the resilience of *Aïda*, *Rigoletto*, *La Traviata*, and *Faust*, but while Verdi's star rose, Gounod's sank, and Bizet's continuing appearance was due solely to the enduring appeal of *Carmen*. The preferences of the audience focused on a decreasing number of composers; the works of the top five accounted for 62.8 per cent of all performances in the first nine years, and 78.2 per cent from 1906 (71.4 per cent overall) while the top three accounted for 51.3 per cent up to 1905 and 69.4 per cent afterwards (Puccini replacing Gounod). Although many novelties were seen during the Syndicate's tenure, the repertory became narrower and more rigid.

As previously, 'star singers' were crucial for the Syndicate's programme and the search for new talent was constant. Of the *prime donne* Nellie Melba

[21] Rosenthal added Giordano's *Andrea Chénier* and Cornelius's *Barber of Bagdad* to this list but they had been previously given by the Rosa Company (2 April 1903, Queen's Theatre, Manchester) and the Royal College of Music (9 December 1891, Savoy Theatre, London) respectively; the Covent Garden performances were the first in the original language (see Rosenthal, pp. 313–15, and below).

[22] Many reviews were lukewarm; see, for example, *MS*, 15 July 1905, pp. 36–7; *Athenaeum*, same date, pp. 90–91; *MT*, 1 August, p. 543. *The Times* (11 July, p. 5) was much more complimentary.

Table 3.2 Operas most frequently performed by the Grand Opera Syndicate at Covent Garden, 1897–1914

1897–1905	**1906–14**	**Overall**
Faust (66)	*Madama Butterfly* (76)	*La Bohème* (106)
Lohengrin (51)	*La Bohème* (72)	*Faust* (93)
Roméo et Juliette (47)	*La Traviata* (48)	*Madama Butterfly* (91)
Carmen (44)	*Rigoletto*/*Tosca* (44)	*Aïda* (77)
Tannhäuser (42)	*Aïda* (42)	*Rigoletto* (76)
Aïda (35)	*Die Walküre*/*Samson et Dalila* (32)	*Carmen* (73)
La Bohème (34)	*Carmen*/*Louise* (29)	*Lohengrin* (58)
Tristan und Isolde/*Rigoletto* (32)	*Faust*/*Pagliacci* (27)	*Tannhäuser* (57)
Die Meistersinger (27)	*Il barbiere di Siviglia*/*Götterdämmerung* (23)	*Die Walküre*/*La Traviata* (55)
Die Walküre/*Don Giovanni* (23)	*Das Rheingold* (21)	*Tosca* (53)

Table 3.3 Performances by the Grand Opera Syndicate by composer, 1897–1914

	Number of works*		**Total performances**			**% of total performances**		
	1897–1905	1906–14	1897–1905	1906–14	Total	1897–1905	1906–14	Total
Wagner	9	10	199	203	402	26.7	22.2	24.2
Puccini	4	5	39	243	282	5.2	26.5	17.0
Verdi	7	6	80	190	270	10.7	20.7	16.2
Gounod	3	2	104	47	151	13.9	5.1	9.1
Bizet	1	2	47	34	81	6.3	3.7	4.9

Note to Table: **Il Trovatore* was only performed in 1905, *Falstaff* only in 1914, and *Hamlet* only once in 1898; *Philémon et Baucis* was given only in 1898 and 1904, and *Les pêcheurs de perles* only in 1908.

reigned supreme, appearing in all seasons bar one between 1897 and 1914. Lilian Nordica also remained popular until her last (unannounced) appearance in 1902, while Miika Ternina was a regular from 1898 to 1906, appearing in both Italian and Wagner operas.[23] Emmy Destinn first appeared in 1904, played Cio-Cio-San in the first performance of *Madama Butterfly* in 1905, and sang at Covent Garden until 1914. Luisa Tetrazzini made her debut in the autumn season of 1907 and appeared annually until 1912. Jean de Reszke's career drew to a close; in his last season (1900) he appeared only five times[24] and his brother Edouard retired at about the same time. Jean's place was taken, intermittently, by Enrico Caruso, who was easily the most popular tenor of the pre-War years although he only appeared in seven seasons (1902, 1904–07 and 1913–14). 'Melba/Caruso nights' were some of the most eagerly anticipated performances of the period. Antonio Scotti (1899–1910) and Mario Sammarco (1904–14) became favourite baritones in Italian repertory. The expansion of music education in the United Kingdom bore fruit and an increasing proportion of the chorus and several principals were British. The English *Ring* cycles conducted by Richter (see below) were dominated by native singers and many British artistes made notable impressions in the grand seasons, including John McCormack (first appeared 1907), Walter Hyde (1908) and Louise Kirkby Lunn (minor roles in 1896 and a principal from 1901). The versatile stalwart Mathilde Bauermeister retired from the Covent Garden troupe in 1905 after 36 years; a benefit was organised for her by Melba.[25]

The Syndicate's early years were not characterised by smooth operation or reception. The directors' lack of musical expertise drew regular criticism, as did the alleged focus on society.[26] The lobby in favour of the establishment of a national opera house and company viewed the Syndicate as an obstacle to its progress (see Chapter 5). Much of the practical criticism directed at the Syndicate related to the performances of Wagner. London music critics placed him head and shoulders above his Italian and French contemporaries,[27] and a passionate interest in seeing his works faithfully and professionally produced became a running thread in

---

23 Ternina (1863–1941) made an impressive Covent Garden debut as Isolde (3 June 1898) and for many critics was the perfect Wagnerian soprano; she also played Tosca in the British premiere of the eponymous opera (12 July 1900).

24 Rosenthal, pp. 292–3.

25 *Era*, 15 July 1905, p. 13. Bauermeister first appeared at Covent Garden in 1869; in addition to her work in the United Kingdom, which went far beyond Covent Garden, she was also a member of the Metropolitan Opera, New York, from 1891 to 1906, and held the record there for the greatest number of performances by a female artist (1,062) until overtaken by Thelma Votipka in the 1950s.

26 *MMR* stated: 'Socially the [1902] season has been brilliant; artistically it is the dullest I can remember' (1 July 1902, p. 134). The coronation of Edward VII had heightened social expectations; due to an emergency appendectomy the ceremony was postponed from 26 June to 9 August.

27 *MS* stated, without irony, 'We are all glad to know that we are to have the *Ring* again … Other opera composers – what are they compared with the great Wagner? Pigmies' (24 February 1906, p. 115).

critical commentary of the Syndicate's early seasons (see below). These demands often extended to the whole of the Syndicate's repertory. The 1897 season illicited many comments on 'routine' performances, last-minute repertory changes and poor stage management.[28]

The *Saturday Review*'s John Runciman unleashed a characteristic tirade: 'It is only too apparent that the dilettante syndicate was overawed by traditions … If it intends to try again I hope it will have the sense … to get a competent man who will direct the artistic policy as cleverly as the business policy is now directed'.[29] Runciman demanded wholesale replacement of orchestral parts in order to eliminate accumulated errors, a revised cuts policy ('the omission of whole numbers – not of three bars here and five bars there in the Costa way'), the dismissal of principals who came to the footlights without justification, the drilling and sprucing up of the chorus (which 'should be washed, the male portion shaved, and the whole attired in something more soothing to the eye than the present unheard of collection of rags and tatters'),[30] the improvement of scene changes ('the present electric bells and boatswains' whistles … should be replaced by a more peaceful mode of communication'), revised lighting arrangements, including the replacement of the electric footlights with gas on the grounds that the former were not dimmable,[31] and the 'voice of the prompter either be tuned or forever stilled'.[32]

Runciman's comments are illuminating regarding stagecraft; although Harris's productions were praised as an advance on those of his predecessors, there were clearly still many faults. The complexities of Wagner's works emphasised this: Francis Neilson told Lady de Grey 'that the stage was a disgrace and that the

---

[28] *Athenaeum* referred to a 'somewhat indifferent performance of *Faust*' (10 May, opening night), while stating that it could 'not be said that … *Roméo et Juliette* on [11 May] was beyond reproach' (15 May 1897, p. 659); *MMR* noted that the Syndicate 'promised *Tristan* twice and gave other operas; it promised *Meistersinger* twice and gave other operas. It has since then substituted *Les Huguenots* for *Le nozze di Figaro*, and *Tristan* for *Siegfried*' (1 July, p. 153).

[29] *SR*, 24 July 1897, p. 84.

[30] The increased interest in 'stage business' may also reflect contemporaneous changes in spoken drama. Changes in theatre design, in which proscenium arches emphasised the 'picture frame' concept of the stage (the first of which had been installed at the Haymarket Theatre by Squire Bancroft in 1880), led actors to play more to each other than to 'break the fourth wall' by addressing the audience (see George Taylor, *Players and Performances in the Victorian Theatre* (Manchester and New York, 1989) and Michael R. Booth, *Theatre in the Victorian Age* (Cambridge, 1981)). The more 'naturalistic' style of acting required in Ibsen and Strindberg and the 'verismo' operas of Mascagni and Puccini may also have influenced a change in critical focus.

[31] Dimmable electric lights were installed in 1902 (*MS*, 3 May 1902, p. 284).

[32] Runciman's views were not universally shared; *MS* implicitly blamed subscribers for demanding too large a repertory: 'What we marvel at is how those in control have managed to do so well! You cannot do without the wealthy subscribers and they desire, naturally enough, to hear several operas during the many weeks the season lasts' (31 July 1897, p. 76).

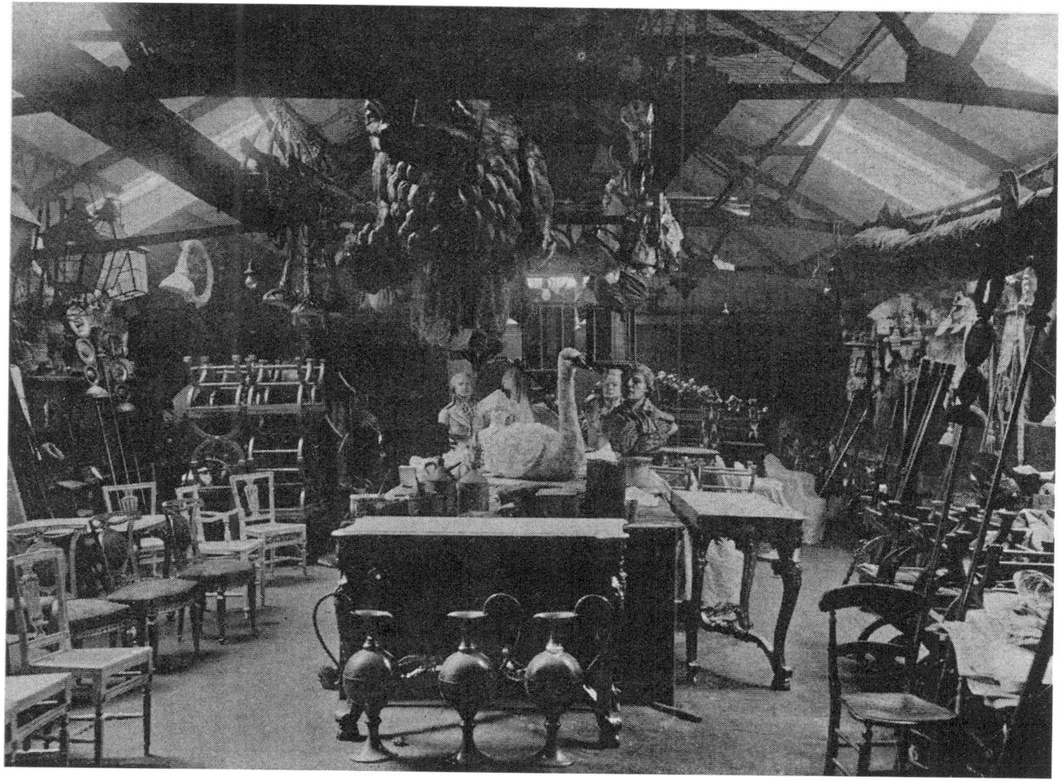

Figure 3.2 The Property Room at the Royal Opera House, Covent Garden (*Royal Opera 50th Anniversary Souvenir Programme*, 1908)

performances, apart from the orchestra and the singers, were not worthy of a metropolitan house'.[33] In 1900–01 the Syndicate, by then owners of the building lease, made extensive alterations to the theatre under the supervision of Edwin Sachs; these included a heightened roof for the easier removal of scenery and backcloths, a rebuilt main stage, a reduced apron with compensatingly expanded stalls and orchestra pit (reducing singers' ability to come downstage to address the audience directly), improved stage lighting, and the remaining auditorium gaslights replaced by electricity.[34] Neilson replaced scenery and properties,[35] and reorganised staging. His opinion of established practice was low:

> There was not a performance which could not have been bettered dramatically. Both the Carl Rosa and the Moody-Manners opera companies performed many of these old [French and Italian] operas in a far more interesting way …
>
> [There was] scarcely any stage rehearsal. In fact, I had to plead all through the second season with artist after artist to come for only an hour or two … in order to make changes which they afterwards admitted were for the better. The amusing part of it was that we carried out some of Wagner's stage directions for the first time, and no one in front knew it.[36]

Staging was steadily refined and more pragmatic commentators gave qualified approval:

> With regard to the stage management … signs of improvement in various ways have not been wanting, but there is still much to be done. With a new man and new machinery everything cannot be set right in one season. What, however, we want, and ought to see, is a steady advance towards perfection and not, as has been the case during the past season, fitful efforts – one thing attended to, another left.[37]

---

33 Neilson, p. 173.

34 See Neilson pp. 183–4, Rosenthal pp. 279–80, and *British Architect*, 24 May 1901, pp. 375–6. For further information on Sachs and photographs of the remodelling, see www.rohcollections.org.uk/CollectionPhotSachs.aspx [accessed 2 November 2012] and also Edwin Sachs and Ernest A.E. Woodrow, *Modern Opera Houses and Theatres* (3 vols, London, 1896–98). Many of these alterations remained *in situ* until the renovation of the building in the 1990s.

35 Much equipment had been in use since Gye's time. Neilson's zeal had only a temporary effect: scenery painted for the 1899 production of *La Bohème* was still in use in 1957 (Rosenthal, p. 289). Although referred to as 'Stage Manager' Neilson's responsibilities extended to many aspects of production. He did not, however, have exclusive responsibility; no fewer than five set designers worked on the 1903 production of *Der Ring* (Rosenthal, p. 280).

36 Neilson, pp. 189–90 and 192.

37 *Athenaeum*, 3 August 1901, p. 167.

A wide range of practices was addressed (though not consistently reformed). In the late 1890s it was not unusual to hear polyglot performances, especially of Wagner, as chorus members sang in their most natural and convenient language;[38] eventually a complete German chorus was employed. Arnold Dolmetsch was employed to play recitatives in *Le nozze di Figaro* on a harpsichord in 1897 although the opera was still cut extensively.[39] The orchestra pit was rearranged for the 1898 season with the brass beneath the stage, improving balance, and the conductor standing against the stall rail in front of the whole orchestra rather than in the middle by the prompter's box.[40]

The most important, though unintentional, change was the engagement of Hans Richter to conduct *Der Ring* in 1903. Although long resident in Britain, and a renowned Wagnerian, Richter had not conducted opera in London since the German season at Drury Lane in 1882 and had never conducted *Der Ring* in a British theatre. Working with Percy Pitt, who was appointed Musical Adviser in 1902 and promoted to Musical Director in February 1907,[41] Richter improved the musical aspects of the Wagner performances, coinciding with the culmination of revised staging. Critical reception was fulsome:

> The artistic success of the three cycles of the *Ring* at Covent Garden has given a new turn to operatic matters in London. Much ink has been thrown on to too much paper in the last few years to prove that the Covent Garden Syndicate was, and ever must be, without virtue … [but] the Syndicate has worked silently and uncomplainingly towards perfecting its opera seasons … [N]ew scenery has been painted and invented for *Das Rheingold* and *Die Götterdämmerung*, and Dr Richter has been given as many rehearsals as he required … Lighting and scenic rehearsals with musical cues were innumerable. For absolute perfection more full rehearsals might have been held, for it was evident that the standards of the performances, apart from the merits of the individual artists, rose from cycle to cycle. Especially this was noticeable in the lighting arrangements … [and] the stage manager at Covent Garden has done wonders with the mechanical difficulties of the *Ring* … [N]ot even at Munich could the casts have been bettered, and the orchestra, under Dr Richter, was superb.[42]

---

38 *MN*, 25 May 1897, p. 521. This practice persisted *in extremis*; when principals were indisposed and substitutes appeared, polyglot performances could still arise.

39 *Athenaeum*, 17 July 1897, p. 106, and *SR*, 24 July, p. 84. Costa had used cellos and basses; subsequently, full strings were employed.

40 *MN*, 14 May 1898, pp. 479–80.

41 *Athenaeum*, 9 February 1907, p. 175. Pitt's role was to organise and run rehearsals, audition and appoint members of the chorus and orchestra and, occasionally, to conduct performances (Rosenthal, p. 278).

42 *MMR*, 1 June 1903, pp. 113–14.

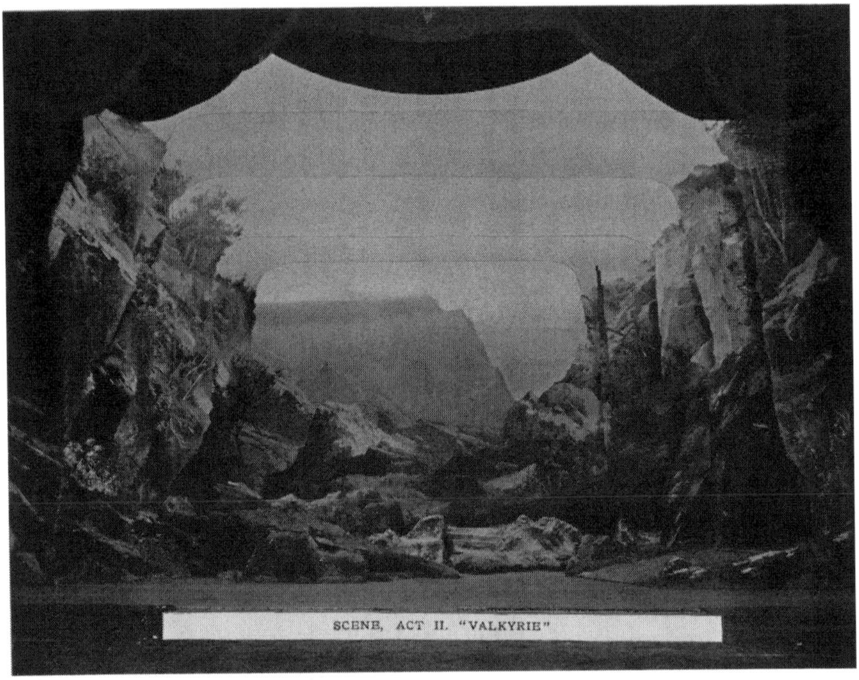

Figure 3.3 Stage set for *Die Walküre*, Act II, at the Royal Opera House, Covent Garden (*Royal Opera 50th Anniversary Souvenir Programme*, 1908)

Richter was re-engaged in 1904 and 1905 and developed a close working relationship with Pitt.[43] His employment completed the division of the grand season into two halves with German operas (now normally sung in their original language) followed by French and Italian works. Richter conducted in May in order to work in Bayreuth in June.

43 See Richter's letters to Pitt (BL, Egerton MSS 3301 and 3302; Richter wrote in German; translations, here slightly modified, form part of MS 3302). From Richter: 'Tell Herr Forsyth *not* to consider the application of the viola player Herr Maurice Speelman, although MS is a first class musician, he is unfortunately not in good health; please also give him the name of the viola player whom you know of as suffering from the same disease; it is sad for the poor fellows but we must not *knowingly* take such a risk' (22 January 1905, MS 3301, f. 11, translation at MS 3302, ff. 94–5); and 'I heard here Herr P. Cornelius from Copenhagen as Siegmund – he is simply *superb* in voice, appearance and acting … Then Frau Gulbranson, whose voice is better than ever, told me she would come to London for *at any rate* two [*Ring*] cycles … [W]e will [also] take Bechstein junior, as the man is called; he is nr. 1 and also sings Kadi and Hirt in *Tristan*. On account of his dear comical figure he will not do of course in *Tannhäuser*.' (23 July 1906, MS 3301, f. 32, translation at MS 3302, ff. 104–5.)

For its first nine years the Syndicate, although often criticised and ridiculed, exercised a virtual monopoly on Grand Opera in the West End. Other companies appeared on an irregular basis and none intended to contest Covent Garden's primacy. The Syndicate extended its activities beyond the main season; aided by improving critical reaction, and following autumn seasons undertaken by the Moody-Manners Company at Covent Garden in 1902 and 1903 (see below), it organised its own Italian autumn seasons from 1904 to 1907; these were given by a company drawn principally from the Teatro San Carlo, Naples, with Melba and Caruso appearing regularly.

From 1907 the activities of Richter and Pitt, the Beechams, and Oscar Hammerstein disrupted the Syndicate. Pitt's appointment as Musical Director strengthened both his and Richter's positions and they quickly took advantage, aiming to mount performances at Covent Garden in English, starting with *Der Ring*.[44] Although the Syndicate occasionally let the theatre to English-language companies, it had no interest in producing vernacular performances, despite pressure from the critical and academic establishments to provide them in order to engender a wider appreciation of opera in Britain (see Chapter 5). The eschewal of English was totemic, marking out the house as an international establishment, and as different from the touring companies. Richter, however, was encouraged by Cosima Wagner who told him that 'a profound influence on the public was only possible through the *national language*'.[45] His final objective was clear:

> An artistic success with the *Ring* would open a wide prospect: *the foundation of a permanent English opera.* By that I mean performances in the English language … If this goal is reached, or at least the way prepared for it, I shall have achieved one of my highest aims and embodied my gratitude for the hospitality which has been unstintingly and unceasingly bestowed on me in this country for thirty years.[46]

In January and February 1907 Covent Garden was leased by a visiting German troupe (see below), whose reception, in winter, was sufficiently encouraging for the Syndicate to decide to support Richter's mounting of two cycles of *Der Ring* in English between 27 January and 8 February 1908. These were well received by large audiences. *The Times* commented that *Das Rheingold* had 'a real sense of artistic achievement about the whole',[47] and remarked on the second performance of *Siegfried*, 'the whole thing reflects the greatest credit on everyone concerned; and is,

---

[44] The project is first mentioned in the Richter/Pitt letters on 4 July 1907 (BL, Egerton MS 3301, f. 55), but their aspirations may have pre-dated Pitt's appointment.

[45] Draft letter from Richter to Higgins, December 1907, sent to Pitt for translation and refinement, with a letter to Pitt dated 4 December 1907 (BL, Egerton MS 3301, ff. 89–91, translation at MS 3302, ff. 117–19); Richter's meeting with Cosima Wagner took place 'on my last visit to Bayreuth', presumably in June 1907.

[46] Ibid.

[47] *The Times*, 28 January 1908, p. 10.

we hope, only the beginning of what Covent Garden intends to give us in the way of opera in English'.[48] The *Musical Times* noted the presence of 'society', and argued:

> It is safe to say that English opera now stands on a totally different footing from that of old days. It has cowered too long Cinderella-like among the ashes; it may now take its place in the palace unashamed. Society has set its seal of approval upon what was formerly esteemed a merely provincial and suburban form of entertainment, and the presence of the King and Queen at Covent Garden reassured the doubters as to the complete correctness of patronizing anything so commonplace as their native language.[49]

Press criticisms were mild, focusing on poor diction, some inadequate singing in minor roles, and occasional staging slips.[50] English-speaking singers were prominent – American-born Clarence Whitehill (already known at Covent Garden) gained especial praise for playing Wotan, as did Canadian Charles Hedmondt, Agnes Nicholls, Edna Thornton, Maude Santley, Walter Hyde, and Frederic Austin.[51]

The success encouraged Richter and Pitt, who started to plan a similar project for January 1909 and extended their ambition to include English-language performances in the grand season.[52] For obscure reasons, Higgins tried to stipulate that the next season include stock operas; *Madama Butterfly*, *Faust*, and *Carmen* were suggested. Richter resisted but could not entirely keep Higgins at bay.[53] The 1909 season (16 January to 16 February) comprised *Madama Butterfly*,[54] three complete *Ring* cycles, *Die Meistersinger* and Naylor's *The Angelus* (see below and Chapter 6).

---

48 *The Times*, 8 February 1908, p. 10.

49 *MT*, 1 March 1908, p. 170. Aspects of the performance recalled practices of an earlier age: in *Götterdämmerung* (1 February) Brünnhilde was played by Maud Perceval Allen, for whom it was, 'her first appearance on any stage' (*The Times*, 3 February, p. 15).

50 See, for example, *Athenaeum*, 1 February 1908, pp. 137–8, and *MS*, 8 February, pp. 83–4.

51 See reviews referenced in notes 47 to 51. Several singers played multiple roles and three different singers played Brünnhilde in the first cycle.

52 'We must throw ourselves with the greatest energy into the English [opera], and without delay: the personnel must be complete before you close [the main 1908 season]. If that is achieved, we can give the English opera in the grand season too.' (Richter to Pitt, 19 July 1908, BL, Egerton MS 3301, f. 152, translation at MS 3302 f. 126).

53 See Richter to Pitt, undated, but probably October 1908, BL, Egerton MS 3301, f. 171, translation at MS 3302, ff. 143–5: 'The artists will be laughed off the stage, for the public will make comparisons which can only be to the disadvantage of our people … If necessary more *Meistersinger* and separate *Ring* nights – even if with cuts – *that* we can do with credit and success'.

54 Richter capitulated as, 'I would rather have *Butterfly* because there is very little chorus in it … Of course I will do my best to dissuade Higgins from *Butterfly* too, so that we can do our own business undistracted … Oh these dilettantes! It is no *diletto* to have to do with them.' (Richter to Pitt, 22 November 1908, BL, Egerton MS 3301 f. 165, translation at MS 3302, f. 148).

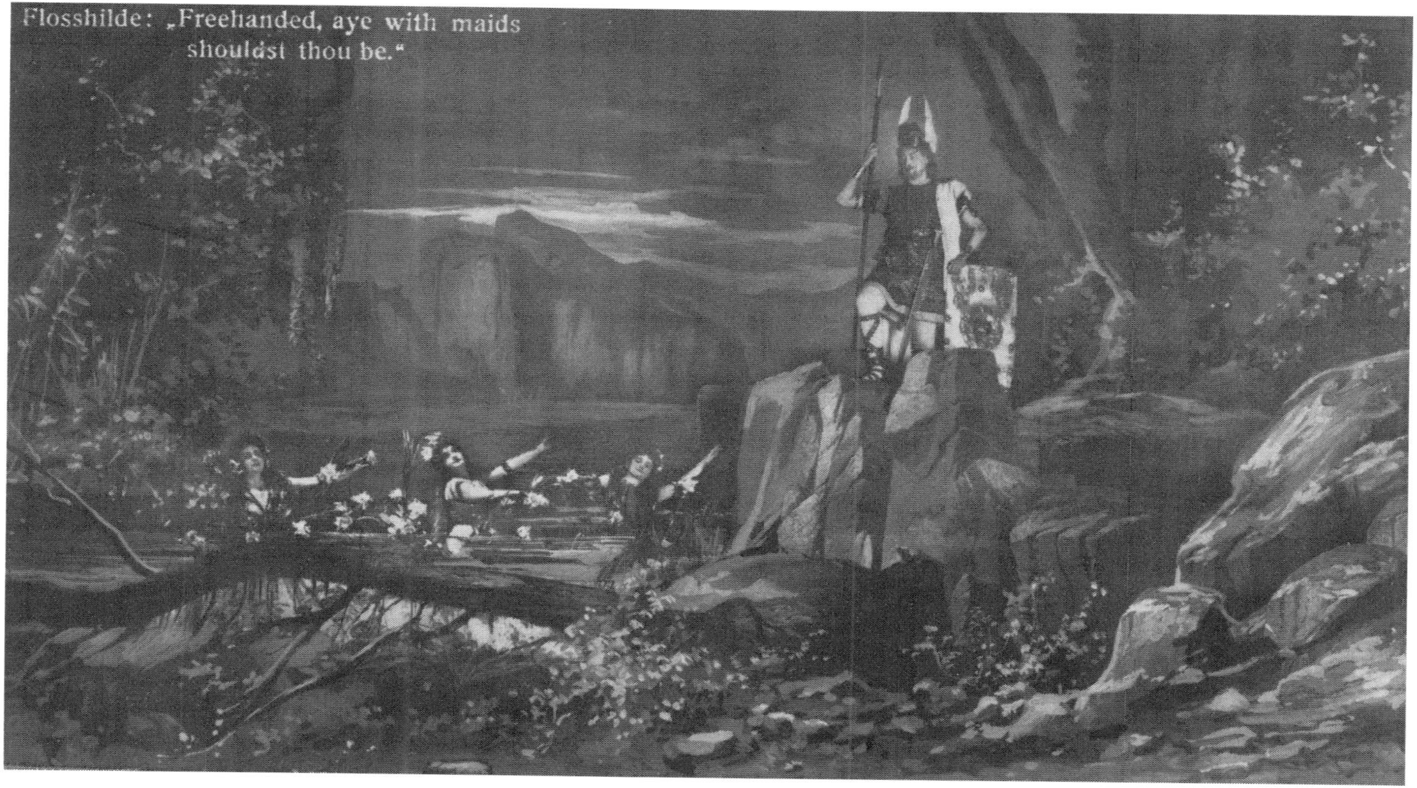

Figure 3.4 *Götterdämmerung* (Act III, Scene 1), from Richter's 'English *Ring*' season, Covent Garden, 1909 (postcard). Peter Cornelius (Siegfried), Wellgunde (Caroline Hatchard), Flosshilde (Edna Thornton) and Woglinde (Alice Prowse).

As Richter feared, the renditions of *Madama Butterfly* were poorly attended, as were those of *The Angelus*: the *Ring* cycles achieved an average box office of £658 per night, with *Die Walküre* on 6 February bringing in £978. *Die Meistersinger* achieved a comparable £650, but *Madama Butterfly* managed only £246 and *The Angelus* a paltry £180.[55] Critical reception of the Wagner performances was again favourable and acknowledged improvements on the previous year.[56]

Despite, or perhaps because of, the success of the 'English *Ring*', the Syndicate almost immediately blocked further performances; a letter from Higgins to Pitt argued that the financial position was insufficiently stable and audiences too unpredictable to justify further support:

> I have been thinking very seriously over my interview with [Richter] and you on the subject of English Opera and before you invite any of your friends to give pecuniary guarantees I strongly urge you both to look the facts fairly and squarely in the face.
>
> On the basis of this year's results you may take it from me that you will not succeed in raising the curtain under £550 per night and I think that it is more probable that that figure will be increased to £600 because it is very improbable that you will again succeed in securing the services of the artists on such good terms as this year. Furthermore you must recollect that in this calculation there is practically no provision at all for new scenery, costumes, etc. …
>
> Now although you can get subscriptions for cycles of the *Ring* and special Wagner performances in limited numbers, it is quite certain to my mind that for the other performances, such as *Orfeo*, *Samson*, *Fidelio* etc., if your receipts average anything over £300 you will be lucky. This has been the experience not only of this season, but of the Italian autumn season in which the only performances that were ever given at a profit were those in which artists like Caruso, Melba or Tetrazzini appeared. There is always a market for stars here and indeed in most countries …
>
> It is not a question of language at all, the fact is that unless for some very special attraction, the London public will not come to the opera in sufficient numbers to make it pay. In the summer it is a different story, but if you deducted the private subscriptions for boxes and stalls which depend to a great extent on fashion, and the seats paid for by foreigners, who certainly constitute nearly forty percent of our audience, I do not believe that the patronage of the British public *proprement dit* exceeds £300 per night on an average even then.

---

[55] These averages are to the nearest pound. A complete list of box office receipts is at BL, Egerton MS 3302, f. 213.

[56] See, for example, *The Times* (19 January 1909, p. 10; 21 January, p. 10; 23 January, p. 12; 2 February, p. 11; 10 February, p. 14; 13 February, p. 13; and 17 February, p. 13); *SR* (23 January, pp. 102–3; 30 January, pp. 134–5; 20 February, p. 235); *MS* (23 January, pp. 52–3; 30 January, p. 67); and *Athenaeum* (30 January, p. 142).

> Under these circumstances I am not prepared to recommend my colleagues, who rely to a great extent on my judgement, to run their head against a brick wall …
>
> If [Richter] likes I am quite willing in 1911 to introduce English opera as a feature of the summer season in place of German. It will be an experiment, but one that we can afford to make. If anything will give an impetus to opera in English, that will …
>
> My conviction is that there is very little demand in England for opera at all outside the season, and that outside the small circle of those who have an axe of their own to grind, the idea that a craving exists for opera to be given in English is an absolute delusion.
>
> If we can do Wagner better in English than in German, by all means let us do it in English; I don't believe the summer public will care one way of the other. We shall see how they receive the *Valkyrie* in May. But beyond that I am not prepared to go unless someone can give me very good reason for thinking that my conclusions are wrong.[57]

Some of Higgins's arguments appear disingenuous. Records of the expenses incurred by the 1909 'English *Ring*' do not survive so the financial outturn is unknown; income figures, however, imply either a break-even or small profit. Certainly audiences could be unpredictable: the Wagner performances did well and must have made money, but Richter and Pitt clearly envisioned an expanded repertory and here the receipts for *Madama Butterfly* and *The Angelus* back Higgins. The issue, therefore, was whether successful performances would be sufficiently profitable to cross-subsidise those which drew smaller audiences.

Richter's initial response was conciliatory:

> Higgins' letter is quite correct and sensible, he is right; but he is not far-seeing, and he underestimates the public's feeling for art: *our* works have made full houses and awakened the greatest enthusiasm, which promised abundantly for the future. So much work, talent, keenness and perseverance to be snuffed out! That Higgins dissents from the idea of an appeal to the art-lovers among the rich is a sign that there is no real wish for the establishment of 'opera in English'.[58]

His position soon hardened and he told Pitt that 'if there is to be no English opera, I will have nothing more to do with the Theatre'.[59] Within weeks, Richter

---

57 Higgins to Pitt, 16 February 1909, BL, Egerton MS 3304, ff. 231–4.

58 Richter to Pitt, 20 February 1909, BL, Egerton MS 3301, ff. 175–6, translation at MS 3302, f. 149.

59 Richter to Pitt, 23 February 1909, BL, Egerton MS 3301, f. 177, translation at MS 3302, ff. 149–50. In fact, four of the last five performances drew box offices from £214 to £313; the final performance, of *Die Walküre*, took £497 (BL, Egerton MS 3302, f. 213).

had all but given up on the prospect of there being more English performances supported by the Syndicate:

> I have renewed my agreement [with the Hallé], for the C[ovent] G[arden] future does not look rosy; if against all expectation another English season be possible – in January or February 1910 – I have left myself a door open … If our enterprise falls through ill-wind and stupidity, the public must be told, ruthlessly! whose is the blame for this discreditable end.[60]

Despite six successful years, Richter was invited only to conduct two performances of *Die Walküre* at the 1909 grand season; the intention to give them in English was thwarted by Clarence Whitehill's being unavailable.[61] By mid-April the enterprise had been abandoned; the *Observer* reported:

> The severest blow that has ever been struck at our pretensions to rank amongst the musical nations has been the abandonment of the [1910] winter season of English opera at Covent Garden. It looks as though we must be for the future content with the skimpy productions of tired-out provincial travelling companies when they pay the metropolis of the world a visit.[62]

Due to illness Richter conducted only one *Ring* cycle in the grand season of 1910, and he did not appear as an opera conductor in Britain again.[63] In 1911 the English opera episode still rankled:

> If the people who ruined *our* English opera knew what they had destroyed, they would be ashamed of themselves … That office – I mean the Syndicate of the opera – demands high-minded holders, with an understanding of art … People who only care for society – names or only for money are not fit to be judges and patrons of art … A pity for those gifted artists who have worked with us so successfully and with so much promise and in such unexpected numbers! How much we had done already! I know of no country, no town, where in such a short time, without long years of preparatory work, such splendid results have been achieved, as 3 and 2 years ago. It was a crime of the worst kind, when the breath of life was forcibly choked out of our English opera, so capable of living.

---

60 Richter to Pitt, 12 March 1909, BL, Egerton MS 3301, f. 180, translation at MS 3302, ff. 150–51.

61 *MS*, 8 May 1909, p. 292.

62 *Observer*, 18 April 1909, p. 6. Richter's winter absences had disappointed the Hallé Society and his renewed contract prevented him from undertaking work outside Manchester between October and March without its permission (*MS*, 10 April 1909, pp. 226–7).

63 He was engaged to conduct the German opera season at Covent Garden in autumn 1911 but had to withdraw again due to poor health (*MS*, 26 August 1911, p. 131).

> Show *this* letter to Higgins; I have not used strong enough expressions when characterising the crime.[64]

Without Richter, the grand season of 1909 swung sharply towards French and Italian works,[65] a trend maintained until 1913. The lack of Wagner generated hostile comment in the press, fuelled by a belief that populism and star singers were exerting a greater influence than artistic probity.[66]

The Syndicate's last pre-War seasons were characterised by a sense of 'business as usual'. From 1910, however, challenges to its dominance appeared. Although the 1910 grand season was one of its longest it was eclipsed artistically by those mounted by Joseph and Thomas Beecham in the winter and autumn (see below). The Syndicate also suffered misfortunes: Richter's illness disrupted the second *Ring* cycle, and the death of King Edward on 6 May resulted in cancelled performances and a dampening of enthusiasm.

The Syndicate maintained its monopoly in the grand season of 1911, its social importance heightened by the coronation of George V on 22 June.[67] Criticism of exclusively French and Italian repertory was countered by the promise of a German season in the autumn;[68] six performances by the Russian Imperial Ballet provided variety,[69] and a similar format was used during the autumn German season and the 1912 grand season.

The Syndicate's artistic achievements in the pre-War years were limited; Nikisch's conducting of *Der Ring* in 1913 was praised, and a special season

---

64 Richter to Pitt, 3 January 1911, BL, Egerton MS 3302, f. 1, translation at ff. 171–2.

65 The first performances of three French operas were taken as some compensation for Richter's absence. On *Pelléas et Mélisande*: 'It is wonderful that with this strangely restricted art, Debussy … should succeed in making the impression … not merely of pleasure but of keen delight … In spite of the scale of six whole tones, and of the constant use of augmented triads, some of the harmonic transitions delight the ear with their musical ingenuity and their appropriateness to the situation, and always the music seems to have been directly inspired by the words' (*The Times*, 22 May 1909, p. 13; see also *MT*, 1 June, p. 386). The first British staged performance of *Samson et Dalila* (opening night, 26 April) was welcomed as it broke the ban on staged representations of biblical stories, raising the hope that Strauss's *Salome* would follow (*MS*, 1 May, p. 275). Queen Alexandra was alleged to have lobbied the Lord Chamberlain; Saint-Saëns supervised rehearsals and attended the first performance.

66 For example: 'The odious vulgarity, the gross, unbeautiful emotionalism, the uninspiring, materialistic coarseness of the younger Italian school, represented by Leoncavallo, Mascagni and Puccini, have again begun to riot and revel at Covent Garden. The octogenarian opera-goer is provided with performances of *La Traviata* with the *impayable* Tetrazzini. The box-holders are enraptured.' (*MS*, 8 May 1909, p. 292). See also *SR*, 1 May, p. 554.

67 See note 15.

68 See *MT*, 1 April 1911, pp. 235–7 and *SR*, 22 April, pp. 483–4.

69 Originally contracted by Joseph Beecham, the arrangement was taken over by the Syndicate (see below). The company made a huge impact even though its more avant-garde productions, such as *The Firebird* and *Petrushka* were omitted.

from 2 February to 10 March 1914 was mounted to present *Parsifal* in Britain for the first time following the expiry of the Bayreuth monopoly. The music was familiar via concert performances but the opportunity to see a staged rendition was enthusiastically taken up with the first presentation selling out well in advance.[70] The Syndicate's 1914 grand season ended just one week before Britain declared war on Germany, as did Beecham's at Drury Lane.

Other Opera Companies in London 1897–1914

Although the Syndicate was dominant it did not desire a monopoly on performances in the West End as long as its grand season was secure. The goal of establishing a national opera house went unfulfilled (see Chapter 5), but various alternatives to Covent Garden were provided by touring companies and, later, by Oscar Hammerstein, and Joseph and Thomas Beecham.

Equally, the touring troupes did not see themselves as rivals to the Syndicate. The uncertain years of the 1880s, when Italian opera virtually collapsed and Carl Rosa had the opportunity to supplant it, had passed. The Syndicate was secure and the touring companies' objective was to provide London with opera at different times to different, less affluent, audiences[71] – visits to suburban theatres were the bedrock of their metropolitan activity.

Several factors deterred touring troupes from appearing in the West End, primarily higher expenses and greater press scrutiny. Wagner created particular problems; critics deemed his works an essential part of the repertory and, while performances drew good audiences, they also required extra resources, particularly in the orchestra pit, and were routinely criticised in the media. The touring companies were also expected by the press to promote new native operas, with these extra burdens often rendering a West End season unprofitable. John Runciman wondered why the troupes bothered, as the audience, he argued, was predominantly suburban and found a visit to theatres in locales such as Kennington and Camden cheaper and more convenient.[72]

---

[70] *The Times*, 15 January 1914, p. 8. Fourteen performances were given (see *The Times*, 3 February, p. 7; *Athenaeum*, 7 February, p. 210; *SR*, same date, pp. 167–8; *MT*, 1 March, p. 187). The main focus for criticism was, again, scenery, some of which deliberately moved as the audience watched; the resulting 'illusion' was not considered successful.

[71] Reflected in their pricing policies; the Moody-Manners Company charged between 1s and 10s 6d at the Lyric in 1907, about one-third of the cost of tickets at Covent Garden.

[72] *SR*, 7 October 1905, pp. 474–5. Quick access from the suburbs to the West End remained elusive until the mid-Edwardian years due to congestion and distant situation of most railway termini. Only with the expansion of tram and 'tube' networks did an evening at a West End theatre come within practical reach of many suburban residents (the crucial parts of the present Central line opened in 1900, and of the Piccadilly, Northern and Bakerloo lines in 1906–07).

The Carl Rosa was the only company which operated continuously from 1897 to 1914. Harris had prevented it from appearing in the West End through much of his tenure at Covent Garden (see Chapter 2) but, following its 1896 season and Harris's death, the company took the Garrick in January and February 1897. The lukewarm press reaction was in stark contrast to the lionising of the 1880s. Performance standards were criticised: the company was inadequately rehearsed and sang too loudly. The *Monthly Musical Record* damned the performers as 'provincial', which became a regular term of abuse:

> They have the unforgivable fault of being old-fashioned; they [display] ... the provincialisms which were affected at Covent Garden ten years ago. Nearly all of the singers thought much too much of the high note ... They sang rapid songs ... far too fast, hoping to bring down the gallery, apparently oblivious to the fact that they were slurring over all the difficulties or dodging them altogether.[73]

An autumn season at Covent Garden in 1897 included the London premiere of *La Bohème* (2 October), and the world premiere of MacCunn's *Diarmid*. The company miscalculated, however, by maintaining a provincial troupe and bringing a reduced company to London. *La Bohème* was received positively ('the music is extremely effective, and in a measure inspired ... as regards the present performance ... we have little but praise'[74]) and *Diarmid* gained qualified approval (see Chapter 6) but a calamitous performance of *Die Meistersinger* on 14 October overshadowed the rest of the season:

> [There were] some good points but some that were inconceivably bad. The work was painfully mutilated, even the great scene of the street disturbance in the second act being expunged ... if an opera depending so much on continuity as that of the Bayreuth master cannot be performed as he intended, then it should be left alone.[75]

The company experienced great instability for the next two years (see Chapter 4); it appeared at the Lyceum for six weeks from 2 January 1899 but MacCunn, acting as Musical Director, resigned just before opening night although he resumed his post soon afterwards.[76] The critics were merciless: 'it is to be regretted that the company did not come more prepared to meet the requirements of the London

[73] *MMR*, 1 March 1897, p. 57.

[74] *Athenaeum*, 9 October 1897, p. 495.

[75] *Athenaeum*, 23 October 1897, p. 567. Whitney Mockeridge (Walther), withdrew at the end of Act II, and was replaced by Barron Berthald, who sang in German. *MN* stated that the performance was 'probably the worst ever given by this company, or indeed, ever heard in London' (23 October, p. 351).

[76] *Athenaeum*, 14 January 1899, p. 58. Subsequently both Frank Osmond Carr (managing director) and Barton McGuckin (stage manager, former principal singer), also resigned (*MN*, 1 February 1899, p. 39, and *MMR*, 1 March, p. 58).

press, and a mistake was made in selecting Wagner's *Tannhäuser* for the opening night, as this work depends so greatly on the orchestra which, on this occasion, was not in satisfactory form'.[77]

After the Van Noorden brothers took over in 1900 the company almost exclusively confined itself to suburban theatres until 1918. There were two further appearances at Covent Garden; a two-week residency, from 26 December 1907, shortly preceded the first of Richter's 'English *Ring*' seasons (see above). The performances gained some condescending praise[78] and the repertory included two rarities, Nicolai's *Merry Wives of Windsor* and Goring Thomas's *Esmeralda* (3 January 1908).[79] Despite lacklustre attendances, the company returned on 18 October 1909 for a four-week season. Attendance improved and reviews were more positive, notwithstanding a more conventional repertory.[80] The Rosa's next appearance in the West End did not take place until 1917 (see below).

The Rosa's role as innovator was partly taken over by the Moody-Manners Company (see also Chapter 4). Manners was active and confident and soon established a good reputation in suburban London. The first season, in 1898, included revivals of Balfe's *Puritan's Daughter* and Wallace's *Amber Witch*.[81] Manners felt the lure of the West End (with which both he and his wife were familiar from their earlier careers), and the company appeared at Covent Garden for five weeks from 25 August 1902. The repertory was criticised, the conventional works being deemed tedious and the ambitious beyond the company's abilities,[82] while stage craft was also censured:

> There has been too great a tendency to sing and act to the audience … Some of the artists have employed all the absurd gestures and tricks of operatic art which have long aroused ridicule. Even the swaying body to express profound emotion

---

[77] *MN*, 7 January 1899, p. 22.

[78] *MS* commented, 'Those of us who follow operatic affairs … are quite aware of the limitations of the Carl Rosa Company, but it must have come as a welcome surprise to many to see the wonderful degree of adaptability shown by both principals and rank and file in settling down to their new conditions' (4 January 1908, p. 10, of *Tannhäuser* on 26 December 1907).

[79] *MS*, 11 January 1908, pp. 21–2. *Esmeralda* was viewed as unsatisfactory, lacking a good libretto and sufficient musical variety and character. See also *Athenaeum*, 11 January, p. 50; *MT*, 1 February, pp. 111–12.

[80] *MS*, 23 October 1909, p. 261; 30 October, p. 283; 6 November, p. 298.

[81] *MN*, 1 April 1899, p. 337, of the performances at the Shakespeare Theatre, Clapham Junction.

[82] The repertory comprised *Carmen*, *Cavalleria Rusticana*, *Faust*, *The Lily of Killarney*, *Lohengrin*, *Maritana*, *Pagliacci*, *Siegfried*, *Tannhäuser*, *Tristan und Isolde*, *Il Trovatore* and a novelty in Pizzi's *Rosabla*.

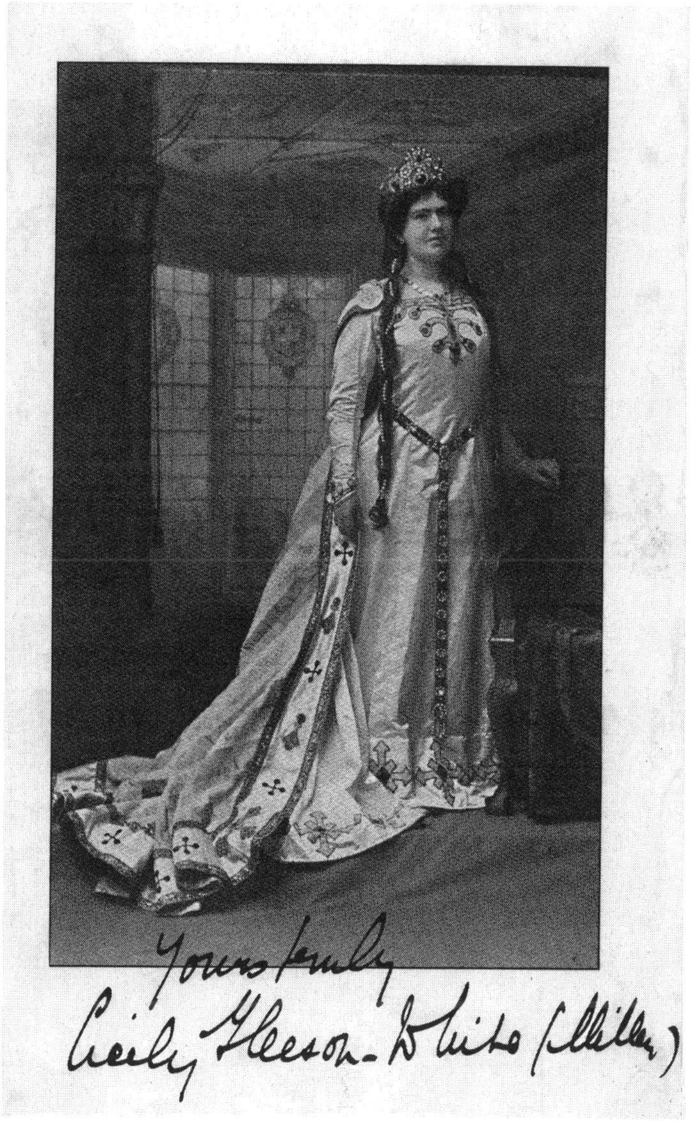

Figure 3.5 Cicely Gleeson-White as Elizabeth (*Tannhäuser*), Carl Rosa Opera Company, Covent Garden, 1909.

was there, and the centre of the footlights was as a lodestone. A certain taint of provincialism ran through all the performances.[83]

[83] *MMR*, 1 October 1902, p. 193; see also *MS*, 30 August, pp. 124–5; and 6 September, pp. 140–41.

The Wagner performances were subjected to particular scrutiny but audiences were buoyant and Manners claimed success at the season's end.[84]

The troupe returned to Covent Garden in 1903 (24 August to 26 September) premiering MacAlpin's *The Cross and the Crescent* (see Chapter 6). Despite losing money,[85] Manners announced a three-month season at Drury Lane from 23 May 1904, placing him for the first time in opposition to the Syndicate. The *Musical Standard* lamented the selection of operas:

> [T]here is no *Siegfried* and also no *Tristan* ... A more drearily hackneyed set of operas ... than those put forward for the first eight weeks it would puzzle anyone to draw up. We cannot say whether the scheme will be popular – very likely it will ... We should have thought that a little less staleness would have been a good thing if only to insure [*sic*] more press criticism, which surely does something in the way of advertisement.[86]

Although the company's core audience was different from the Syndicate's, attendances were poor and the season finished early, on 23 July. Manners was subsequently more cautious and gave annual seasons at the Lyric from 1906 to 1909, starting in July or August.[87] Revivals of *Eugene Onegin* (1906), Halévy's *La Juive* (1908) and *Rienzi* (1909) were praised, the introduction of Onegin's suicide in the first work notwithstanding.[88] The company also premiered Löhr's *Sarenna* (1907) and Maclean's *Maître Seiler* (1909) (see Chapter 6). A great self-publicist, Manners proposed a season of English Opera at Drury Lane in May 1909 to include the premieres of Coleridge-Taylor's *Thelma* and MacAlpin's *Ingomar*, but the scheme, if it was ever seriously contemplated, collapsed through lack of support.[89] Possibly due to the presence of Thomas Beecham and Oscar Hammerstein, Manners retreated to the suburbs until 1914 when the company gave its final West End season at the Prince of Wales, which included the first London performance of Kienzl's *Der Kuhreigen* (13 July, opening night).[90] Originally planned as a seven-week venture, the season was terminated when war was declared.[91]

---

84 *Era*, 27 September 1902, p. 15.

85 *The Times*, 8 December 1903, p. 15; *MS*, 12 December, p. 367.

86 *MS*, 30 April 1904, p. 271.

87 Located on Shaftesbury Avenue, the theatre opened in 1888 and is still in operation.

88 See *The Times*, 30 July 1906, p. 12; *Athenaeum*, 5 September 1908, p. 279; and *The Times*, 28 August 1909, p. 11.

89 See *The Times*, 2 January 1909, p. 10, and 16 February, p. 13. *Ingomar* has never been performed; *Thelma* was finally given at Croydon in February 2012 to mark the centenary of the composer's death. .

90 *Athenaeum*, 18 July 1914, p. 86. The theatre was located on Coventry Street, near Leicester Square; opened in 1884 and rebuilt in 1937, it is still in operation.

91 *MT*, 1 August 1914, p. 508, and *SR*, 7 November, p. 414.

Other attempts at producing Grand Opera in the West End were sporadic and, other than those made by Beecham and Hammerstein, need only be mentioned in passing. Following his Covent Garden season in 1895 (see Chapter 2), Charles Hedmondt appeared in 1897 at Her Majesty's, performing *Hänsel und Gretel*, Somerville's *Prentice Pillar* (see Chapter 6) and Leoni's *Rip van Winkle* (4 September, British premiere).[92] A season of Italian opera and drama organised by Henry Russell to inaugurate the Waldorf Theatre (22 May to 15 July 1905), included the premiere of Amherst Webber's *Fiorella* (see Chapter 6).[93] The Castellano Italian Opera Company, which, like the Rosa and Moody-Manners troupes, operated primarily in the provinces and London suburbs, introduced Leoncavallo's *Zaza* (Coronet, Notting Hill, 30 April 1909) and Monleone's *Cavalleria Rusticana* (10 May) and transferred to Drury Lane from 31 May and received several good reviews.[94] Another season of standard Italian operas was mounted by C. de Macchi in September 1910,[95] while the composer Raymond Rôze leased Covent Garden for a six-week season (1 November to 13 December 1913), the primary purpose of which was to give his own *Joan of Arc* (see Chapter 6) although there were also performances of *Tristan und Isolde*, *Lohengrin*, *Tannhäuser*, *Hänsel und Gretel* and *Carmen*. While he managed to draw an impressive array of subscribers, the performances drew varying criticism, and the closing night, attended by the king and queen, was disrupted by a suffragist demonstration.[96]

Of greater importance were two German seasons mounted in 1907. The first, by the 'Winter German Opera Company', organised by the Belgian tenor Ernest van Dyck, introduced Artúr Nikisch to Britain as an opera conductor (*Tristan und Isolde*, 15 January).[97] Although dominated by Wagner, the season also included rare revivals of *Fidelio*, *Der Freischütz*, *The Merry Wives of Windsor* and *The Bartered Bride*.[98] Despite good press reviews the company experienced financial difficulties and was placed in Receivership.[99] This unfortunate end was compounded when 16 members of the troupe were drowned when returning to Germany.[100] The second

---

92 For reviews see *The Times*, 6 September 1897, p. 5; *MN*, 11 September, p. 225; *MT*, 1 October, p. 689; and *MMR*, 1 October, p. 233.

93 See, for example, *MT*, 1 July 1905, p. 476. Located on Aldwych, the theatre is still in operation; it was renamed the 'Novello' in 2005.

94 See *MS*, 5 June 1909, p. 355, and 12 June, pp. 380–81.

95 See *MT*, 1 October 1910, p. 658.

96 For the subscribers' list see *The Times*, 14 October 1913, p. 10; for reviews see *The Times*, 3 November, p. 12; 10 November, p. 13; 17 November, p. 12; 1 December, p. 70; 15 December, p. 5; *MT*, 1 December, p. 806; and 1 January 1914, p. 42.

97 See *MS*, 19 January 1907, p. 37; *Athenaeum*, 19 January, p. 83.

98 *MT*, 1 February 1907, p. 112; *MS*, 9 February, p. 84.

99 *MS*, 23 February 1907, p. 117; 2 March, p. 131; and *MT*, 1 March, pp. 178–9.

100 The Great Eastern Railway's steamer *Berlin* was lost on 21 February near the Hook of Holland; of 140 passengers and crew, 12 people were rescued, including three members of the German company. See *The Times*, 22 February 1907, p. 12, and 23 February, p. 5.

season, at the Adelphi, introduced the Berlin Komische Oper and Offenbach's *Tales of Hoffman* (17 April), a work which became hugely popular with audiences and touring companies alike.

Of similar importance were three short seasons mounted by the mezzo-soprano Marie Brema at the Savoy between April 1910 and February 1911. These included highly praised renditions of Gluck's *Orfeo*, an innovative adaptation of Handel's *L'allegro e il penseroso*, and the British premieres of Emánuel Moór's *Wedding Bells* and *La Pompadour* (both 26 January 1911). Rutland Boughton praised Brema as an opera producer, valuing her work as much as the theatrical productions of Gordon Craig and suggesting that she was the first person in Britain to understand and implement the Wagnerian credo of integrating all aspects of the production.[101]

Two further activities deserve mention. Firstly, the London music colleges all mounted occasional opera performances during this period; several less well-known works were performed, and premieres of works by students were also given (see also Chapters 2 and 6). Secondly, and of ultimately greater impact, was the commencement of opera performances at the 'Old Vic'.[102] Located on New Cut, near Waterloo station, the Royal Victoria Hall had opened as a temperance music hall in 1881; under the management of Emma Cons, occasional recitals of opera in costume were given from 1889. After the 'Old Vic' acquired its full theatre licence in 1912, under the management of Cons's niece Lilian Baylis, complete performances were given. This was the only venue in London to perform opera for a predominantly working-class audience, with pre-War ticket prices ranging from 2d to 2s – it was often known as the 'twopenny opera'. It is impossible to build up a full account of these productions: the musical press paid little attention as the 'Old Vic' was not patronised by its middle-class readership, and neither did *The Stage* and *The Era* (the latter was also the trade journal of the licensed victuallers).[103] The staged performances are known to have been given, at their greatest extent, on Thursdays and Saturdays each week between October and May each year, with an orchestra of around 20, directed from 1899 by Charles Corri, who made his own arrangements of the scores, and a repertory similar to that of the smaller touring companies, such as Rousbey and Turner (see Chapter 4). The

101 *MS*, 4 February 1911, pp. 68–9; for further reviews see, *The Times*, 13 April 1910, p. 10; *SR*, 16 April, pp. 492–3; *Athenaeum*, 16 April, p. 471; *MT*, 1 December, p. 789; and *MS*, 3 December, p. 352. Marie Brema (1856–1925) established an operatic career in the 1890s, appearing in the British premiere of *Cavalleria Rusticana* in 1891, and also at Bayreuth, Covent Garden, and the Metropolitan, New York. She also appeared as the Angel at the first performance of *The Dream of Gerontius* at Birmingham in 1900. Her second and third Savoy seasons were conducted by Frank Bridge.

102 For fuller, though still brief accounts, see Peter Roberts, *The Old Vic Story, A Nation's Theatre 1818–1976* (London, 1976); George Rowell, *The Old Vic Theatre: A History* (Cambridge, 1993); and Susie Gilbert, *Opera for Everybody* (London, 2009).

103 Baylis also promoted Shakespeare; these performances received more press attention.

few substantive press reviews were more interested in the novelty of a working-class audience for opera, but are still informative:

> An opera night at the 'Vic' is not to be missed … the hall, which holds something over 2,000, is always crammed. It is an astonishing sight. Imagine, or preferably go to see for yourself, a building as large as Queen's Hall, packed with a dense mass of working men and women, listening with a keen appreciation to the 'Swan Song' in *Lohengrin*. In the matter of quiet attention this audience could set an example to Covent Garden … You will find all types – small shopkeepers, clerks, artisans, railway workers, foreign waiters, all the grades down to the labourer with just enough in his pocket to pay for his ticket. He stands at the back of the gallery, smoking a clay pipe, and if you are lucky you can encourage him in the intervals to compare intelligently the relative merits of famous Lohengrins. For many of these men have been coming week after week for many years … and they know their favourite operas by heart. *Faust* and *Carmen* are the most popular, but Wagner runs them close and *Lohengrin* and *Tannhäuser* always mean crowded houses …
>
> [W]hat strikes one most, apart from the audience, is the quality of the performances … The band is more than competent, and the general ensemble is excellent. As the price of admission is so low, and only artists of good standing are engaged, it can easily be understood that the work cannot exist without liberal help from outside.[104]

Recurrent financial difficulties were overcome, and the 'Old Vic' performances continued throughout the war years (see below). The company developed, and came into its own in the 1920s, before relocating to Sadler's Wells in 1931, the Coliseum in 1968, and being renamed 'English National Opera' in 1974.

Only from 1910 did the Syndicate come under any serious pressure from alternative providers. Although Joseph and Thomas Beecham entered the fray before Oscar Hammerstein, discussing the latter's activities first contextualises those of the former. Hammerstein had been active as an impresario in New York for some years;[105] in 1906 he entered into direct competition with the Metropolitan Opera to the financial detriment of all and, in 1910, accepted $1.2m in return for withdrawing from opera production in the United States for 10 years,[106] and turned his attention to the world's other great centre of commercially run opera, London. Accustomed to building theatres, Hammerstein negotiated a lease on vacant land

---

[104] *Review of Reviews*, 1 December 1913, p. 467. See also *Review of Reviews*, 1 March 1911, p. 296; *MT*, 1 July 1915, p. 496.

[105] Hammerstein (1847–1919) was born in Stettin, Prussia (now Szczecin, Poland) but emigrated to the United States in 1864; he made a fortune in tobacco manufacturing and used this to build eight theatres in New York between 1889 and 1906.

[106] *MT*, 1 June 1910, p. 365; at the prevailing exchange rate of $4.78/£1, the amount was just under £250,000.

in the new Kingsway development.[107] Scepticism as to the viability of the project was widespread,[108] but Hammerstein was neither poor nor deterred:

> Opera is the costliest form of entertainment known, and the manager who hesitates in spending money is lost. Cheap opera is no opera at all ... There is no commercialism in my plans for the production of opera, except for the natural fact that I should not like them to run at a loss.[109]

Hammerstein did not waste time: building work started on 17 October 1910 and the theatre was completed a year later.[110] It opened on 13 November (two days later than advertised) with the British premiere of Nouguès's *Quo Vadis*, and a repertory comprising 32 operas drawn overwhelmingly from the French and Italian repertories; ticket prices were comparable to those at Covent Garden with the most expensive boxes costing 10 guineas and the cheapest gallery seats 2s.[111] For the initiated, potential problems were, surely, already evident: the repertory was unbalanced, containing no Puccini (the exclusive British performing rights were held by the Syndicate[112]) and, initially, no Wagner, but seven operas by Massenet. Four novelties (including *Quo Vadis*) were promised but none by well-known composers,[113] the company, though cosmopolitan, included no 'stars', and the season was to last an unprecedented 20 weeks. It is unclear as to whether Hammerstein was naïve or rash.[114]

---

107 *MS*, 19 October 1910, p. 239. Hammerstein paid annual ground rent of £4,875 on a 99-year lease. Kingsway was intended by the London County Council to clear slums and provide a new link between Holborn and Aldwych; the road was completed in 1905. The London Opera House was acquired by Oswald Stoll in 1916 and demolished in 1957. The LCC had been recommended in 1899 to consider reserving a plot on the Kingsway for a national opera house (see Chapter 5) but Hammerstein's enterprise was unconnected to this.

108 Colonel Henry Mapleson said: 'he will fail because he cannot force the aristocracy to attend, and Covent Garden is the traditional *rendez-vous*. Besides, all the best singers are pledged to Covent Garden' (*MH*, 1 August 1910, p. 242); see also *MS*, 17 September, p. 184. Joseph Beecham stated, 'I doubt the success of such a venture. In London the opera is a social function ... Many attend to see their friends or to be seen ... Mr Hammerstein may have no difficulty in filling his cheaper seats, but that will not make opera. You know it is rather an expensive undertaking' (*MS*, 19 November, p. 329, quoting from *Musical America*).

109 *MS*, 1 October 1910, p. 208, quoting an interview in *DN*.

110 *MS*, 22 October 1910, p. 267; *The Times*, 28 October 1911, p. 8; the latter includes a description of the building's size and appointments.

111 *MS*, 15 July 1911, pp. 35–6, and *The Times*, 30 October, p. 13.

112 The Syndicate later highlighted publicly its possession of certain performing rights in an attempt to undermine Hammerstein's 1912 season; see *The Times*, 30 January 1912, p. 9.

113 The others were Hubay's *The Violin Maker of Cremona*, Giordano's *Siberia*, and Bretón's *La Dolores*.

114 He certainly recognised the importance of star singers, having contracted both Melba and Caruso in New York.

The production of *Quo vadis* was universally acclaimed with even John Runciman stating that 'the orchestra was excellent, the scenery gorgeous, [and] the stage management beyond reproach',[115] but the work itself was largely dismissed; the *Athenaeum* deemed it 'pleasing' but the *Musical Standard* proclaimed it 'flat, feeble [and] very mediocre'.[116] Revivals of *William Tell* and *Norma* failed; the critics at least viewed these not as interesting rediscoveries but as hackwork.

Although many social figures attended the opening night,[117] interest was insufficiently sustained;[118] in January 1912 Hammerstein reduced all ticket prices by about half which encouraged patronage but did not eliminate losses.[119] The theatre closed on 3 March with many operas unperformed, but a new season, operating in direct competition with the Syndicate, at Syndicate prices, was promised.[120] A supporting committee was formed and the prospectus included Holbrooke's *The Children of Don* and Drysdale's *Fionn and Tera*, in order to secure the financial and social support of their respective librettists, Lord Howard de Walden and the Duke of Argyll.[121]

The season ran from 22 April to 15 July and Hammerstein lost money heavily. Previous weaknesses were emphasised when Covent Garden was also open. Holbrooke's opera was received badly (see Chapter 6) and Drysdale's was not produced. Herman Klein declared:

> His intentions are excellent … his fighting interests are so strong that he cannot refrain from challenging Covent Garden on its own ground … He may scoff at the indifference and dullness of London opera-goers, but he must at least admit that, with all his experience and acumen, he has failed to discover exactly what they want or to offer them something worth having that they cannot obtain elsewhere.[122]

---

115 *SR*, 18 November 1911, p. 638.

116 *Athenaeum*, 18 November 1911, p. 637; *MS*, 18 November, p. 319; see also *SR* (as previous note); *MT*, 1 December, pp. 785–6; and *The Times*, 14 November, p. 8.

117 *The Times*, 14 November 1911, p. 8; several of those present were regular Covent Garden subscribers, for example, the American, Portuguese, and Austro-Hungarian Ambassadors, the Duchess of Westminster, Lady Charles Beresford, Lady Mary Cunard, Lady Alexander Paget, Lady Edgar Speyer, Sir Harry Waechter, and Leopold de Rothschild.

118 *MS*, 30 January 1912, pp. 35–6; and 10 February, p. 83; *MT*, 1 February, pp. 95–6.

119 *The Times*, 3 February 1912, p. 8; revised prices were implemented in January.

120 *MS*, 9 March 1912, pp. 147–8.

121 *The Times*, 17 February 1912, p. 11; the committee also included the Duke of Norfolk, Lord Harewood and Helen, Countess of Radnor. See also *MT*, 1 March 1912, pp. 166–8, and Chapter 6.

122 *MT*, 1 August 1912, pp. 515–16.

On the last night, Hammerstein announced to the audience he had lost £45,000 but that he would, nevertheless, try again in November 1912.[123] The *Era* exemplified general scepticism:

> Mr Hammerstein's speech was an illogical, though doubtless very natural, attempt to scold the British public. He found fault with them for not insisting upon grand opera being subsidized, and a voice answered, 'We have enough taxes already'. He called the British public uneducated and yet later on said he did not believe that anywhere else in the world they had so much inborn love of music as in this country …
>
> For an entrepreneur to come over from America, and build a beautiful opera house, without having guarantees from Society of its sustained patronage of the enterprise, with the prospect of having to face the very strong competition of an existing establishment, and without any superlatively strong attractions to fight the latter with, showed more courage than judgement.[124]

Shortly afterwards Hammerstein abandoned his enterprise, stating candidly that he could not lose more money: 'I bear no resentment. The absolute lack of support from those wealthy people who should endow grand opera, and in some quarters of the London press the decided personal hostility to me, have caused the venture's abandonment'.[125]

It is difficult to view many of Hammerstein's actions as anything other than foolish: he assumed that he could move from New York to London despite weaknesses in his scheme which he would surely not have tolerated in Manhattan. Although he had not been, 'a manager who hesitates in spending money', a circumscribed repertory, lack of 'star' singers, and variable production standards all undermined him. Possibly too there was some resentment (and also an element of anti-semitism) directed at an extrovert Prussian-Jewish American who presumed to show a variety of vested interests how to mount opera in the heart of the British Empire.[126] Whatever the truth, the venture was doomed from the start.

Hammerstein caused the Syndicate little actual difficulty. A far more serious challenge was posed by Joseph and Thomas Beecham. Attention has focused on the latter, as a charismatic conductor, but the role of his father was crucial: his financial resource and acumen gave the Beecham seasons a potency and sustainability unequalled by any operatic enterprise in London other than that of the Syndicate itself, and Joseph was extensively involved in the organisation of the seasons and commented on them publicly. John Lucas's study traces in detail

---

[123] *Era*, 20 July 1912, p. 13.

[124] Ibid, p. 17.

[125] *The Times*, 22 August 1912, p .4.

[126] Vincent Sheehan argued that Hammerstein's direct manner did not help him in London, and that he unintentionally offended several supporters and singers; see *The Amazing Oscar Hammerstein* (New York and London, 1956), pp. 310 and 327–30.

the activities of both men; here the focus is on their operatic activities.[127] The family's wealth came from its pharmaceutical business. Ambitious for his sons, Joseph sent them to good schools and Thomas went briefly to Oxford. Father and son fell out over Joseph's mistreatment of his wife and they did not meet for some 10 years. Thomas meanwhile pursued his musical ambitions, focusing on orchestral conducting although in 1902 he conducted a modest touring company in the London suburbs.[128] In 1909 Thomas formed the Beecham Orchestra and its manager, Thomas Quinlan (who also managed touring opera companies; see below and Chapter 4), effected a meeting between Joseph and Thomas which led to a reconciliation. The orchestra was specially engaged for the first British performances of Smyth's *The Wreckers* (see Chapter 6), enabling Thomas to appear again as a conductor of opera. A command performance attended by the king and queen brought extra attention.

A direct consequence of the reconciliation was Joseph's decision to mount a one-month season of opera at Covent Garden in February and March 1910.[129] The proposed programme showed flare and ambition: works included *The Wreckers*, a revival of *Ivanhoe*, the first British performance of Delius's *A Village Romeo and Juliet*; *Elektra* (the first Strauss opera seen in Britain), *Carmen*, *Tristan und Isolde*, *Hänsel und Gretel* and Debussy's *L'enfant prodigue*.[130] *Salome* was hoped for but the Lord Chamberlain withheld permission.[131] Attention focused overwhelmingly on *Elektra* (19 February, opening night);[132] two subsequent performances were conducted by Strauss himself, and, importantly for the Beechams' reputation, all the operas promised were given and production standards praised across the board. For the first time, it appeared that the Syndicate had a serious potential rival, whose artistic and financial strengths could stay the course. By the end of the

127 John Lucas, *Thomas Beecham: an Obsession with Music* (Woodbridge, 2008).

128 See Lucas, pp. 20–22; the company included Joseph O'Mara, Blanche Marchesi and Zélie de Lussan. Beecham wrote that 'Some of the singers, of course, were excellent ... but of attempt ... at production there was none, and both scenery and dresses were atrocious ... The chorus ... was accurate but toneless, and the orchestra the most incompetent I have known anywhere' (*A Mingled Chime* (London, 1944), p. 47).

129 It is often unclear who was responsible for particular decisions. In general, while Thomas managed artistic matters, Joseph exercised financial and managerial control.

130 *MS*, 15 January 1910, p. 35.

131 *MS*, 4 December 1909, p. 355–6; *Observer*, 23 January 1910, p. 13; and Lucas, pp. 53–5.

132 Reviews were mainly positive: *MS* described *Elektra* as a 'marvellous edifice of sound. Its proportions are perfect' but expressed disappointment that Strauss 'has not given us a new tone in music' (26 February 1910, p. 127); *MT* deemed it 'one of the most beautiful things in all musical literature' (1 March, p. 158). *The Times* was more equivocal, referring to the Hoffmansthal's book as a 'squalid modern play' (21 February, p. 10), as was the *Athenaeum* (26 February, pp. 256–7).

year, however, through a combination of over-confidence and wilfulness, Thomas was in a very different position.

The Beechams were determined to maintain momentum. Before the end of the first season, a run of lighter operas at His Majesty's from May to July was proposed, and a second grand season at Covent Garden in the autumn.[133] The plan for a light opera season was shrewd: it did not challenge the Syndicate directly as it was to be a repertory season of *opéra comique* in English, including several rarely performed works: *Shamus O'Brien, Così fan tutte, Die Entführung aus dem Serail, Werther*, Méhul's *Joseph, Die Fledermaus* and the British premiere of Missa's *La Muguette* were all proposed.[134] The British premiere of Strauss's *Feuersnot* and world premiere of Clutsam's *A Summer Night* and Mozart's *Der Schauspieldirektor* were subsequently added. The season delivered almost all that was promised[135] and the productions of the all-but-unknown *Così fan tutte*, and *Die Entführung* aided a long-term rise, albeit sporadic, in Mozart's popularity which had consequences in Britain throughout the twentieth century. *The Tales of Hoffman* became Beecham's trump card with the audience, and was performed 34 times; *A Summer Night, Werther* and *Der Schauspieldirektor* appeared only once.[136] The predominantly English cast drew praise in most productions, as did the orchestra (conducted not only by Beecham but also by MacCunn, Cuthbert Hawley and Emil Kreuz).[137]

Two months later the Beechams re-opened at Covent Garden (3 October); by the last performance (31 December), 19 operas had been performed including *The Tales of Hoffmann, Il barbiere di Siviglia, Tristan und Isolde* and *Elektra*. *Salome* was finally introduced (8 December) and given 10 performances.[138] Not

---

[133] Before the end of the summer season there were press rumours that grand opera, in direct opposition to Covent Garden, would be mounted at Drury Lane in the main season of 1911 (*Observer*, 26 June 1910, p. 9).

[134] See *Observer*, 3 April 1910, p. 7.

[135] Méhul's *Joseph* (based on Exodus, and not an *opéra comique*) was not given and may only have been proposed to highlight the continuing ban on *Salome*; in fact the ban on staged representations of Old Testament material had already been broken by the Syndicate's production of *Samson et Dalila* in 1909; *Salome*, however, is based on the New Testament. See also note 138.

[136] *Observer*, 31 July 1910, p. 5.

[137] The company included Maggie Teyte, Caroline Hatchard, Edith Evans, Zélie de Lussan, Walter Hyde, Robert Radford, Joseph O'Mara, Frederic Austin, Frederic Ranalow, an orchestra of 70 and chorus of 50 (*Observer*, 3 April 1910, p. 7).

[138] The sometimes surreal debate with the Lord Chamberlain is described by Lucas (pp. 65–9) and, in a colourful but less accurate way, by Beecham (pp. 97–9 and 102–5). As with Massenet's *Hérodiade* (see Table 3.1, note 2), all biblical references were removed, the characters renamed and the location of the opera shifted, this time to ancient Greece. The severed head of John the Baptist was replaced firstly by a sword and then an empty tray. The delay in production did not neutralise critical responses to the play, many of which were hostile; Strauss's score generated a more muted response than that of *Elektra*. For sample

everything ran smoothly: the other novelties, D'Albert's *Tiefland* and Leroux's *Le Chemineau*, were not so enthusiastically received and on several occasions the published schedule was altered due to various singers' indispositions. Audiences were variable and even the *Musical Standard*, which became one of Thomas's most stalwart supporters, stated:

> It cannot be pretended that Mr Beecham has had great experience in the running of opera. He should have started his season with a well thought out plan: he should have calculated more minutely the drawing powers of operas. For instance Debussy's *Pelléas et Mélisande* was played at the end of the season and drew a large audience on the occasion of its single performance. It might easily have been made a feature of the season, and proved, we believe, a second *Tales of Hoffmann*. The way good operas become successful is not by the system of performing them once or twice and then dropping them, but by constantly according them a presentation.[139]

Thomas was displeased; he declined to make the conventional speech after the last performance and refused a floral wreath from principal soprano Aïno Ackté. Shortly afterwards a representative of the *Observer* asked him if he was satisfied with the results of the year's work.

> 'Profoundly dissatisfied,' he answered emphatically.
> 'Why? Because nobody ever comes to see my productions. You can't run a grand opera house for the benefit of a hundred persons … For years everyone has been crying out and grumbling at the lack of opportunity. Now they have had it for a year and they never come anywhere near the place.'[140]

This outburst was not a fair summary. As the *Manchester Guardian* argued:

> Considering the qualified success of former Autumn seasons at Covent Garden of much shorter duration [the variable audiences] were by no means surprising. Among indifferent performances were many of excellent value and effect … The lack of sufficient rehearsals was perhaps the greatest drawback. But with so extensive and varied a repertoire in four languages, this was unavoidable.[141]

reviews see: *The Times*, 9 December 1910, p. 10; *MS*, 10 December, pp. 367–8; *Athenaeum*, 17 December, p. 774; *Academy*, same date, pp. 594–5.

[139] *MS*, 31 December 1910, p. 416.

[140] *Observer*, 3 January 1911, p. 9.

[141] *MG*, 3 January 1911, p. 5.

Almost immediately afterwards some of the company appeared in a series of operatic selections at the newly opened London Palladium.[142] Poorly organised, the arrangement ended after only two weeks. Actions for wrongful dismissal followed, as did disagreements between father and son as to the style of opera they should mount (Joseph advocating 'popular opera at popular prices', Thomas a more rarified and artistically ambitious approach).[143]

A beneficial cessation of activity occurred; Thomas had over-extended himself mentally and physically, and the seasons had lost money. Although not public knowledge at the time, Lucas shows that Thomas had little financial sense: when petitioning the Lord Chamberlain for permission to perform *Salome*, the Beechams' manager, Albert Archdeacon, claimed that the first two seasons of 1910 had lost £50,000 and that there was a projected loss on the autumn season of £30,000.[144] Despite almost limitless resources, Joseph refused to finance any further seasons, putting paid to a rumoured appearance at Drury Lane in 1911. Meanwhile, in an attempt to neutralise them, the Grand Opera Syndicate offered Thomas a place on their board in November 1910.[145] Judging by its subsequent actions, Beecham failed to have any influence on its workings and never expected to: 'I am a young man, and some of [the other directors] are older, and I may want to go further than they are disposed to go. I have a tendency that way, but, still, they are very nice people'.[146] As a *quid pro quo*, Joseph handed on to the Syndicate the contract he had made with the Russian Imperial Ballet, which was integrated into the 1911 grand season (see above).

Joseph and Thomas then both withdrew from opera in London for the next two years and Thomas undertook some provincial touring (see Chapter 4).[147] After Hammerstein's failure and perhaps inspired by the success of the Russian ballet seasons he had almost inaugurated, Joseph returned to take Covent Garden for a

---

[142] The theatre, on Argyll Street, Oxford Circus, was conceived as a large and up-market music hall offering a wide variety of programmes; it is still open.

[143] See Lucas, pp. 71–3.

[144] Lucas, p. 67. Possibly these figures were exaggerated in order to sway the Lord Chamberlain; Archdeacon's letter stated: 'in the event of your not giving permission for the opera to be given, there is no doubt whatever that this will be Mr Beecham's last attempt to give opera in London, as no one, however rich he may be, can stand so huge a drain on his purse'.

[145] *MS*, 26 November 1910, p. 347.

[146] *St Helen's Newspaper and Advertiser*, 25 November 1910, quoted in Lucas, p. 77. It remains unclear how Beecham's joining of the Syndicate affected either his or Joseph's plans: it does not appear that they withdrew from West End opera performances in 1911 and 1912 in especial consideration of a conflict of interest. The Syndicate's motivations, however, are obvious.

[147] To complicate matters, in October 1911 Thomas was the correspondent in a bitter divorce case (see Lucas, pp. 78–83); despite condemning Joseph's treatment of his mother, Thomas replicated his father's behaviour on several occasions.

short six-week opera season in early 1913, combining opera and Russian ballet. The operatic repertory was restricted; only five works, all German, were given, including the British premiere, conducted by Thomas, of *Der Rosenkavalier* on the opening night (29 January).[148] Once again the Lord Chamberlain's office refused to allow the opera on stage as originally conceived, beds and bedrooms being eliminated. Although the season was unprofitable,[149] the Beechams' growing social connections proved useful: a list of subscribers published in *The Times* shows a selection of society members as extensive as any of the comparable lists published for the main Covent Garden seasons.[150]

Enthusiasm restored, Joseph gave a run of Strauss's *Ariadne auf Naxos* at His Majesty's in May,[151] and a combined season of opera and Russian ballet at Drury Lane from 24 June to 25 July.[152] This encroached upon the Syndicate's territory to the greatest extent so far but it opted for peaceful co-existence.[153] During the grand seasons of 1913 and 1914 the repertories selected by the two organisations were almost entirely different, partially ameliorating the impact of simultaneous performances. Joseph's 1913 season was one of the most innovative ever mounted in London: it included the British premieres of *Boris Godunov*, *Khovanshchina*, and *The Maid of Pskov* and also of *Le sacre du printemps* and *Jeux*. The Russian bass Feodor Chaliapin, although unknown in London, stole the show, and even Caruso, appearing for the first time since 1907, was swept into the shade. The success was not just Chaliapin's – all three operas were proclaimed in the press, with the *Musical Times* producing a useful summary:

> *Boris Godunov* … at once made a deep impression. It was splendidly mounted, the colour scheme being often dazzlingly vivid and it was wonderfully well performed. The originality of the music combined with its comparative simplicity and directness of expression made an instant appeal … A great feature of the presentation was the singing and acting of the chorus. Rarely, if ever before, has such chorus-singing been heard at an English opera house … The agonising remorse, culminating in the madness and death of the guilty Boris … was brought out with terrible fidelity by M. Chaliapine …

---

148 The *Ballets Russes* gave the first British performance of *Petrushka* on 4 February, and a choreographed version of *L'après-midi d'un faune* on 17 February.

149 Lucas, p. 95.

150 *The Times*, 20 January 1913, p. 9. Joseph was knighted in the 1912 New Year's Honours, and Thomas was having an affair with Lady Maud Cunard, a well-known hostess who acted, as Lady de Grey did for the Syndicate, as an unofficial promoter in social circles.

151 See Lucas, pp. 95–6.

152 The Syndicate had decided not to re-engage the *Ballets Russes* in 1913.

153 Thomas resigned from the Syndicate in either 1913 or 1914: Rosenthal stated that he left in early 1913 (p. 374), Lucas slightly later (p. 100), while *The Times* referred to him as 'very recently resigned' on 13 May 1914 (p. 6).

> [In *Khovanshchina*] the development of the story is full of variety and Mussorgsky repeatedly shows his power to secure a thrill of emotional expression, sometimes by surprisingly simple means. His use of folk-song and folk-song idiom has great charm … [and] the rhythmic appeal of his music is always strong and sometimes fascinating … Again M. Chaliapine was superb …
>
> Although [*The Maid of Pskov*] is always full of interest because of its strength and clarity, it does not rise to supreme heights until the last act … The music is always born of the dramatic demands, and does not stoop to make effects for their own sake. Again we have to note the all-round excellence of the performance, and to record the outstanding ability of M. Chaliapine.[154]

Joseph expressed satisfaction; on being asked about the future he replied, 'we have been discussing possibilities … I can say nothing just now except this, that the public has so greatly appreciated the present season, that I can only hope that it may be the forerunner of others'.[155]

In 1914 Joseph took Drury Lane for 10 weeks, running concurrently with the second and third months of the Syndicate's season. German opera was added to Russian ballet and opera, but the last of these once again took centre stage, with Chaliapin leading the company once more, as four more Russian operas were introduced (see below). Press reception was mainly positive towards all the new works but the premiere of Holbrooke's *Dylan* was received indifferently (see Chapter 6).[156] At the end of the season, Joseph appeared on stage and hinted that there would be more to come.

The record of first performances mounted by the Beechams is ample demonstration of their importance (see Table 3.4). Thomas showed an ability to pick works which 'stuck' with audiences and, consequently, his choices had a profound impact on shaping British operatic tastes for decades to come, not only in his promotion of Strauss and Russian opera, but also in his love of Mozart. As a practising musician he had an advantage over the Syndicate, which picked winners more by accident than design.

Thomas generally had the backing of the media and this gave him an advantage over the Syndicate, which always contended with some press hostility. Nevertheless, it is clear from accumulated coverage that the companies in which he was involved took a thorough and serious approach to their work. Aided by

---

154 *MT*, 1 August 1913, p. 535. Of the music of *Le sacre du printemps* the same journal stated, 'to say that much of it is hideous as sound is a mild description. There is certainly an impelling rhythm traceable. Practically it has no relation to music at all as most of us understand the word'. The two Mussorgsky operas were performed in Rimsky-Korsakov's edited version; Act 3 ('the Polish act') was omitted from *Boris Godunov* (*MG*, 25 June, p. 10).

155 *Observer*, 27 July 1913, p. 9.

156 This work was not mentioned in advanced publicity and may have been produced in recognition of support Thomas had received from its librettist, Lord Howard de Walden (Lucas, p. 107).

Table 3.4 Opera premieres produced by Thomas and Joseph Beecham 1909–1918 (* World Premiere; otherwise British)

Composer	Opera	Date
Smyth	*The Wreckers*	22 June 1909
Strauss	*Feuersnot*	9 July 1910
Clutsam	* *Summer Night*	23 July 1910
Strauss	*Elektra*	19 February 1910
Delius	*A Village Romeo and Juliet*	22 February 1910
Strauss	*Salome*	8 December 1910
Missa	*La Muguette*	25 May 1910
D'Albert	*Tiefland*	5 October 1910
Leroux	*Le Chemineau*	12 October 1910
Strauss	*Der Rosenkavalier*	29 January 1913
Strauss	*Ariadne auf Naxos*	27 May 1913
Mussorgsky	*Boris Godunov*	24 June 1913
Mussorgsky	*Khovanshchina*	1 July 1913
Rimsky-Korsakov	*The Maid of Pskov*[1]	8 July 1913
Borodin	*Prince Igor*	8 June 1914
Rimsky-Korsakov	*Le coq d'or*	15 June 1914
Stravinsky	*Le Rossignol*	18 June 1914
Rimsky-Korsakov	*Le nuit de mai*	26 June 1914
Holbrooke	* *Dylan*	4 July 1914
Lehmann	* *Everyman*	28 December 1915
Stanford	* *The Critic*	14 January 1916
Smyth	* *The Boatswain's Mate*	28 January 1916

Note to table: [1]Usually performed by Beecham as *Ivan the Terrible*.

generous subsidies, the Beecham troupes were in a position to pay greater amounts than their competitors for stage designs and costumes which, especially in the war years, when 'stars' such as Chaliapin were unavailable, led to some of the most coherent and innovative productions ever seen in London.

Opera in the Great War

The impact of the Great War on London's operatic culture was as unexpected as the war itself was by many citizens. The changes which took place, while not having many long-term repercussions, provided, if only briefly, an interruption to the Harris/Syndicate-dominated model of the preceding 25 years.

Britain's opera companies operated as usual in the first eight months of 1914. Their approach is unsurprising: planning for the future could not be suspended because a war was *possible*, while many – including members of the British cabinet – assumed there would be no conflict at all. The consequences for domestic life of previous campaigns, most recently the Second Boer War (1899–1902), but also other skirmishes around the Empire during the Victorian era, had been negligible. Even those who expected war did not anticipate its scale and impact.[157] The Syndicate and the Beechams mounted full-length seasons (see above), which ended only a few days before Britain declared war. The German and Austro-Hungarian Ambassadors, Prince Carl Lichnowsky and Count Albert Mensdorff, both regular Covent Garden subscribers and popular in aristocratic and political circles, attended regularly. The Moody-Manners Company appeared at the Prince of Wales (see above). Meanwhile Joseph Beecham entered upon an ambitious venture to buy the Covent Garden estate from the Duke of Bedford for £2,000,000; he irrevocably committed himself to its purchase six days before war broke out, a decision which had consequences for the Beecham family for years to come.[158]

Advanced planning also carried on as usual: the Quinlan company returned to Britain after a year-long world tour in April 1914 with plans for a similar venture starting in October in place.[159] Joseph Beecham too expected to mount another season,[160] and in July the *Musical Standard* reported plans for grand opera at

---

157 Engagement in previous conflicts was undertaken by a regular army and navy occasionally boosted by expanded volunteer recruitment; tangible domestic consequences were largely limited to the impact on the families of those serving. Beyond reading newspaper reports, the day-to-day life of the average British citizen carried on unaltered with no threat, for example, to food or fuel supplies. About 450,000 men were involved in the Second Boer War, of whom 250,000 were members of the regular army; fewer than 6,000 were killed in combat although a further 16,000 died of disease, and 23,000 were wounded. By the end of the Great War, 887,000 British and Irish troops had died, with a further 1,663,000 wounded. By way of context, just over 1,000 people were killed annually in reported industrial accidents in the United Kingdom between 1900 and 1909.

158 The estate, comprising not only the opera house but the market and surrounding streets, had been on the market since 1910; Joseph hoped to make a quick profit by immediately selling it to a Manchester stockbroker, Alexander Ormrod. Capital transfers were quickly restricted, however, and Ormrod was unable to complete his purchase, while Joseph could not withdraw from his; it took eight years for the Beechams to resolve the situation. See Lucas, pp. 111–13, and *passim*.

159 *Stage*, 2 April 1914, p. 22. By July 1914 this tour had been either postponed or abandoned and a season at the Lyceum followed by a provincial tour proposed instead (see *Stage*, 16 July, p. 20); the domestic plans too were rapidly abandoned and the company dissolved.

160 *The Times*, 27 July 1914, p. 11

Covent Garden under American management in February 1915.[161] On 8 August the *Musical Standard* noted that Harrison Frewin planned to launch a touring opera company (see Chapter 4), and a week later related the experiences of the tenor John Coates, who had travelled to Bayreuth to hear *Parsifal* on 1 August, and visited both Wagner's grave and Hans Richter before returning post-haste to London, arriving in the early hours of 4 August.[162]

Only the Moody-Manners Company was performing in London on the day war was declared and the season was promptly terminated. Across the entertainment industry there was an initial panic but, within two or three weeks, the sector declared that 'carrying on' was best. The mass mobilisation of troops was disruptive – 750,000 men signed up by the end of September, meaning that the number directly involved had already exceeded, in two months, the total who served in the three and a half years of the Boer War – and briefly made travel around the country difficult. For the vast majority, however, domestic life carried on largely unchanged. Although Winston Churchill did not publicly use the phrase 'business as usual' until November, the musical and theatrical media, and the opera companies, adopted the policy within weeks of war being declared. The *Stage* argued:

> It is necessary as far as possible to keep the working stage in being, even at the expense of heavy pecuniary sacrifices. It is necessary for the sake of the bulk of the actors and other artists, who, if suddenly deprived of their means of livelihood have, after the summer vacation, no resources on which to fall back … And the 'carry on' is equally necessary in the cause of public welfare. In these anxious days it is for the stage to play a tonic part – to help to divert, cheer and brace the minds and hearts of the people.[163]

Opera troupes acted accordingly: the Carl Rosa commenced its annual tour on 7 September (see Chapter 4); Arthur Spizzi mounted a season of lighter Italian and French operas at the New Middlesex Theatre which opened on the same night;[164] the O'Mara Company opened at the King's Theatre, Hammersmith, one week later; and the Moody-Manners Company reappeared briefly at the New Theatre in the West End just before Christmas.[165]

---

161 *MS*, 11 July 1914, p. 33.

162 *MS*, 8 August 1914, p. 115, and 15 August, p. 125. The composers Edgar Bainton and Benjamin Dale, also at Bayreuth, were detained and subsequently interned at Ruhleben, near Berlin, for the duration of the war.

163 *Stage*, 13 August 1914, p. 18.

164 *Era*, 9 September 1914, p. 12; *MS*, 5 September, p. 182, and 19 September, p. 212. MacCunn was one of the conductors and the repertory proposed included *Faust*, *Carmen*, *Rigoletto*, and *Il Trovatore*.

165 *MS*, 26 December 1914, p. 439. The New Theatre, St Martin's Lane, was renamed the Albery in 1973 and the Noel Coward in 2006.

Only the Syndicate eschewed 'business as usual'. Uniquely, it mounted a truly 'international' season, employing artists from across Europe and beyond. While the proportion of British artists involved had increased, the perception that the company recruited the world's best was a big attraction for subscribers. With many artists no longer available, one of the principal *raisons d'être* of the Covent Garden season was removed. By November rumours were circulating that the 1915 season would be abandoned. The *Musical Standard* reported:

> All contracts which had been made for the season with singers, players and staff are, of course, void by reason of a clause covering war, strikes or any other national calamity ... Meantime it has been suggested that the present is an excellent opportunity to rebuild 'the Garden' ... Is it not, however, a much better opportunity to rebuild opera, rather than the mere shell of it? ... We need a national opera house where operas by native musicians, sung by native 'stars' and accompanied by native orchestral performers, will have a certainty of production. It is the fashion just now to decry everything German – but they do give opera a chance! Can't we?[166]

Two weeks later, however, the same journal declared that, 'we can hardly imagine that if the present horrible waste of human life continues until next May anyone other than the openly heartless will have the effrontery to indulge in ... nights at the opera; and, if all is over, it will surely be more fitting to attend *en bloc* as a nation solemn services of thanksgiving and humble contrition'.[167] Thus not only practical difficulties gave the Syndicate pause for thought; a grand season was also felt to be inappropriate. Activities were suspended, the theatre, with occasional exceptions, was closed and, in January 1917, requisitioned by the government for furniture storage.[168] The organisation was deprived of one of its principal employees when Neil Forsyth drowned while salmon-fishing on 29 April 1915,[169] and Lady de Grey devoted herself to charitable work, principally at the King George Hospital, Southwark, until her death on 27 October 1917.[170]

---

166 *MS*, 7 November 1914, p. 317.

167 *MS*, 28 November 1914, p. 365.

168 *Stage*, 20 September 1917, p. 19. As this article, which reports legal proceedings by the Syndicate against the government in order to secure compensation for lost rental income, makes clear, it was not the intention to close the theatre for the duration of the war; in 1914 and 1915 'things were bad in the operatic world and at the beginning of 1916 the manager was not anxious to let, because things had not settled down,' but, by late 1916, the situation had improved and the Syndicate was negotiating with the Carl Rosa Company for a three-month tenancy to start at the end of that year, and also believed that Beecham might have taken the theatre in 1917.

169 *The Times*, 30 April 1915, p. 10, and *Era*, 5 May, p. 8.

170 Lady de Grey's son-in-law was killed in action in October 1914. See her obituary in *The Times*, 1 November 1917, p. 9.

The Syndicate's suspension of activities created a gap in the West End calendar. For the touring companies, though, 'business as usual' meant continuing in the provinces and London suburbs rather than in the West End. Neither of the Beechams showed any immediate interest and the opportunity to produce opera in the West End in 1915 was taken by two very different tyros, the actor-manager Robert Courtneidge and Russian tenor Vladimir Rosing.

Courtneidge, although inexperienced as regards opera, had almost 20 years of general theatre management behind him, including production of musical comedies. Furthermore, he was working with Henry Phillips, who managed the Beecham Opera Company for a few months in 1912. Why Courtneidge alighted upon opera at this time is unknown[171] – probably he saw an unclaimed opportunity. Given his background his different approach from that of the established companies was unsurprising. His season of opera in English opened at the Shaftesbury on 6 February 1915 comprising solely *The Tales of Hoffman*, rather than a typical repertory season. Only after a month was *Madama Butterfly* introduced (10 March). *Rigoletto* and *La Bohème* were also added, and the season closed on 15 May. Despite only four operas in a season of 104 performances, Courtneidge's debut was largely well received. Summing up, the *Musical Times* stated 'it is impossible to speak too highly of the admirable way in which these [works] were staged. Every artist and member of the chorus and orchestra worked for a perfect ensemble and the results achieved were often remarkable'.[172] The financial results were not as good as hoped,[173] but Courtneidge and Phillips had protected themselves by working with the 11 principal singers on a shared-profits basis.[174]

Rosing's season of Russian opera at the London Opera House was, by contrast, disastrous. Aged 25 in 1915, his singing career was in its infancy and he had no experience of operatic management but acted as both principal tenor and company manager.[175] His plans were naively ambitious, and included the British premieres of half a dozen, mainly Russian, operas.[176] Rosing hoped to replicate the successes of

[171] He barely mentions this aspect of his career in his autobiography (*I Was an Actor Once* (London, 1930)).

[172] *MT*, 1 June 1915, p. 359. See also *MS*, 20 February, p. 140, and 20 March, p. 220; *The Times*, 8 February, p. 10, and 11 March, p. 5.

[173] *Observer*, 15 May 1915, p .6.

[174] *MS*, 27 March 1915, p. 230 and *Era*, 14 July, p. 13.

[175] Rosing (1890–1963) came from a wealthy cosmopolitan background. He was engaged by the Vienna Imperial Opera in 1914 but, resident in London and married to an Englishwoman, remained in England when war broke out. He was one of the first regularly recorded singers; after 1918 he moved to the United States but visited Britain regularly and was an influential and innovative opera producer in both countries.

[176] In addition to the two given (see below), *Mademoiselle Fifi* (Cui), *Mozart and Salieri*, and *The Tsar's Bride* (Rimsky-Korsakov), *Marriage* (Mussorgsky), and *La légende du point d'Argentan* (Félix Fourdrain) were all mentioned (see *MS*, 24 April 1915, p. 310, and 15 May, p. 369; *The Times*, 29 May, p. 9).

the Beechams' Russian seasons and to capitalise on the sympathies of the audience by relying on Russian, French, Belgian and British artists. The British premiere of Tchaikovsky's *Queen of Spades* (29 May, opening night) received a generally good reception despite disorganisation, characterised principally by long intervals,[177] but Rosing soon encountered difficulties: audiences were poor, the orchestra went on strike due to a pay dispute,[178] and production costs had not been controlled. The engagement of Japanese soprano Tamaki Miura to sing in *Madama Butterfly* (31 May) did not redeem the situation and the first Zeppelin raid of the war on London occurred later the same evening. Although damage was slight, the absolute novelty of hostile action against the capital subsequently deterred many potential audience members.[179] The season collapsed on 7 June, making it shorter even than Mapleson's Patti season of 1885. With help from others, a number of benefit performances to support the performers were put on during July and August, including the British premiere of Rachmaninov's *Aleko* (15 July).

Press dissection of Rosing's fate highlighted not only his naivety ('His first eye-opener was the price of labour. "Heavens! What it costs!" was his remark to an interviewer from an American paper'[180]) but also contrasted the season's ambitious nature with Courtneidge and Phillips's populist approach. Deterred by air raids and possibly also the mainly unknown repertory, audiences stayed away. The *Era* concluded that 'love of opera as a fine art is a negligible quantity in this country', and argued that until a national opera which performed indigenous works that were 'largely imitative of foreign schools ... then, and only then, will a love of music-drama awaken in the people'.[181]

In September 1915 it was reported that Thomas Beecham and Courtneidge were to collaborate at the Shaftesbury.[182] According to Lucas, Beecham's involvement

177 *Stage*, 3 June 1915, p. 21; *MS*, 5 June, p. 430.

178 *MS*, 29 May 1915, p. 419.

179 Five people were killed although property damage was slight; the press and War Office were deliberately vague regarding locations which doubtless heightened anxiety (for example see *The Times*, 2 June 1915, pp. 2 and 3). Air raids commenced in January 1915 and regular raids started in April but, although London was a primary target, poor navigation and the Zeppelins' susceptibility to strong winds led to bombs falling from Newcastle to Dover. Of 20 raids in 1915, five were on London; the last, on 13 October, damaged the Lyceum and Strand theatres (at the Shaftesbury, Courtneidge appeared halfway through *La Bohème* to reassure the audience (*Stage*, 21 October, p. 22)). Three raids were made on London in 1916 and one in 1917 but, from March 1917, Germany employed more effective Gotha IV aircraft; the first attack on London on 13 June 1917 killed 162 people. Regular raids continued until February 1918; the last, isolated, attack was on 19 May.

180 *Era*, 7 July 1915, p. 13, possibly in response to an opening night carpentry bill of £500 (*Era*, 2 June, p. 8).

181 Ibid.

182 *MS*, 1 September 1915, p. 184.

was limited to artistic advice, and he conducted only two performances,[183] but his influence was evident in the proposed repertory of nine operas.[184] The season opened on 2 October: 'It is hoped that adequate public support will be forthcoming, in which case it is intended to continue the season throughout the winter months. The first subscription list already contains most of the names which are usually associated with operatic efforts in this country'.[185] By any measure the season was successful; it lasted for five months, closing on 26 February 1916, a West End record. Three world premieres were also included (see Table 3.4 and Chapter 6). *The Times* lauded 'evidence of a striking adaptability and enthusiasm, which has to a large extent surmounted the difficulties of previous inexperience'.[186] The challenge was to carry on:

> If this company can continue under Sir Thomas Beecham's guardianship, and develop its corporate style and be ready to extend its productions to works written with a view to its special capabilities … something of lasting value will be done for the unhappy cause of British opera. There have been plenty of good starts made before; it is good continuance which is wanted.

This second Shaftesbury season was important for two particular reasons. Firstly, of necessity the cast and orchestra was almost exclusively British, many artists acquiring opportunities they might not otherwise have had. Secondly, despite his peripheral involvement, the success encouraged Beecham, who became the dominant provider of opera in London for the remainder of the war. And yet, just as British opera seemed about to turn a corner, the impact of the war was felt much more keenly.

The primary challenge was the growing scarcity of men. Initially the forces relied on volunteers encouraged by propaganda and societal coercion but recruitment rates declined steadily; the Military Service Act introduced conscription for healthy single men aged 18 to 41 from 2 March 1916, excluding those in reserved occupations,[187] with married men added in May 1916, and men up to age 51 in 1918. In the first six months, however, almost as many men appealed against their call-up as accepted it. One possible reason was that a man's occupation was of vital economic importance to the country. The *Stage* argued:

> We trust that the claims of the stage in this respect will meet with the consideration they merit … Amusements are among the necessities of life, and they are particularly called for in helping to support the spirits of the general

[183] Lucas, p. 125. The bulk of the conducting was undertaken by Percy Pitt, with Eugene Goossens II and III, Landon Ronald, Julius Harrison and MacCunn appearing.

[184] Ibid.

[185] *MS*, 25 September 1915, p. 229.

[186] *The Times*, 19 February 1916, p. 11.

[187] Ireland was excluded from conscription due to the inflamed political situation.

> public … But there is also their economic place. The stage … represents a great industry … Immense numbers of men and women are dependent upon it for a livelihood. In rent-paying, tax-paying and wage-paying its turnover runs into millions a year … If all stage workers of every sort … are conscripted, the traffic [that is, audience attendance] will largely fall to pieces.[188]

Theatres were already adapting but difficulties were real, if unevenly felt. The variety stage moved towards the plotless revue, allowing the proportion of women participating to increase, while automation eliminated some heavy work behind the scenes. Nevertheless the lack of male artists and skilled backstage staff was evident. Orchestras were also affected for while women occupied some vacant places there were instruments which women had yet to take up in large numbers. Similarly, the female conductor was still inconceivable for many, not least players themselves. For opera companies, however, it was the shortage of male singers that posed the greatest problem. Although touring companies were hardest hit (see Chapter 4), London was not exempt, not least because touring companies provided most of the city's opera performances. Others, especially with social connections, contrived helpful postings: the conductor Julius Harrison, perhaps with the help of his employer Thomas Beecham, served in the Royal Flying Corps and was normally based near London, and was able to conduct evening performances, appearing in uniform.[189] Beecham himself, though liable for conscription was, it appears, not even approached, even though his case was raised in the House of Commons.[190]

Other issues included inflation and taxation. On 15 May 1916 an *ad valorem* tax on theatre tickets was introduced although audiences remained mainly resilient.[191] Curfews were introduced on 2 April 1918, requiring blackouts at 10.30 pm. Theatres had to be cleared by this time, with performances starting up to one hour earlier than normal, depending on the work performed.[192]

Much evidence relating to how the war affected opera companies is anecdotal and sometimes contradictory. It remains the case, though, that British opera companies, despite difficulties, prospered and only the Syndicate and Moody-Manners Company suspended operations as a direct result of the conflict (see Chapter 4). London enjoyed some of its longest ever seasons and the number of active touring companies was as great as during the Edwardian decade. For all the challenges, residents of major British cities had greater access to opera performances, at more affordable prices, than at any time previously.

---

188 *Stage*, 11 May 1916, p. 16.

189 Lucas, p. 140.

190 See Lucas, p. 139 and House of Commons proceedings, 27 November 1916, vol. 88, columns 21–2: http://hansard.millbanksystems.com/commons/1916/nov/27/sir-thomas-beecham [accessed 3 November 2012].

191 *The Times*, 15 May 1916, p. 11. The levy averaged 13 per cent and was increased to 20 per cent from 1 July 1917.

192 *The Times*, 1 April 1918, p. 2.

The effect on repertory was less than might be expected. The West End experienced the greatest change, for four reasons: the suspension of the Syndicate's activities; changes to Beecham's programming policy (discussed below); the absence of the pre-War Russian opera and ballet seasons; and a more cautious approach from all companies regarding the extent of their repertories. The established core works were largely unaffected: Puccini, Verdi and *Faust* remained essential; lighter operas such as *Le nozze di Figaro*, *Die Zauberflöte*, and *The Tales of Hoffman* were also consistently popular. A backlash against German music was inevitable but its impact on the opera companies was limited because German works formed a proportionally small part of the repertory. The West End saw the greatest changes because it was here that German opera had been strongest in the pre-War years. Strauss's operas disappeared in a wave of anti-German sentiment, although they had first appeared only in 1909. Wagner's works were somewhat less vulnerable: while they were initially dropped, from 1916 a more nuanced attitude prevailed with an implicit ban being placed only on works by living German composers and on operas which necessitated payments to German or Austrian companies (also affected by the Trading with the Enemy Act 1914). The complex theatrical requirements of Wagner's output caused practical difficulties, but *Tannhäuser*, *Lohengrin* and *Tristan und Isolde* were all performed from 1916. Nevertheless, regular *Ring* cycles disappeared, as did *Die Meistersinger* and *Parsifal*. Other, less frequently performed works, such as *Hänsel und Gretel*, were also withdrawn as companies concentrated on the popular. *Pelléas et Mélisande* suffered the same fate, suggesting that finances were at least as important as politics when it came to repertory choices. For purely practical reasons the Russian repertory also diminished initially but Beecham revived it to an extent (see below). An unusual success was Bruneau's *L'attaque du Moulin* which had made no impact when first performed in London in 1894,[193] but became attractive due to its narrative of French heroism in the Franco-Prussian War. British repertory continued to be represented unevenly. Premieres were inevitably infrequent and the optimism provoked by Beecham's production of three new works (see above and Chapter 6) was misplaced (see below) and the touring companies were reluctant to expend resources on unknown quantities with only a few exceptions (see Chapters 4 and 6), relying instead on the 'evergreen' *Bohemian Girl* and *Maritana* to represent indigenous composers. At Glastonbury, Rutland Boughton launched new works but his entire organisation was unique and he neither desired nor was able during the war years to expand beyond his own corner of Somerset (see Chapters 4 and 6).

From 1916 to 1918, Beecham almost entirely held sway in the West End as well as being active in Manchester. He took the Aldwych, owned by Joseph, for three weeks from 15 April 1916, and from 14 June to 5 August and conducted

[193] Harris gave the British premiere at Covent Garden on 4 July 1894 and revived it in 1897.

regularly.[194] The second season included the first West End performances of Wagner for almost two years (*Tristan und Isolde*, first given on 15 June). *The Times* noted 'that the London public has gone without its Wagner is apparently … only due to lack of opportunity, not to any self-denying ordinance, or to revulsion from the Wagnerian fever. There was a very large and exceedingly enthusiastic audience.'[195] Beecham also revived *Boris Godunov* but of the three British operas only *The Boatswain's Mate* was repeated; the almost exclusively British troupe gained extensive praise.[196] A third stint at the Aldwych lasted four months (14 October to 10 February 1917) but only Charpentier's *Louise* was added to the repertory, while *The Boatswain's Mate* was dropped. Francis Barrett, however, had positive words for Beecham:

> At last he has done the thing that London wanted. Too long has he expended his time – and its equivalent – on putting before the public works he thought it would like to hear … But the London public – unlike the provincial public – is something of a spoilt child in matters operatic. It will go to what it wants to see and will stay away religiously from what it does not want to see. Now Sir Thomas Beecham seems to have at last recognised this fact and for the first time in history we have seen displayed outside the Aldwych Theatre the dual legend 'Opera in English – House Full'.[197]

Two further seasons, sandwiched between short provincial excursions ran at Drury Lane from 30 May to 28 July and 22 September to 24 November; the first of these overlapped with a Carl Rosa season (see below). The repertory was steadily expanded: *La fanciulla del West*, *Il Trovatore* and Bizet's *Fair Maid of Perth* were added in the first season, *Ivan the Terrible* and *Khovanshchina* in the second.

A claim that the second season would include the premieres of three or four British operas was left unfulfilled (see below). When accused by George Clutsam of neglecting British works, Beecham retorted:

> All the English operas I have produced in the last few years have been unsparingly condemned by the majority of London critics, and far away the most ferocious of the band has been Mr Clutsam himself … My only answer … is that I now have in course of preparation four other British operas which I confidently expect will receive the same kind of treatment.
>
> But my object in writing … is to challenge directly his suggestion that there are [*sic*] quite a number of British operas of merit in existence that cannot obtain

194 Lucas, p. 133.

195 *The Times*, 16 June 1916, p. 11.

196 See, for example, *MT*, 1 July 1916, p. 341; *Athenaeum*, 1 July, p. 349, and 1 August, pp. 392–3; and *MS*, 5 August, p. 103.

197 *MT*, 1 March 1917, p. 123.

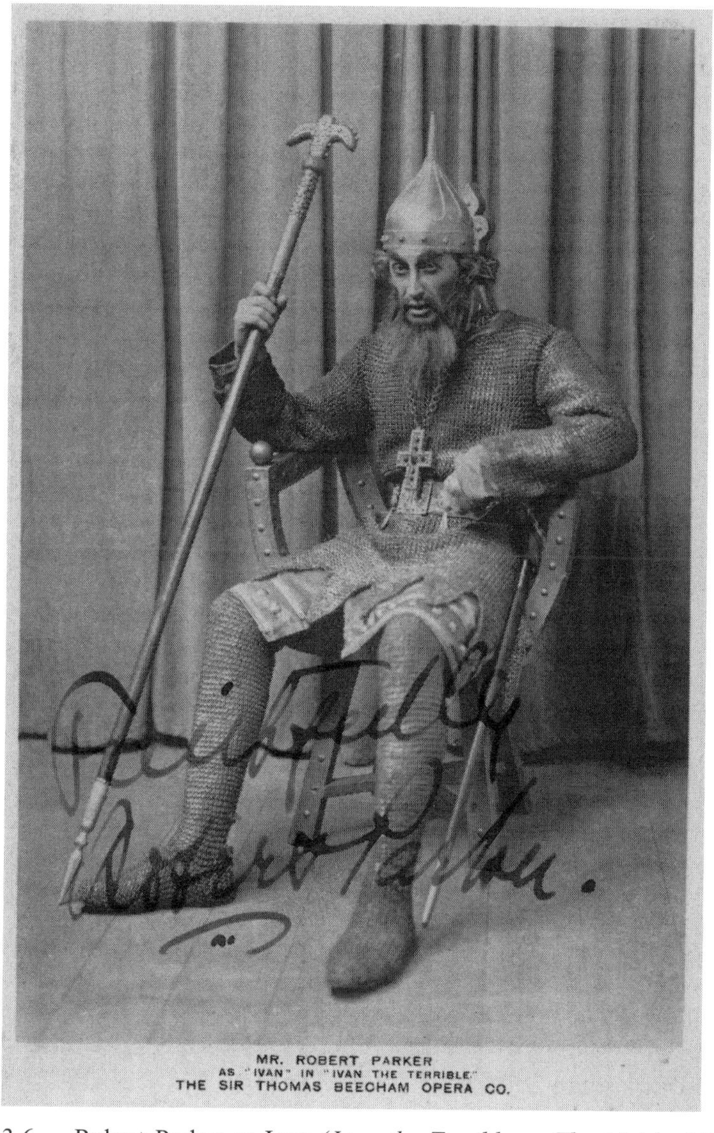

Figure 3.6 Robert Parker as Ivan (*Ivan the Terrible* or *The Maid of Pskov*), Beecham Opera Company 1917

a hearing. Frankly I do not believe in the existence of these works … I now challenge Mr Clutsam to allow me one new English opera … which can be performed on the stage of Drury Lane without bringing discredit on the cause of English music … the work should at least be up to the standard of certain other English operas I have already given. Furthermore I shall be pleased to give a

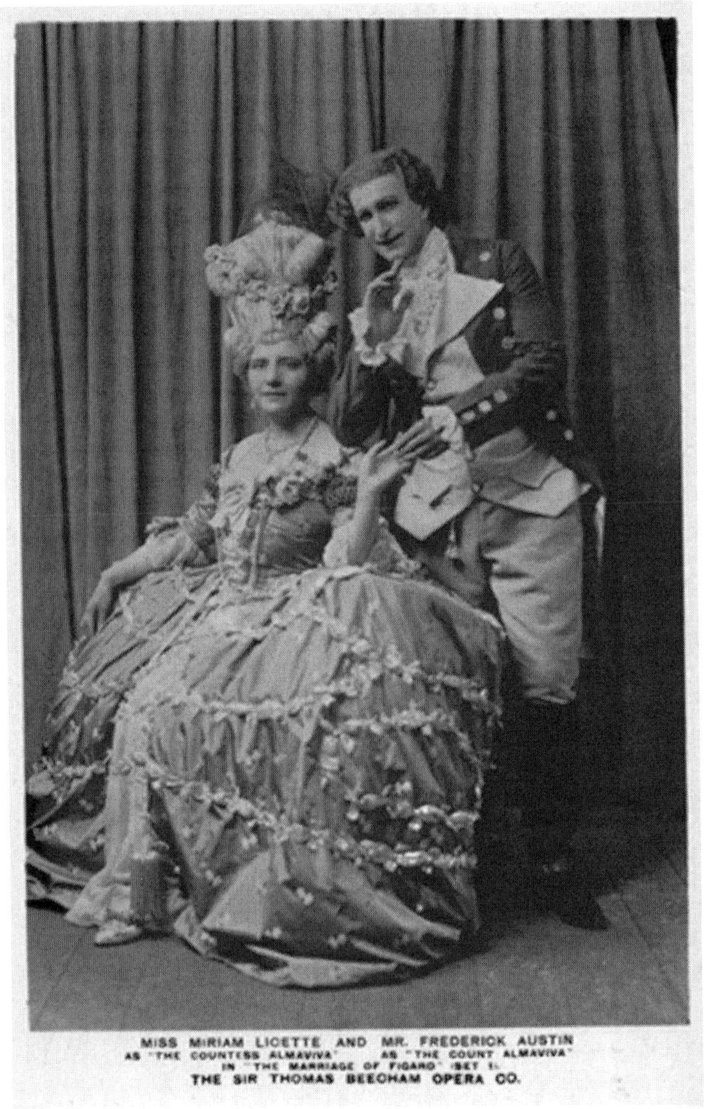

Figure 3.7 Miriam Licette and Frederick Austin as Countess and Count (*Le nozze di Figaro*), Beecham Opera Company, 1917

prize of £250 to the composer and, of course, at the earliest possible moment the work itself shall be produced.[198]

[198] Beecham to *Observer*, 24 June 1917, p. 10. Beecham probably had Clutsam's *Summer Night*, which he produced in 1910, in mind when referring to 'certain other English operas', but, if Smyth, Stanford or Lehmann saw his letter, they would surely have been

Nevertheless, the seasons continued to receive good reviews and healthy attendances provoked some philosophising:

> Why opera in English should succeed in war time after having failed to establish itself for generations of leisured pace is not to be answered by the critics ... Here, however, is the fact. Opera in English at Drury Lane and simultaneously [by the Carl Rosa] at the Shaftesbury is for the moment a success. At a time when most of our theatrical managers have agreed to assume that the public is too tired and depressed for anything but the trashiest revue the public has inconsequently made up its mind to enjoy *Boris Godunov*, *Faust* [and] *Aïda* ... There is, at any rate, no doubt at all that the audiences assembled to hear *Aïda* and *Boris* at Drury Lane are as big and as joyful as the audiences assembled to hear *Chu Chin Chow* at His Majesty's Theatre ...
>
> [*Boris Godunov*] was tastefully mounted and well sung ... There was no suggestion of competing principals grouped against a background of listless supernumeraries ... The individual members of the company at Drury Lane now begin to be well known, but they do not presume on our favour ... Producer, conductor, singers, the chorus and the scene-painter, by simply working together without display or fuss ... contrive to present us with an opera without needlessly emphasising the fact that opera is a highly conventional hybrid form of art which, by all the laws of right reason, ought never to have been invented.[199]

The *Musical Standard* suggested that audiences, segregated socially before the War, were, although not sitting side by side, coming together in the same theatre:

> Society at first seemed a little nervous, but now it takes its courage into its hands and flocks to Drury Lane. One of the season's old *habitués*, an old dowager of the possessing class, turning her lorgnette on the house and surveying it *in extenso*, as if it were only another portion of her vast privileged preserve, exclaimed 'Who are these people, my dear? There is not a familiar face to be seen. They look like artists and people of that sort.' That was at the beginning. The old familiars have come along since ... The heavenly eminence where the Olympians at one and twopence suffer like gods at feast, and the bottomless abyss, where the two and eightpenny middle class stew to death, were both

---

disappointed. A rebuttal by Clutsam (same issue, p. 5) blamed poor libretti in part (see also Chapter 5). The reference to four (sometimes three) new English operas was repeated subsequently; see *MT*, 1 August, p. 371; *Observer*, 16 September, p. 3; *The Times*, 22 September, p. 9.

199 *SR*, 30 June 1917, p. 594. Asche and Norton's musical comedy *Chu Chin Chow* opened at His Majesty's on 3 August 1916 and ran for a record 2,238 performances, closing in 1921.

> crammed. One wonders at the amazing enthusiasm which induces people to endure such horrible discomfort.[200]

The autumn 1917 season was not trouble free; on opening night *Ivan the Terrible* was introduced in English and 'notabilities were to be seen everywhere,'[201] but air raids disrupted the week, diminishing attendances, and the season closed two or three weeks earlier than expected.[202] The (still unnamed) British operas Beecham had mentioned did not appear:

> 'I have refrained from producing them,' said Sir Thomas, 'in consequence of the inauspiciousness of the moment ... English audiences would put down an empty house to a bad opera and not to any other cause.' That is not altogether a fair argument. London audiences showed years ago that they knew how to appreciate (and differentiate between) the new English operas of their day ... [S]urely it must be the constant high purpose of the British impresario to encourage British talent and, even at some pecuniary risk, to strive to identify 'Grand Opera in English' with English Grand Opera.[203]

But Beecham was in financial difficulties. Rumours circulated, although few knew the losses amounted to about £1,000 per week,[204] attributed to various reasons: air raids, the dour subjects of *Ivan the Terrible* and *Khovanshchina*, the attraction of cinema, and the Entertainment Tax encouraging attendees to 'trade down' to cheaper seats. Disentangling reasons for the losses from Beecham's provocative and contradictory statements, and his own tangled finances, is beyond the scope of this study.[205] Beecham claimed that exceptional circumstances hampered a fair assessment of his latest season and went on:

---

[200] *MS*, 4 August 1917, p. 82.

[201] *MS*, 29 September 1917, p. 210.

[202] Improving anti-aircraft defences caused the Germans to switch to night-time raids in September 1917. On 24 September falling bombs were audible inside the theatre and the upper gallery was cleared; on 1 October *Tristan und Isolde* was temporarily suspended during the first act with audience and performers taking refuge in the corridors (see Lucas, pp. 142–3). See also note 179.

[203] *SR*, 1 December 1917, p. 435; the verbatim quotes from Beecham are taken from the *Observer* interview referenced in note 198 (16 September, p. 3).

[204] Lucas, p. 145.

[205] Joseph Beecham died on 22 October 1916 leaving a massive estate but, while he bequeathed Thomas 46 per cent of the family business, he restricted his access. Thomas was allowed an annual income of £8,000 but this was dwarfed by his expenditure. Nevertheless, his credit remained good and his debts continued to rise; in 1921 he was brought to the Bankruptcy Court (see *The Times*, 17 February 1917, p. 3, and Lucas, pp. 157–61). Lucas notes that the opera company's accounts even under Joseph's management were vague and that losses amounted to around £30,000 each year (p. 148).

> 'During the raids … the theatre was empty, but the last week was good. One can always count on the last week!'
> 'Are you coming back,' he was asked, 'at Easter?'
> 'It is not quite certain. We shall certainly come back some time' …
> And then, sounding a more encouraging note, Sir Thomas added that there is some very strong hope that when better times return it will be possible to give regular seasons in London.
> 'I think the ground is all prepared for them. I am not pessimistic about London at all. At the same time London people must not run away with the idea that they are supporting the opera. They are not. They have not even begun to support it yet.'
> 'And by support you mean – ?'
> 'Reducing the loss to a reasonable figure.'[206]

Beecham reappeared, however, running two seasons in 1918 (five weeks at Drury Lane from 2 March and 3 June to 27 July). He returned again, along with a revived Grand Opera Syndicate, in 1919.

Partly because of the absence of competition, Beecham's seasons enjoyed both longevity and press support, if not financial success. Of the touring companies only the Rosa ventured into the West End. That they did so successfully, giving seasons in 1917 (from 3 May at the Garrick, transferring to the Shaftesbury on 4 June and closing on 7 July) and 1918 (6 May to 15 June at the Shaftesbury) raises the question as to why others did not follow suit but, with the exception of the defunct Moody-Manners, the Rosa was the only troupe with previous West End experience so, in the face of Beecham's sustained presence, others probably decided to work elsewhere. The Rosa seasons focused on standard repertory but included *Jeanie Deans*, and the first staged London performance of Philpot's *Dante and Beatrice* (7 June 1918; see Chapter 6). Meanwhile, the 'Old Vic' continued its twice-weekly performances of opera throughout the war years; Saturday matinees were introduced in January 1916,[207] and the 1916–17 season comprised 70 performances of 17 standard operas.[208]

Conclusion

With the exception of the war years, opera in central London from 1897, and by extension the operatic culture of the country, was dominated by Covent Garden. Its audience may have been elite, elitist, and wholly atypical, as were its performers, but it retained the role of dominant arbiter of taste and repertory. A frequently critical press, through its consistent and comprehensive coverage, only reinforced Covent Garden's position. Only Thomas and Joseph Beecham

---

[206] *Observer*, 25 November 1917, p. 11.

[207] *Stage*, 17 February 1916, p. 18.

[208] *Stage*, 26 April 1917, p. 15.

came close to usurping the Syndicate and, indeed, in the early Georgian years they achieved this, at least as far as defining operatic repertory was concerned. In the war years Thomas Beecham had a clearer run although prevailing circumstances only allowed him to take limited advantage of his opportunity. The 1910s also saw the establishment, at the 'Old Vic', of a company that became one of the major players in British opera in the twentieth century. Between these two extremes the middle classes were catered for through the solid if unspectacular work of the touring companies in smaller West End theatres and the suburbs. Although West End opera prospered as never before in the war years, and inspired hopes of a new golden age, the atypical circumstances created a false dawn. After the armistice, fashion and finance once more became the rulers of opera in central London.

Chapter 4
Opera in the Provinces

While operatic culture in the British Isles was largely shaped by the West End of London, activity beyond this area was extensive and often distinctive. Throughout this chapter the term 'provincial' should be taken as including suburban London, as it was the West End which was unusual rather than the metropolis as a whole. Provincial performances in this period were provided by touring companies and this chapter focuses on them; no town had a resident troupe similar to those found in many continental cities. Although touring companies all had a base, in practice this was only a contact address and storage facility; most of the year was spent 'on the road'. Performers who maintained a permanent residence were usually based in London to maximise employment if touring work was not available. A comprehensive survey of all provincial operatic activity is impractical and consequently particular reference is made to four towns (Birmingham, Dublin, Huddersfield and Norwich) to give a cross-section of the provincial experience; Birmingham and Huddersfield exemplify the rapidly growing industrial towns of the north and Midlands; Dublin and Norwich represent older settlements which expanded only slowly in the nineteenth century and whose economies were focused more on non-manufacturing activities.

Touring Companies

In terms of longevity, status and innovation, the dominant troupes between 1875 and 1918 were the Carl Rosa and Moody-Manners companies; there were many others but the majority survived fewer than five years before either collapsing or reforming under another name. The sum of activity is impressive: in this period, and especially in the Edwardian decade, more people had an opportunity to see Grand Opera (albeit often in a highly modified form) at affordable prices than either before or since.

The Carl Rosa was the only opera troupe which operated continuously from 1875 to 1918 and survived until 1960. Its pre-1918 activities can be separated into three phases: from its foundation in 1873 to Rosa's death in 1889; an uneasy decade culminating in liquidation and re-establishment in 1900; and the regaining of consistency under the management of brothers Alfred and Walter van Noorden.[1]

---

1 For further literature see Chapter 2, note 56.

Due to ample financial resources[2] and an absence of competitors in its early years, Rosa's troupe became almost immediately the leading provincial company, a status retained until the late 1890s; during the 1880s it posed a serious threat to the Italian operations in London (see Chapter 2). Only when the Moody-Manners Company was established in 1898 was the Rosa troupe's pre-eminence undermined. Rosa's death in 1889 robbed the company of its dynamo; the commissioning policy of the 1880s ceased, although works in progress, such as Cowen's *Thorgrim*, were performed as promised. The agreement in 1890 with Augustus Harris that it would not perform in central London for some years was, in retrospect, a major mistake and gave the impression of a retreat from the high-profile activities of the 1880s. First performances almost dried up (the British premieres of Godard's *La Vivandière* (Liverpool, 10 March 1896) and *La Bohème* (Manchester, 22 April 1897) and of MacCunn's two operas (see Chapter 6) were rare exceptions) although the company continued to expand its repertory and take works to the provinces, such as *Aïda*, *Die Meistersinger*, and *Hänsel und Gretel*, which had recently been given in London. Finances gradually declined from 1890 and, after losing heavily at Covent Garden in autumn 1897 (see Chapter 3) and on the provincial tour in spring 1898, shareholders opted for voluntary liquidation,[3] although a reformed company was soon back on the road. Another difficult West End season in early 1899 followed and the company almost collapsed again later that year,[4] but the Van Noorden brothers' management brought much-needed stability and, although no new works were commissioned, performance standards stabilised, more operas were added to the repertory (for example, *Siegfried*, *La forza del destino*, *Andrea Chénier* and *La Gioconda*), and the company regained ground. The death, on 14 April 1916, of Walter van Noorden, who also acted as principal conductor, was a blow,[5] but the tour underway continued and the organisation prospered in the later war years, taking over H.B. Phillips's company in 1918.

---

2 Rosa's capital seems to have come from lucrative tours of the United States in the early 1870s. The successful flotation as a limited company in 1887 (see Chapter 2, note 54) suggests that Rosa made substantial investments in the early years and that handsome profits were generated. Rosa's estate was valued in 1889 at £79,000; by contrast, Harris left only £24,000.

3 Occasional press comments reveal the company's financial decline. In 1888 an operating profit of £8,637, an overall profit (after deductions for depreciation, goodwill, and capital expenditure) of £5,502 and a dividend of 8 per cent were reported (*MW*, 9 March 1889, p. 147). By 1896, the operating profit had fallen to £188, with a loss on the main provincial tour of £475 (*Minim*, 1 July 1897, p. 232). In 1897 a loss of £6,600 was recorded followed by a further £3,000 in the first six months of 1898 (*MS*, 18 June 1898, p. 398).

4 *Era*, 2 September 1899, p. 12: 'Matters came to a dreadful head a few days since, the members of the troupe declining to go on. Since then conferences have been held ... and one more attempt will be made to carry on the concern.'

5 A brief obituary is at *Stage*, 20 April 1916, p. 22. Before 1900 Van Noorden had conducted the D'Oyly Carte company; he was educated at the Guildhall School of Music.

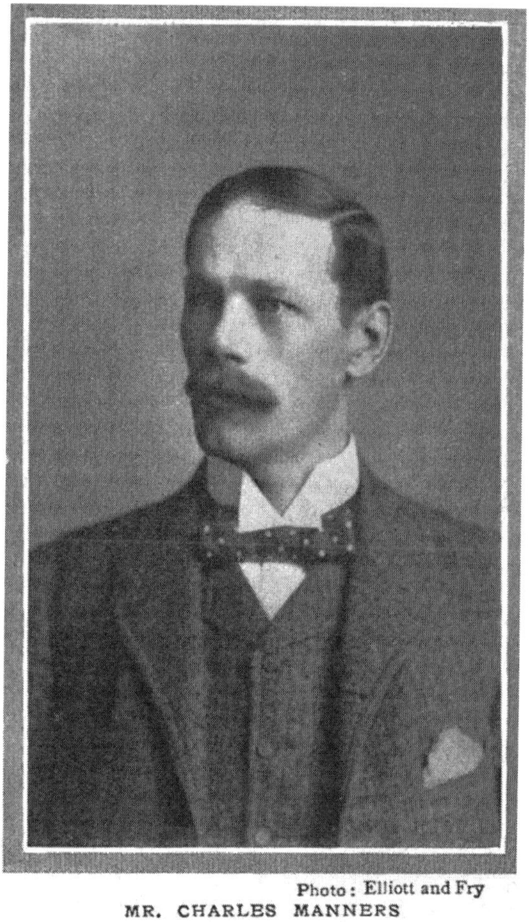

Figure 4.1 Charles Manners (*Black and White*, 21 September 1907)

The Rosa's difficulties in the late 1890s created an opening which was rapidly filled by a former member, Charles Manners, and his wife, Fanny Moody.[6] Within weeks of the Rosa's voluntary liquidation, the new Moody-Manners Company was inaugurated (5 September 1898). It soon became popular and by 1900 was as highly regarded as the Rosa. It expanded rapidly and, by 1905, Manners had four separate

---

6 Manners (1857–1935, born Southcote Mansergh) trained at the Royal Irish Academy, Royal Academy and in Florence. From 1881 he sang professionally in grand and light opera. Fanny Moody (1866–1945) studied with Charlotte Sainton-Dolby; originally intending a concert career, she joined the Rosa Company in 1887 and married Manners in 1890. For further anecdotal information see Perceval Graves, 'The Moody-Manners Partnership', *Opera*, 9 (1958), pp. 558–64.

Table 4.1 Touring Opera Companies in the United Kingdom 1875–1918

Company Name/Manager	Years known to be active
Charles Durand	1865–80
(Royal) Carl Rosa	1873–1960
Campobello-Sinico Italian	before 1875–78; 1881–82
Walsham	1875–78; 1888–90; 1897; also known as the Telma-Walsham company; may have been renamed National Grand Opera Company, active 1881
Blanche Cole	1877–79
G.W. Traverner	1880
Frederick Archer	1880
Royal English	1882–86
Cave Ashton	1884–85
Dalmaine	1885
Sydney Leslie	1886
James Turner	1886–1918 and beyond
Arthur Rousbey	1887–99
Ilma Norina	1889–94
Valentine Smith	1889–96
Grand National Opera Company / Grand English Opera Company / [Mrs Gordon] Hicks	1890–95 (renamed Hicks Opera Company in 1893)
Burns-Crotty	1892–93
Neilson	1895–1904
John Ridding	1897–1924*
Moody-Manners	1898–1916
F.S. Gilbert	1899–1905; possibly still active in 1908
National Grand Opera Company (unrelated to above)	1899
Elster-Grime	1900–07
Hilton St Just	1904–05
Castellano Italian / Castellano English	1909–15 (renamed Castellano English in 1915)
Ernst Denhof	1910–13
Quinlan	1911–14
Beecham	1911–20

Joseph O'Mara	1912–34
Empire English / Allington-Charsley	1915–21 (renamed Allington-Charsley in 1917)
Harrison Frewin	1915–17 (taken over by H.B. Phillips)
H.B. Phillips	1917–19 (taken over by Carl Rosa)
Brisan	1916–17 (performed only in Ireland)
McNally	1918–19 (only traced in Ireland)

Note to table: *In some years active only as a 'costume recital' company, playing semi-staged, condensed versions of standard operas.

troupes with a fifth promised.[7] 'A' company, with over 100 members, visited the biggest towns, focusing on industrial northern England, and had an 'Academy of Music' attached through which operatic hopefuls could gain experience and training (on payment of a fee). 'B' company, comprising about 60 members, favoured medium-sized towns especially in southern England; 'C' company (about 30 employees), and 'D' company (overseas), did not survive long and the proposed 'E' company does not appear to have started. Manners was interested in English opera and premiered several new works (see Chapter 6). Despite his success, Manners suspended operations in April 1916, initially temporarily, then with a promise to resume after the war, but the cessation was permanent.[8]

Many other troupes operated during this period but most were short-lived (see Table 4.1). Singers, players and conductors transferred on a regular basis and singers also moved between Grand Opera and operetta/musical comedy. Most companies operated in a similar manner, distinguished primarily by size; itineraries are a good indicator of employee numbers and performing standards, with the most modest troupes appearing in smaller market or county towns, lesser seaside resorts, and minor industrial centres. Repertories comprised established operas and few companies attempted to expand by adding new works. The first priority was to break even, encouraging a 'safety first' approach.

7 *Era*, 7 January 1905, p. 3, and below. In order to strengthen the impression of magnitude, quoted company numbers usually included non-performing personnel.

8 Graves (note 6) gave the final performance as 1 May 1916. Manners wrote: 'I see Mr W.W. Kelly [manager of the Shakespeare Theatre, Liverpool] announced that I have disbanded my company for the duration of the war. This is not the case. I have disbanded my company only until I find it feasible to run it under the proper conditions' (*Era*, 24 May 1916, p. 13). In May 1918, however, Manners put the company up for sale (*Era*, 15 May 1918, p. 4) and in September all its properties were auctioned, though Manners claimed that resumption was imminent: 'Retiring? Who's talking about retiring? … We are making a clearance of everything because – after the war – we mean to make a fresh start on a new plan … a new national opera scheme, with a proper system of stable income and pensions for everybody concerned' (*Era*, 25 September 1918, p. 9).

The companies founded by the singers James Turner and Arthur Rousbey are representative examples of medium-sized enterprises. Both men established reputations with other groups before setting up own their own (the latter was briefly a member of the former's company); neither aimed at the level of innovation of the Rosa or Moody-Manners but both gained a sufficiently loyal following to continue for several years.

Rousbey formed his company in spring 1887. Although intended initially to run only for a few months,[9] Rousbey's energy gave his troupe momentum. Often playing only two or three nights in a theatre before moving on, his successful first tour encouraged him to establish a full-time company.[10] Modest in size, it did not exceed 30 members (singers, players, and support staff) and, while Henry Wood and Eugene Goossens wrote disparagingly of its standards (which were, nevertheless, typical – see below) and its repertory was dominated by safe and popular choices, it took occasional risks, giving the world premieres of Christensen's *Belphegor* (26 October 1889, Theatre Royal, South Shields), Bucalossi's *Massaroni* (23 January 1894, Leinster Hall, Dublin) and Pellegrini's *Mercedes* (11 January 1896, Leinster Hall, Dublin), and the first British performance of Puccini's *Le Villi* (24 September 1897, Comedy Theatre, Manchester).[11] Rousbey's unexpected death, on 30 October 1899 while sailing back to England from a tour of South Africa, brought activities to a premature end.[12]

James Turner founded his company in 1886; although he died in 1913, it carried on after the end of the Great War.[13] Turner dominated his troupe into his sixties – in 1905 the *Birmingham Daily Post* commented, 'His voice wears wonderfully well, but the nasal quality becomes more pronounced; his management of it is really remarkable,'[14] and, in 1910, at Bolton, 'Mr Turner appeared as Count Rupert [in *Satanella*] and, notwithstanding his seventy years, his vigour of action and

---

[9] *Era*, 11 November 1899, p. 13.

[10] In August 1887 the company played in at least nine towns in Devon and Cornwall in a masterpiece of planning, starting at Penzance and ending in Exmouth, via Camborne, Redruth, Devonport, Teignmouth, Ilfracombe, Bideford, and Barnstaple, typically playing two nights in each (see weekly advertisements in *Stage*, August 1887).

[11] The Puccini performance came only five months after the British premiere of *La Bohème* by the Rosa (see above), which may have inspired Rousbey's choice; for reviews see *Stage*, 30 September 1897, p. 17, and *MS*, 9 October 1897, p. 237. Rousbey also revived Suppé's *Galatea* (1893), *Ernani* and Balfe's *The Sleeping Queen* (both 1894).

[12] Rousbey's name first appeared in reviews of music hall turns (see *Era*, 20 July 1873, p. 14, and 13 September 1874, p. 5); he sang in a variety of companies including the Royal English Opera, and for one season in Turner's troupe. For obituaries see *Stage*, 9 November 1899, p. 20, and *Era*, 11 November, p. 13.

[13] Turner's career was less varied than Rousbey's. His first major engagement was on a world tour; he joined the Rosa Company in the mid or late 1870s and stayed with them until setting up his own troupe; see *Stage*, 23 January 1913, p. 26, and *Era*, 25 May 1892, p. 10.

[14] *BDP*, 21 November 1905, p. 11.

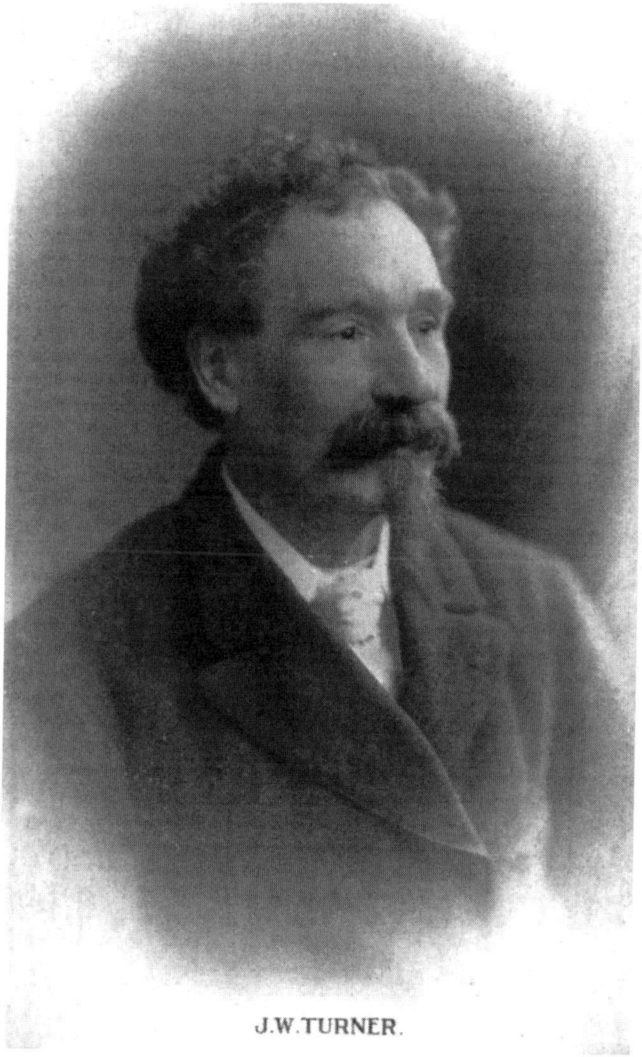

Figure 4.2 James Turner (postcard)

rich tone of voice were truly remarkable'.[15] Like Rousbey, Turner stuck largely to tried and trusted repertory but also produced such rarely performed works as Macfarren's *Robin Hood* and Auber's *La Dame Blanche* for several years, and gave several performances of Philpot's *La Gitana* (1897) and the world premiere of Philpot's *Nigel* (see Chapter 6).

15 *Stage*, 22 September 1910, p. 5; Turner was actually 63.

Organisation of Touring Companies

In the early 1800s more affluent provincial theatre-goers tended to confine their attendances to a limited number of patent theatres, each served by a 'stock' company.[16] While these groups could operate self-sufficiently, 'star' actors toured the country taking leading roles, with locals stepping down to supporting parts. Stock companies maintained a large repertory in order to give audiences varied entertainments; actors were expected to sing and regularly appeared in 'opera' as well as spoken drama. The few extant touring troupes offered specialist performances, such as productions including animals.

Spurred by social and legal changes, the stock system declined. Population growth, urbanisation and the expansion of the railways extended the practical and financial advantages of touring beyond 'niche' troupes. The Theatres Act 1843 devolved responsibility for licensing to local authorities resulting in increasing numbers of legitimate venues, which also made touring more attractive. The Dramatic Copyright Act 1833 enabled authors to sell the rights of representation on stage of plays and, under the Copyright Act 1842, this was extended to musical compositions. A trade developed in which troupes bought exclusive performing rights of new plays and operas, encouraging the formation of single-work touring companies secured by a performance monopoly.[17] The touring system became self-perpetuating: companies were self-sufficient and the stock system declined as local troupes became both unfashionable and redundant for increasing proportions of the year and as the stock companies disbanded, theatres became dependent on visiting groups. By the 1880s the 'touring' system dominated British and Irish theatre.

Touring opera companies had, like animal and acrobatic troupes, first appeared in the 1820s and '30s. Initially limited in their activities, they expanded in number, size, and scope as touring became more attractive.[18] Unlike most touring

---

16 Patent theatres, the only ones legally entitled to play spoken drama, were licensed by the crown. Originally confined to London, several provincial 'Theatres Royal' opened during the eighteenth century. While the patents did not provide the bulk of theatrical entertainment, they were, as the only legitimate theatres, the primary venues for such expensive genres as opera. In order to circumvent the law, however, many other venues performed 'operas' as a cover for the production of spoken drama (for example, by selling tickets for a 'concert' during which a play would be given for 'free'. Still more basic entertainments were given in penny gaffs and portable theatres.

17 This trade subsequently developed with 'sub-licenses' being sold to other companies once they were more valuable than a monopoly. The rights of operas were especially complicated as scores and libretti were separate legal entities, as were English-language translations of the latter.

18 For an account of touring opera companies in Dublin between 1830 and 1870, see Paul Rodmell '"The Italians are Coming": Opera in mid-Victorian Dublin' in Rachel Cowgill and Julian Rushton (eds), *Europe, Empire and Spectacle in Nineteenth Century British Music* (Aldershot, 2006) pp. 97–112. For an account of a single provincial tour see E. Bradley Strauchen-Scherer, 'Lost Luggage: Giovanni Puzzi and the Management

companies, however, opera troupes, in one respect, continued the 'stock' tradition by playing a repertory of works.[19]

Touring was a precarious activity requiring skilled organisation and some luck. Local theatre managers contracted troupes for a fixed period, typically one week, on either a rental or 'shared takings' basis; in the former instance the touring company took all the financial risk and any resulting profit, while in the latter risk was shared with the theatre manager, reducing losses in poor weeks but also profits in successful ones. Records from the Theatre Royal, Huddersfield, show that 'shared takings' were preferred, with touring companies receiving between 40 and 70 per cent of box office income; opera troupes were at the higher end with James Turner's company taking 60 per cent and the Carl Rosa the tacit maximum of 70 per cent (see also Table 4.14).[20] The most prestigious theatres operated almost continuously and drew high-profile stars and companies; in smaller towns theatres could stand empty for several weeks. The classified sections of the trade journals *The Era* and *The Stage* were the conduits used by interested parties to ensure optimum bookings and employment:

> Miss Somerville's Comedy-Bouffe Company with standard comedies and a new *opéra-bouffe* by Charles Lecocq entitled *Una* … Theatre Royal, Leeds, April 12th; St George's Hall, Bradford, April 19th; Theatre Royal, Huddersfield, April 26th; Theatre Royal, Shrewsbury, May 10th. Applications for dates and terms to be addressed *en route* to Mr Thomas W Charles, Acting Manager …
>
> Mr Henry Haigh's English Opera Recitals Company (Directress Madame Haigh-Dyer) … Theatre Royal, Oxford. First vacant date 31st May …
>
> Mr Joseph D. M'Laren, Business Manager, Carl Rosa Grand Opera Company, will be disengaged early in May. Town address care of A. Austin Esq, St James's Hall, Piccadilly …

---

of Giovanni Rubini's Farewell Tour in 1842', in Rachel Cowgill and Peter Holman (eds), *Music in the British Provinces 1690–1914* (Aldershot, 2007), pp. 237–51. Other, anecdotal, accounts of early provincial tours are included in: Thomas Willert Beale, *The Light of Other Days Seen Through the Wrong End of an Opera Glass*, (London, 1890); Walter Maynard [alias of Thomas Willert Beale], *The Entertaining Impresario* (London, 1867); and Luigi Arditi, *My Reminiscences* (London, 1896).

19 Most spoken drama (but not Shakespeare), operetta, and musical comedy companies were run on the 'single work' principle; the D'Oyly Carte troupes started from this basis but, as the 'Savoy Opera' oeuvre grew they moved to a repertory system.

20 See Theatre Royal, Huddersfield, Box Office Records and Accounts, WYAS, B/HTR; the records cover the periods April 1901 to August 1902, April 1906 to February 1917, and August 1918 onwards.

> Bedlington (Northumberland), New Gaiety Theatre (Proprietor Mr J. Dowson). The above theatre at liberty from April 7th to 24th for opera, Christy Minstrel or concert companies on sharing terms or rental …
>
> Dublin Queen's Theatre of Varieties (Sole Lessee and Manager Mr Arthur Lloyd) … Mr A. Lloyd will be happy to hear from first-class travelling companies. No vacancies for music hall artistes. Quite full for the year. Three days' silence a courteous negative …[21]

In the 1870s the system was fluid; arrangements were typically made at short notice and companies could extend residencies if business was good. In later years, however, practices became more rigid. Many theatres passed into group ownership and arrangements covering several theatres could be made as one booking and fixed-length engagements became normative. By the end of the Great War, Huddersfield's theatre was booking opera companies between 12 and 18 months in advance.[22]

Personal employment contracts were often also short-term. Singers and players were typically contracted for a single tour, lasting anything between three and eleven months, with the latter becoming normative in later years. There is little extant primary source evidence but surviving records give selective insights. At the top of the scale, the contract between Carl Rosa and Charles Santley for Rosa's 1875 tour illustrates the treatment of a star principal singer.[23] Santley was employed from 14 September to 23 December 'at such places in England, Scotland and Ireland as the said Carl Rosa may from time to time desire'. His salary was £120 per week in London (the West End and the Standard Theatre, Shoreditch), and £130 elsewhere, with all travelling expenses borne by Rosa; Santley was to perform up to four times each week but not in consecutive performances, and to provide his own costumes. Operas were to be chosen by 'mutual consent'.[24] The two men agreed that Santley would perform in neither *The Bohemian Girl* nor *Il Trovatore* although he gave way on the latter. Santley's experiences with Rosa were unhappy and, when Rosa proposed a renewal of the contract in 1877 Santley refused, declaring that 'I have had enough of the theatre and have firmly resolved

21 *Era*, 4 April 1875, pp. 16, 19 and 20. The English Opera Recitals Company (often known as the Haigh-Dyer), gave 'opera recitals in costume' in smaller towns in the south of England.

22 The Rosa troupe was booked in December 1917 for a one-week residency in February 1919 and the smaller Allington-Charsley Company in November 1918 for performances in December 1919 (WYAS, B/HTR/g). Less prestigious companies worked to shorter timeframes.

23 Employment agreement between Carl Rosa and Charles Santley, 16 February 1875, Liverpool Record Office, 920 SAN 2/17.

24 These terms are favourable compared to two contracts made between Santley and Mapleson for Italian opera in 1872–73; Mapleson paid between £360 and £400 per month for up to 16 performances, provided costumes, and added £10 per week for accommodation outside London (Liverpool Record Office, 920 SAN 2/15 and 16).

never to enter one again as a performer'.[25] These conditions were exceptional: during the Great War the Harrison Frewin Company's total weekly salary bill for more than 20 principal singers was only £120 (see below).[26]

Terms and conditions for chorus singers and orchestral players were very different; they were required to appear in six evening performances and one or two matinées each week. In 1905 the Moody-Manners Company paid chorus members £1 17s 6d (sopranos and altos), £2 2s 6d (basses and baritones) and £2 5s (tenors) per week and stated that 'Extra Salaries are paid for Small Parts which are all exclusively played by the Chorus'.[27] The orchestral players of the Harrison Frewin Company appear to have earned an average weekly wage of £2 18s in 1916.[28]

Companies varied greatly in size: in 1898 the Moody-Manners comprised 70 people[29] and, by 1905, its 'A' troupe exceeded 115;[30] the smallest organisations employed fewer than 30. The largest companies operated in the early 1910s, when those of Ernst Denhof and Thomas Quinlan exceeded 150 (see below). Nevertheless, touring troupes were rarely self-sufficient. In addition to resident backstage staff (for example, fly operators and limelight men), most companies used local performers as a supplement where necessary. The choruses could be reinforced and orchestras augmented by the resident theatre band. Local singers were gradually discarded – as stage business became more complex and 'realistic' the training of local extras became impractical. Of necessity, however, the practice re-emerged during the Great War (see below). The combination of travelling and resident orchestras was standard practice and attracted little comment, but occasional notes are illuminating:

> A marked feature in the [Royal English Opera] company's organisation is the exceptional quality of its orchestra. Mr Edwards carries no less than fourteen of

---

[25] Charles Santley, *Reminiscences of my life* (London, 1909), p. 136. For an account of his tours with Rosa see pp. 104–36.

[26] John McCormack was offered £8 per week as a principal tenor by Manners in 1906; McCormack wanted £10, but Manners refused as the singer had little stage experience. No engagement was undertaken (see Gordon Ledbetter, *The Great Irish Tenor: John McCormack* (Dublin, 2003), p. 55.

[27] *Era*, 2 September 1905, p. 3. For the 1906–07 season rates increased by 2s 6d (*Era*, 2 March 1907, p. 3) but by 1913 rates for male singers had reverted to 1905 levels (*Era*, 12 April 1913, p. 2). In 1903 Manners stated that after three years singers could graduate to (sub-)principal roles and receive £4 per week (*MH*, 1 June 1903, p. 166).

[28] Derived from the total expenditure on players' wages shown in the company's accounts (Table 4.13), and an orchestra of 21 members, as advertised in *Stage*, 19 August 1915, p. 18 and *IT*, 24 February 1916, p. 4.

[29] *Stage*, 16 June 1898, p. 22. The company comprised 14 principals, two of whom were tyros; a chorus of 33; an orchestra of 12; two conductors; four dancers; stage manager; general manager; two wardrobe staff; and a 'baggage and supermaster'.

[30] *Era*, 7 January 1905, p. 3.

his principals with him and with a liberal augmentation from the best local talent is able to do full justice to the most exacting score.[31]

The [Moody-Manners 'A'] company numbers 120 and includes … a band of thirty first-class instrumentalists … to augment the local orchestra.[32]

Thus even large companies relied on local players. Accounts from Huddersfield invariably show wages for the local orchestra as an expense during opera weeks and surviving agreements from the war years specify how many players the Theatre Royal would provide.[33] The complexities of the scores of such composers as Puccini and Wagner, however, posed difficulties and some organisations eschewed local players who, like chorus singers, could not be adequately rehearsed in advance. The Denhof and Quinlan companies became entirely self-sufficient with their own orchestras of 50 to 60 players; smaller companies' performances of more challenging works were often ragged, although the relatively static repertory (see below) helped to preserve standards.

While press reports often complimented the orchestras, the recollections of Eugene Goossens III and Henry Wood, both of whom conducted the Rousbey Opera Company in the 1890s, tell a different story:

The 'locals' were chosen ahead of time by the advance representative of the company … The job of rehearsing … [them] can well be imagined. For over twenty years father [Eugene Goossens II] always undertook this task himself. Every morning … he would rehearse apprehensive little groups of players (never more than seven or eight in number) in the stuffy bar of the theatre, in order that they should be tolerably familiar with the opera to be played that night. The execrable sounds produced at some of these rehearsals were unbelievable, yet at the performance, with the help of the regular players, the 'locals' usually managed to give a fair account of themselves. Father relates that in one small town, after a spell of bad business, the company's finances were so slender that he was reduced to conducting a performance of *Cavalleria* [*Rusticana*] with five players – harmonium, cornet, horn and two violins. The following day even the horn and cornet players deserted, and he had to conduct *Tannhäuser* with two

31 *Era*, 1 May 1886, p. 16, reviewing the company at Norwich. The Rousbey and Moody-Manners 'B' companies were of a similar size (*Era*, 6 November 1897, p. 22; 28 October 1905, p. 9, respectively).

32 *Era*, 9 September 1905, p. 16, reviewing the company at Leicester.

33 The regular orchestra comprised about 10 players with extras employed as required (see WYAS, B/HTR/as). The Carl Rosa contract for February 1919 stipulated the provision of at least 16 local players; for the Allington-Charsley Company in December 1919 eight players were to be found (B/HTR/g).

violins and a harmonium. This performance prompted the manager's wife to remark that she had never heard the woodwind 'so well in tune'.[34]

> The full [Rousbey] company assembled at Charing Cross station, and I found myself with a chorus of forty, a travelling orchestra of six, ten principals, a wardrobe master and mistress, an advance booking agent, and a stage manager – all bound for Ramsgate …
>
> The orchestra – as usual – was hopeless. I fear I became sarcastic and upset things a little by asking the violins whether they were sure they were playing on the right string. The woodwind played so out of tune that I begged them not to transpose – a remark that did not go down very well …
>
> The climax, however, came on the opening night. The stage band for the march in *Faust* was a local affair … [M]ost of them appeared to be a little 'Saturday-afternoonish', the bass drummer especially. The band sometimes played on the pier and consisted of two cornets, two saxhorns and a bass drum. Not having to appear until the third act these gentlemen retired for further refreshment. And a fine sight they made at their entry, the drummer wearing his cap at a rakish angle! He played his part abominably, landing after the beat rather than on it, with special effects on each bar-line.[35]

Companies were not only reliant on personnel from outside. Smaller groups often rented costumes, and scenery and large props were provided by theatres.[36] The preference, however, was for companies to own as much equipment as

[34] Eugène Goossens [III], *Overture and Beginners* (London, 1951), pp. 27–8. The Goossens family was extensively involved in opera in Britain: Eugène I (1845–1906) was a conductor with the Carl Rosa (1883–93) and his wife Sidonie a choreographer. Eugène II (1867–1958) played violin in the Rosa and Covent Garden orchestras and conducted the Burns-Crotty, Rousbey, Moody-Manners, Rosa, and Beecham Companies up to 1918.

[35] Henry Wood, *My Life of Music* (London, 1938), pp. 72–4. Touring with the Rosa he had a travelling orchestra of 10 (p. 77). According to Walter van Noorden, 'The vast majority of provincial orchestras are composed of persons who are cobblers or tallow-chandlers by day, and musicians by night … Scores and scores of times have I been told in the course of a rehearsal that, "I'm not dependant on this for a living," or "I can't get away from my business to rehearse"' (*MS*, 13 October 1900, p. 224). Members of the Huddersfield orchestra received between £1 2s 6d, and £1 15s per week playing for Turner in 1907 (WYAS, B/HTR/as/1), rising to an average £1 17s in 1916, much less than the estimated £2 18s Frewin paid his permanent musicians (see above).

[36] Hired equipment could be seized if payments were not kept up; the Campobello-Sinico suffered this fate at Rochdale when Augustus Harris and his brother Charles, employed by their costumier mother 'Madame Auguste', 'each sat on a large basket of the costumes and refused to allow them to be opened or any costume used till some instalment was paid' (James Glover, *Jimmy Glover, His Book* (London, 1911), pp. 105–6). This company also experienced the embarrassment at Huddersfield of 'the desertion at a moment's notice of the conductor and large part of the band' (*Era*, 28 May 1876, p. 6).

Table 4.2 Provincial tours by James Mapleson, Frederick Gye/Julius Benedict and Carl Rosa, 1875 (six performances per week, Monday to Saturday, unless otherwise stated)

<table>
<tr><th>Week commencing</th><th>Gye/Benedict</th><th>Mapleson</th><th>Rosa</th></tr>
<tr><td>1 March</td><td></td><td>Newcastle 1 – 3 Mar
Edinburgh 4 – 6 Mar</td><td></td></tr>
<tr><td>8 March</td><td></td><td>Glasgow</td><td></td></tr>
<tr><td>15 March</td><td></td><td>Liverpool</td><td></td></tr>
<tr><td>22 March</td><td></td><td>Manchester</td><td></td></tr>
<tr><td>29 March</td><td rowspan="6">(London season from 30 March to 17 July)</td><td></td><td rowspan="3">Dublin</td></tr>
<tr><td>5 April</td><td></td></tr>
<tr><td>12 April</td><td rowspan="4">(London season from 10 April to 24 July)</td></tr>
<tr><td>19 April</td><td>Liverpool</td></tr>
<tr><td>26 April</td><td>Leeds</td></tr>
<tr><td>3 May</td><td>Birmingham</td></tr>
<tr><td>13 September</td><td></td><td></td><td rowspan="7">(London season from 11 Sept to 30 October)</td></tr>
<tr><td>20 September</td><td></td><td></td></tr>
<tr><td>27 September</td><td></td><td></td></tr>
<tr><td>4 October</td><td rowspan="2">Dublin</td><td></td></tr>
<tr><td>11 October</td><td></td></tr>
<tr><td>18 October</td><td></td><td></td></tr>
<tr><td>25 October</td><td></td><td></td></tr>
<tr><td>1 November</td><td>Glasgow</td><td></td><td>Birmingham</td></tr>
<tr><td>8 November</td><td>Newcastle</td><td>Liverpool</td><td>Sheffield</td></tr>
<tr><td>15 November</td><td rowspan="2">Liverpool (to 25 Nov)</td><td>Dublin</td><td rowspan="3">Manchester</td></tr>
<tr><td>22 November</td><td>Glasgow</td></tr>
<tr><td>29 November</td><td></td><td>Glasgow 29 Nov – 1 Dec
Newcastle 2 – 4 Dec</td></tr>
<tr><td>6 December</td><td>Manchester</td><td>Manchester</td><td rowspan="2">Dublin</td></tr>
<tr><td>13 December</td><td></td><td>Birmingham 13 – 15 Dec</td></tr>
<tr><td>20 December</td><td></td><td></td><td></td></tr>
<tr><td>27 December</td><td></td><td></td><td>Liverpool 26 Dec – 15 Jan</td></tr>
</table>

possible – in the war years Frewin's company needed only to hire wigs and to use local properties and scenery.[37] Larger companies used dedicated transport; interviewed in 1901, Manners explained that,

> [Touring] involves the chartering of special trains and steamers … the weight of our paraphernalia is so enormous that our train is almost invariably drawn by two engines. Why, our clothes alone turn the scales at seventeen tons. They fill a hundred and eight huge baskets. Then we have all our own musical instruments even down to the pianos.[38]

The core season ran from September to June. Only resort theatres were normally open in July and August, although, later, practices changed and tours lasted up to 11 months.[39] A few performers moved to the West End 'Grand' seasons but this did not cause significant disruption. Although pantomimes were traditional after Christmas, in larger towns opera was viewed as an attractive alternative, and for all touring companies box office receipts from Boxing Day to the end of January were usually higher than average and could help to eliminate losses made at other times.

Companies tried to base itineraries on sensible routes, as moves between venues normally took place on Sundays.[40] Extended stays, although preferable in practical terms, were uncommon; as the touring system became embedded, weekly moves became standard practice. In 1875, the Rosa, Mapleson and Gye/Benedict troupes confined themselves to the biggest and most affluent cities (Table 4.2); note Mapelson's truncated visits to Newcastle, Edinburgh and Birmingham, which required midweek moves.[41]

---

37 Wig hire is an expense in the company accounts (see below); Huddersfield agreements in 1917 and 1918 require the theatre to provide stock scenery and props (WYAS, B/HTR/g). Frewin bought the costumes and properties of the Quinlan Company when it was liquidated in 1915.

38 *MS*, 24 August 1901, p. 127. From 1896 touring companies were given a standard 25 per cent discount on railway fares and favourable terms for freight (see *Stage*, 6 August 1896, p. 11).

39 Some companies took a break before Christmas and reopened on Boxing Day. Theatres normally closed on Ash Wednesday and in Holy Week, although by 1914 only Maundy Thursday and Good Friday were observed; in some instances opera companies replaced staged performances with concerts of sacred music.

40 Under the Sunday Observance Act 1780 theatres remained closed. Manners observed: 'We are bound to [travel on Sundays] but the arrangements I make always allow of the members of the company going to church … We wind up at each town we visit on a Saturday night. Immediately the curtain falls the baggage men set to work, and by midnight everything is out of the theatre. The scenery and baggage are placed on the railway trucks forthwith and soon after breakfast we are on the road' (*Era*, 24 August 1901, p. 127). For further commentary see D.T. Timins, 'How theatrical companies travel', *Ludgate*, 1 January 1900, pp. 222–9.

41 Manchester was disadvantageously overwhelmed: a three-week season by Rosa (in which he was 'gleaning fame, if not gold' (*MW*, 27 November 1875, p. 810)) was immediately

Table 4.3 Moody-Manners 'A' and 'B' companies' tour schedule 1906–07

Week commencing	'A' Company	'B' Company
3 September 1906	Kennington	Llandudno
10 September	Coronet, Notting Hill	Norwich
17 September	Camden	Tunbridge Wells
24 September	Middlesbrough	Aldershot
1 October	Sunderland	Hastings
8 October	Edinburgh	Folkestone
15 October	Glasgow	Bournemouth
22 October		Swindon
29 October	Hull	Bath
5 November	Sheffield	Exeter
12 November	Birmingham	Torquay
19 November	Hanley	Worcester
26 November	Bolton	Crewe
3 December	Liverpool	Eccles
10 December	Burnley	(*free*)
17 December		
26 December	Dublin	
31 December		Woolwich
7 January 1907		
14 January	Cork	Ipswich
21 January		King's Lynn
28 January		Kendal
4 February	Oldham	Preston
11 February	Leeds	Blackpool
18 February	Glasgow	Carlisle
25 February		Lincoln
4 March	Edinburgh	Dewsbury
11 March	Middlesbrough	Halifax

followed by the simultaneous appearance of the two Italian companies: 'it is surely a misfortune that Mr Gye's and Mr Mapleson's troupes are going to play here in the same week and on the same nights. The amateurs who wish to see Mdme Nilsson as Marguerite and Mdlle Albani as Amina, are compelled to make a choice, as these operas will not be repeated, and they are to be given on the same night' (*MW*, 4 December 1875, p. 831).

<table>
<tr><td>18 March</td><td>Liverpool</td><td>Bury</td></tr>
<tr><td>25 March</td><td colspan="2">(Holy Week)</td></tr>
<tr><td>1 April</td><td rowspan="2">Nottingham</td><td>Birkenhead</td></tr>
<tr><td>8 April</td><td rowspan="2">Southampton</td></tr>
<tr><td>15 April</td><td>Birmingham</td></tr>
<tr><td>22 April</td><td colspan="2">Sheffield (companies combined)</td></tr>
<tr><td>29 April</td><td>Peckham</td><td>Cambridge</td></tr>
<tr><td>6 May</td><td rowspan="2">Coronet, Notting Hill</td><td rowspan="2">Crystal Palace</td></tr>
<tr><td>13 May</td></tr>
</table>

In the same year, the smaller Durand company, which visited more modest towns, undertook a much more itinerant tour.[42] The Rosa and Moody-Manners 'A' troupes also moved every week, and although short journeys were preferred some long leaps were inevitable (Table 4.3).

As Tables 4.2 and 4.3 show, there were exceptions to the weekly residency. In Ireland, especially Dublin, more prolonged stays were typical due to the cost of the sea crossing and, in bigger cities, particularly Liverpool and Manchester, residencies could extend to over a month; in the war years, when transport costs increased greatly, touring companies sometimes stayed in bigger towns for much longer.[43]

Provincial and suburban audiences were far less socially segregated than in London's West End. Touring companies charged 'standard prices' for their performances, meaning that opera tickets cost the same as for any other production in the same theatre, bringing them within reach of most of the local population as the lowest price was typically 6d. Whereas in the West End audiences were segregated by theatre (venues aimed explicitly at different social classes), elsewhere social segregation was maintained between different seating areas in one building. Only the Italian companies at the beginning of this period, and the Denhof, Quinlan and Beecham troupes at the end, adopted different pricing policies.

The four sample towns experienced differing levels of opera provision and repertory (see below), influenced by their particular circumstances and theatrical

---

42 The company opened at Norwich on 29 March, where it played for four weeks, before proceeding, usually for one-week residencies, to Leicester, Oldham, Middlesbrough, Grimsby, Hull, Rotherham, Whitehaven (twice), Newcastle-upon-Tyne, Darlington, Barrow-in-Furness, Scarborough, Edinburgh (twice), Aberdeen, Stockton-on-Tees (twice), Sunderland, Lancaster, Limerick, Cork, Kendal, Carlisle, Dalton-in-Furness, and Preston (source: *Era*).

43 The trend for long seasons in Liverpool originated with Rosa, whose company was based at the Royal Court Theatre and typically gave six- or seven-week seasons. Usually opening on Boxing Day, these extended runs were maintained by a succession of companies until 1918; starting in December 1917, W.W. Kelly, manager of the Shakespeare Theatre, gave opera for 24 consecutive weeks (of which 19 were given by the Phillips Company; see *Era*, 9 October 1918, supplement, p. 12, and *MS*, 11 May 1918, p. 279).

resources. The populations of the two industrial towns grew by over 200 per cent between 1861 and 1921 (Birmingham from 296,000 to 922,000, Huddersfield from 35,000 to 111,000) but Norwich grew by only 63 per cent (74,000 to 121,000) and Dublin by just 23 per cent (410,000 to 505,000 in 1926).[44]

In addition to its own growth, Birmingham was also the dominant regional centre, with several neighbouring towns subject to its influence (although many had their own theatres). The Theatre Royal, founded in 1774 and a patent from 1807, mounted opera regularly; it was rebuilt in both 1820 and 1904 before closing in 1956. The town's rapid growth allowed the addition of the Prince of Wales (1856), and Grand (1883), both of which hosted opera companies, and also Queen's (later Metropole, 1886), and Lyceum (later Alexandra, 1901) theatres; there were also several music halls, variety palaces, and suburban venues.

As Ireland's capital, Dublin had had a patent Theatre Royal since the seventeenth century which, from 1821, was sited on Hawkins Street. This burnt down in 1880 and was not rebuilt until 1897. Rebuilt again in 1935, it finally closed in 1962. Other central Dublin theatres were the Queen's Royal (later Queen's, 1844), Gaiety (1871), Leinster Hall (1886), and Abbey (1904), plus several music halls. The principal venues for opera were the Royal, Leinster Hall and, from 1880, the Gaiety. As in Birmingham, several smaller townships fell under Dublin's influence; they were increasingly the preferred residences of the professional classes. Although Dublin's potency as a capital diminished after the 1801 Act of Union it was still the largest city in Ireland and home to the Irish legal system, civil service, military establishment, and a substantial ecclesiastical community. While these professionals dominated cultural life, residual landed gentry and the viceregal establishment at Dublin Castle wielded significant influence.

Provision of theatres in Huddersfield and Norwich was more limited. In the former, the Theatre Royal was constructed in 1861 but functioned primarily as a lecture room until rebuilt as a dedicated theatre in 1880;[45] the Huddersfield Hippodrome opened in 1905. Huddersfield's catchment area was much smaller than that of either Birmingham or Dublin: 'satellite towns' were smaller and fewer, and many other competing towns lay close by (Halifax, Wakefield, Leeds, Bradford, Rochdale and Oldham are all within 20 miles). Conversely, Huddersfield's geographical position made it a popular destination since it was *en route* to many other theatres in the West Riding of Yorkshire and Lancashire. In Norwich there was only one theatre, another patent, opened in 1758. Satellite communities were small and few, but, unlike Huddersfield, Norwich was isolated geographically. Great Yarmouth and Lowestoft are over 20 miles away and the

---

44 Source: National Censuses. The comparisons are imperfect as civic boundaries were periodically redefined; Birmingham, for example, incorporated several adjoining suburbs at the end of the nineteenth century. The trends, however, are clear.

45 See Stanley Chadwick, *Theatre Royal: The Romance of the Huddersfield Stage* (Huddersfield, 1941).

nearest towns with significant cultural activity, Ipswich and Cambridge, are 40 and 60 miles distant respectively.

Population growth was only one of many factors influencing provision of venues: devolution of licensing to local authorities, changing social attitudes to theatre attendance, economic conditions and particular local circumstances all played significant roles. It is notable, for example, that Dublin, despite only a modest growth in population, experienced an expansion of theatre provision comparable to that of Birmingham, a development which must be attributable to factors peculiar to the city.

Access to theatres varied considerably. In 1875 the greater part of the audience would have lived in the immediate vicinity and would either walk or travel by carriage; suburban access was more restricted as public transport was less comprehensive. By 1887, however, it was possible for many residents in the greater Birmingham area (up to 10 miles from the city centre) to attend the theatre as the last trains on most lines left at about 11pm; in Dublin provision was less generous with only some routes offering late evening services, but in Huddersfield such trains were only provided on certain days of the week, while in Norwich there were no late evening services at all.[46] In the late Victorian period tram services were launched in all four towns but again provision was variable. In Birmingham and Dublin trams appeared in the 1870s and both networks were extensive by 1900; Huddersfield established the country's first municipal service in 1882, but trams only arrived in Norwich in 1900.[47]

Birmingham and Dublin were usually visited by at least one company each year. In Huddersfield one visit was normative, with occasional fallow years and biannual visits. In Norwich, where the theatres often operated in difficult circumstances, fallow years were more common although there is only one substantive gap, from April 1901 to October 1905; biannual visits also occurred.[48] Although trends can be outlined there are frequent variations, exacerbated by gaps in press coverage which render a complete survey impractical. In Tables 4.4 to 4.6,

---

46 Information collated from *Bradshaw's August 1887 Railway Guide* (Newton Abbot, 1968).

47 The challenge of late-night travel was ubiquitous; of a performance of *Tristan und Isolde* given by Beecham in Manchester on 19 May 1916 the *Musical Standard* commented: 'Though the curtain rose on Wagner's masterpiece soon after seven o'clock, the end was not in sight until long after eleven p.m. Last trains Cheshire-wards left at eleven-twenty and thus cut off the glorious finale, which no one would miss for worlds. At the station, feeling ran high. One lady … came out with a startling military swear-word. A man who arrived breathless a few minutes before the last train, laughed out aloud, as he recognised a whole platform full of people in the same plight. Each arrival asked of the last whether he or they had heard the end. None had.' (27 May 1916, p. 394).

48 For further commentary, see Michael and Carole Blackwell, *Norwich, Theatre Royal* ([United Kingdom], 2007), pp. 73–82.

Table 4.4 Opera seasons in Birmingham, Dublin, Huddersfield and Norwich in 1876

Week commencing	**Town, theatre, length of season**	**Company**
21 February	Huddersfield, Theatre Royal, 2 weeks	Charles Durand
13 March	Dublin, Theatre Royal, 3 weeks	Campobello Italian
10 April	Norwich, Theatre Royal, 4 weeks	Charles Durand
16 May	Birmingham, Theatre Royal, 1 week	Carl Rosa
16 May	Huddersfield, Theatre Royal, 3 nights	Campobello Italian
23 May	Huddersfield, Theatre Royal, 4 nights	Campobello Italian
19 June	Dublin, Queen's Theatre, 2 weeks	Telma-Walsham
7 August	Dublin, Gaiety Theatre, 2 weeks	Blanche Cole
4 September	Norwich, Theatre Royal, 1 week	Crystal Palace (Blanche Cole)
24 September	Dublin, Theatre Royal, 2 weeks	Her Majesty's Italian (Mapleson)
24 September	Huddersfield, Theatre Royal, 4 nights	Imperial Italian (Signor De Rialp)
17 October	Birmingham, Theatre Royal, 1 week	Her Majesty's Italian (Mapleson)
11 December	Birmingham, Theatre Royal, 1 week	Carl Rosa

Sources: *Era*; *FJ*; *HC*; *BDP*.

opera performances are summarised in years from the beginning, middle and end of the period: 1876, 1896 and 1916.

In 1876 Norwich (five weeks) and Dublin (nine weeks) were unusually well served by touring companies and saw more opera than either Birmingham or Huddersfield. Large and enthusiastic audiences made Dublin an attractive destination,[49] despite the extra travelling expenses. By contrast, the population of Birmingham was chastised by local critics for its failure to support Mapleson's troupe:

49 See Rodmell, 'The Italians are Coming'.

Table 4.5 Opera seasons in Birmingham, Dublin, Huddersfield and Norwich in 1896

Week commencing	Town, theatre, length of season	Company
26 December (1895)	Dublin, Leinster Hall, 8 weeks	Arthur Rousbey
6 January	Norwich, Theatre Royal, 1 week	Valentine Smith
23 March	Birmingham, Queen's, 1 week	Neilson
6 April	Birmingham, Grand, 4 weeks	James Turner
6 April	Norwich, Theatre Royal, 2 weeks	Arthur Rousbey
29 June	Dublin, Queen's Royal, 1 week	Neilson
17 August	Dublin, Gaiety, 4 weeks	Carl Rosa
28 September	Dublin, Leinster Hall, 4 weeks	Neilson
26 December	Dublin, Leinster Hall, 5 weeks	Arthur Rousbey

Sources: *Era*; *Stage*; *BDP*; *HC*; *FJ*.

> To the disgrace of the town, however, the inhabitants of which pride themselves on being music-lovers of a high degree, the attendance has been ridiculously small compared with the merits of the company.[50]

> The attendance, though somewhat larger than on the first evening, was not, we regret to say, very satisfactory. The Birmingham musical public evidently believe more in artistes than in music, and are attracted rather by names than by things.[51]

Twenty years later the pattern of seasons had not changed much other than in the disappearance of the Italian language companies (see below). Long seasons by Arthur Rousbey in Dublin contributed to a total of 17 weeks of opera performances, dwarfing Birmingham's five weeks, and three weeks in Norwich. For Huddersfield 1896 was a fallow year. Also notable is the absence of the Rosa company from Birmingham: it did not visit the town between December 1895 and March 1899, a remarkable gap even allowing for Birmingham's unsympathetic reputation.

Performances in 1916 were inevitably affected by the war. Despite difficulties, opera companies appeared in three of the towns; in this year there were no performances in Norwich. Dublin still enjoyed the best provision despite the additional encumbrances of hazardous sea crossings[52] and the Easter Uprising,

[50] *Era*, 8 October 1876, p. 6

[51] *BDP*, 19 October 1876, p. 6, of the performance of *Lucia da Lammermoor* on 17 October; Lucia was played by Alwina Valleria.

[52] Disrupting shipping between Ireland and Great Britain was not a priority for the German navy, which concentrated its activity on the North Sea and trans-Atlantic traffic,

Table 4.6 Opera seasons in Birmingham, Dublin, Huddersfield and Norwich in 1916

Week commencing	Town, theatre, length of season	Company
28 February	Dublin, Gaiety, 2 weeks	Harrison Frewin
3 April	Huddersfield, Theatre Royal, 1 week	Harrison Frewin
28 August	Dublin, Queen's Royal, 2 weeks	Brisan
30 October	Dublin, Gaiety, 2 weeks	Carl Rosa
4 December	Huddersfield, Theatre Royal, 1 week	O'Mara
4 December	Birmingham, Prince of Wales, 1 week	Carl Rosa
11 December	Birmingham, Repertory, 1 week	Raybould's *Sumida River*

Sources: *Era*; *Stage*.

which was followed for several weeks by an evening curfew. Although conditions were less than ideal, the Carl Rosa played in Dublin for two weeks in November to good audiences.[53] Provision of opera in Birmingham remained limited for so large a city. The performances of Raybould's *Sumida River* in December were an atypical addition, and attributable to his being a local composer.

Although the pattern of performances varied each year, the overall arrangement was consistent. Dublin attracted touring companies due to supportive audiences, with only Manchester and Liverpool equalling or exceeding it; for many years a biannual pattern was followed with an opera season in late August heralding the end of the summer holidays, and a post-Christmas season of equal popularity. Birmingham, by contrast, was a challenging environment; there is no obvious explanation although the more irregular distribution of seasons across the year cannot have helped. Late autumn was popular, but not observed consistently, and only James Turner, lessee of the Grand Theatre from 1893 to 1906, ran longer seasons.[54] Provision in Huddersfield and Norwich remained modest; the timing of seasons was unpredictable and substantial gaps occurred as neither town was a high priority for touring companies. Before 1900 Arthur Rousbey was the most frequent visitor to Norwich; the Carl Rosa seems only to have appeared there in 1899 and 1900, and the Moody-Manners typically sent its smaller 'B' troupe. Huddersfield was visited by a greater variety of

but attacks occurred sporadically.

53 See *Stage*, 2 November 1916, p. 10, and 9 November, p. 3.

54 Turner gave seasons lasting at least four weeks on many occasions between 1890 and 1904, typically starting just after Christmas; his longest lasted 11 weeks, commencing on Boxing Day 1893.

companies, with the Carl Rosa appearing several times in the 1880s and 1900s, but visits by all were irregular and it is the cumulative provision that gave the town more frequent performances than Norwich.

Repertory and Performance Practice

With few exceptions, the language of performance in provincial opera was English. When local stock companies gave operas the repertory was initially indigenous and, as foreign operas, such as those by Rossini, Mozart and Weber, were introduced, they were performed in the translations used in London.[55] Gradually stars of London's Italian companies ventured into the provinces, with Italian opera being advertised as the latest fashionable entertainment – and more exclusive, for premium prices were invariably charged – such that a modicum of metropolitan sophistication could be enjoyed in the provincial hinterlands.[56] The visits of Italian companies remained sporadic until the 1850s when Mapleson started organising tours to the largest towns on a regular basis, a practice he maintained for the next 20 years. In 1875 theatre-goers in such places as Manchester, Glasgow, and Dublin were as likely to see opera performed in Italian as in English (see Table 4.2); in smaller centres, however, English was invariably used.

By the late 1870s the appeal of Italian opera was waning. The 1875 Gye/Benedict tour lost money heavily, deterring Benedict from touring again.[57] Mapleson toured the United Kingdom in 1876 but then crossed the Atlantic and did not mount any further provincial tours until 1886 and 1887 after which he abandoned them for good. In Mapleson's wake, Augustus Harris organised Italian

---

[55] In Birmingham the first traced performances of foreign operas are of *Don Giovanni* and *The Marriage of Figaro* in October 1819 (both presented in Henry Bishop's adaptations, the latter as *The Libertine*), *The Barber of Seville* in August 1822 (also adapted by Bishop), and *Der Freischütz* in October 1824 (see playbills of the Theatre Royal, Birmingham, BL, shelfmark mic.c.13137/playbills).

[56] The first 'Italian' performances in Birmingham were in November 1827 (*Il barbiere di Siviglia* and *Il turco in Italia*) and in October 1829 in Dublin (*Il Turco in Italia, La gazza laddra, Tancredi, Otello, L'italiani in Algeri*, and Paer's *Agnese*).

[57] Although always referred to in the press as Gye's tour, he had no direct involvement in its management. Gye only mounted opera outside London in 1857, during the reconstruction of Covent Garden. Towards the 1875 tour's end Gye noted: 'Benedict came and complained very much of the bad engagements which Vianesi [the conductor] had made for the tournée and of his great neglect in making the various arrangements for the band, chorus, &c &c. to which he (B[enedict]) attributed his large loss on the speculation which he said would be near £3,000.' (Gye's diary, 8 December 1875, ROHA). Albani and some other artists gave a concert in the Albert Hall to help Benedict; Gye allowed him to repay his debts by regular salary deduction in 1876.

tours in 1888, 1893 and 1894.[58] The Grand Opera Syndicate, which after 1896 was the only organisation capable of mounting a similar venture, showed no interest in operating anywhere other than at Covent Garden and so, after 1894, foreign-language performances disappeared from the provinces with the exception of those given by the Castellano Grand Italian Opera Company, which commenced operations in 1909.[59] As overseas troupes rarely visited England (for exceptions see Chapter 3) and never ventured outside London, there was no other provision for the performance in a language other than English.[60]

Although English was the language of performance, the repertory in 1875 was dominated by Italian works familiar in the West End. Interest in Italian opera in the 1850s and '60s was such that all companies had to give works by Verdi, Donizetti, Bellini and Rossini in order to flourish. By 1875 French operas such as *Les Huguenots*, *Faust* and Auber's *Fra Diavolo* were also included. English-language companies also played native works, although the heyday of the early 1860s, when the Pyne-Harrison troupe performed new works by Balfe, Macfarren, Loder and Barnett, were long gone and the native operas given were largely reduced to the trio later known, disparagingly, as the 'English Ring': *The Bohemian Girl*, *Maritana* and *The Lily of Killarney*. Nevertheless, in the late 1870s Durand's troupe also performed *Satanella* and *The Rose of Castille*, both by Balfe, and Blanche Cole gave Balfe's *Puritan's Daughter* and Macfarren's *Robin Hood*. Other mid-century British operas were occasionally revived in subsequent decades.[61]

With the exception of the Rosa and Moody-Manners companies (see below), touring troupes tended to add new operas to their repertories only after they had been successful in London and, in this sense, the West End companies remained the primary developers of taste. The slow expansion of the repertory is not solely attributable to companies being overly cautious in the face of audience conservatism; while performances of such staples as *The Bohemian Girl* and *Faust* almost invariably drew large audiences, there were additional costs associated with producing new or neglected works. Although sets and costumes were commonly reused, new orchestral parts and perhaps a translation of the libretto would be required, and rights of representation had to be secured. With popular operas the last of these could be expensive and it was not unusual for companies to retain

58 Harris allegedly lost £4,000 on the 1888 tour; see Luigi Arditi *My Reminiscences* (London, 1896), p. 269.

59 It included English-language performances from 1913, was renamed the Castellano English Opera company in 1915, and collapsed shortly afterwards.

60 The only traced exceptions are the ill-fated Russian tour in 1888 (see Chapter 2) and some war-time Beecham performances when a pragmatic decision was made to perform some foreign operas in their original language.

61 For example, Rosa gave Wallace's *Lurline* in 1878 and 1890, and Balfe's *The Siege of Rochelle* in 1877 and 1879, as did James Turner in 1892. Turner also gave *Robin Hood*, *Satanella* and *The Rose of Castile*; the last of these was also performed occasionally by Rousbey and Gilbert. The Moody-Manners revived Wallace's *Amber Witch* in 1899.

exclusive rights of performance for many years in order to draw as much profit as possible from their monopoly.[62]

It was the biggest companies that normally took these risks, indeed, they needed to do so to maintain their reputations as leaders of the field, and the reduced number of novelties and revivals given by the Rosa in the 1890s after the dynamism of the previous decade contributed to a perception of lost impetus. Even in his enterprise's earliest years Rosa had tried out several new or forgotten operas. Up to 1880 these included Cowen's *Pauline* (see Chapter 6) and Hérold's *Zampa* (1876); *Der fliegende Holländer*, Auber's *Masaniello*, and Brüll's *The Golden Cross* (1877); Thomas's *Mignon*, and *Carmen* (1879); and *Lohengrin*, *Aïda*, Goetz's *The Taming of the Shrew* and Flotow's *Stradella* (1880). The Moody-Manners troupe was less adventurous but nevertheless performed Halévy's *La Juive* (1900); *L'étoile du nord* and *Siegfried* (1901); *La Gioconda* (1903); and *Eugene Onegin* (1906); and gave the first provincial performances of both *Madama Butterfly* (1907) and *Tosca* (1909). Many of these works were only performed in larger towns and were dropped after one or two seasons, just as works were dropped by the West End companies. The economics of provincial touring made the establishment of a new work particularly challenging as this meant, in effect, a premiere every week as companies moved from town to town. In a week's residency comprising up to eight performances, even one set of poor takings could be problematic if repeated on a weekly basis – that the Grand Opera companies played works on a repertory basis heightened this problem, as a substantial part of the audience, which might attend perhaps a maximum of three performances in a week, generally preferred to spend money on familiar works certain to entertain. Only new works that came with some form of perceived reliability, for example composer reputation or evidence of popularity elsewhere, were safe choices.

Arising from these pressures, smaller troupes especially were bound to a much more restricted repertory, often leading to accusations of staleness. James Turner addressed this criticism:

> Sometimes critics will complain that our repertory contains too large a proportion of hackneyed old favourites. The fact is, that to obtain novelties worthy of our efforts, or even obtain permission to perform some well-known masterpieces, would be so costly as to be prohibitive. It is an essential condition of the existence of my company that it must pay.[63]

---

62 See above regarding the legal creation of the 'right of representation'. On floatation in 1887, the Rosa Company claimed the exclusive rights of representation of 25 operas in its financial assets; in many cases this was the right to use a particular translation or to perform the opera in English (see Chapter 2, note 54).

63 *Era*, 21 May 1892, p. 10; Turner acknowledged Rosa's generosity in allowing him to perform several operas for which Rosa had exclusive rights.

Table 4.7 Selected operas performed in Birmingham by the Turner Opera Company

Dates and Venue	Operas Performed (titles in bold not performed in seasons listed in Table 4.8)
4 January to 27 February 1892 (eight weeks), Grand Theatre	*Maritana*; *The Bohemian Girl*; *The Lily of Killarney*; *Il Trovatore*; *Faust*; *Martha*; *Don Giovanni*; *La Sonnambula*; *Fra Diavolo*; *Lucia da Lammermoor*; ***Der Freischütz***; ***Robin Hood***; ***The Siege of Rochelle***.
24 to 29 November 1902 (one week), Grand Theatre	*Maritana*; *The Bohemian Girl*; *The Lily of Killarney*; *Carmen*; *The Puritan's Daughter*; *Satanella*.
27 March to 1 April 1911 (one week), Palace Theatre, Bordesley	*Maritana*; *The Bohemian Girl*; *Il Trovatore*; *Faust*; *Martha*; ***Tannhäuser***; ***La Figlia del Regiment***.

Sources: *Era* and *Stage*[64]

Unsurprisingly, therefore, a comparison of Turner's repertory in selected Birmingham seasons between 1892 and 1911 (Table 4.7) shows few changes when compared to the operas listed in Table 4.8 below. Works added to the repertory were all in familiar styles even if not well known.

On forming his company in 1915, Harrison Frewin stated:

> I must admit that I would prefer to conduct *Tristan and Isolde* to *The Bohemian Girl*; but nevertheless I would rather see a house full of happy, contented people who were thoroughly enjoying themselves than a few disgruntled enthusiasts with scores in their hands and fads in their heads scattered about a discontented-looking theatre.[65]

Nevertheless, he endeavoured to extend his repertory beyond standard operas, and delivered on his promise to give the premieres of his own *Gay Lothario* and Barkworth's *Romeo and Juliet*, and to mount Bruneau's lesser-known *L'attaque du Moulin*, Halévy's *La Juive*, and the staged version of *Elijah* he had produced while employed by the Moody-Manners Company.

An analysis of the operas performed in the seasons listed in Tables 4.4 to 4.6 confirms the existence of a small and stable core repertory (Table 4.8). In 1876 *Il Trovatore*, *Faust*, *Le nozze di Figaro*, *Lucia di Lammermoor* and *La Sonnambula* were virtually essential (and equally popular in the West End), with *The Bohemian Girl* and *Maritana* also obligatory for the English-language companies. To this core was added works of a similar nature, many by the same composers.

64 Of the 1902 season: 'Wisely enough, the present week is wisely devoted to old and well-tried friends ... Surely a generous, if familiar programme' (*Stage*, 27 November 1902, p. 3).

65 *MS*, 24 July 1915, p. 69.

Table 4.8 Operas performed in Birmingham, Dublin, Huddersfield and Norwich, 1876, by company

Performed by more than one company: Key: Ca – Campobello Italian; Co – Blanche Cole; D – Charles Durand; I – Italian Imperial; M – Mapleson Italian (Her Majesty's); R – Carl Rosa; T – Telma-Walsham				
Opera	Birmingham	Dublin	Huddersfield	Norwich
Balfe *The Bohemian Girl*	R	Co; T	D	Co; D
Balfe *The Rose of Castile*		Co	D	D
Bellini *La Sonnambula*		Ca; T	Ca; D	D
Donizetti *Lucia di Lammermoor*	M	Co; M	Ca	
Gounod *Faust*	M; R	Ca; Co; M	Ca	D
Mozart *Don Giovanni*	M	M	I	
Mozart *Le nozze di Figaro*		Ca; Co; M	I	
Verdi *La Traviata*	M	Ca	I	
Verdi *Il Trovatore*	R	Ca; Co; M; T	Ca; D; I	Co; D
Wallace *Maritana*	R	Ca;[1] Co; T	D	Co; D
Performed by one company only:				
Campobello:	Flotow *Martha*; Meyerbeer *Les Huguenots*; Mozart *Die Zauberflöte*; Rossini *Guillaume Tell*[2]			
Blanche Cole:	Auber *Masaniello*; Balfe *The Puritan's Daughter*			
Charles Durand:	Auber *Fra Diavolo*; Balfe *Satanella*; Rossini *La Cenerentola*; Ricci *The Brewer of Preston*[3]			
Italian Imperial:	(none)			
Mapleson:	Bellini *Norma*; Donizetti *Lucrezia Borgia*; Rossini *Il Barbiere di Siviglia*; *Semiramide*; Verdi *Rigoletto*			
Carl Rosa:	Benedict *The Lily of Killarney*; Cherubini *Les deux journées*; Cowen *Pauline*; Hérold *Zampa*;			
Telma-Walsham:	Wallace *Lurline*			

Notes to table: [1] Given in Italian (*FJ*, 22 March 1876, p. 1). [2] Performed only in Dublin on 25 March and claimed as a premiere (*Era*, 2 April 1876, p. 6). [3] Originally *Il birrajo di Preston* (1847).

Sources: *Era*; *BDP*; *HC*; *FJ*.

Table 4.9 Operas performed in Birmingham, Dublin, Huddersfield and Norwich in 1896

Operas in the repertory of more than one company:	
Balfe *The Bohemian Girl* Benedict *The Lily of Killarney* Donizetti *La fille du regiment* Gounod *Faust* Leoncavallo *Pagliacci* Mascagni *Cavalleria Rusticana* Mozart *Le nozze di Figaro* and *Don Giovanni* Verdi *Il Trovatore* Wallace *Maritana*	
Operas in the repertory of one company only:	
Company	Operas
Rosa	Bizet *Carmen*; Collinge *Grace Darrell*; Godard *La Vivandière*; Thomas *Mignon*; Wagner *Der fliegende Holländer*, *Die Meistersinger*, *Lohengrin* and *Tannhäuser*.
Rousbey	Adam *Le Chalet*; Auber *Fra Diavolo*; Donizetti *Lucia di Lammermoor*; Flotow *Martha*; Pellegrini *Mercedes*.
Turner	Auber *La Dame Blanche*; Macfarren *Robin Hood*; Verdi *Rigoletto*; Weber *Der Freischütz*.
Neilson and Valentine Smith	none

Sources: *Era*; *Stage*; *BDP*; *HC*, *FJ*

Twenty years later there had been few changes (Table 4.9). *Cavalleria Rusticana* and *Pagliacci* were added while Donizetti, Rossini, Bellini and Meyerbeer were largely expunged. Several other works were revived regularly, including *Martha*, *Fra Diavolo*, *Don Giovanni*, and *Robin Hood*. Rousbey showed a sense of adventure in giving Adam's *Le Chalet* and the world premiere of Pellegrini's *Mercedes*,[66] while the Rosa company added *La Vivandière* to its repertory and obliged a local Dublin composer, F.C. Collinge, by giving his *Grace Darrell* (see Chapter 6). In view of the practical challenges it is unsurprising that only the Rosa gave Wagner's operas, although Rousbey added *Tannhäuser* to his repertory in 1897. The importance of performing rights is shown by the Rosa's apparent monopoly on English-language presentations of *Carmen*: despite its being one of the most popular operas of the time, no performances by any other company have

[66] The opera was described as 'distinctly and emphatically a success … [it] is nothing if not melodious … though the music rarely shows genius, there is not a weak bar in it from beginning to end' (*MS*, 18 January 1896, p. 42).

Table 4.10 Operas performed in Birmingham, Dublin, Huddersfield and Norwich in 1916

Operas in the repertory of more than one company:	
Balfe *The Bohemian Girl* Benedict *The Lily of Killarney* Bizet *Carmen* Gounod *Faust* Leoncavallo *Pagliacci* Mascagni *Cavalleria Rusticana* Verdi *Il Trovatore* Wagner *Tannhäuser* Wallace *Maritana*	
Operas in the repertory of one company only:	
Company	Operas
Harrison Frewin	Barkworth *Romeo and Juliet*; Halévy *La Juive*; Verdi *La Traviata* and *Rigoletto.*
Joseph O'Mara	Puccini *Madame Butterfly*
Carl Rosa	Mozart *Die Zauberflöte* and *Le nozze di Figaro*; Offenbach *The Tales of Hoffman*; Verdi *Aïda*

Sources: *Era*; *Stage*; *IT*; Huddersfield Theatre Royal archives

been traced before Charles Manners included it in his tour in 1900. Turner appears to have given the opera from 1902 onwards.[67]

In 1916 the repertory had contracted slightly, as companies inclined to popular works in order to ensure survival. The core operas were mainly the same as 40 years earlier with the addition of *Tannhäuser*. 'Peripheral' works were reduced in number but most companies tried to monopolise at least one opera to distinguish them from their competitors although not all works appeared in all towns. Frewin, for example, did not give *L'attaque du moulin* in Dublin in 1916, replacing it with *La Traviata.*[68]

It would be wrong to infer that the 'operatic diet' outside London was stagnant; in Dublin and Birmingham especially, and other large cities, many works were given but very few appeared more than two or three times (Table 4.11). In Huddersfield and Norwich such occurrences were far fewer, but not unknown.

Table 4.11 shows the unplanned way in which new operas appeared in particular towns; as works were usually dropped within a couple of years, it was easy to 'miss out' if the relevant company did not visit; *Falstaff* was performed in Birmingham because Harris included the town in the relevant tour but, as he did not visit Dublin, audiences in the Irish capital did not see Verdi's last opera; the

67 The Italian version used by Mapleson and Harris was subject to different rights.

68 *IT*, 11 March 1916, p .5.

Table 4.11 Premieres of selected operas in Birmingham and Dublin 1875–1918

Opera	**First performance and company**	
Key: B – Beecham; D – Denhof; H – Harris; Ma – Mapleson; Mo – Moody-Manners; Q – Quinlan; R – Carl Rosa		
	Birmingham	Dublin
Bizet *Carmen*[1]	5 May 1879 (Soldene)	9 September 1878 (Ma)
Boïto *Mefistofele*	16 October 1884 (R)	21 August 1884 (R)
Charpentier *Louise*	18 November 1912 (Q)	31 December 1912 (Q)
Corder *Nordisa*[2]	22 February 1887 (R)	18 August 1887 (R)
Cowen *Pauline*	11 December 1876 (R)	Not performed
Cowen *Thorgrim*	24 October 1890 (R)	1 September 1890 (R)
Debussy *Pelléas et Mélisande*	19 September 1913 (D)	Not performed before 1918
Glinka *A Life for the Tsar*[3]	26 July 1888 (Russian)	Not performed before 1918
Goetz *The Taming of the Shrew*	27 November 1897 (R)	7 April 1880 (R)
Humperdinck *Hänsel und Gretel*	28 May 1895 (R)	15 August 1895 (R)
Leoncavallo *Pagliacci*[4]	16 October 1893 (R)	23 August 1893 (R)
MacCunn *Jeanie Deans*	12 December 1894 (R)	12 September 1895 (R)
Macfarren *Robin Hood*	28 November 1877 (R)	22 August 1877 (R)
Mackenzie *Colomba*[5]	18 October 1883 (R)	2 May 1883 (R)
Mascagni *Cavalleria Rusticana*[6]	16 January 1893 (Turner)	15 August 1892 (R)
Massenet *Manon*	13 October 1885 (R)	20 August 1885 (R)
Mussorgsky *Boris Godunov*	14 May 1917* (B)	Not performed before 1918
Puccini *La Bohème*	16 September 1907* (Mo)	25 August 1897 (R)
Puccini *La fanciulla del West*	6 November 1911* (Q)	4 January 1912 (Q)
Puccini *Madama Butterfly*[7]	16 September 1907* (Mo)	2 January 1908 (Mo)
Puccini *Tosca*	21 May 1917* (B)	31 December 1909 (Mo)
Rimsky-Korsakov *Le coq d'or*	20 November 1918 (B)	Not performed before 1918
Saint-Saëns *Samson et Dalila*[8]	24 October 1910 (Mo)	11 January 1910 (Mo)

Opera	First performance and company	
Stanford *The Canterbury Pilgrims*	20 May 1884 (R)	19 August 1884 (R)
Stanford *Much Ado About Nothing*	Not performed	2 January 1902 (Mo)
Strauss *Elektra*	16 September 1913 (D)	Not performed before 1918
Strauss *Der Rosenkavalier*	20 September 1913 (D)	Not performed before 1918
Sullivan *Ivanhoe*	30 May 1895 (R)	7 September 1895 (R)
Tchaikovsky *Eugene Onegin*	30 April 1906 (Mo)	11 January 1907 (Mo)
Tchaikovsky *Mazeppa*	10 September 1888 (Russian)	Not performed before 1918
Thomas *Mignon*[9]	23 October 1879 (R)	18 August 1879 (R)
Thomas (Goring) *Esmeralda*[10]	10 October 1883 (R)	27 April 1883 (R)
Thomas (Goring) *Nadeshda*	18 February 1886 (R)	26 August 1885 (R)
Verdi *Aïda*	28 November 1888 (H)	13 November 1888 (H)
Verdi *Otello*	1 June 1893 (R)	2 September 1893 (R)
Verdi *Falstaff*	Not performed before 1918	11 October 1894 (H)
Wagner *Der fliegende Holländer*	17 April 1877 (R)	9 August 1877 (R)
Wagner *Götterdämmerung*	3 May 1913 (Q)	16 May 1913 (Q)
Wagner *Lohengrin*[11]	17 October 1881 (R)	11 October 1875 (Gye)
Wagner *Die Meistersinger*	20 September 1909* (Mo)	10 October 1894 (H)
Wagner *Das Rheingold*	30 April 1913 (Q)	12 May 1913 (Q)
Wagner *Rienzi*	30 May 1894 (R)	8 September 1894 (R)
Wagner *Siegfried*	11 September 1901 (Mo)	6 December 1901 (R)
Wagner *Tannhäuser*[12]	4 June 1893 (R)	30 August 1893 (R)
Wagner *Tristan und Isolde*	23 March 1899 (R)	29 November 1901 (R)
Wagner *Die Walküre*	6 November 1911* (Q)	5 January 1912 (Q)

* week commencing; date unconfirmed.

Notes to Table 4.11: [1] First performed at Huddersfield, 20 October 1881 (R); Norwich in the week commencing 16 April 1900 (R). [2] Huddersfield, 11 May 1888 (R). [3] Huddersfield, 2 August 1888 (Russian). [4] Huddersfield, 2 March 1894 (Rousbey). [5] Huddersfield, 13 December 1883 (R). [6] Huddersfield, 8 May 1893 (Rousbey); Norwich, 10 April 1893 (Rousbey). [7] Huddersfield, 8 December 1916 (O'Mara); Norwich, week commencing 21 September

1908 (Mo). [8] Huddersfield, 4 April 1910 (Mo); Norwich, week commencing 3 October 1910 (Mo). [9] Huddersfield, 19 October 1881 (R). [10] Huddersfield, 11 December 1883 (R). [11] Huddersfield, 21 September 1881 (R); Norwich, 30 August 1899 (R). [12] Huddersfield, 13 January 1902 (R); Norwich, 1 September 1899 (R).
Sources: *Era*; *Stage*; *BDP*; *IT*; *FJ*.

converse applies to *Die Meistersinger*.[69] First performances sometimes came in a rush, perhaps resulting in audience fatigue: in Birmingham the first performances of *Elektra*, *Der Rosenkavalier* and *Pelléas et Mélisande* took place within five days. Table 4.11 also shows the extent to which the Rosa and Moody-Manners companies controlled the expansion of the repertory before 1910. With the vast majority of new operas being introduced by these two troupes, local audience experiences depended hugely on management decisions within these organisations.

Only after 1910, when Quinlan and Denhof entered the fray, was the Rosa and Moody-Manners's control of the provincial repertory broken. The newcomers brought many operas to the country's biggest cities for the first time and emphasised their companies' size and ability to perform works previously seen only in the West End.

Ernst Denhof's original mission was to mount the first performances in Edinburgh of *Der Ring*. Although he had long organised concerts in the city,[70] he only ventured into operatic management in March 1910, making extensive use of artists from Richter's production at Covent Garden (see Chapter 3). The scale and financial risk were audacious:

> The circumstances of the production are remarkable and, indeed, may be fairly said to constitute a 'record' in the history of dramatic speculation in Scotland ... An orchestra of nearly eighty, made up of nearly all the Scottish Orchestra, supplemented by some extra instrumentalists from Covent Garden, has been engaged ... The costumes and the scenery have been specially made for the production in Germany. The cost of the entire production is estimated locally at between £8,500 and £10,000 ... What is most remarkable of all, however, is that the production ... has been worked out by a local pianoforte teacher, Mr Ernst Denhof. Unsupported by any guarantee, and unaided by any committee, he has worked out all the details ... and, as far as can be judged by appearances, with reasonable prospects of financial success.[71]

69 The most curious instance is that Huddersfield was one of only six towns in the United Kingdom to see Russian opera before the Great War; see Chapter 2.

70 Denhof appeared as a pianist in London in 1890 and in Edinburgh in 1893 (*MW*, 28 June 1890, p. 517, and *MO*, 1 November 1893, p. 94); he organised chamber concerts in Edinburgh from 1897.

71 *Stage*, 3 March 1910, p. 16. The chorus came mainly from the Rosa troupe, with the addition of 'specially selected singers from the local choral societies in Edinburgh' (*Stage*,

Despite the risks, Denhof was successful, showing that, in favourable circumstances, large-scale operations could pay. Encouraged, he then mounted performances of *Der Ring* in Leeds, Manchester and Glasgow in spring 1911,[72] and *Elektra, Die Meistersinger, Tristan und Isolde, Der fliegende Holländer* and *Orfeo* in spring 1912 at Hull, Liverpool, Manchester, Leeds, Glasgow and Edinburgh.[73] In autumn 1913 he undertook his most ambitious project, a provincial tour intended to take in Birmingham, Manchester, Sheffield, Leeds, Liverpool, Newcastle, Edinburgh, Aberdeen and Glasgow, and a repertory comprising all the operas above plus *Der Rosenkavalier*, *Pelléas et Mélisande*, and *Die Zauberflöte*. The Denhof troupe numbered over 200, making it the biggest touring opera company in the country's history, and included an orchestra of up to 82 drawn from the Scottish, Covent Garden, Beecham and London Symphony Orchestras, a chorus of 90, and ballet of 24; Thomas Beecham was one of the two conductors.[74]

Unfortunately Denhof miscalculated and, within three weeks of the tour starting, it collapsed with reported losses of over £4,000. Despite previous successes Denhof was castigated for embarking 'recklessly upon an enterprise that he had not the means to carry through'.[75] Opening in Birmingham on 15 September, cautious optimism that 'the fortnight's visit will attract all the patronage it deserves' was tempered by ticket prices being up to five time as high as usual.[76] Perhaps Denhof should have remembered Birmingham's reputation for ambivalent support of opera, not least after he was unable to mount *Der Ring* there in 1911. He should also have noted that Quinlan had given the complete cycle for the first time just six months earlier (see below). Audiences were poor;[77] the company transferred to Manchester, where attendances were as bad and, before the end of the first week, Denhof could not pay all the wages due. On Friday 3 October the troupe was told that it would cease operations after the two Saturday performances and, that evening, Denhof refused to appear before the curtain despite a sympathetic audience.[78] Beecham dashed from London with a promise to rescue the company,

10 March, p. 3). The Rosa Company played other operas in the same theatre on non-*Ring* evenings. See *MG*, 24 February, p. 10, for further discussion of the scheme's genesis.

72 *The Times*, 29 March 1911, p. 7; 3 April, p. 10; and *Stage*, 6 April, p. 23. Denhof appealed for guarantees in Birmingham and Newcastle but to no avail (see *MT*, 1 October 1910, p. 660, and 1 November, p. 738).

73 *MS*, 10 February 1912, p. 87.

74 *Stage*, 31 July 1913, p. 18.

75 *Stage*, 9 October 1913, p. 24.

76 *Stage*, 18 September 1913, p. 24; Denhof, however, stated that, although higher than standard theatre prices, his charges were the same as for his previous tours (*Observer*, 5 October 1913, p. 11).

77 *MT* stated: 'Although the public was blind to the fact, the Denhof operatic season at Birmingham was artistically an unqualified success, especially as regards the orchestra, which was the finest combination yet heard in opera in this city' (1 November 1913, p. 748).

78 There are several press accounts; *Stage*, 9 October 1913, p. 24, is representative.

and it appeared in Sheffield shortly afterwards and made most of its remaining planned appearances. Beecham was portrayed as a hero in the press but his rash financial commitment renewed tensions with his father, whom he had not consulted.[79] Denhof, chastened and humiliated, disappeared from public sight.[80]

The collapse of the company was the biggest and most high-profile since the difficulties in London in the 1880s; the sheer size of Denhof's operation had attracted the press, but so too had his enterprise in bringing new operas to a variety of provincial cities. The episode generated debate regarding the receptivity of non-metropolitan audiences, and to how such large undertakings could be made sustainable. Beecham gave a frank and provocative interview to the *Manchester Guardian*:

> He remarked that 'he had not much opinion of Manchester as a musical city, or indeed,' he added, sadly, 'of any part of the North of England ... I have no opinion of any town as a musical centre except London. London, of course, is so huge a place that we are bound to do better, simply because we have seven millions of population to draw on'.[81]

A few weeks later the rescued company returned to Manchester to much improved attendances; Beecham declared that, 'After all the terrible things I said ... three weeks ago I am almost ashamed of appearing before you tonight ... I am all the more gratified to say that, judging by our business in Manchester at the present time, it is the best we have done in our tour'.[82] Beecham reinterpreted these difficulties as a challenge and returned to Manchester during the war years, determined to foster a more consistent appreciation of opera among its citizens (see below).

Thomas Quinlan's company, which had a slightly smaller total complement of about 160, including an orchestra of 55, was equally ambitious but more stable and with a different *modus operandi*; in its short life it circumnavigated the globe twice and spent more time overseas than in the British Isles.[83] Its home appearances caused considerable interest, however, due to the inclusion of works in its repertory not seen outside London previously, including *La fanciulla del West* and *L'enfant prodigue* (both 1911) and *Louise* (1912); Wagner was also strongly represented and

---

79 For a full narrative of Beecham's involvement, see John Lucas, *Thomas Beecham: An Obsession with Music* (Woodbridge, 2008), pp. 102–7.

80 He gave a brief interview to the *Observer* (see note 76), stating that 'The people of Manchester and Birmingham would not support the enterprise so it is not possible to go on ... I think that grand opera will have to be confined to London. I wanted to give the public here a Covent Garden experience but Manchester has shown beyond all doubt that it will not support grand opera on a grand scale'. See also *MG*, 6 October 1913, p. 9.

81 Quoted in *MG*, 11 October 1913, p. 9.

82 Speech to the audience of the Theatre Royal, Manchester, quoted in *MG*, 4 November 1913, p. 8.

83 For coverage of the company's activities in Australia see Alison Gyger, *Opera for the Antipodes: Opera in Australia 1881-1939* (Sydney (Australia), 1990).

Quinlan gave the first performances of *Der Ring* in Liverpool, Birmingham, Dublin and Newcastle in spring 1913.[84] Although Quinlan was more prudent than Denhof, and always included several standard operas in his repertory, his focus on overseas touring proved his undoing as the outbreak of war inevitably made foreign travel much more difficult; Quinlan put his company into receivership in February 1915.[85]

The aspect of provincial performance hardest to document successfully, as in London, is how audiences saw and heard operas performed. Theatrical and musical memoirs inevitably focus on the bad, strange, accidental or farcical which, while amusing and sometimes informative, relate the exceptional rather than typical. Contemporaneous press reviews were extensive but often used coded language, leaving ambiguities for the historian:

> In such parts as that of Arline [in *The Bohemian Girl*] ... Miss [Julia] Gaylord had little more to do than look pretty, act gracefully, and sing sweetly, all of which she does, of course, as naturally as a duck swims. But the part of Mrs Ford [in *The Merry Wives of Windsor*] affords some scope for humour and delineation of character, and Miss Gaylord last night showed her appreciation of the fact ... by assuming a distinctive and consistent individuality, which added immensely to the charm and dramatic value of her performance. There was real finesse in the pretended struggle between modesty and love with which she first receives the amorous advances of the greasy knight, and her malicious delight and affected grief and indignation at the kindling suspicions of her jealous husband, marked the possession of genuine humour. The scene in which she mocks and defies the jealous fury of her husband in the second act was admirably rendered.[86]

> The Blanche Cole Company ... cannot perhaps, compare in magnitude of resources with some of the operatic troupes which periodically visit Birmingham, but the organisation is an excellent one so far as it goes and some of the principal artists are second to none who have appeared here in English opera ... The band, consisting of some five-and-twenty performers, was fairly adequate to the locale and the occasion, though an extra rehearsal would not, perhaps, have been superfluous.[87]

Reviews couched in more specific terms are unusual and typically note the whimsical, unexpected or inappropriate. While these comments, like those of theatrical memoirs, often deal with unrepresentative events, their immediacy lends them a greater degree of credibility:

---

[84] In addition to undermining Denhof's performances of *Der Ring* in Birmingham, the appearances by Quinlan's company may also have contributed to poor attendances during Denhof's visits to Liverpool and Newcastle after Beecham had taken the company over.

[85] *Stage*, 18 March 1915, p. 21.

[86] *BDP*, 22 November 1877, p. 8.

[87] *BDP*, 30 September 1879, p. 8.

[*Faust* (Mapleson, Birmingham, 1875):] The *mise-en-scène* was incongruously comic. The 'Kermesse' was backed up by a sort of Greek temple (which, at first sight, might have been taken for the Birmingham Town Hall), and buildings of hybrid architecture, while one Gothic wing was faced by an old English shop front with the legendary 'M. Brown, Butcher'. The church scene was represented by wings of a banqueting hall, with Norman arch at the back, seen through which was a table with a dingy red cloth, surmounted by a tea-tray with a painted cross. The brass band of the soldiers was evidently native talent, the big drum displaying the words 'Police Band' in gilt letters so that the scenic illusion was not entrancing.[88]

[*The Bohemian Girl* (Rosa, Huddersfield, 1881):] With the exception of the superb singing of Mr Barton McGuckin in the character of Thaddeus, the performance did not answer our expectations. Mr Ludwig … was too tremulous in his rendering of his principal songs, although he acted with all his old fire and verve … The disappointment of the night centred in the debutante Miss Frances Carr. This young lady has a sweet voice, and will no doubt make her way on the operatic stage, but for Mr Carl Rosa, on a fashionable night in Huddersfield to present a young lady for the first time before the patrons of opera, was certainly a bold adventure … we consider that great liberties were taken with the Huddersfield public in selecting this town for the debut of a girl in the character of Arline. The opera, throughout, lacked the spirit which only an experienced and talented soprano can infuse into it.[89]

[*Carmen* (Rosa, Birmingham, 1883)]: [Marie Roze's] Carmen combines all the pertness, vivacity, and coquettish abandon … with traits of tenderness, intensity, and nobility which are missed by too many representatives of the character. Whilst never wanting in becoming vigour and robustness, Madame Roze observes a certain measure of moderation in her rendering of the vulgar airs and graces of the fickle gypsy, which are necessary to raise the assumption to an artistic level … Her most cunning effects are achieved with an appearance of spontaneity which might be readily mistaken for momentary impulse … The confident smile, elastic step, and saucy swagger with which she enters in the first act, with hand on hip, mischievous rolling eyes, and her favourite rose between her lips, struck at the outset the key note of her assumption.[90]

[*Faust* (Turner, Birmingham, 1894):] Its production puts the company to a severe test, and while it serves to display the talent possessed by the combination, it

88 *MW*, 25 December 1875, p. 871. For a further example of the use of inappropriate local equipment, see Wood pp. 74–5, which relates the transformation of a wooden cow into the Commendatore's horse in *Don Giovanni*.

89 *HC*, 24 September 1881, p. 5.

90 *BDP*, 9 October 1883, p. 8.

also shows up the weaknesses and shortcomings. With the principals engaged in last night's performance there was little fault to be found ... The chorus also did its best but was not equal to the demands placed upon it ... In the great soldiers' chorus ... the valiant army of a dozen did wonders, but had to fall back upon the ladies to aid in the climax, being deprived of that auxiliary, the band on the stage ... It was in the orchestra that the shortcomings were most evident. Not that there was any bad playing. Far from that, all did well – but in the strings – having to do the work of many, there was an absence of that delicacy, combined with richness of tone, that should characterise the sensuous strains of Gounod's captivating music. So long as Mr Turner is content with an inadequate and incomplete orchestra so long must his enterprise be regarded as below those claiming first rank.[91]

[*Faust* (Moody-Manners, Dublin, 1900):] [Mr John Child's] 'make-up' [as Faust] was anything but suitable or attractive and ... he was greatly handicapped ... by his singularly unpicturesque and unbecoming costume ... The opera was fairly well mounted. Still there were many strange incongruities. When Mephistopheles [Charles Manners] sang the 'Calf of Gold' he stood on a modern, particularly up-to-date chair, which is not much in its way, but the absurdity could be easily avoided. The Garden Scene was made almost ridiculous by the fact that the bed of flowers to which Siebel has to direct attention was just like a little round specimen of a poor decorative device; then the use of electric light to intensify the flowers was a poor and meretricious kind of device in an opera of the kind; and finally the turning on of the limelight whenever Mme [Ella] Russell [as Marguerite] came on the scene was, no doubt, a well-intentioned performance, but in the case of the close of the garden scene it had simply a ridiculous effect. When she appeared at the window, what seemed like a miniature search-light was thrown on her, and the effect was almost ghostly. Certainly it was not artistic.[92]

[*The Bohemian Girl* (Moody-Manners, Dublin, 1900):] [Lizzie Burgess, as Arline] looked the part, and acted it with a grace, modesty and naturalness quite delightful ... The 'dream song' has never been given in Dublin more sweetly or sympathetically ... Mr Child is an ideal Thaddeus ... He sang 'When other lips' very beautifully and with all due sympathy and grace ... [On Charles Manners as Devilshoof:] No doubt in many respects his performance was good but he displayed an objectionable disposition to overdo the comic 'business' ... The climax of incongruity was certainly reached when in the drawing room scene he, to the amazement of the audience, stepped forward to the footlights and sang

91 *BDP*, 2 January 1894, p. 4.

92 *FJ*, 10 April 1900, p. 5; this journal's partiality is demonstrated by its contrast with the *Irish Times*'s review: 'The scenery and accessories and mounting of the opera generally were quite up to the requirements of the most exacting in those respects', although it did notice the lack of a band on stage for the soldiers' chorus (10 April 1900, p. 3).

> 'In cellar cool'. Why or wherefore he is not satisfied with what Balfe has written for the part is a mystery ... The proper place for the effort is obviously on the concert platform. But to drag it into *The Bohemian Girl* is enough to make poor Balfe rise from his grave in protest.[93]

Without more specific, consistent and explicit evidence it will remain difficult to gain a strong sense of the audience experience. London critics' reviews of the Rosa and Moody-Manners troupes in the Edwardian period sometimes accused them of such 'provincialisms' as a tendency for principal singers to come to the footlights for solo items (see Chapter 3), a practice for which Nellie Melba, however, was also criticised. Companies were undoubtedly much more 'accident-prone' than a century later and there was far greater scope for errors: rehearsals were fewer, orchestral standards lower, a more liberal interpretation of the score routine (particularly as regards cuts, and instruments absent from the orchestra), and there was rarely a unified production design. Above all there was great variability in *mise-en-scène* and stage business. Conversely, however, audiences and critics alike were far more indulgent of such 'imperfections' as long as the 'fundamentals', especially the principal singers, were found to be adequate: the greatest opprobrium was reserved for poor intonation and tone quality, weak or inappropriate 'characterisation', the presentation of tyros, and inadequate choruses and orchestras.

Finance

The finances of the touring troupes are largely unknown: most provincial companies existed for relatively short periods and their records have not survived. Press reports occasionally mention the affairs of the larger companies but give little detailed information (see note 3 regarding the Rosa company). There are, however, exceptions: the summary accounts of the Harrison Frewin and Phillips companies survive,[94] covering the period August 1916 to August 1918, and, despite their summative nature, give an insightful overview of the expenses incurred by a modestly sized company. Although the Phillips troupe in particular was adversely affected by the war, many details can reasonably be assumed to apply to touring companies throughout this period. Surviving records of the Theatre Royal, Huddersfield, give a further indication of touring company finances via box office receipts.

---

93 *FJ*, 17 April 1900, p. 5. 'In cellar cool' ('Im tiefen Keller') was composed in 1802 by Ludwig Fischer. The *Irish Times* was more allusive: 'The artiste was rather original at times, and it is doubtful whether some of his lines ever found a place in the libretto' (17 April 1900, p. 6).

94 The accounts are contained within the archive of Brett and L'Estrange, solicitors of Belfast, at the Public Records Office, Northern Ireland, deposit D1326/25/3. All subsequent references are drawn from this archive unless otherwise stated.

Frewin decided to form his own opera company in August 1914[95] – the early effects of the war did not deter him (see below). The company was officially registered on 6 March 1915,[96] and acquired the theatrical properties of the defunct Quinlan company.[97] It comprised 105 staff: 27 principals and small part artistes, a chorus of 40, ballet of six, orchestra of 21, and 13 other members.[98] It gave its first performance on 30 August 1915 in Brighton, before commencing a tour of England and Ireland.[99] Despite Frewin's optimism (see below), favourable press reports, and claims of good business,[100] the company was soon in difficulties and was bought on 5 August 1916 by the impresario Henry Phillips and his partner Lavens Ewart[101] for £1,750; on 1 April 1917 it was legally reconstituted as the H.B. Phillips Opera Company, and was appeared as such from the next month. Frewin transferred to the Allington-Charsley troupe.

Under Phillips's management, losses grew (Table 4.12). The causes are not entirely clear. An accountants' report on 12 March 1918 noted that 'a large part of the loss incurred between June and December 1917 arose during the London season in October and November when business was practically at a standstill owing to air raids,' but losses had already been increasing: the deficit from 1 April to 31 May 1917 was as great as that in the previous seven and a half months. Shortly before Christmas 1917 the company appeared at Liverpool and returned to profit but, from February to April 1918, it lost on average £64 per week. A possible contributory factor was the number of fallow weeks: up to March 1917 there was only one non-performing week out of 34 but, between April and December 1917, the troupe rested for 16 weeks out of 37. Additionally, however, principal singers' wages rose substantially (from an average of £120 per performing week before April 1917 to £169 from mid-February 1918), as did directors' salaries and

95 *MS*, 8 August 1914, p. 115.

96 *Stage*, 18 March 1915, p. 21.

97 *Era*, 2 June 1915, p. 2.

98 *Stage*, 19 August 1915, p. 18.

99 Ibid.

100 For example: (at Birmingham), 'The operas, which terminated on Saturday with a capital performance of *The Lily of Killarney*, have been remarkably successful' (*Stage*, 28 October 1915, p. 3); (at Middlesbrough) 'The Harrison Frewin company … must be complimented on the general excellence of their performance. Both artistically and financially the engagement has proved a big success' (*Stage*, 6 January 1916, p. 16); and 'we are informed that the Harrison Frewin opera company during the past three weeks have broken all records at two theatres (Darlington and Grimsby) and have beaten the night's record for present prices for a third (Burnley)' (*Stage*, 3 February 1916, p. 19).

101 Lavens Ewart was the grandson of Sir William Ewart, one of Belfast's biggest linen manufacturers. An enthusiastic musician, Ewart went into partnership with Phillips in 1915; they operated both the opera company and a concert management agency. See also his obituary (*The Times*, 23 September 1939, p. 8).

Table 4.12 Losses of the Frewin and Phillips Opera Companies, August 1916 to May 1918

Period	**Playing weeks (Actual weeks)**	**Recorded loss to nearest £**	**Average loss per playing week to nearest £**
As Harrison Frewin Opera Company 12 August 1916 to 31 March 1917*	33 (34)	£1,318	£40
As H.B. Phillips Opera Company 1 April 1917 to 9 February 1918	29 (45)	£4,387	£151
1 April to 30 June 1917	Not specified	£1,315	Not specified
1 July to 15 December 1917	Not specified	£3,352	Not specified
1 April to 15 December 1917	21 (37)	£4,467	£222
16 December 1917 to 9 February 1918	8 weeks	£280 profit	£35 profit
10 February to 25 May 1918	15 (15)	£960	£64

Note to Table: *This period included a record-breaking 16-week season at the Shakespeare Theatre, Liverpool, from December 1916 to April 1917 (see Stage, 12 April 1917, p. 12).

expenses.[102] In August 1918 Ewart terminated his partnership with Phillips and the Carl Rosa bought the company for £3,000; it appeared under Phillips's name until August 1919 but was then entirely absorbed into the Rosa organisation.[103]

While both troupes were affected by empty weeks in 1917 arising, at least in part, from air raids, the accounts suggest that box office receipts remained consistent when they were on stage; for the three principal periods average weekly receipts for playing weeks were £352, £335 and £383 respectively.[104] Costs, however, exceeded income, with wages comprising the greatest element of expenditure; although there are minor variations, a breakdown of the Harrison Frewin's

102 In the first period Phillips's combined salary and expenses averaged £12 per week, rising to £47 in the second period, and falling to £15 in the third period.

103 Although losses were substantial, they are dwarfed in proportion by the £4,000 Denhof allegedly lost in just three weeks in 1913 (see above).

104 The accounts are not comprehensive; the summary figures show that the company received about 65 per cent of gross ticket sales over the whole period, a proportion confirmed by Huddersfield box office records. A small additional income came from programme and libretto sales.

Table 4.13 Frewin Opera Company expenditure 12 August 1916 to 31 March 1917

Recipient/Cost	Amount			Percentage
	£	s	d	
Principal Singers	3,956	6	2	30.5
Conductors and Repetiteurs	576	10	0	4.4
Chorus Gents	1,061	2	4	8.2
Chorus Ladies	1,106	8	11	8.5
				(Total chorus 16.7)
Orchestra	2,025	1	6	15.6
Ballet	368	14	5	2.8
(Total wages performers	*9,094*	*13*	*4)*	*(Total performers 70.0)*
Stage Staff and Managers	337	14	0	2.6
Wardrobe Staff; Dressers; Call Boy	163	1	9	1.2
Supernumeraries/Extras	31	11	9	0.2
(Total wages production staff	*532*	*7*	*6)*	*(Total production staff 4.0)*
Directors' Travelling and Entertaining Expenses[1]	400	6	8	3.1
Business Managers	418	3	0	3.2
Advance Agent; Press Agent	73	15	0	0.6
(Total other staff costs	*892*	*4*	*8)*	*(Total other staff 6.9)*
(Total all staff wages	*10,118*	*8*	*10)*	*(Total all staff wages 80.9)*
Printing and Advertising	708	2	4	5.6
Stage Expenses and Wig Hire	401	13	2	3.1
Performing Right Fees; Music purchase and hire; Stage Band	368	4	3	2.8
Transport Costs	549	0	7½	4.3
General Expenses[2]	430	12	3½	3.3
(Total non-staff costs	*2,457*	*12*	*8)*	*(Total non-staff 19.1)*
TOTAL EXPENDITURE	**12,986**	**8**	**2**	

Notes to Table: [1] Phillips drew no salary but all his hotel and travelling expenses were paid by the company. [2] Including insurance, legal fees, bank changes and agents' costs.

expenditure is representative (Table 4.13). With over 80 per cent of outgoings attributable to staff costs, mainly spent on performers, and almost one-third on principal singers alone, costs could clearly be reduced only by compromising the manner in which operas were performed.

In a wider context these figures demonstrate the challenges faced by all touring companies as it is unlikely that, in proportions, expenses were substantially different during peace time. Although the reliance on principal singers was substantial, wages were not generous; the mean weekly payment for a principal singer was £4 9s. Non-staff costs were equally difficult to reduce as expenses such as travel, insurance, and performing rights could only be diminished by a limited extent in the overall context. Good box office receipts were crucial, and a bad run could easily lead to insolvency.

The records of the Theatre Royal, Huddersfield, include box office receipts and show how erratic the companies' income could be. The Rosa troupe appeared in the week commencing 13 January 1902 and total receipts were an impressive £615 11s, of which the company took 70 per cent (£413 17s 8d); takings varied from £82 2s for Monday's *Tannhäuser* to £113 11s for Saturday night's *Maritana*; *The Bohemian Girl* on Thursday also took over £100. Such figures were, however, exceptional for Huddersfield until the post-war years, by which time inflation had taken its toll. Typical weekly receipts at the theatre were between £100 and £300 in the Edwardian years, but could fall to £30, and exceed £600 for the most popular musical comedies. Opera companies always achieved amounts within the typical range, but with much variation (Table 4.14). The Saturday evening performance was particularly important and always devoted to a 'crowd-puller'. Of the Turner company's five visits from 1907 to 1913, the last performance accounted on average for a quarter of the week's takings; *Maritana* and *The Bohemian Girl* were each given twice and *The Lily of Killarney* once.

The figures imply that a prolonged break between seasons may have augmented receipts. Conversely, though, in 1913, a bumper year with four weeks of opera, takings did not collapse, suggesting that 'audience fatigue' was not inevitable. An examination of the operas performed, together with their receipts, implies that audiences were unpredictable; of the 18 works given, while *Maritana* (11 performances, average receipts £36), *Il Trovatore* (10, £29), and *Faust* (9, £24) occurred the most frequently, it was *Maritana*, *The Bohemian Girl* (5, £45), *Carmen* (3, £36) and *Tannhäuser* (2, £38) that brought in the biggest average receipts. The unpredictability is further shown by the range: *Maritana* achieved between £14 and £92, while *The Bohemian Girl* ranged between £37 and £61. When the Castellano troupe gave the first traced performance of *La Traviata* since 1882 it brought in only £12, while, on introducing *Samson et Dalila*, which also affronted some sensibilities due to its subject matter, the Moody-Manners achieved an average for two performances of £31. Trying to anticipate which operas would entice, and to reconcile this with other practicalities was a challenge, and miscalculation easy.

Table 4.14 Box office receipts for touring opera companies at Theatre Royal, Huddersfield, 1907–13

Week commencing	Company	Gross Box Office receipts to nearest £	Company share	Company share to nearest £
7 January 1907	Turner	£313	60% of first £200, then 65%	£195
14 October 1907	Turner	£269	As above	£165
5 October 1908	Turner	£174	60%	£104
4 April 1910	Moody-Manners	£273	70% with £200 minimum	£200
7 November 1910	Castellano	£153	65%	£99
13 November 1911	Turner	£221	62.5%	£138
6 January 1913	Castellano	£183	65%	£119
21 April 1913	Turner	£116	62.5%	£72
29 September 1913	Castellano	£191	65%	£124
24 November 1913	Castellano	£167	65%	£109

Source: WYAS, B/HTR/as

Without more evidence, definitive conclusions remain elusive. The high staff costs of the Frewin and Phillips companies suggest that cuts could only be achieved by reducing the number of performers, which may have caused more harm to the companies' reputation than was worthwhile. Erratic box office receipts at Huddersfield suggest that liquidity could often be a problem and that companies were vulnerable to factors beyond their control. Even when circumstances were favourable, touring was a risky and unpredictable business,but nevertheless, when Charles Manners put his company up for sale in 1918 he claimed that in 21 years it had never made an annual loss.[105]

Provincial Opera during the Great War

At the outbreak of war concerns arose that theatrical life would be disrupted but the touring companies soon embraced the 'business as usual' mantra (see also Chapter 3). Walter van Noorden, interviewed in the *Daily Telegraph*, said:

> When the appalling news of the war burst on us, naturally our first impulse was to cancel our forthcoming tour, or, at least, the first portion of it. On reflection,

[105] *MS*, 25 May 1918, p. 293.

however, the thought of over one hundred artists being thrown out of work … made us reconsider the matter, and we decided to make a start in the ordinary manner. The expenses of an opera company are, however, so very great that it will be impossible to continue if business is bad for very long.[106]

The Rosa accordingly started in suburban London before moving into the provinces. Likewise, Joseph O'Mara put his faith in the public:

It has been decided to carry through this season's tour if possible. If the business is not sufficiently strong to meet all the expenses of such a large company, then the artists on their part agree to accept a reduction in salary to an extent to allow Mr O'Mara to fulfil all his contracts, unless something very unforeseen occurs. The strength of the company will be in no way diminished … So anxious is Mr O'Mara to keep the company in engagements that he himself has forfeited all salary both as manager and artist.[107]

Results were uneven and unpredictable but mainly encouraging. When the Rosa and O'Mara troupes appeared in Manchester in late spring 1915 both drew large audiences.[108] Critics were usually keen to emphasise the maintenance of pre-war standards – of the Rosa's two-week season in Edinburgh in April 1915, the local critic stated:

Never have I known the Carl Rosa company to give better stage productions, and as regards the singers, Mr Van Noorden has again, perhaps even more so than ever, stipulated for aesthetic and executive ability quite irrespective of the fact of their already possessing a name or reputation.[109]

The launch of Frewin's company in 1915 exemplifies the spirit of determination that the touring companies embraced, an ethos encouraged by the press:

Of Mr Harrison Frewin himself we can speak from experience, and with an assurance that 'the goods he carries' will be good goods … [A]s to the sense and sensibility of 'another opera company' in war-time, it is significant that whilst the only operatic failure of this year was the immature experiment [by

---

106 *MS*, 22 August 1914, p. 148.

107 *MS*, 12 September 1914, p. 196.

108 *MS*, 24 April 1915, p. 317, and 8 May, p. 358. A year later, when both companies reappeared in Manchester 'full houses were the rule. It would seem that the public, far from moping at home, means to make the most of such opportunities as arise in the way of healthy and invigorating diversion' (*MS*, 6 May 1916, p. 340).

109 *MS*, 10 April 1915, p. 281.

Vladimir Rosing] in Kingsway, the provincial opera companies all report satisfactory houses.[110]

Frewin was confident of success:

> Many people have expressed the opinion that we are doing an unwise thing in starting during the war ... There is, in my opinion, no ground for apprehension as regards the welfare of opera ... I have been able to book one of the best first-season tours ever known.[111]

As shown above, however, Frewin's optimism was misplaced, and the company lost money almost from the outset.

As the impact of war was felt more keenly, touring companies were inevitably affected. Staffing was the greatest problem as men joined up and conscription was introduced (see Chapter 3). Touring was hard work and it seems that many male chorus singers and orchestral players left for military service readily. Later press reviews make irregular but increasingly frequent reference to gaps on stage and in the pit. Adaptation of practices, together with press and audience stoicism, were crucial – when Frewin's company appeared at Leeds in October 1916, it was noted that:

> the chorus has lately been depleted to such an extent that at the present time the entire male section is composed of substitutes, [and] the orchestra has suffered similarly, yet they are giving performances which compare very favourably with anything we are accustomed to in the provinces.[112]

Orchestras were particularly affected due to the practice of amalgamating touring and resident bands venue by venue. The depletion of local orchestras made it harder to predict where gaps would be. Despite a successful season at Liverpool in early 1916, Charles Manners stated to the audience that:

---

[110] *MS*, 24 July 1915, p. 65. For commentary on Rosing, see Chapter 3.

[111] Quoted ibid, p. 69. Frewin's plan included visits to Belfast, Birmingham, Brighton, Buxton, Cork, Dalston (north London), Dublin, Harrogate, Huddersfield, Middlesbrough, Nottingham, Reading, Scarborough, St Helens, Swindon, Warrington, and Wolverhampton; novelties were promised in the larger towns.

[112] *MS*, 4 November 1916, p. 334. A later assessment of the O'Mara Company at Leeds stated that 'the performances have been very good on the whole. As is inevitable in these times, the chorus is not well-balanced, but there is no lack of capable principals. The orchestra has been quite efficient' (*MS*, 29 September 1917, p. 212). In 1918, the same critic said of the company's performance of Halévy's *La Juive*: 'the performance was an adequate one and the cast efficient ... When it is once more possible to have a chorus of sufficient numbers on the male side there will doubtless be a great gain in general effect' (*MS*, 12 October 1918, p. 126).

> A difficulty lay in the fact that so many men were being called up for Army service. Last week the orchestra had had to do its part without the assistance of a cello or a flute, and it was probable that as many as eight or ten members of the company might have to go at one rush … Unlike the modern revue, men were essential in opera; they could not, for example, represent Valentine or Mephistopheles with ladies.[113]

Manners disbanded his company soon afterwards (see above). Others companies, however, continued by enlisting the support of non-serving men. Charles Hedmondt, for example, reinvigorated his career as a leading tenor, singing for the Carl Rosa, O'Mara and Allington-Charsley companies during the war years, despite reaching the age of 60 in 1917.[114] Nor did the number of companies decrease: in 1916 there were seven troupes touring the country, although, in some cases, their activities were intermittent.[115]

While substantial, the effects of military service were neither consistent nor insurmountable. Rutland Boughton, for example, tried to claim exemption from his call-up as he was 'indispensable to the productions contemplated' at his Glastonbury Festival, which was of 'national importance'.[116] The Military Appeals Tribunal disagreed, but helpfully did not deliver its verdict until after the 1916 festival had finished. Boughton duly joined up and remained in uniform until the end of the war.[117] Irishmen were exempt from conscription, but it is impossible to discover if there was a consequently greater Irish participation in theatre work.

The press was supportive throughout the war, despite periodic warnings of calamity. In August 1917, *The Era* reported that:

> The near future – the autumn – will see at least six 'grand' opera companies at work in the country, all giving opera in English or English opera with English-speaking artistes … Some of the companies – the Carl Rosa, the O'Mara, and the Harrison Frewin – are well-established organisations that do their yearly round of the provinces with the regularity of clockwork. All of them appear to be in flourishing condition, in spite of the … depletion of the male ranks of the chorus,

113 *Stage*, 9 March 1916, p. 16.

114 An exceptional example of an extended career is that of John Cornwall, a chorus singer with the Rosa company until he died in 1915, aged 78; Cornwall had sung with the Pyne-Harrison Company in the 1860s (*MG*, 17 April 1915, p. 6).

115 The companies were the Rosa, Frewin, Turner (no activity from March to October), O'Mara (no activity from May to October), John Ridding, Moody-Manners (ceased April) and Empire; gaps in activity may be attributable in part to incomplete listings (source: collated from 'On the Road' entries in *Stage*, 1916).

116 *MS*, 8 July 1916, p. 31.

117 For further commentary see Michael Hurd, *Rutland Boughton and the Glastonbury Festivals* (Oxford, 1993), pp. 102–4.

> and the 'calling up' of soloists and conductors … there is a real public need for the fare these companies provide.[118]

Rising taxes and living costs presented further challenges. As in London the effect of the Entertainment Tax was uneven.[119] Greater difficulties arose in relation to transport; pressure on the railways was immense, and touring troupes were not their first priority. The opera companies' 25 per cent discount on fares continued, but fares in general increased by 50 per cent on 1 January 1917, and luggage restrictions were imposed.[120] Of greatest practical impact was the difficulty in transporting scenery and props:[121]

> It is one thing to bring the play, the company, the wardrobe, and a reasonable amount of printing [i.e. programme books], and another thing to bring the whole production, often with tons of scenery and properties, and sometimes with extra working staff and extra musicians … The railway companies profess their ability to get a company into a town in time for the opening on the Monday night, but they accept no responsibility for the due delivery of scenery etc.. As an official of one of the great railway companies said … last week, "[A] manager must not expect that he will be able to get his scenery over a long stretch of country on Sunday and unload it on Sunday evening … We should only under dire pressure hook a coach off a train and put it on one side while there were people in it … [but] in the event of trains being too heavy to lift both passengers and scenery, the trucks will be taken off and left behind."[122]

Theatres were exhorted to provide more scenery and properties to enable companies to 'travel light'; Huddersfield agreements with the Rosa and Allington-Charsley companies require the theatre to provide stock scenery and properties. Touring troupes adjusted as necessary; opera companies in particular often stayed in larger towns for longer, and runs of several weeks became more common, especially in Manchester and Liverpool. Managers reacted with a mixture of stoicism and resignation. Charles Manners cited transport difficulties compromising the quality of productions as one reason for suspending operations,[123] but Joseph O'Mara was more pragmatic:

---

[118] *Era*, 8 August 1917, p. 11.

[119] See *Stage*, 18 October 1917, p. 15, and below for box office receipts at Huddersfield.

[120] *Stage*, 4 January 1917, p. 15.

[121] Ibid. One truck per company was allowed but not guaranteed.

[122] *Stage*, 8 February 1917, p. 14. O'Mara encountered this problem: he intended to give the first performance at Leeds of *Manon Lescaut* but substituted another work when the required scenery did not arrive (*MS*, 12 October 1918, p. 126).

[123] *Era*, 3 January 1917, p. 1.

> I asked all the members of the company to reduce their private luggage as low as possible [*sic*] … This has been no easy task, as the tour of this company extends from the first week of September to about the end of May, and they have to take more than the ordinary amount of personal luggage. I have also reduced my scenery and baggage as far as I possibly can without in any way interfering with the proper staging of the different operas we produce … [The railway companies] have at all times given every facility to theatrical companies travelling, and now that the country demands the curtailing of services I am sure the theatrical professions will be the first to relieve the railway companies of any extra trouble.[124]

That most companies survived demonstrates that audiences continued to turn out. Box Office returns from Huddersfield show a steady increase in receipts for the war-time seasons although in part this is attributable to increased ticket prices (Table 4.15).

The war-time repertory contracted slightly (see Table 4.6) with a tendency to focus even more on works that drew large audiences. Managers also wanted to show, though, that 'carrying on' meant continuing to perform less well-known works and even to give new ones. While premieres reduced in number some new works appeared. In addition to those mounted by Beecham and Boughton (see Chapter 3 and below), Manners brought out MacAlpin's *The Vow*, Frewin produced his own *Gay Lothario* and Barkworth's *Romeo and Juliet*, and Phillips gave Lyon's *Storm Wrack* and Price's *Nuns of Ardboe* (see Chapter 6).

The performance of works of German origin was a further issue (see also Chapter 3). This affected opera companies less than concert promoters and provincial audiences saw even less change than in the West End as the operatic repertory was dominated by works of French, Italian and British/Irish origin. The tacit policy of banning operas by living German composers changed almost nothing: although, since 1910, operas by Strauss, Kienzl and Waltershausen had been performed in London, none of their works had become part of the established provincial repertory.[125] The next potential casualties were Humperdinck and Wagner; *Hänsel und Gretel* had been given by several companies since the 1890s but was a peripheral work and easily discarded, leaving only Wagner as a 'problem'. Charles Manners was quoted as saying that:

> [In Liverpool] this season he had not given them any of the heavier operas. He had purposely left these out because, first of all, they were mainly German – although he looked upon Wagner's operas as operas for the world, and quite

124 Ibid.

125 Denhof and Quinlan both gave operas by Strauss outside London but neither operated during the war; the Moody-Manners troupe performed Kienzl's *Der Kuhreigen* in August 1914 but this was immediately dropped.

Table 4.15 Box office receipts for touring opera companies at Theatre Royal, Huddersfield, 1915–18[126]

Week commencing	Company	Gross receipts to nearest £*	Company receipts to nearest £
1 February 1915	Castellano	£189	£123 (65%)
4 October 1915	Frewin	£416	£270 (65%)
3 April 1916	Frewin	£261	£174 (66.67%)
4 December 1916	O'Mara	£281	£188 (66.67%)
12 October 1918	Allington-Charsley	£483	£314 (65%)
22 February 1919	Rosa	£871	£610 (70%)
20 December 1919	Allington-Charsley	£430	£279 (65%)

Note to table: *These figures do not include the Entertainment Tax, which was accounted for separately.

> above any questions of nationality. The other reason was that he found that certain percentages would have to go to Germans and German composers now living.[127]

Yet within months both companies and audiences seem to have reached an unspoken consensus that Wagner was acceptable and performances of *Tannhäuser*, the most popular of his works outside London, continued throughout the war: Frewin performed it regularly from the outset.[128] When the Rosa company performed *Tannhäuser* in Edinburgh in March 1918 a local critic wrote:

> The intelligent and interested manner in which all the beauties of the opera were marked and applauded by the huge audience that filled every available seat in the theatre, is a curious commentary on the proposal in certain circles to ban German music entirely. Clearly it cannot be done. We might as well admit the fact the Wagner – even the Wagner of *Tannhäuser* – is a classic, and the people will have him whether or not.[129]

Performances of *Lohengrin* decreased; other Wagner operas were given rarely, as they had been before 1914.

[126] No records survive for February 1917 to July 1918; the Allington-Charsley Company visited Huddersfield in the week commencing 15 October 1917.

[127] *Era*, 24 February 1915, p. 10.

[128] Frewin was still sensitive to local feeling: before giving *Tannhäuser* in Liverpool in 1917 the local theatre manager held an informal plebiscite with the result favouring performance (see *Stage*, 15 March 1917, p. 14).

[129] *MS*, 2 March 1918, p. 146.

Much of the evidence as to how the war affected the opera companies is anecdotal and sometimes contradictory. Despite the challenging environment many troupes did well during the war years and only one, the Moody-Manners, suspended operations as a direct result of the conflict, with two others, the Castellano and Quinlan companies, dissolving, the latter due to its focus on overseas work. For all the difficulties and privations, many provincial towns and cities enjoyed regular opera seasons throughout the war.

In addition to the ongoing activities of the touring companies, two other significant ventures operated outside London during the war years, those of Thomas Beecham and Rutland Boughton. Both were unusual and made distinctive impacts on Britain's operatic culture in the short-term.

Thomas and Joseph Beecham started their provincial activities in a very modest fashion. Two operas from the 1910 *opéra comique* season at His Majesty's (*The Tales of Hoffman* and *Die Fledermaus*) toured from September 1910 to March 1911 with satisfactory results, although Sheffield was excoriated by Beecham for lack of enthusiasm,[130] and in 1912 Joseph organised a troupe which put on popular operas in music halls in a manner reminiscent of that of the 'Old Vic' (see Chapter 3).[131] Thomas was subsequently involved with the Denhof company (see above) and rumoured to be one of the conductors of the Quinlan troupe's abandoned autumn tour in 1914.[132] After war broke out he became involved with the Hallé Orchestra,[133] and at the society's annual meeting in June 1915 suggested that:

> Manchester's next development in music might be in the direction of opera … 'I think it would be quite easy for you in Manchester to make yourselves the centre of an inspiring centre of a great English opera movement. It cannot be done in London. London people are far too busy with fifty things, but the more sober intellectual life of Manchester gives you more time to think about these things … In pleasanter and more peaceful times there will no doubt be an opportunity for going into the details of the question'.[134]

In part such proposals were typical bluster but Beecham brought his Shaftesbury Theatre company to Manchester for five weeks from 9 May 1916 with a reduced repertory but including two of his three new British operas (*The Critic* and *The Boatswain's Mate*), the first provincial performance of *Boris Godunov* (opening

---

130 See Lucas, p. 74.

131 See *MT*, 1 November 1912, p. 741.

132 *MS*, 1 August 1914, p. 96.

133 The orchestra's permanent conductor, Michael Balling, was in Bayreuth when war was declared and could not resume his post; Willem Mengelberg, engaged for most of the 1914–15 season, was unable to leave Holland, so several guest conductors, including Beecham, were engaged.

134 *MG*, 30 June 1915, p. 3. These remarks contrast with those made after the collapse of the Denhof company two years earlier (see above).

night), and also *Tristan und Isolde*. Beecham argued that the war was acting as a catalyst in changing attitudes to both opera and culture in general:

> There is no doubt that one of the results of the war is the startling change of opinion that is taking place in nearly every branch of our intellectual and economic life … Nowhere has this right-about-turn of public attitude been more marked than in the musical world … It has always been one of my definite ambitions to establish grand opera permanently in this country and … it has been my particular desire that Manchester should lead the way in the achievement of this object.[135]

In his Manchester seasons, Beecham employed the Hallé and the professional chorus was supplemented by a specially formed body of 80 amateurs. After a shaky start, performances settled and reached a high standard.[136] It is probable that Beecham lost money; in an end-of-season speech he stated that 'if the visits of his opera were to be anything more than occasional … he thought that a firmer support from the moneyed people of Manchester would be necessary. The theatre had been well filled, but mostly in the cheaper seats'.[137]

Beecham returned in 1917, visiting Birmingham (where he was involved in the campaign to establish a permanent orchestra) as well as Manchester.[138] At the end of the latter's six-week season he declared that 'the advance in public interest in this season over the last is something that has surprised even me'.[139] Further seasons followed and other towns were visited. Beecham also proposed to build an opera house in Manchester if the council would provide a site.[140] The company experienced financial troubles, however, and collapsed in 1920; the opera house scheme also stalled.[141] Beecham's financial recklessness limited his impact as his company was short-lived. He did, however, like Denhof and Quinlan before him, introduce new operas to a part of the provincial audience, and gave performances at a standard superior to those of the other companies. After 1920, however, he played no part in the promotion of opera outside London.

Rutland Boughton's activities were very different and had, in many respects, a greater influence over a longer period. By the beginning of 1914 Boughton had two operas ready for performance. His idealistic socialism, however, inclined him to a production method very different from that of conventional opera

---

135 Quoted in *MG*, 8 April 1916, p. 8.

136 *MG*, 10 June 1916, p. 6.

137 *MG*, 12 June 1916, p. 4.

138 *MG*, 9 March 1917, p. 10.

139 Quoted in *MG*, 14 May 1917, p. 8

140 *MG*, 19 September 1917, p. 4. A formal offer was not made to the council for another year (*MG*, 31 October 1918, p. 4); Beecham proposed to give the building to the city after 10 years, but was always to have control of its management.

141 *MG*, 1 August 1919, p. 12; see also Lucas, pp. 148–56.

companies.[142] In 1912 Boughton settled on the concept of a 'festival' comprising a residential school with public performances.[143] By spring 1914 he was ready to produce his most recently completed work, *The Immortal Hour*, in a festival to be held at Glastonbury in August 1914.[144] Although Glastonbury's Assembly Rooms were small, permitting only modest scenery and stage effects, and the international situation caused problems (Beecham's orchestra could not perform and the accompaniment was instead provided by two pianos), the first performance of Boughton's opera, the centre-piece of the festival, took place one day after Britain declared war on Germany. Boughton was well known to the press and his supporters were also proficient at networking and generating publicity, so both the festival and the new opera gained some valuable attention in the midst of war-related coverage. Despite starting at an inauspicious time, a series of festivals was initiated which continued, intermittently, until 1927.

Subsequent war-time festivals included the premieres of Boughton's *Bethlehem* and *The Round Table*, Bainton's *Oithona* and Raybould's *Sumida River* (see Chapter 6) and these also attracted press interest.[145] Boughton's call-up (see above) necessitated changes after the 1916 festival; although his partner, Christina Walshe, organised performances at Glastonbury complete operas were impractical until Boughton returned in peace-time to mount a full festival in August 1919. Although the new operas, with the exception of *The Immortal Hour*, did not survive in the repertory longer than other British operas premiered before 1918, they were well received. Perhaps the greatest long-term impact of the festivals, however, was that they provided a different model for the production of opera to that practised in the West End and by the touring companies, and supplied a template for others to follow subsequently, most notably Benjamin Britten and Peter Pears at Aldeburgh.

---

[142] Boughton had played in the pit orchestra of the Haymarket Theatre (Hurd, pp. 22–3); although bringing practical knowledge, the gruelling work may also have instilled a dislike of the 'conventional' theatre world, which he avoided until *The Immortal Hour* was produced in London in 1922.

[143] A first attempt at Hindhead, Surrey, in August 1912 was cancelled; Boughton moved to Glastonbury in 1913 and a more ambitious plan was conceived (involving the erection of a temporary theatre and the employment of Beecham's orchestra), but postponed when funds could not be raised. A modest project at Bournemouth in August 1913 gave two extracts from *The Birth of Arthur* (Hurd, pp. 52–62).

[144] The original intention was to perform *The Birth of Arthur* but *The Immortal Hour* was substituted. The Glastonbury festivals comprised not only operas (which included works by Purcell, Blow, Gluck, and extracts from Wagner), but also plays, lectures, debates, readings, and children's activities.

[145] For example, see *MT*, 1 September 1915, p. 539; *The Times*, 16 August 1916, p. 9 (a review of *The Round Table* as long as those of many Covent Garden premieres).

Conclusion

The late nineteenth century witnessed a substantial expansion in the provision of opera in suburban London and beyond. As the touring system bedded down and stock companies closed, dedicated opera troupes expanded in number and activity, bringing performances to a greater number of people than ever before – and, quite possibly, ever since. Although most organisations were modest in size and did not always give performances of the highest standard, the volume of their activities is impressive. The challenging financial conditions in which the companies operated – lacking the large subscription guarantee and social cachet enjoyed by the Covent Garden-based troupes and their equivalents – impacted on both performance standards and repertory selected. The latter, influenced also by performing rights, was based on a small core of popular works which evolved only very slowly between 1875 and 1918. While, therefore, provincial audiences enjoyed the greatest number of opportunities to see opera, they saw a largely static selection of works, with new compositions being presented selectively and only occasionally. Thus much the greater part of the United Kingdom's opera-going public experienced little in the way of broadened horizons, a contrast, in the case of the biggest cities, with a more rapidly developing concert repertory. Aspirations, after 1910, to provide West End-like experiences in terms of repertory and quality, proved unsustainable. Even Thomas Beecham, with access to great personal wealth, could not make such activities pay in the longer term.

For the companies, circumstances were often difficult and while many troupes proved remarkably tenacious and enterprising, their existences were rarely comfortable. The troupes' resilience is impressive. Their desire to survive, if not to prosper, maintained a steady provision of opera performances around the British Isles in conditions unique in western Europe. For audiences, the opera companies provided widely welcomed entertainment. For all their imperfections, their appearances were anticipated positively up and down the country, and opera as a genre came nearer at this time in the United Kingdom to being a mass entertainment than at any other.

Chapter 5
'The Operatic Problem'

In 1902 William Galloway published a slim volume entitled *The Operatic Problem.*[1] The title reflected a sense of unease and dissatisfaction within the music profession and among its supporters that opera was failing to flourish and take its place within British society, either as a source of entertainment and edification, or as a part of the country's wider 'growth' as a musical and cultural nation. Unease focused on two particular aspects: firstly, its organisation and, secondly, the perceived failure of native composers to produce a corpus of successful works. The debate arising from this disquiet focused on the twin questions of how opera might be better managed to bring it to a wider audience and play a role in 'improving' British society, and how native composers could be enabled to establish a repertory equal to that of other European nations, and worthy of a great imperial power. Commentary focused primarily on supporting structures. Relatively few writers were willing to tackle two crucial but nebulous questions: why did native composers seem unable to produce operas of lasting value, and, how could they create works that were truly national? At a time when national characteristics were commonly believed to be biologically determined, the need for art forms to 'speak' to their respective peoples became a widespread credo. This chapter examines these debates, traces their development, considers the ideological positions of the protagonists and the solutions put forward. Despite a persistent and occasionally intense discourse, almost invariably coloured by its English and London-centric nature, there was little agreement and still less was achieved; the fundamental intellectual and practical positions remained largely static between 1875 and 1918.

Galloway succinctly set out reasons for structural change, and was representative of those advocating a new approach:

> Opera has, since its origin, been considered the highest form of theatrical pastime. The very appellation 'opera' indicates that in the land of its birth it was looked upon as the 'work' *par excellence*, and to this day it is the form of Art which is invariably honoured by exalted patronage, and one that people pay the most to enjoy ...

[1] William Galloway, *The Operatic Problem* (London, 1902). Galloway (1868–1931) worked in his family's boiler-making business and served as Conservative MP for Manchester South West from 1895 to 1906.

> [Historically] England alone in civilised Europe remained indifferent, and took no active part either in fostering or patronising the new form of art … England was satisfied to import spectacles and performers from abroad, just as she would have imported any other commodity … Our failure to create a body of art comparable with that of Germany, Italy and France has sometimes been attributed to inherent lack of the dramatic instinct in music, but that view is contradicted by the historical facts. From the time of Purcell … neither the impulse to write on the part of musicians nor the capacity to appreciate on the part of the public has been lacking … Again and again English or British composers returned to the task with significant, if temporary, success …
>
> I have long desired that Opera should be placed within the reach of those whose purses are not able to bear the strain of the high prices charged in England … in providing National Opera for the people we can assist in the higher education of the community.[2]

In essence Galloway made three points: (a) opera was the highest musico-dramatic form of art; (b) Britain had artists able to compose and perform opera just as well as those of nations perceived to be leaders in the field, if only they were adequately supported; and (c) opera performances of the highest standard should be accessible to everyone without regard to income as they were an agent of civilisation and improvement. An implicit fourth point, that the language of performance should be English, appears to have been so obvious in Galloway's mind that it was left unstated.

Galloway believed that a crucial part of the solution to the 'operatic problem' was the creation of a national opera house (his proposals are discussed below). He was not its first advocate; a growing source of frustration was the failure to achieve this goal and a national opera house became both a mascot and a cure-all. Disunity and lack of support, however, prevented progress, despite frequent declarations of intent. Given its centrality within discussion of the 'problem', it is important to examine the arguments for and against the establishment of a national opera house and to consider why little progress was made.

Galloway might easily have written his pamphlet in 1875, as British opera was then viewed by many as being in a parlous state. Barely any works that aspired to 'rise above' the light comic operas of composers such as Sullivan and Frederic Clay had been premiered since the collapse of the Pyne-Harrison Company and its short-lived successor, the English Opera Association, in 1864 and 1866 respectively, and most of the composers who had benefited from those enterprises had either died soon afterwards or focused subsequently on other activities.[3] Concurrently, there was a lack of confidence in the native product, and

---

[2] Galloway, pp. 7; 11–13; 3 and 5–6.

[3] Wallace and Loder died in 1865, and Balfe in 1870; Macfarren and Benedict showed no interest in composing opera later in their careers, although Benedict's cantata *Graziella* was produced in a staged version (29 September 1883, Crystal Palace). Between 1865

a combination of resignation and resentment that British composers and artists seemed destined to play second fiddle to the Italian companies based in the West End. The lack in the capital of an equivalent to the national theatres and opera houses found in many European cities was perceived as an oddity at best and an embarrassment at worst. Charles Gruneisen, reflecting on London's 1870 season, prefaced his remarks, which necessarily focused almost entirely on the activities of Gye and Mapleson, with a lament on the lack of a national theatre. It was not, he argued, due to a dearth of native talent:

> It is the organisation which is required; it is the formation of a really national opera house which is the necessity of the day; it is faith on the part of the public, to have more confidence in our artists, and not to place such unbounded reliance on singers because they declaim in a foreign language.[4]

This *cri de coeur* was hardly unique; an articulate manifestation appeared in the *Irish Times*:

> A great deal has been said and written recently respecting the decline of English Opera, the denationalized condition of the English operatic stage, and the apathy with which the whole subject seems to be regarded ... For some years past attempts, somewhat spasmodic in character, have been made to elevate the condition of the lyric drama in England ... There have been a number of companies got together, some exceptionally good, ... some moderate, some wretchedly bad ... [T]here seems to be an ample supply of material; but there is a want of cohesiveness in the individuals which prevents anything permanently great or good being achieved. Thus excellent companies have been brought together, have appeared for a brief season, and, dissolving once more into the separate individualities, as a company have been heard of no more ... And so, private speculation being unequal to the task, there is no national opera.[5]

In the 1870s this apathy and the lack of supporting structures were the most common reasons put forward for the failure of British opera; few wanted to entertain the possibility that there was insufficient audience interest or native talent (discussed below). More trenchant writers, though, were prepared to criticise; an exchange of letters in the *Musical Standard* included some succinct remarks:

---

and 1875 Charles Deffell's *The Corsair* (25 March 1873, Crystal Palace) and Balfe's *The Talisman* (11 June 1874, Her Majesty's) are the only traced exceptions in the interregnum which lasted until the appearance of Cowen's *Pauline* in 1876. Neither presaged a great future: Deffell's work was a critical failure (although it was revived in 1877) and Balfe's a posthumous premiere performed in an Italian translation (see Chapter 1).

[4] Charles Gruneisen, 'The Opera Season of 1870', *Era Almanack 1871*, pp. 16–22 (p. 16.)

[5] *IT*, 17 August 1874, p. 2; reproduced in *MW*, 26 September, p. 640.

> It cannot be maintained that there is any existing school of opera in this country worthy of the name. Balfe's and Wallace's operas are little more than collections of ballads; they are in all respects weak … [By] giving us Italian and German operas with English words [Carl Rosa] is at least allowing us to hear good music … If Englishmen have written no operas of merit in the last sixty years, why are we to suppose that they are likely to do better in the next sixty?[6]

> Surely one can suggest very easily a reason for the failure of almost all the operas that have been produced on the English stage for the last forty years. This is the abominable silliness of the stories and the meanness of the words. Could anything be more stupidly ridiculous and conventional than the incidents, or more supremely bad and unpoetical than the words, of such libretti as those of *The Bohemian Girl*, *The Siege of Rochelle*, *Maritana* &c.[?][7]

Such bald criticisms were, however, relatively rare. When Rosa mounted his first West End season in 1875, *The Times* argued that this latest venture could succeed:

> The Carl Rosa company has long been talked about in circles where the necessity of reviving English opera is discussed … Those who think, as we do, that the non-existence of … [a permanent English Opera house] is discreditable to a populous city like London, where music of almost every kind is brought forth in such abundance, and who regard the lyric drama as one of the most engaging forms of artistic expression, hail with satisfaction this new and spirited endeavour to revive it.[8]

Rosa's company was viewed, therefore, as a stepping stone to the establishment of a national opera. But what did a 'national opera' comprise? Advocates, throughout this period, looked to continental cities with opera houses and resident companies. The link between performers and a physical space distinguished operatic organisation in France, Germany and Italy from that in Britain, where companies were either itinerant or, if based in London, effectively reconstituted each year, an unavoidable consequence of the brevity of the grand season. British visitors to continental Europe perceived, especially in Germany, an opera house in every major town, open for most of the year, performing operas in the vernacular to a creditable standard without the need for star singers, drawn from an international repertory but with a strong national bias, and the regular production of new works. More controversial aspects, such as subsidy and state, aristocratic or royal interference, were glossed over. With the greatest of these theatres in such cities

6 *MS*, 21 October 1876, p. 268; another correspondent accused the writer of being a foreigner such was his bias and turn of phrase (28 October, p. 283).

7 *MS*, 28 October 1876, p. 268.

8 *The Times*, 14 September 1875, p. 6.

as Berlin, Paris and Vienna, it was an embarrassment that the United Kingdom – richer and more powerful than Germany, France or Austria – did not possess even one institution of a similar nature, supporting native artists and promoting an indigenous repertory performed in a language 'understanded of the people'. A 'national opera' would, it was believed, provide the opportunities that composers, performers and audiences all lacked; the musicality of the British people was such that the success of a national opera was all but assured.

Given this logic, Mapleson's proposal in 1875 to construct the 'Grand National Opera House' on the Victoria Embankment in London would appear to have been the perfect solution.[9] In truth, however, the name, and other aspects of the project, were skilful manipulations on Mapleson's part to mask what was, first and foremost, an attempt to acquire a permanent base from which to rival and undermine Gye at Covent Garden, in order to continue Italian opera in the accustomed manner. If supporters of British opera perceived this, they failed to lobby for the founding of a national company, betraying a lack of confidence in the viability of their idea. 'Thaddeus Egg' (Joseph Bennett) viewed Mapleson's proposal at best as a stepping stone but did not argue that Mapleson's approach could be altered:

> We have never yet had a national operahouse [*sic*], nor, in the fullest sense of the term, are we likely to have one for a long while. Opera in England must, under present circumstances, be either foreign, *pur et simple*, or foreign in an English dress. This, however, should not hinder any effort to change the circumstances, and the new enterprise contemplates, besides the performance of English or quasi-English operas during the off-season, the establishment of an academy for the training of native artists, both vocalists and dancers ... Let these essentials be provided – in other words, let our composers have a chance for their productions, and we believe the musical talent of England will make English opera a very different thing to what it now is.[10]

The sense of resignation in Bennett's statement is notable: there is tacit acknowledgement that British opera was inferior to Italian in his acceptance of its performance only during the 'off-season', and in his belief that Mapleson's scheme was only the first stage in resuscitating a moribund art form. This 'chicken and egg' question – which should come first, the national repertory to justify a national opera, or a national opera to facilitate the creation of a national repertory – was repeatedly batted back and forth, contributing to the paralysis which pertained beyond 1918.

While Bennett's remarks exemplify a recurrent lack of confidence in British opera, there was also a degree of optimism. The United Kingdom's status as an

[9] For further discussion see Paul Rodmell, 'James Mapleson and the National Operahouse' in Paul Rodmell (ed.), *Music and Institutions in nineteenth-century Britain* (Aldershot, 2012), pp. 99–117.

[10] *MW*, 6 February 1875, p. 100.

imperial power encouraged a belief that a cultural renaissance was imminent and that a nation conscious of its political and commercial status would not allow itself to be bettered in matters artistic by poorer and less powerful countries. This was coupled with a sense, expressed even before the watermark date of 1880 commonly taken as heralding the 'British Musical Renaissance', that receptivity to music and musicians was growing. Francis Hueffer, newly appointed music critic of *The Times*, argued in 1879 that things had already changed for the better, and gave cause for further optimism:

> Mr Rosa's successful season at Her Majesty's Theatre has brought the question of the permanent establishment of English opera in London into the foreground once again. Thoughtful musicians and amateurs ask themselves, 'Why should we not have an opera in our own tongue, sung more or less by our own people, and produced at least in reasonable proportion by our own poets and composers … ?'
>
> The most superficial observer of social and artistic matters in London cannot but have noticed the change that in late years has come over the spirit in which music is listened to and practiced by English amateurs. Not only does the interest taken in it exceed that granted to all other arts in conjunction, but the character of this interest itself is becoming more and more divested of the attributes of a fashionable pastime. A glance at the crowds which gather to listen to Beethoven's quartets at St James's Hall, and to his symphonies at the Crystal Palace would be alone sufficient to establish the point. And in equal measure as the taste of our audiences has become more serious and refined, it has also broadened in scope. The exclusive admiration of Handel and Mendelssohn, on the one hand, and of the school 'of the future' on the other is gradually being merged into intelligent appreciation of all good music to whatever school or country it may belong … A glance at the rise which the national development of music has of late taken in such remote countries as Russia and Norway … naturally awakens the desire that England also should occupy her proper place among musical nations …
>
> It is at such times of national art-revival that the demand for a national opera, in the sense above specified, becomes irresistible.[11]

Hueffer's view was in part tactical: confidence that things would improve, and that failure to encourage such changes would be a source of national shame, were essential elements in his lobbying for a new, more modern, intellectual and liberal approach to music. Nevertheless, his optimism sprang in part from a genuine belief that British attitudes were starting to incline towards his own.

Others were more circumspect; in 1880 Charles Salaman pointed out that Rosa had hitherto been only a promoter of opera *in* English, Cowen's *Pauline* being

[11] Francis Hueffer, 'The chances of English opera', *Macmillan's Magazine*, 40 (1879), pp. 57–65 (p. 57). Similar comments appear in the opening chapter of his *Half a Century of Music in England 1837–1887* (London, 1889).

the only new indigenous work he had produced. Salaman argued that Rosa had more to do: he should not only support new composers, but revive more British operas of the recent past, such as *Robin Hood, Helvellyn, The Amber Witch, The Mountain Sylph* and *Fair Rosamond.* Salaman concluded that 'English Opera has confessedly not been fairly represented under his operatic management; public opinion has not yet been freely tested; there is no evidence that the taste for English opera *has* revived; and, therefore, none that Mr Carl Rosa has conduced to its revival'.[12]

Calls for a 'permanent English opera' – variably defined but based on the concept of a theatre with a resident company – appeared occasionally in the 1870s and '80s but gained no momentum. In 1883 the *Era* declared that 'a National Opera is a national want', and argued that Britain had no lack of performers, composers, and supportive audiences,[13] but this was not part of a wider, sustained process. The absence of more consistent and co-ordinated lobbying was primarily due to the perception that Britain had, in Rosa's troupe, effectively acquired a national company. The restiveness regarding Rosa's efforts exemplified by Salaman dissipated following his production of Mackenzie's *Colomba* and Thomas's *Esmeralda* in 1883. Those in favour of a national opera house were disposed to wait and see: Rosa seemed to be delivering the goods and, while his West End seasons were short, this was only because of his company's popularity in the provinces. The simultaneous disintegration of the Italian companies encouraged the belief that the country's operatic culture had turned a corner with further improvements simply a matter of time. Rosa himself stated that 'I am firmly convinced that the time is not far distant when a national opera house will be a necessary and generally recognised institution in the country',[14] adding that there were enough native performers, sufficient compositional talent, and more than enough demand (massaging his readers' egos by asserting that the English had a better sense of pitch than the Germans, and a greater interest in the dramatic aspect of opera than the Italians).

Occasional appeals and initiatives arose: in 1886 Mackenzie called for the establishment of a national opera, permanent orchestras in all towns comprising populations over 100,000, and better music education.[15] Two years later the Lord Mayor of London inaugurated a committee to investigate how best to train graduates of the London musical colleges for stage careers (it appears to have

---

12 *MW*, 24 January 1880, p. 55.

13 *Era*, 24 November 1883, p. 13.

14 Carl Rosa, 'English Opera', *Murray's Magazine*, 1 April 1887, pp. 460–70 (p. 470).

15 Alexander Mackenzie, 'The Aspects and Prospects of Music in England', *Quarterly Musical Review*, 1 February 1887, pp. 38–50 (reproduction of a speech given to the National Society of Professional Musicians, in Manchester, 15 December 1886).

achieved nothing),[16] and in 1889 Stainer reiterated the call for the creation of a national opera at his inaugural lecture as Professor of Music at Oxford.[17]

In the mid-1880s, therefore, optimism prevailed. A series of events between 1888 and 1892, however, undermined the fragile façade and the dynamic of the national opera debate changed. The first setback was Rosa's death in 1889. Although not the only producer of new native operas, he was the only one with a national reputation, who operated regularly in the West End, and whose performance standards were deemed comparable to those of the Italian companies. After 1889 his troupe showed less interest in promoting new work; the decline of the company's finances undermined its ability to produce them, and absence for several years from the West End reduced its status (see Chapters 2, 3 and 4).

The second setback, the failure of Carte's Royal English Opera in 1892 (see Chapter 2), was not unexpected; the enterprise had been criticised after its initial good reception, sometimes unfairly, but it had appeared at first to exemplify a national opera house: a native cast performing an opera by one of the country's leading composers on a national subject in the vernacular in a dedicated theatre. The shortcomings of both *Ivanhoe* and Carte's management, however, rendered sustained success all but impossible. On re-opening the theatre in December 1891 for his final attempt to make the project work, Carte promised reduced prices and new operas in due course by Thomas, Cowen, MacCunn and Sullivan, but nevertheless remained sanguine: 'The permanent success of the English opera scheme is … now in the hands of the public; it depends upon the public and the public alone; if they support it and fill the theatre … the enterprise can be carried through'.[18] The conversion of the theatre a few months later to a venue for high-class variety and music hall entertainment, by a company chaired by none other than Augustus Harris, must have struck many observers as ironic.

Although Rosa's death and Carte's failure are emblematic events, the role played by Harris is in many respects more important, for his activities, incrementally, cumulatively and unintentionally, did most to undermine the optimistic spirit of the mid-1880s. Not only was Harris responsible for keeping the Rosa company out of the West End, he also rescued Italian Opera at Covent Garden which, by 1891, had recovered all the ground lost in the previous decade. Harris's success was a major

---

16 Reported in *Era*, 7 July 1888, p. 7; amongst those serving on the committee were the Lord Mayor (Polydore de Keyser), George Grove, Mackenzie, Stanford, Rosa, William Hayman Cummings (professor of singing at the Royal Academy), Viscount Folkestone (see Chapter 2, note 54), and Lord Charles Bruce (former Liberal MP).

17 John Stainer, 'The Present State of Music in England', *MS*, 18 January 1890, supplement pp. 64–65 (reproduction of the first part of his Oxford lecture, given on 13 November 1889).

18 Carte to *The Times*, 3 December 1891, p. 7. On finally withdrawing *Ivanhoe* during the previous month, Carte made a speech to the theatre audience which drew an excoriating attack from T.L. Southgate, who argued that Carte blamed everyone except himself for the project's difficulties (*MN*, 11 December, pp. 817–19).

setback: it ensured that English-language performances in the West End continued to be perceived by society as a second-rate middle-brow alternative to the 'real' thing as practised in the grand seasons. To complicate matters, although Covent Garden's social and linguistic elitism was resented in many quarters, a triumphant performance there was still the most highly-sought prize for British composers, not only for itself, but because it was believed that a success there might open doors across Europe and North America. Harris, however, partly in deference to his subscribers' wishes, showed little interest in producing native works at Covent Garden: in nine 'grand seasons' he produced only seven operas by British composers (see Chapters 3 and 6). Of these only Cowen's *Harold* and Maclean's *Petruccio* were performed in English, the latter being confined to a single matinée performance. The production of the others in either Italian or French served only to heighten the resentment of Covent Garden felt by many members of Britain's music profession. While Harris may have fallen victim at Bow Street to his subscribers, he also failed to encourage British composers in his English-language seasons at other venues and this must be attributable to a lack of confidence in the product: Harris was, first and foremost, a businessman, and felt no patriotic obligation to produce British works. That he had interests in many West End venues and choked off potential competitors demonstrates a ruthless and unsentimental approach.

Before moving further towards the twentieth century, when the dynamic of the debate altered, an examination of the philosophical and ideological points behind Galloway's argument summarised at the opening is advisable since it was increasingly on these that the debate turned. Galloway's first point, that opera was the supreme theatrical art form, was rarely deployed as an argument in such specific terms but a broader view, that music could be an agent of social improvement and civilisation, rather than a source of idle amusement, was increasingly accepted in the United Kingdom in the later nineteenth century.[19] A belief that the educated and affluent minority had a moral and parochial responsibility to elevate taste and to draw the majority away from crass and sometimes immoral popular music was also articulated.[20] That opera was theatre-based caused some difficulties as

---

[19] The evolving views of John Ruskin on music are emblematic of this change. From scepticism, expressed in his unpublished essay, *An Essay on the Relative Dignity of the Studies of Painting and Music* (1838), Ruskin moved to a more nuanced position by 1870: 'Music is thus, in her health, the teacher of perfect order, and is the voice of the obedience of angels, and the companion of the course of the spheres of heaven; and in her depravity she is also the teacher of perfect disorder and disobedience' (John Ruskin, *The Queens of the Air, being a study of the Greek Myths of Cloud and Storm*, quoted in William Gatens, 'John Ruskin and Music', *Victorian Studies*, 30 (1986), pp. 77–97). Other writers held a consistently positive view of music's aesthetic and moral attributes; see, for example: Walter Pater, 'The School of Giorgione' in *The Renaissance: studies in art and poetry* (2nd ed., London, 1888) and Hugh R. Haweis, *Music and Morals* (London, 1871). Hueffer's views, quoted above, exemplify the common perception that public attitudes to music were 'improving'.

[20] See, for example, Hubert Parry, *Style in Musical Art* (London, 1911), pp. 106–51; and Charles Stanford, 'The Case for National Opera' in *Studies and Memories* (London,

resistance on moral grounds to theatrical entertainments remained, especially in certain churches, but this view was decreasing in potency, and such views made little impact on the general debate. Among the musical establishment and its supporters this argument was not considered seriously, but there were occasional nods to the feelings of those 'outside'.[21]

Galloway's second point, regarding the predilection for foreign entertainment and failure to support native talent was, together with the associated but unstated issue of the language of performance, the most easily carried, both in terms of an appeal to patriotic sentiment and the citation of historic circumstance. The perception that Britain had allowed its musical culture to be dominated by foreigners to its own disadvantage was frequently reiterated during the late nineteenth century; due to the dominance of the Italian companies in London in no area was this felt more strongly and demonstrated more easily than in relation to opera. Playing on the sense that Britain was emerging from a musical 'dark age' was a tactic often deployed from the 1870s onwards, allowing as it did an appeal to national pride. Despite frequent use, and undoubted ease of comprehension, this point was in certain respects the weakest, as some of these desiderata were coming about without intervention: improvements in musical education led to more native performers on stage and in the orchestra pit, while, with the virtual ending of provincial touring by the Italian companies in the late 1870s, the language of opera performances was, with the sole exception of two or three theatres in the West End, invariably English. While the repertory remained dominated by foreign works, and British composers had to work hard to get their operas on stage, this aspect of the argument shows how the debate largely took place within a small, London-based, academic and musical elite which was driven as much by an obsession with Covent Garden as it was by a wider knowledge or perspective.

Given that the first of Galloway's points was uncontentious and that the second was easily advanced, if also inadequately scrutinised, it is apparently curious that the debate dragged on for so long. Up to around 1890 this was attributable to a lack of confidence in native artists and composers, to a recurrent feeling that good times were just around the corner, and that lobbying was almost enough in itself.

1908), pp. 3–23.

21 Galloway dismissed this concern out of hand, arguing that 'this battle was fought by Molière in the seventeenth century ... who is there today who will deny that Molière helped to correct the follies of his age by exposing them to ridicule' (Galloway, p. 5). For discussion of changing perceptions, see Michael Booth, *Theatre in the Victorian Age* (Cambridge, 1991), pp. 21–6, which notes the trend towards accepting the theatre as 'respectable' through various practices including a gradual enticement of middle class attendance; segregation of audiences both within individual theatres and, especially in the West End, by creating an implicit class-based hierarchy of venues; the perception of actor-managers such as Kean, Bancroft and Irving as gentlemen; and the production of such morally uplifting plays as Barrett's *The Sign of the Cross* (1895). For a specific focus on religious attitudes to the theatre see Richard Foulkes, *Church and Stage in Victorian England* (Cambridge, 1997).

Those such as Mackenzie and Stainer, arguing for a more interventionist approach, were in a minority. In the 1890s the mood changed: the three factors highlighted above (Rosa's death, Carte's failure, and Harris's ambivalence) led many to conclude that a more pro-active approach was needed. With the foundation of the Grand Opera Syndicate further removing Covent Garden from the influence of the musical profession, and the resultant increase in resentment, advocates of a national opera alighted increasingly on a further distinctive feature of the management of continental opera houses, the provision of public financial support. It is largely due to a complete ideological fracture on the question of subsidy (or 'subvention', the more commonly used contemporaneous term), spurred by the petition to the London County Council (LCC) in 1898 (see below) that no progress was made until long after 1918. Even those who supported the creation of a national opera often baulked at the idea of public financial support being provided, and it was the failure to win the argument for subvention that resulted in schemes remaining nothing more than proposals.

Arguments in favour of subvention of a national opera had been put forward periodically before 1898. Alfred Bunn had pointed out the advantages subsidy conferred on opera houses in other countries in his autobiography published in 1840, although he also stated that he did not think it was 'compatible with the disposition of this country, that its places of public entertainment should be upheld by any grant from Government ... it is nevertheless true, that if such were the case, we should not complain as we do, of the great dearth of dramatic talent'.[22] In 1853 Thomas Beale had argued that some of the profits from the Great Exhibition should be devoted towards supporting and promoting music,[23] and he also argued for subsidy in a volume of memoirs and anecdotes published in 1867.[24] These arguments, however, ran counter to the prevalent belief in market economics which held that if a well-run company had a good product at an acceptable price it would usually succeed. Conversely, a company that struggled financially should not be bailed out. Contrasting the self-supporting nature of opera in Britain with the subsidised system common on the continent was on occasion a source of pride and demonstration of superior British initiative: in 1875, Lord Alfred Paget was proud to note that Mapleson's national opera house was being built without any financial aid from the state, an implicit criticism of the massive sums committed by the French government to the rebuilding of the Grand Opéra in Paris, which

[22] Alfred Bunn, *The Stage: both before and behind the curtain* (3 vols, London, 1840), vol. 1, p. 34.

[23] See Thomas [Willert] Beale to *The Times*, 25 March 1853, p. 3. Beale criticised the failure of the Royal Commission of Fine Art, which was responsible for managing the Exhibition's profit of £186,000, to include music in its activities.

[24] See Walter Maynard [alias of Thomas Willert Beale], *The Entertaining Impresario* (London, 1867), pp. 26–39.

opened in the same year.[25] Others, though, did make a link between the purely commercial basis of British music-making and its apparent backwardness; two letters to the *Musical Standard* in 1876 suggested advantages that could be achieved by intervention in the free market:

> The reason [for] … this absence of high class English music appears to me to arise from and be consequent upon *fiscal* causes, and not from any incapacity in English blood to produce high musical genius. In Germany music is cultivated in almost every small town, as well as in Berlin, Vienna [*sic*] and the like. Every little capital of every little province has its opera and a good team of singers and players. I have heard *Der Freischütz* performed at the little town of Darmstadt as well as I ever heard it performed in London.
>
> In England there is but one *locale* for the effective performance of operas, viz., London …
>
> In Germany there are [also] a great many musical appointments such as that of kapel-meister which fall to the lot of musicians not overladen with gold and which enables them to live and to cultivate their taste for composition if so gifted. In England we hear nothing of the kind.[26]

> As long as the culture and care of English opera is left in the hands of private enterprise, we must not expect so-called English operas to consist of anything except collections of ballads written expressly for the purposes of trade.
>
> If this wealthy city of London for instance would follow the example set by the small towns of Germany and guarantee a fixed sum per annum, sufficient to cover all the working expenses of a theatre where operas in English and English operas would be performed nightly at the ordinary playhouse prices all the year round … the public would gradually learn to appreciate this class of entertainment …
>
> A new school of art cannot be built up in a day; it will be the result of years of patient and enduring labour. It is to our young and unknown composers we must look for the establishment of a national school of opera, if we are ever to have anything worthy of the name.[27]

While statements in favour of subsidy appeared occasionally in the 1870s and early '80s, they were unusual and attracted little attention; the predominant belief was that, if well managed and free of the exorbitant wage demands of star singers, opera companies, supported by an increasingly enlightened and educated

---

25 See Rodmell, *Music and Institutions*, pp. 112–13, and *MP*, 8 September 1875, quoted in *MW*, 11 September, p. 100.

26 *MS*, 11 November 1876, p. 315.

27 *MS*, 28 October 1876, p. 284.

audience, would pay their way.[28] The primary arguments against subsidy were that there was no sustained lobby for it and parliament would therefore never approve it, and that its receipt would come with too many conditions, interfering with managerial freedom. An extensive article in the *Era* in August 1881 admitted that money paid in subsidy in many European towns demonstrated an appreciation of the performing arts, but concluded that the obligations placed upon managers – specific works to be played and people employed, and bureaucratic scrutiny – made the system unattractive.[29] The author concluded: 'We need only look much nearer home to find an example of the highest theatrical success achieved without state or other aid. Mr [Henry] Irving's career at the Lyceum is a brilliant illustration of what may be done by private enterprise, courage, and perseverance, allied with abilities of the first order'. Rosa stated that: 'State subvention for Art purposes in this country is unobtainable. The English are a practical nation. The people prefer to build up important institutions through private enterprise; and that this is preferable in some instances, the system of management upon the great railways here gives the greatest proof'.[30]

Some musicians, such as Mackenzie and Stainer, declared themselves in favour of subsidy. Mackenzie did, however, wish to pacify those who opposed subsidy on principle:

> State aid is most desirable – some of us consider it absolutely necessary. But I cannot bring myself to think that subsidy is, at first, at least, indispensable; that it would not be possible to make a beginning supported only by private individuals who agreed to guarantee the undertaking against loss for a certain number of years. Nay, I am even confident that, with careful management, English opera might soon enough gather strength to pay its own way.[31]

Stainer, however, was unapologetic in his support for subvention as he believed that one factor precluding the success of native operas was:

> the absence of a national opera house or houses, subsidized by the central government or by local municipalities, in which new operas by native composers could be produced without the risk of sending a friendly impresario to the workhouse. Surely the time is ripe for the serious consideration of this question.

---

28 In neither the article by Francis Hueffer nor the editorial in favour of a national opera in the *Era* cited above is the possibility of state support even contemplated (see notes 11 and 13).

29 *Era*, 6 August 1881, p. 15. The subsidy figures quoted are taken from Percy Fitzgerald, *A World Behind the Scenes* (London, 1881), pp. 161–2.

30 Rosa, p. 460.

31 Mackenzie, pp. 45–6.

> Annual grants are made to the National Gallery, the British Museum, and other educational institutions; why is there no grant for a National Opera?[32]

Two papers in favour of the establishment of a national opera house demonstrate the thinking of its supporters in the 1890s. Arthur Hutton's argument, published in 1895, was straightforward: private enterprise, Hutton stated, 'does what it can for us in this matter, but its failure to provide what is wanted is sufficient proof of its inability to meet the case'.[33] Hutton proposed that government should provide a site and fund the building of an opera house upon it, that the LCC should maintain it, and that the building should be let out, at a nominal rent, to impresarios, subject to strict conditions regarding frequency of performance, ticket prices and repertory.[34]

Fuller Maitland, writing in 1898, argued on similar lines: 'Some kind of grant or subvention from without is absolutely essential if opera as an institution is to do a really useful work, or to take a place among national enterprises'.[35] Maitland did not outline a specific scheme, but did make the same ideological case for support:

> In all parts of the continent the intellectual value of the opera is recognised, just as much as that of non-theatrical music or of the other arts. In England alone there still survives the curious impression that music, and more especially the opera, has some element of dissipation about it.[36]

Maitland was not afraid, either, to attack sections of the audience, one of which he accused of comprising 'the wealthy few who are not too particular about the selection of operas given as long as they can be assured that the music they hear is really fashionable'.[37] Such a focus on the wealthy was not new (see Chapters 2

---

32 Stainer, p. 65.

33 Arthur Hutton, 'A National Opera House', *Contemporary Review*, 68 (1895), pp. 58–64 (p. 59). Hutton (1848–1912) served as a priest in both the Anglican and Roman Catholic churches; he also acted as librarian at the National Liberal Club. His published writings included a biography of Cardinal Manning (1892) and he edited the six volume series *The Lives of the English Saints* (1901–02).

34 He said nothing about either the language of performance or the employment of native artists; he may have thought these were implicit in his scheme.

35 John Fuller Maitland, 'Wanted – An Opera', *Nineteenth Century*, 1 June 1898, pp. 977–84 (p. 981).

36 Maitland, p. 979.

37 Maitland, p. 977. The 'lower middle classes' were also criticised; although praising them for consistently supporting Rosa, Maitland argued that this had led to the company keeping 'alive certain traditions which [have] sadly hindered the cause of English opera. The silly dialogue of the days of the poet Bunn is still relished by the kind of audience to which English Opera is ... supposed to appeal; and any educated person, not especially musical ... would very naturally wonder at the tolerance of a West-end public towards a style of declamation that would disgrace the transpontine theatres' (p. 979). Although he referred to the 'lower middle classes', Maitland's criticism was actually directed at a more

and 3) but attacks on Covent Garden's elitist dilettantism became a regular feature of press criticism after Harris's death.[38]

In supporting subsidy, however, the argument both men viewed as their strongest was that the principle was already established in relation to galleries and museums, and simply needed extending to music:

> The general principle of State or municipal aid for various things lying outside the domain of practical business life, is already acknowledged in many ways, and accepted as a fact of our national existence. It would require a very bold politician indeed to bring in a bill for the abolition of the grant to the National Gallery or the British Museum, yet in truth these are not more strictly educational in their intention than such institutions as the great opera houses of the continent.[39]

Maitland's article acted almost as a curtain-raiser for the submission of a memorial presented to the LCC on 21 June 1898 urging the authority's support – both practical and ideological – for the establishment of a national opera house in the capital.[40] This first direct approach to a public authority transformed the possibility of public subsidy from an abstract concept to a potential reality. From this point on, the question of financial assistance dominated all arguments for and against the establishment of a national opera. Ironically, the memorial itself was vague:

---

affluent middle class which considered itself cultured but could neither afford comfortable seats at Covent Garden nor accept the conditions pertaining in cheaper ones.

[38] An anonymous author commented that: 'The Syndicate does not even know the names of the instruments of the orchestra. Not one of its members can read a full score. If some unknown composer in his innocence were to offer a new opera to the management even if it were worth ten *Tristans* and a dozen *Lohengrins*, the management would be none the wiser. Who would look at it? Mr Grau would hand it to Mr Forsyth, Mr Forsyth would pass it on to Mr Higgins, who would give it to Lord de Grey. Lord de Grey immediately would see it to be neither a gun nor a target for anyone else but the critics, and he would give it to Lady de Grey. Lady de Grey would see that there were more than the treble and bass clefs to which she had been accustomed in piano music, and she would hand the score back to Mr Grau, who could scarcely be blamed if he dropped it into the waste-paper basket. All these people are excellent people, and they do their work excellently. What we wish to point out is that not opera, but providing an evening's amusement for society, is their work.' (*Chord*, 1 September 1899, pp. 7–12 (pp. 8–9)).

[39] Maitland, pp. 981–2.

[40] The committee that drew up the memorial included Mackenzie (Chairman), Stanford, Parry, Cowen, Corder, Grove, MacCunn, Stainer, Sullivan, Paolo Tosti, George Martin, Walter Parratt, Alberto Randegger, Joseph Bennett, Frederick Bridge, William Hayman Cummings and Edward German; supporting signatories, totalling over 140, included several aristocrats, headed by the Duke of Westminster, and also Herbert Asquith, Joseph Chamberlain, Henry Irving, Squire Bancroft, Arthur Conan Doyle, Hans Richter, Maitland, J.M. Barrie, G.F. Watts, Arthur Wing Pinero and Alma Tadema.

> 1. That in this, the richest capital in the world, there exists no means whereby the highest class of operatic music can be systematically brought within the reach of the great mass of the people.
> 2. That under existing conditions the very classes of the community which would benefit most constantly by the presentation of the greatest operatic masterpieces are now debarred from such a privilege, and the musical education of the public is thereby much restricted.
> 3. That for this reason little encouragement is offered to young artists to pursue the highest paths of their profession, and little opportunity is afforded for their advancement in them.
> 4. That the development of native operatic art is seriously hindered and discouraged by the lack of any permanent establishment where the works of native composers can be produced.
> 5. That in most of the important towns in Europe it has been found practicable, with the assistance of the public authorities, and at no great cost to the public exchequer, to make provision for the systematic representation of the best class of opera, which has thus, by long established usage, become part of the life of the people.
> 6. That it would be possible for your council, by an annual grant of money of no excessive amount, to bring about the establishment of a permanent opera house in London, which would fulfil the requirements herein before set forth and thereby promote the musical interests and refinement of the public and the advancement of the art of music.
> Your petitioners therefore humbly pray as follows:– That your council should take such steps as to them seem advisable to ascertain how the great want referred to above can be best supplied; and if deemed necessary to obtain powers to obtain some portion of their funds to assist in the maintenance of an opera house for the promotion of the highest form of musical art.[41]

The superiority of opera as an art form, the value of music as a civilising tool, widening access, and the implicit appeal to patriotism were all cited as usual, together with the moral obligation to provide employment for those trained as musicians by the expanding education system (which also employed several of the signatories). The petitioners neatly placed the responsibility on the LCC to work out how the provision of a national opera house might best be achieved.[42]

Even at the outset, reaction to the petition was qualified. Edward Baughan, editor of the *Musical Standard*, doubted that the LCC would act, and attacked the

[41] Memorial to the LCC, reproduced in many newspapers and journals including *MS*, 25 June 1898, p. 401; and *MN*, 2 July, p. 13.

[42] This may in part have been because the council would have had to ensure that it had the power to commit resources to any project; local authorities exercise power on the *ultra vires* principle, that is, actions are only legal if explicitly allowed in law.

proposal for financial support in both principle and practice.[43] Ratepayers were already too highly taxed, he stated, although the amount required to support opera would be minimal (see below), and it was unfair to require those who did not like music to subsidise it; if money was to be spent on supporting music it should be used for education. On two further points Baughan was especially vehement; he turned the argument that Britain was lagging behind the rest of Europe practically on its head by quoting a speech given by Kaiser Wilhelm:

> 'I made it my object,' [the Kaiser] said the other day, 'that the Royal Theatre should become the tool of the monarch, like the schools and the university, whose task it is to train the growing generation, and prepare them for the work of maintaining the highest spiritual possessions of our grand German Fatherland … The theatre is also one of my weapons. It is the monarch's responsibility to look after this theatre … because it can be a tremendous power in the Sovereign's hands' … At the bottom of the Emperor's utterances there is an idea that is quite foreign to the British nation. It is that he considers himself a ruler by divine right and that he looks upon himself as a shepherd who has been called to guide the interests, both moral and material, of his flock. To a certain extent our State takes the same view of its duties, but so far as possible it has been our creed, as it has been the source of our strength, that the satisfying of individual needs should be left in the hands of individuals.[44]

This was scaremongering, but the argument that to advocate state support was virtually unpatriotic because it undermined individual freedom was one that would be deployed effectively, with variations, by other opponents of public subsidy.

The reasoning that the government already supported museums and galleries was dismissed, on the basis that:

> every man and woman, be they aristocrats or plebeians, statesmen, princes or mechanics, can avail themselves of the rich stores of mental education and recreation to be found in our public museums and picture galleries, and do so avail themselves of the opportunity of improving their minds … [A]dmission is free to all classes, so that all classes are on a level and share in the advantages purchased with their money.

An opera house, Baughan contended, could never, for practical reasons, be free, and it was unreasonable to force people who could never attend to contribute to its support.[45] The answer in the first instance was that the memorial's richer

---

43 *MS*, 25 June 1898, pp. 401–3 (p. 401).

44 Ibid, p. 402.

45 This argument could have been undermined by pointing out that many municipalities already supported bands and organ recitals, for which admission fees were charged (see note 58).

signatories should act as philanthropists, with the Prince of Wales taking the lead; 'as to the working of the scheme,' he concluded, 'there is time to think of that when the money has been subscribed'.

F. Gilbert Webb was also sceptical. Like Baughan, he challenged the idea that a national opera could be equated to museums and art galleries as:

> the sums granted to the National Gallery and like institutions are primarily for the preservation of acknowledged works of art, and it can scarcely be said that any operas are in need of special means of preservation. Even the argument of Free Libraries is scarcely sound. These institutions possess an educational influence which opera can never hope to have.[46]

Webb too argued that the responsibility for establishing a national opera should fall to 'the intellectual members of London society. If they are sufficiently numerous and sufficiently in earnest, they can stimulate native art, and give pleasure to thousands of less fortunate ones than themselves'.[47]

The LCC appointed a subcommittee to consider the petition. In March 1899 Stanford, perhaps fearful that momentum was flagging, wrote to *The Times* to draw attention to the issue. The arguments were reiterated, and practical needs listed: a site, £100,000 to build a suitable house, and about £60,000 to endow it and ensure survival in its first three years. After that, Stanford thought, the institution might well be self-sustaining and, if not, 'a national opera should be kept going for the general good, whether it supports itself or not'.[48]

This generated much comment; the arguments for and against public support were reiterated. S.A. Herbert's response put the ideological case against subsidy forcefully, and neither Stanford nor subsequent supporters of subvention were able to refute it successfully. Indeed, the two men's points remain central to the debate on public support for the arts over a century later. Herbert wrote:

> What we all desire to see accomplished is the establishment of English opera on the same firm footing as English drama. The drama is not subsidized, and is probably the better for it. There is a healthy prejudice in the minds of most Englishmen against state subsidies … for undertakings which ought to and can flourish by the ordinary commercial methods if efficiently managed. The signatories to the County Council petition … do not like to be told that what is sauce for the dramatic goose ought to sauce for the operatic gander … Oratorios

46 *MN*, 2 July 1898, p. 13.

47 Another sceptical article asked if grand opera would ever appeal to the 'mass of the people', expecting it 'to be a long while yet in England before *The Ring* and *Tristan* and *The Meistersingers* take a strong hold upon any but a limited and cultivated class' (*Speaker*, 25 June 1898, p. 787); like Baughan and Webb, the anonymous author proposed that philanthropic giving by the rich was the way forward.

48 *The Times*, 11 March 1899, p. 10.

> flourish without state aid, orchestral music in London was never so good a speculation as it is today, the concert rooms are still crowded, grand opera in the Covent Garden season now pays [a dividend of] 35 per cent and is now asking for more capital. Why then alone among all the undertakings of the dramatic or musical impresario, can English opera not pay its way in England?[49]

Herbert alleged that 'even "opera in English" is hardly existent as yet', underlining the persistent metropolitan bias of the debate, forgetful as it was that almost all opera outside the West End was performed in English. Stanford's reply argued that pure commercialism in this instance led to the pursuit of the lowest common denominator:

> Mr Herbert says oratorios flourish without State aid; they do if the societies who produce choral works invariably put on the *Messiah* and *Elijah* to pay for the deficit on anything new or unfamiliar, otherwise there is a loss. He says orchestral music in London was never so good a speculation as it is today; true, if the programme consists mainly of excerpts from Wagner's operas, with Tschaikowsky's 'Pathetic Symphony'. If it does not, only a star pianist can avert a deficit. He says grand opera in Covent Garden pays 35 per cent. It does, provided that the managers play Wagner as often as possible and rely on star singers at enormous salaries, with a corresponding maximum charge for seats. The majority of the Covent Garden public go to hear a singer, not the work in which the singer is but one of the interpreters.[50]

Other letters moved the debate no further, as 'facts' and anecdotal evidence were exchanged.[51] Herbert's principal point, that a good product would be commercially successful, obviating the need for public intervention,[52] remained the most potent, together with the argument that, if the intellectual elite believed so powerfully in the civilising effects of music, it would and should find private

---

49 *The Times*, 1 April 1899, p. 10.

50 *The Times*, 4 April 1899, p. 6.

51 See *The Times*, 27 March 1899, p. 8 (Mackenzie); 28 March, p. 15 (Lord Dysart); 6 April, p .6 (F.B. Money Coutts); 8 April, p. 9 (William Boosey); 11 April, p. 10 (Herbert); and 19 April, p. 4 (Stanford). Other commentary on Stanford's first letter appeared in: *MN*, 18 March 1899, p. 283–4; *MH*, 1 April, p. 107; and *MS*, 8 April, pp. 209–10. A further letter from Edward Speyer (*The Times*, 27 May, p. 6) drew responses in *MS*, 3 June, pp. 344–5; and *Outlook*, 3 June, p. 583.

52 Herbert's faith in market economics was absolute: 'It will not improve the taste of the public to offer them something which they do not want … Nor does it do any good to talk contemptuously of their inability to accept certain works which have failed to please them … by what miraculous power is it supposed that … [the] public will be induced to sit out operas which bore them?' (*The Times*, 11 April 1899, p. 10).

endowments to provide it, as had been the case in art with such recently-founded institutions as the Tate Gallery and Wallace Collection.

When the LCC subcommittee reported it effectively sidelined the memorial. While expressing sympathy and support for the petitioners' objectives, it stated that: 'we are not able to advise the Council to take any step towards establishing a permanent opera house at the expense of the ratepayers until the general public shall have acquired a greater interest in the question'.[53] Contributions from central government and private individuals should also be required to support any future project. A small beacon for the petitioners was that the council was recommended to reserve a plot of land on the new Kingsway development so that private speculators could, if they wished, build an opera house there.[54] In response, the petitioners expressed the hope that as 'so excellent an opportunity has never been given to our national music by a representative public body as is now offered by the generosity of the London County Council … the public will not allow it to be lost'.[55] No further progress was made.

The memorial undoubtedly stimulated debate. The amount of press space devoted to the subject in the Edwardian decade was far greater than before, but in neither practical nor ideological terms were there any advances. Music journalists themselves expressed both frustration and boredom with the subject on several occasions.

Galloway's pamphlet published in 1902 supplied the most extensive examination of practical issues; he described managerial methods in France, Germany and Italy, and gave examples of how much money was provided and by whom. Galloway advocated the adoption of the French system, in which an impresario managed the theatre and was given financial support, in return for which he was subject to a list of responsibilities and obligations, which could relate to the language of performance, new productions, a fixed number of national works in the repertory, and so on.[56]

Although attracting favourable comments in respect of his research, Galloway's brief and somewhat patronising dismissal of the ideological issues, especially that of subvention, did not move the debate forward. In 1903 Galloway initiated the first debate in the House of Commons on music with the motion: 'That, in the opinion of this House, with a view to directing the musical taste of the people into proper channels, it is desirable that National Opera Houses under public control should be established in the principal cities of the United

53 Report reproduced in *Era*, 20 May 1899, p. 8.

54 Oscar Hammerstein did build an opera house on Kingsway (see Chapter 3) but received no favourable terms.

55 *MS*, 10 June 1899, p. 357. Further commentary on the subject can be found in *SR*, 10 June, pp. 711–12; *MN*, 17 June, p. 646; *MOMTR*, 1 July, pp. 670–71.

56 The French system had been previously described in some detail by Maynard in 1867 (see Maynard, pp. 27–8) and also advocated, in brief, by 'Progress' (see *MS*, 28 October 1876, p. 284); Hutton's proposal in 1895 (see above) is also remarkably similar.

Kingdom'.[57] Galloway noted that the principle of public subsidy for music had already been established as the LCC and other municipalities had long sponsored band concerts in public parks; the LCC alone had spent £12,000 on this in the previous year.[58] The parochial argument was again deployed: 'In every class of the community there was some knowledge of, and some desire for music; and if the Government would only step forward ... it would not be long before they found a much greater improvement in the people'. No-one spoke against Galloway but Sir William Anson, for the government, stalled by asking him to await the publication of a parliamentary paper detailing subsidy levels in other countries; Galloway withdrew his motion which, as the house was inquorate, could not be voted on in any case. The parliamentary paper was published later in 1903,[59] and showed that in every country for which information was available (most in Europe, and many in South and Central America), with the exceptions of Honduras, Venezuela, the United States and United Kingdom, some public support for opera at either municipal or state level was forthcoming.[60] While Stanford once again tried to use the publication to revive the debate, nothing happened.[61]

The issue continued to exercise commentators, but now almost invariably refracted through the prism of public subsidy. Papers by Fuller Maitland, J. Cuthbert Hadden, and Stanford (all in favour), and Hugh Arthur Scott (against) re-covered the same ground, and Galloway returned to the fray in 1910 in *Musical England*.[62] Parallels existed with the debate in favour of the establishment of a

57 House of Commons Debate, 7 April 1903, vol 120, columns 1333–44: *http://hansard.millbanksystems.com/commons/1903/apr/07/national-opera* [accessed 22 August 2012]. As a Manchester MP, Galloway was more sensitive than many to the existence of an audience beyond the West End.

58 Park concerts were not the only instance of municipal support for music. Resorts, for example, saw the provision of music as a means of encouraging tourism: Bournemouth established a municipal band established in 1876 which developed into the Bournemouth Municipal Orchestra in 1893. Several towns sponsored organ recitals; for examples see Rachel Milestone, '"A Melodious Phenomenon": The Institutional Influence on Town-Hall Music-Making' in Rodmell, *Music and Institutions*, pp. 55–78; see also William Galloway, *Musical England* (London, 1910), pp. 45–65.

59 House of Commons, Parliamentary Papers: *Miscellaneous. No. 6 (1903). Return as to financial support given from state or municipal funds to dramatic, operatic, or musical performances in foreign countries* (http://gateway.proquest.com/openurl?url_ver=Z39.88-2004&res_dat=xri:hcpp&rft_dat=xri:hcpp:rec:1904-004354 [accessed 4 September 2012]).

60 Amounts and types of assistance varied from substantial and consistent support given in many European countries to minimal and sometimes sporadic assistance such as that available in the Argentine, which comprised solely the Buenos Aires municipality exempting visiting opera companies from local taxation in the main, winter, season.

61 Stanford to *The Times*, 28 December 1903, p. 6.

62 See J.A. Fuller Maitland, 'Music versus the Opera', *Nineteenth Century and After*, 51 (1902), pp. 112–22; J. Cuthbert Hadden, 'The Question of Subsidised Opera', *Gentlemen's Magazine*, 1 March 1905, pp. 295–304; Stanford, 'The Case for National

national theatre, which had sporadically erupted over several previous decades and which reached its highest pitch between 1908 and 1914,[63] and in Frederick Verney's call for the establishment of a municipal concert hall in London.[64] That the debate continued to focus on the principle of subsidy for music performances when it already operated, modestly, in many provincial centres, illustrates the continuing metropolitan bias of the debate, alongside an unspoken sense that opera was too elitist and expensive to justify support, even if the principle itself might be conceded. The positions of both sides were entrenched with little evidence that the debate changed many minds; Edward Baughan's *volte face* was a rare event.[65]

Despite, or rather because of, the lack of progress, the 'national opera' issue refused to die, and supporters continuously grasped at straws which might signal that change was afoot. Richter and Pitt's performances of *Der Ring* and other operas in 1908 and 1909 were, for example, cited as a step forward, as the English language finally stormed the operatic Bastille of Covent Garden for an entire season: here was tangible evidence that, even at Britain's most exclusive theatre, opera in the vernacular, supported by the Syndicate itself, could be successful. It was not long, however, before Harry Higgins put the lid firmly back on the Pandora's Box the Syndicate had briefly opened (see Chapter 3). Whatever the

---

Opera' (note 20); Hugh Arthur Scott, 'Against a Subsidised Opera', *Nineteenth Century and After*, 55 (1904), pp. 752–64.

63 For discussion of campaigns to establish a national theatre see James Woodfield, *English Theatre in transition 1881–1914* (London, 1984) and also extensive coverage in *The Times* from 1908 onwards; the ability to perform Shakespeare adequately was a constant factor and the later campaigns aimed at opening a national theatre in time for his tercentenary in 1916. A motion in favour of establishing a state-supported National Theatre was debated by MPs in 1913 but adjourned without a vote. Francis Neilson, former Stage Manager at Covent Garden, spoke in favour; Galloway had ceased to be an MP. (*House of Commons Debate, 23 April 1913, vol 52, columns 454–95* (http://hansard.millbanksystems.com/commons/1913/apr/23/national-theatre-in-london [accessed 13 September 2012])). See also William Caird, 'A Plea for National and Municipal Theatres', *Westminster Review*, 1 May 1913, pp. 562–74.

64 Frederick Verney, 'A Municipal Concert Hall for London', *Nineteenth Century and After*, 58 (1905), pp. 561–9.

65 For Baughan's arguments against subsidy see above; he did not acknowledge the alteration in his views, but his statement in favour of state support was unequivocal: 'As a nation we have been inclined to look on all but the plastic arts as mere amusement and to consider them … as the fad of dilettanti. With our exaggerated love of individual action, it has seemed only reasonable to us that both music and drama should be the enterprise of the individual and, with some muddled idea of the great truth of Supply and Demand, we have thought that when the public wants a thing it will be given it … If [however] you consider the history of any artistic movement you will find, I think, that there has always been a leader who has found his public waiting for his lead … It may at least be said that the art of music has every right to claim rank besides the plastic arts … It is clear, I think, that a nation which subsidises painting cannot logically refuse to subsidise music' ('The Subvention of Music', *MMR*, 1 February 1904, pp. 23–5 (p. 23)).

Syndicate's motivations, the perception that Covent Garden was the enemy within was reinforced.[66] Similarly, rumours that circulated in summer 1909 that Joseph Beecham was prepared to donate £300,000 towards the founding of a national opera house – just the sort of sum those advocating philanthropy needed – created excitement but turned out to be another false dawn.[67]

The outbreak of war resulted in a temporary end to calls for subsidy for the performing arts; *grands projets* were put on hold and campaigns for state or municipal support were subordinated to the war effort. Thomas Beecham's call for Manchester Council to provide him with a site upon which to build an opera house after the war ended was the last proposal for a publicly supported venue made before 1918. This project made no progress (see Chapter 4).

In the Edwardian years the establishment of a national opera became, for many, the panacea for Britain's 'operatic problem'; such an institution, in providing opportunities for native composers and performers, high-class productions in the vernacular, long seasons and cheap tickets, would, it was argued, generate its own momentum, Britain would be transformed into a nation of opera lovers, drawn from all social classes, who would regularly support performances of both revived and new works in a language they understood, and based on subjects which 'spoke' to them in a way that foreign operas did not. Thus the difficulties were structural: if the appropriate framework could be created, the 'operatic problem' would solve itself.

This was a simplistic approach. The commercial environment of British opera undoubtedly hampered the establishment of a local canon: the constant and short-term financial pressures experienced by opera troupes, issues relating to performing rights, the lack of a prestigious house in which reputations could be made and sustained, and the relentless focus of the country's leading theatre, Covent Garden, upon foreign works, all created difficulties whereby even operas which enjoyed some measure of mass popularity, such as Thomas's *Esmeralda*, were dropped within a few years. These difficulties created a demoralising sense that the effort required was disproportionate to the likelihood of success; it is notable how few British composers and librettists sustained a consistent interest in opera writing, forgoing development in the light of accumulated experience. But, in spite of these challenges, the number of new British and Irish operas produced in this period is impressive. On average two or three works appeared each year between 1875 and 1918, the vast majority of which were first produced in the

---

[66] It is tempting to conclude that the Syndicate simply did not want opera in English, and even worse, English opera, to gain a permanent foothold at Covent Garden.

[67] See *MG*, 6 July 1909, p. 14 and 7 July, p. 6; *MS* 10 July, pp. 19–20, and 17 July, pp. 35–6. These reports were only rumours, but Joseph did little if anything to dampen them. Henry Mapleson, son of James, stated that £500,000 was the figure necessary for the complete project (a massive increase on the figure of £160,000 Stanford had proposed ten years previously) and that Beecham's promised donation was contingent on other rich men and investors making up the balance. Similar rumours appeared in 1913; see John Lucas, *Thomas Beecham: An Obsession with Music* (Woodbridge, 2008) p. 100.

British Isles.[68] And yet, with the exception of Boughton's *The Immortal Hour*, none achieved a contemporaneous success sustained for more than two or three seasons at most, and many went almost unnoticed except by the audiences present at the one or two performances most works received, or by those who combed through press reviews.

The structural problems were particular as well as general. Firstly, it was difficult to secure a production in the all-important West End; success in a central London theatre, with the attendant press coverage, was widely and correctly seen as the best way for an opera to be launched. Secondly, the crucial repeat performances needed to build a reputation and subsequent longevity with due admission to the – enduringly hypothetical – canon of British operas, were few and far between. Resentment of these two difficulties – with especial opprobrium directed at Covent Garden – festered continuously and contributed to a feeling that native operas were not given a fair chance. The lobby for a national opera is therefore understandable but, while it would certainly have made a difference, the transformative expectations vested in such an institution were wholly unrealistic: it could never have provided all the production opportunities desired and, just as in France, Germany and Italy, replete with subsidised theatres, the majority of new works would have been discarded, as they were in the United Kingdom's commercially based system. Nor could a single institution create mass enthusiasm for opera. Indeed, a suspicion of the opponents of the scheme was that it would merely provide a subsidised playground for a composers' cartel to produce operas which would be seen by the 'usual suspects' while the remainder of the populace was unaware even of its existence.

Commentators were keen to suggest that the foundation of a native canon was imminent and cited contemporaneous works that would be included; looking back, however, they were usually dismissive of almost all previous efforts. In dismissing earlier attempts, the standard justifications were that the product was either weak, or derivative, or both. But why did so many British operas fail? Steadily there appeared an uncomfortable feeling that structural problems were not the sole explanation. This in turn raised questions regarding what a British opera was meant to look and sound like in order to make it both distinctive and appealing, as

[68] Contemporaneous claims that native composers needed to go to abroad, especially to Germany, are exaggerated, although they apply in certain instances; Stanford was told by Carl Rosa that he should get *The Veiled Prophet* 'first produced in Germany. Its success will (unfortunately) have much greater chances here if accepted abroad' (Rosa to Stanford, 11 February 1879, RCM MS 4253, item 122). Smyth's first three operas were also premiered in Germany, and most of De Lara's first produced in France; all three composers, however, had overseas contacts, an advantage held by relatively few British composers. The impression that continental productions were easier to secure has been more recently reinforced, perhaps inadvertently, by Eric Walter White (see *A History of English Opera* (London, 1983) pp. 335–64).

audiences were neither inclined nor to be expected to support composers solely on the grounds of shared nationality.

The issue of professional training was considered: inadequate facilities to prime composers and performers had been cited in the late Victorian period as a crucial reason for Britain's failure to meet the musical achievements of its continental neighbours (in all genres) and for the ubiquity of foreign musicians in its orchestras and theatres. With the founding of the Royal College, expansion of the Royal Academy and music education within universities, however, this argument weakened as greater numbers of trained musicians passed through their doors.[69] Curiously, the point that neither the College nor the Academy devoted significant resources to opera was rarely made.[70]

The issue of the quality and nature of the product itself remained unresolved. When, in the late 1870s, new British operas started to appear after the post-Pyne-Harrison interregnum, a sense that something new was afoot took tentative hold. A new generation of composers, it was hoped, would set Britain on a new path. While there was considerable audience affection for the works of Balfe, Wallace and their contemporaries, the *cognoscenti* felt that to carry on in this established style was unacceptable. Thus the musical amalgam of early nineteenth-century Italian *opera buffa*, English glees and ballads, and a little French *opéra comique*, combined with a slight story frequently involving an innocent girl whose fortitude in the face of adversity was eventually rewarded by living happily ever after with her heroic suitor, while the villain of the piece was either killed, humiliated, or redeemed, all expressed via a libretto comprising almost entirely rhyming couplets, had to be discarded.[71] Continental opera had moved on to more realistic, tragic and epic veins, best exemplified in Britain's theatres by *Carmen*, the developing style of Verdi and the rise of Wagner. A belief formed that if British composers were to stand equal to their most successful continental contemporaries, scenarios had to become more naturally dramatic, rely less on clichéd character stereotypes, dispense with the moralising plots and twee, almost pantomimic, spoken dialogue and, instead, embrace continuous music, and a more symphonic, integrated musical

---

69 Stanford turned this back on itself by arguing that the creation of a national opera house was needed in order to provide employment for the professional musicians the country was producing: 'We have begun at the wrong end. The education which has been thrown open to the musical youth of England has been regally endowed, but the career in which the bulk of their years is spent has been totally uncared for. It would have been safer to have provided the career first, and trusted to its inducements to foster the desire for education. But if the mistake has been made it is happily one which can be repaired; and the establishment of a national opera will repair it' (Stanford to *The Times*, 11 March 1899, p. 10).

70 Neither Stanford nor Corder, principal teachers of composition at the College and Academy respectively, prioritised opera in their courses; Stanford, at least, believed that mastery of small forms was essential before larger and more flexible genres could be tackled.

71 For further discussion of stock mid-century plots and characters see George Biddlecombe, *English Opera from 1834 to 1864* (New York, 1994), pp. 17–36.

structure which, while it certainly did not have to be overtly Wagnerian, especially in its tonal language – a step too far for many critics of the 1880s – had at least to demonstrate large-scale musical planning and a desire to move 'beyond' the regular periodisation and simple formal structures that characterised British operas of the earlier Victorian years.[72] Overt and strong criticisms of Balfe, Wallace, and their librettists, such as those quoted above were relatively rare, but there was a sense that a new work such as Cowen's *Pauline* (1876) did not 'advance' sufficiently on earlier models, despite its strengths. Prout commented that,

> when he tries to write after the pattern of *The Bohemian Girl* he produces what is of little value ... [whereas] the duet between Claude and Pauline, 'A palace lifting to eternal summer', is one of the very best numbers of the opera. Here, for the first time in the work, the influence of Wagner is to be clearly seen, not in the music itself, but in the connexion between it and the text.[73]

It was not only European 'progress' that induced a feeling that British opera had to change. The rise of operetta, followed by musical comedy, as a distinct and popular genre in the last 30 years of the century further emphasised in the minds of the *cognoscenti* the need to move on from the mid-century style: Gilbert and Sullivan and Alfred Cellier were viewed as the successors to Balfe and Wallace and, if 'grand' opera in Britain was to distinguish itself from its lighter and aesthetically inferior comic cousin, its musical and dramatic structures had to change accordingly.[74]

The enduring popularity of *The Bohemian Girl* and *Maritana*, however, illustrates a divide between commentators and audiences, and created further problems for both composers and companies; while the new generation of internationally educated composers that appeared in the 1880s (supported by London-based critics) was inclined to experiment with structural and tonal innovations and more graphic dramatic scenarios, audiences were less enthusiastic – perhaps not least

---

72 A common late Victorian criticism of Balfe et al. was that they acceded to commercial pressure to write operas from which items could be extracted for publication, resulting, in the words of Ebenezer Prout, in works in which 'the separate numbers might be shaken up in a bag, and then put together in whatever order they happened to be drawn out without any detriment whatever to the musical effect' (*Academy*, 2 December 1876, p. 553). Similar sentiments were expressed in the *Athenaeum*'s review of Thomas's *Esmeralda*: 'the English Opera of the future must be planned on a larger basis [than that of Balfe, Wallace or Loder], with more attention to dramatic detail, and less regard to the needs of the music shop' (31 March 1883, p. 417).

73 Ibid.

74 Sullivan in particular suffered from this mentality, with a long-running perception that he was wasting his talents on his collaborations with Gilbert; for example, Stainer stated that 'all those that have the true progress of English music at heart must hope that Sullivan's genius will some day take a higher flight' and that he would eventually attempt to 'produce the more ambitious type of opera' (quoted in *MS*, 18 January 1890, p. 65).

because, especially outside the West End, there were few opportunities to see the contemporaneous continental works that influenced the new generation – and this rendered the new operas financially unviable, leading to their rapid retirement. Stanford's *Canterbury Pilgrims*, and Mackenzie's *Colomba* and *The Troubadour* all suffered in this respect for, whatever their strengths, audiences did not embrace them. Thomas's *Esmeralda*, exhibiting the influence of Gounod and Ambroise Thomas, and evincing more readily its number-based structure, was received more positively, and was the most successful of the Rosa commissions.[75] When Corder's *Nordisa* was produced, however, its overt reliance on mid-century British opera (as well as *opéra comique* and *Spieloper*) generated audience enthusiasm but sneering criticism in the metropolitan press and it was dropped after one season.

British operas of this period exhibit a diverse range of influences. While orchestral and choral music was subjected most strongly and consistently to German models and approaches, fitting neatly with the aesthetic values of most composers and critics, the prevalent belief in the 'racial affinity' of the 'north European nations', and the healthy presence of German music and musicians in Britain's concert life, this was much less the case with opera, where the French and Italian schools were equally important due to their dominating the repertory performed in Britain, and despite their representing the 'foreign' and 'exotic' Latin nations of southern Europe. Conversely, the absence in the British repertory of a strong German opera tradition,[76] and the conflicted reception of Wagner until well into the 1890s, diluted the strong Anglo-German relationship felt in other genres. Consequently, until the 1890s, composers educated at home generally stuck to the form and musical language of mid-century models (themselves influenced by continental works). Edwards's *Victorian*, for example, nods to Rossini, Bizet and earlier Verdi, but not to Wagner; Cole's *Romance of the Harem* and Selby's *Adela*, similarly stick resolutely to early nineteenth-century structures. Overt Wagnerianism, such as that seen in *The Canterbury Pilgrims*, *The Troubadour*, Bantock's *Caedmar*, Tolkien's *Adela* and Clutsam's *King Harlequin* (which verges at times on the Straussian) was relatively rare, but, from the 1890s, many composers responded, as French and Italian composers also did, to Wagner's works by moving towards a less rigid number structure, employing shorter single-

[75] Stainer grouped the three men together, while maintaining that there was a gap between them and their audience, stating that they had 'secured a certain amount of success as opera writers, and they would probably have attained still greater success had they not been over-anxious to prove in their writings their allegiance to the new and most advanced order of operatic style' (as previous note, pp. 64–5).

[76] The only German composers whose operas featured regularly in the repertories of British companies in the second half of the nineteenth century were Mozart, Beethoven, Weber and Nicolai, the last three being represented by single works, and thus not a viable basis for a new British school of opera composition. The only contemporaneous German composer other than Wagner who might have provided some inspiration, Hermann Goetz, died prematurely in 1876 at the age of 36.

section arias, passages of arioso, more frequent modulations between both closely and more distantly related keys, more irregular periodisation, reminiscence motifs, and aspiring towards a more continuous musical and dramatic impulse.[77]

The popularity of *Cavalleria Rusticana* and *Pagliacci*, followed by the growing reputation of Puccini, led some composers to attempt 'verismo' operas, for example Maclean's *Petruccio* and Löhr's *Sarenna*, while Wagner's influence was felt most strongly in scenarios, with mythical or Celtic pre-Christian subjects becoming more popular, such as in Holbrooke's trilogy *The Cauldron of Annwn*, Boughton's *The Immortal Hour*, Butler's *Muirgheis*, and MacCunn's *Diarmid*, although all these works also exhibit elements of Wagnerian musical style. Other composers, styles and subgenres were also influential: Massenet and Saint-Saëns in the works of de Lara and Bunning's *Princesse Osra*; a combination of Gounod and Wagner in Rôze's *Joan of Arc*; Märchenoper in Holbrooke's *Pierrot and Pierrette*, Esposito's *The Tinker and the Fairy*, and Smyth's *Der Wald*; overt exoticism in Holst's *Sāvitri*, Pritchard's *Kunacepa* and Raybould's *Sumida River*; and a lighter 'post-Singspiel' in Stanford's *Shamus O'Brien*, Smyth's *Boatswain's Mate*, and Sullivan's *Beauty Stone*.

In terms of stylistic distinctiveness, it is hard to trace either the emergence of one preferred style borrowed from abroad, or the development of a musical language which might be termed distinctly national (be that English, Welsh, Scottish, Irish or British – see below). This eclecticism, although showing erudition, was both the cause and illustration of the problem faced by producers and consumers alike. Whereas in operetta and musical comedy a more homogeneous, though variegated, style emerged and developed in the 1870s, grand opera scores remained diverse. Originality was also valued to a greater extent in serious music and so, increasingly, the sense that British operas were too derivative was used as an explanation for their failure. Furthermore, the popularity of the thesis that national characteristics were biologically determined encouraged the conclusion that British composers would continue to fail until they cast aside foreign influences. That this became an issue was due to perception rather than actuality: commentators wanted an explanation and a solution for the 'operatic problem'. Many opera-goers, however, simply wanted to enjoy themselves, and were happy to use a set of established reference points similar to those widely perceived to exist in musical comedy to measure a work's success.

Paradoxically, and despite this perception of enslavement to overseas influences, there was little pressure before the Great War to establish an overtly national operatic style comparable to that of Russia or Bohemia, via the use of native myths and stories, traditional melodies, dance forms and instruments. The situation was further complicated by the United Kingdom's tetra-national structure. It was, albeit inconsistently, among the three smaller nations that interest in a national outlook comparable to that of Russia first emerged. The results, however, were variable:

[77] Many late Victorian critics indiscriminately tagged operas superficially exhibiting any of these characteristics as 'Wagnerian', regardless of any other aspects or affinities.

Joseph Parry struck out first with *Blodwen* (1878), a Welsh story set to a Welsh language libretto, but the music could hardly be described as either national or distinctive. Parry's impact was almost entirely confined, as much by design as by accident, to Wales and its diaspora, and there were no immediate successors to develop the tentative manifesto he had set out.[78] A similar situation prevailed in Scotland: MacCunn and Drysdale both composed works which tried to embody a distinctly Scottish outlook, but Drysdale's were not performed, and MacCunn did not sustain his activity. Mackenzie, notably, showed no interest in participating in such a movement in his operas and no-one continued the fledgling style MacCunn attempted in *Jeanie Deans*. Irish composers were, together, the most successful in creating a distinctive style before 1918, but again their efforts were inconsistent. Stanford, for all his Anglo-Irish heritage, set down a marker in *Shamus O'Brien* and, spurred by the late nineteenth-century growth of interest in Irish history, folklore and language, more Irish operas appeared in the Edwardian decade, mainly based on folklore. A lack of performance opportunities and a London-centric musical press, however, meant that these works attracted little attention outside Ireland and, within the country itself, there was insufficient momentum to develop these ideas for some time subsequently. Despite being the largest and most advantaged of the four nations, England was weakest in terms of creating (or even being interested in) a national style. Cosmopolitanism reigned (reflected as much in the varied settings of musical comedy as in grand opera) and interest in English subjects and musical styles rarely appeared. The fledgling folksong revival and 'Pastoral School' made virtually no impact on English opera before 1918. The indigenous theme most consistently employed by English composers was actually that of the 'Celtic Fringe', exemplified by Boughton, Bainton and Holbrooke. The works that came closest to a human (as opposed to mythical) English outlook were such varied examples as Sullivan's *Ivanhoe*, Smyth's *The Wreckers* and *The Boatswain's Mate* and, ironically, the Anglo-Irish Stanford's *Canterbury Pilgrims* and *The Critic*, but works of such varied subject, musical language, and chronology could hardly be deemed an emerging style. Indeed, the wide variety of geographical and historical locations chosen by composers from across the British Isles highlights their cosmopolitanism and interest in the possibilities of 'local colour': from France (*Pauline*, *Esmeralda*, *Joan of Arc*, *The Troubadour*) to India and Persia (*Sāvitri*, *The Light of Asia*, and *The Veiled Prophet*), the Far East (*Sumida River*), Scandinavia (*Thorgrim* and *Nordisa*), Italy (*Dante and Beatrice* and *Signa*), and the Gulf of Mexico (*Petruccio*), to Greece (*Soléa*), and from the mythical pre-Christian (*Oithona* and *The Cauldron of Annwn*), medieval (*Ivanhoe*, *The Prentice Pillar*, *Duke or Devil?* and *Harold*), and recent past (*The Wreckers*, *Shamus O'Brien* and *Jeannie Deans*), to the virtual present (*The Boatswain's Mate* and *Naïl*).

In the Edwardian years this perceived lack of a distinctively national approach was more frequently cited as a reason for British opera's failure. Contributions to

---

[78] Vincent Thomas's operas represent an attempt but, an amateur resident in London, he was unable to tap into the support networks Parry had accessed so successfully.

the debate were often vague, such as when Boughton presented Bainton's *Oithona* as an example of British opera of the future:

> We must have opera of the noblest and most elevating nature which is just as much to the Anglo-Saxon race of the present and future as *Maritana* and *The Bohemian Girl* [!] have been in the past – opera which shall go right down into the soil for its being, and dig there from the ever-fruitful Mother all that is best and true – opera that shall weld the vigour of the man of action, the tenderness of the lover, the happiness of the child, and a conviction of spiritual truth into one great dissoluble whole …
>
> [U]ntil the Folk recognize themselves and their conditions in stage productions nothing but a more or less elevated species of amusement can result. But the day is not far distant … when opera will be as important a factor in the higher education of our People … This will be when the young British school of composers, now fast attaining command of their mother-tongue in music, have arrived at maturity and are enabled thereby to give utterance to the long-pent songs of manliness and deep emotion which for many years have struggled for birth.[79]

In a less florid manner and at greater length in his 1911 volume *Music and Nationalism*, Cecil Forsyth posed the question 'why have the English people never been able to develop a school of national opera?' and suggested several reasons, including Britain's sustained overseas exploration and imperial ambitions.[80] While explaining the past, however, Forsyth, like Boughton, had little practical advice to offer composers for the future:

> So began the long line of operas for whose failure all the old familiar excuses have been, and are still, solemnly trotted out. The injustice and ignorance of the critics; the squabbles of the singers; the badness of the Opera books; the wickedness of the lower classes, who were too stupid to know anything (except perhaps what they did not want); the equal wickedness of the upper classes, who were so clever that they knew exactly what they did want … all these and a dozen similar excuses have been paraded in English journals and in English literature from the first years of the eighteenth century till the year of grace, 1911; and the operas on whose behalf they have been coaxed out make their

[79] Rutland Boughton, 'British Opera – And its Future. With an Example', *MS*, 13 February 1903, pp. 113–15 (p. 113)). Boughton blamed Covent Garden's bias towards French opera on the 'preponderating influence of Norman blood' within the aristocracy; his use of the term 'Folk' implies an acquaintance with Wagner's prose works.

[80] Cecil Forsyth, *Music and Nationalism: A Study of English Opera* (London, 1911), p. 15. Exploration and empire-building led to musical failure (and similar situations in Holland, Spain and Portugal) due to the nation turning 'outwards', whereas 'inward-looking' countries such as Germany and Austria-Hungary had thrived; the inconsistencies in this thesis are too numerous to discuss here.

> awkward, unconvincing, little bows before the public have all been made of Brummagem stuff, made in imitation of to-day in Italy, or of last-week in France, or of yesterday-fortnight in Germany …
>
> To develop [popular English opera] further our composers must, once and for all, put off their high-and-dry, detached attitude of mind and determine, at whatever sacrifice to themselves, to write Opera which is 'accessible and intelligible' to the people …
>
> It will be an opera such as Purcell imagined – an opera in which the Drama is poetry, and the Music is employed to 'exalt the poetry' … The procession of the Drama itself can be … restricted to such broad developments as we see in *Tristan and Isolde*, while the movements of the actual characters on the stage can be, and ought to be, confined to those expressive 'ceremonial movements' each one of which has a definite bearing on the Drama. In an Opera of this sort we stretch hands, as it were, across two centuries to Henry Purcell. The 'emotion of the character' and the 'emotion of the music' become blended into a single conception, in which the two parts are presented simultaneously to the audience …
>
> The essential preliminary to the foundation of a School of English opera is the production of English works written, not with the object of outraging the English prejudices in the matter, but in the frank and healthy determination to accept these prejudices, and to offer the public an art-form satisfactory to both itself and to the composer.[81]

Faced with such nebulous counsel, British composers might be forgiven for not creating a distinctive operatic style more or less instantly.

The futile circularity of this debate can be illustrated by reference to two further articles. Almost 20 years before Forsyth, John Runciman had attempted to define 'national opera'.[82] Runciman dismissed the Rosa commissions and *Ivanhoe* as being 'not English in spirit … without exception the music was in form, structure and feeling (where there was any feeling) thoroughly German'.[83] National opera, he argued (specifically excluding the works of Gilbert & Sullivan and other comic operas as 'their purpose is not artistic but antipathetic to that – commercial'), needed to be 'acceptable and accessible to a whole nation', with the former meaning 'common to one nation … nor likely to become common to other[s]'. Acknowledging that national traditions were usually adaptations of pre-existing forms, German opera was preferred as a basis since 'that is the form wherein has found completest expression the life of the nation more nearly resembling the English than any other which exists'. Runciman then also lapsed into nebulous generalities: as the English were dramatic where the Germans were

---

81 Ibid, pp. 103, 120, and 122–3.

82 John F. Runciman, 'English National Opera', *MoM*, 1 July 1893, pp. 161–3, and 1 August, pp. 188–9.

83 Ibid, p. 161.

mystical, 'it seems certain that opera fitted to around noblest English feeling to the highest pitch will be full of action'. But he could then only manage to say that

> I leave it to more imaginative spirits to speculate on the exact matters with which it will be concerned. But I venture to suggest that … it could not leave untouched … the tragedy of woman's life, the tragedy of man's life also, and the longing of both for the larger freedom; the ancient, ever-fresh puzzle of freedom versus necessity, the mysteries of fate and of the destinies of the individual and the race, [and] the greater mystery of the world and human existence.[84]

As regards the music, Runciman was equally unforthcoming:

> All that can be said is that English music must possess the subtle qualities necessary to make it acceptable to the English people. That is to say … that truly English music can only be produced by an Englishman, a consummate musician, thinking the noblest thought and experiencing the deepest emotions of the English; he, taking the musical structures and forms of Beethoven and Bach, as Goethe took the dramatic form and expression of Shakespeare, will produce English music, replete with English feeling – music which will act like magic on the English speaking nations.[85]

Concluding with a call for better music education in schools, the foundation of multiple municipal opera houses, a socialistic rallying-cry for collective action to replace selfish individualism, and the inaccurate statement that Wagner was to be the model because his 'are the most popular of all operas with the English', Runciman declared – like many others – that good times were just around the corner.[86]

Although the primary focus of commentators was music, the work of librettists did not escape attention. Indeed, a desire to discard the mid-century styles and structures of Alfred Bunn and Edward Fitzball was felt perhaps even more intensely than the need to move on from Balfe and Wallace. Just as the appropriate inheritors of the mid-century musical style were felt by most commentators to be the comic opera composers, so the rhyming couplets of Bunn and Fitzball were viewed as best developed by that genre's librettists, such as Gilbert, Stephenson, Burnand, and Farnie. With no other native libretto tradition, however, authors,

---

84 Ibid, p. 162.

85 Ibid, pp. 162–3. Fugues, imitative counterpoint, and word-painting were, however, explicitly excluded.

86 Another contribution to this debate came from Charles Maclean, who concluded, in contrast to Runciman, that the English ballad 'is destined to be one of the principal stones in the arch of future English opera', and, in respect of dramatic subjects, that 'the key to English emotion is home-life, for in England woman is honoured more than in any other country; and the music which will dominate the future stage will be that which derives its initial force from the domestic hearth' ('More English Opera', *MS*, 18 February 1899, pp. 98–100).

like composers, could either only continue the mid-century approach in a more sentimental or melodramatic vein than was used in comic opera (for example in Oxenford's libretto for *Herne*, Sketchley's for *A Romance of the Harem*, and Corder's much-maligned *Nordisa*) or effectively start again from scratch, necessitating the use of ideas and conventions from continental models and indiscriminately selected literary sources.

Even more so than with composers, few who tried their hand at libretto-writing attempted the task more than once or twice, so inexperience was a constant problem, and established playwrights were rarely tempted to contribute.[87] The combination of unschooled authors and absence of acceptable models resulted in libretti that frequently failed. Common faults were wordy and artificial construction, difficult to understand even as spoken drama; tortuous manipulation of word order; antiquated expressions and constructions; an inability to create distinctive yet credible characters; a failure to understand dramatic pacing by the strategic distribution of climaxes; and an emphasis on static spectacle rather than dramatic action. That few composers demanded more of their librettists exacerbated the problem; some had the added disadvantage of working with aristocrats with literary pretensions, such Lord Howard de Walden (Holbrooke's trilogy *The Cauldron of Annwn*), John Campbell, Duke of Argyll (MacCunn's *Diarmid* and Drysdale's unperformed *Fionn and Tera*) and Sir Edward Malet (Cowen's *Harold*). Composers who wrote their own libretti rarely fared any better, replicating the same errors as independent authors. Not all operas were marred by poor prose and structure but successes were rare: Julian Sturgis did a good job in adapting Shakespeare for Stanford's *Much Ado About Nothing*, Smyth produced an effective libretto for her own *Boatswain's Mate*, and being a tyro did not necessarily spell disaster as the simple yet eloquent work by Douglas Hyde for Esposito's *The Tinker and The Fairy* shows.

The 'libretto problem' was often cited as a factor in Britain's failure to produce successful operas but, while many writers opined on the subject, few made any practical suggestions for improvement. In 1888, Frederick Crowest stated that 'the librettist would appear to be the chief mischief-worker ... Each new librettist adopts these old [Italianate] lines and when the composer comes by he feels it no duty of his to improve the libretto. That there is no possible departure from this state of things is absurd and the new era librettist will do well to cast about for some improvements upon his very antiquated model'.[88] George Clutsam was more specific but still imprecise:

> [The librettist's] text will be to the point – terce, pregnant lines, poetical if possible, but discreetly selected in the matter of the actual words used, and

[87] The forlorn state of British playwriting in this period did not help matters; the brittle and intricate wit of Oscar Wilde would hardly have been suitable for a grand opera libretto.

[88] Frederick Crowest, 'English Opera *in nubibus*', *National Review*, 1 October 1888, pp. 185–201 (p. 188). Most of Crowest's article was later derided by Charles Graves, but not the comments on librettists (see *MT*, 1 November, pp. 650–53).

> action will be supreme. Closely-nit [*sic*], vivid moments on the stage, each brief scene all of opportune significance, the story almost entirely capable of being understood by pantomime alone, and when the text is all important a consideration and reticence on the part of the composer that will permit of every word being understood, are essentials that cannot be neglected if English opera is to gain any sort of attention.[89]

The long-established observer Herman Klein replied in despair:

> Throughout the length and breadth of the land we do not possess one solitary specimen of that primary essential … 'the first-class opera librettist'. It is very well to say that librettists must be found, that they must 'come fresh to their work', that they must be 'informed'. Where are they?
>
> How can Mr Clutsam … believe for a moment that we as yet have available in this country writers who will compare with the men who have made libretti for Verdi (Ghislanzoni and Boïto), for Puccini (Giacosa and Illica), [and] for Mascagni (Tozzetti and Menacci) … ? I mention only these popular Italian masters because their opera books are in many respects the best that are written …
>
> But to talk of finding librettists as though they were to be discovered under a blackberry hedge, is surely futile … The first thing to do … will be to search among our poets and dramatists for a genius of this type, and next proceed to develop him.[90]

More optimistically, Cecil Forsyth devoted a chapter to the subject in *Music and Nationalism* but, while arguing that the libretti of the preceding 30 years were an improvement on those of Bunn, Planché and Fitzball, he acknowledged that there was a long way to go.[91] Nevertheless, the dearth of experienced and good librettists was a persistent issue; few highly-regarded authors were tempted, perhaps understandingly, given the relative thanklessness of the task.[92] Such a well-known lover of opera as George Bernard Shaw showed no interest. Indeed, Shaw forbade adaptations of his plays after seeing *Arms and the Man* re-presented by Oscar Straus as *The Chocolate Soldier*. Neither was the talented translator Edward Dent, whose English-language version of *Die Zauberflöte* was widely commended on its appearance in 1911, drawn to writing new libretti.

89 George Clutsam, 'National Opera and its Prospects', *MT*, 1 January 1913, pp. 13–15 (p. 15).

90 Herman Klein, 'National Opera and its Prospects: A Rejoinder', *MT*, 1 February 1913, pp. 92–93 (p. 92).

91 Forsyth, pp. 152–84; Forsyth accused librettists of 'Wardour-Streetism', that is, a literary style reliant on artificial archaisms, 'similar to the fake-antique trade which is supposed to flourish in Wardour Street [Soho]' (p. 181).

92 Forsyth argued that a crucial step was for composers and librettists to be viewed by all as artistic equals (ibid., p. 183).

Despite being a subject of continuous interest and concern, no solution to Britain's 'operatic problem' was found between 1875 and 1918. The environment for composers remained challenging throughout and did not encourage the establishment of a native canon of works. Nevertheless, a constant stream of operas appeared and many more were composed but not performed; there was a consistent interest in the genre, even if most composers were quickly deterred from sustained effort. It is unlikely that the creation of a national opera house would have radically altered the situation, for all that composers and commentators saw it as a comprehensive solution. British observers forgot, or did not notice, that many operas premiered in France, Germany and Italy were discarded as readily as their British equivalents despite the assistance of subsidised theatres with a remit to promote native works. A national opera house could, however, have provided a structure to incentivise composers to a greater extent and encourage them to return to opera more regularly and to learn from accumulated experience. This would not have guaranteed the creation of a more dynamic and successful native tradition, but could not have hindered it. Many composers were discouraged by the lack of a national forum in which their works could be seen; while the composers of oratorios and cantatas could look to the annual and triennial festivals around the country for national exposure, albeit often fleeting, the conspicuous lack of an operatic equivalent was a strong disincentive. The absence, for much the greater part of this period, of sympathetic English-language companies in the West End of London, and the conspicuous lack of support from Covent Garden, handicapped composers consistently. For many, the lack of production opportunities in central London, with their attendant publicity and cachet, caused a decision to focus on other, more promising, activities.

The idea that a national opera house, on its own, would have transformed the British into a country of opera enthusiasts was, however, clearly fallacious. More likely, this would have come to be seen as a rival to Covent Garden and the desire to maintain a prestigious venue for the production of new operas would have resulted in a new institution with its own elite audience. In any case, a single venue, beyond the reach of the vast majority of the population, could never have influenced attitudes in the way its advocates claimed. In this respect, sceptics were right to believe that a national opera house would be run with the interests of London's professional musicians at its centre. Beyond the West End, the issue was one of unstable structures; although touring companies provided increasing opportunities to see opera across the country, their precarious existence discouraged innovation and led to a largely static repertory, making it difficult for even accessible new works to gain a foothold.

The lack of structural stability militated against the establishment of a dynamic and successful school of native operatic composition but does not entirely explain its difficulties. Although there was a desire to create a canon of works which would stand comparison with those of Europe's leading musical nations, there was no shared sense of purpose and no consensus regarding the nature of British opera: did it need, simply, to be as engaging and popular as the best continental works or did it have to do more, and 'speak' to the populace in a manner distinct and exclusive? And, if the latter, how was this new musical language to be constructed? No composer or commentator could articulate a convincing answer to these questions, still less produce an opera which fulfilled these criteria. It would be surprising to find it had been otherwise – the desire to find an easy and quick solution to the 'operatic problem' was perhaps the single greatest reason for its remaining.

Chapter 6
Operas by British and Irish Composers premiered 1875–1918

This chapter details operas by British and Irish composers known to have been premiered between 1875 and 1918. On average two or three new works were set before the public each year, with the total number of new works exceeding 100.[1] The works themselves varied greatly in style, from grandiose Wagnernism to short, light, romantic-comic works. The criteria for selecting works are given in the Introduction. Previously published research on individual works varies greatly in quantity: a few have been the subject of detailed studies and this chapter does not aim to supplement or supersede them; other operas are referenced for the first time. In many cases the music is untraced and the information given is derived from press coverage but, nevertheless, a large amount of musical material survives. As the focus of this study is opera in the public domain in Great Britain and Ireland, works for which there are no traced performances may be omitted or mentioned only in passing; works composed between 1875 and 1918 but premiered afterwards may also be alluded to. Operas which were only performed overseas are included for completeness, while for those premiered overseas with a subsequent pre-1918 British production, the bulk of the commentary focuses on the latter. In the main text of this chapter operas are ordered by composer. Table 6.1 lists the works in chronological order of premiere.

Bainton, Edgar (1880–1956)

Oithona

Libretto	Presumed by Bainton, after James Macpherson's *The Works of Ossian*
Premiere	11 August 1915, Assembly Rooms, Glastonbury
Principal cast	Gaul – Frank Mullings Oithona – Marjorie Ffrangçon-Davies

[1] This is a significantly larger corpus than that listed in Eric Walter White, *A register of first performances of English operas and semi-operas: From the 16th century to 1980* (London, 1980).

Synopsis	One act; two scenes: Pre-Christian Britain or Ireland. Oithona is abducted by Dunrommath; Gaul, her betrothed, and her family sail to the island where she is held to rescue her. In the ensuing battle Dunrommath is killed and Oithona, disguised as a soldier, is also fatally wounded.

Bainton's first and only pre-1918 opera was completed by 1903, either during or shortly after his studies at the Royal College, but was not performed until Rutland Boughton produced it at his second Glastonbury Festival, when Bainton was interned at Ruhleben (see Chapter 3). The music is lost; an article by Boughton quotes nine themes and implies a Wagnerian style employing leitmotifs;[2] although orchestrated, the premiere was accompanied by a piano. The *Musical Times* described *Oithona* as having 'considerable dramatic force' and being 'quite modern in style', but suffering from 'a rather too strained feeling, with a constant climactic effect'.[3]

Bainton completed a children's opera, *Walooki the Bear*, by 1912. A second music-drama, *The Crier by Night*, was completed in piano score by 1912 but not orchestrated until 1919; a studio performance was broadcast in Australia in 1942.[4]

Bantock, Granville (1868–1946)

Caedmar

Libretto	Composer
Premiere	18 October 1892, Crystal Palace, London (Crystal Palace Opera Season) 25 October 1892, Olympic Theatre, London (Lago)
Sources	Vocal Score: London Publishing Company (London, 1892) Autograph score: University of Birmingham, MS GB3/1/1
Cast	Caedmar – Mr Wareham Andred – Mr Marcil Hulda – Marie Duma
Synopsis	One act: Ancient Britain. Caedmar, an errant knight, rests by a tree in a forest and is found asleep by Hulda, Andred's wife. She accidentally wakes him and their attraction is mutual. Andred and Caedmar fight over Hulda; she is accidentally stabbed by Andred, who is killed by Caedmar. Hulda dies shortly afterwards; Caedmar prays for her soul.

Despite a life-long interest in dramatic music, Bantock composed few operas and only *Caedmar* was produced professionally before 1918. The slight story

---

2 See *MS*, 21 February 1903, pp. 113–5.

3 *MT*, 1 September 1915, pp. 539–40.

4 http://www.musicweb-international.com/bainton/bainton.htm [accessed 20 September 2012].

necessitates a succession of soliloquies and one duet; the only dramatic incidents are confined to a passage of only 25 bars late in the work. The Crystal Palace performance attracted little press attention but many critics reviewed *Caedmar* at the Olympic. The *Academy*'s comment that 'almost everything seems borrowed from Wagner'[5] is an exaggeration, but Bantock's debt is obvious in both scenario and musical style (harmony, leitmotifs, pulsating rhythms, orchestration, eschewal of a number-based structure, and occasional pastiche); a few passages, such as the Elves' Dance, are incongruous. Wagner's influence notwithstanding, Bantock's potential was acknowledged; the *Musical Standard* noted 'passages of some originality', and concluded by 'expressing our hope that we shall again hear Mr Granville Bantock'.[6]

Barkworth, John (1858–1929)

Romeo and Juliet

Libretto	Shakespeare, reduced by the composer
Premier	7 January 1916, Grand Opera House, Middlesbrough (Harrison Frewin)
Sources	Vocal score: MacDonagh, Capdeville & Co (?London, 1926)
Principal cast	Juliet – Myfanwy Newell Nurse – Gwen Cartmell Romeo – William Boland Mercutio – Lewis James Tybalt – Harry Tremayne Friar Lawrence – Kingsley Lark
Synopsis	Four acts; 14 scenes. A compressed version of Shakespeare's play; the libretto uses only Shakespeare's original text.

Yorkshire-born, and educated at Oxford, the Royal College and in Berlin, Barkworth's only known opera employs reminiscence motifs and a Brahmsian harmonic style in a flexible number-based structure which includes many diegetic dances. Positively reviewed in the *Stage* ('a refreshing flow of melody throughout' and displaying 'much dramatic skill'),[7] the opera was revived in 1920 (Surrey Theatre, London, Miln-Fairbairn Company)[8] and 1926 (Royal College).[9]

5 *Academy*, 29 October 1892, p. 394, of the performance at the Olympic Theatre.

6 *MS*, 29 October 1892, p. 348. See also *The Times*, 26 October, p. 6.

7 *Stage*, 13 January 1916, p. 23.

8 *SR*, 17 April 1920, p. 3 (a critical review).

9 *MT*, 1 January 1927, p. 65.

Boughton, Rutland (1878–1960)[10]

The Immortal Hour

Libretto	'Fiona McLeod', pseudonym of William Sharp
Premiere	26 August 1914, Assembly Rooms, Glastonbury, Somerset (staged, with piano) 7 January 1915, Winter Gardens, Bournemouth (semi-staged, with orchestra)
Sources	Vocal Score: Stainer & Bell (London 1920) Full Score: Stainer & Bell (London, 1923) Autograph full score: BL, Add MS 50963 Autograph vocal score: BL, Add MS 69445–6
Principal cast	Dalua – Rutland Boughton Etain – Irene Lemon Eochaidh – Frederic Austin Manus – Neville Strutt Maive – Agnes Thomas Midir – Arthur Jordan
Synopsis	Two acts; three scenes. Dalua, Lord of Shadow, sees Etain, an entranced princess of the faery Land of Youth, wandering aimlessly through a forest. Dalua foresees a king falling in love with her. After Etain leaves, Dalua waits for Eochaidh, the king, whom Dalua draws further into the forest. Etain takes shelter with the peasants Manus and Maive; Dalua leads Eochaidh to them and he falls instantly in love with Etain. A year later, Etain and Eochaidh celebrate their love. A stranger arrives, and kisses Etain's hand; her memory returns and the stranger is revealed to be Midir, her faery lord. Joyful, she departs with him, leaving Eochaidh stricken.

Although Boughton's work had generated press interest for several years, the premiere of *The Immortal Hour* was inevitably overshadowed by the outbreak of war. The Bournemouth performances were more extensively reviewed and Boughton's work received much positive comment: the *Musical Times* referred to 'the best piece of work Mr Boughton has yet given us … there are many moments of real charm and beauty',[11] while *The Times* commented that Boughton 'has much to say that is beautiful and original'.[12] The use at Glastonbury of the chorus as 'dancing scenery' also attracted interest.[13] Boughton's devotion to his festivals separated him

[10] For a full account of Boughton's career and music, see Michael Hurd, *Rutland Boughton and the Glastonbury Festivals* (Oxford, 1993).

[11] *MT*, 1 February 1915, p. 107.

[12] *The Times*, 8 January 1915, p. 6.

[13] *MT*, 1 October 1914, p. 625.

from the operatic mainstream and *The Immortal Hour* only came into its own during the record-breaking production at London's Regent Theatre in 1922.[14]

One of the most musically successful pre-1918 British operas, it is easily superior to other 'Celtic' operas of the period. Sharp's essentially undramatic story – there is little passionate or aggressive confrontation – was treated sympathetically and listeners were readily drawn into its unreality. Combining a quasi-Wagnerian subject, an extensive system of reminiscence motifs, an animated 'Greek' chorus (allowing effective employment of several diegetic choral numbers), and technical skill in both orchestration and harmony (incorporating pentatonicism and modal inflections but always remaining tonally grounded), Boughton's work was more accessible, distinctive and coherent than that of many contemporaries. Although the regular periodisation and number division at times undermine narrative flow, they also aided the work's popularity; it is one of very few pre-1918 operas with a substantial performance history.

Bethlehem

Libretto	Based on part of the Shearmen and Taylors' Pageant from the Coventry Mystery Plays
Premiere	28 December 1915, Street, Somerset
Sources	Vocal Score: Curwen & Son (London, 1920) Autograph Score: BL, Add MS 50966
Principal cast	Mary – Irene Lemon Gabriel – Christina Walshe Joseph – Bernard Lemon Shepherds – David Scott, Tom Gilbert, Percy Holley Wise Men – Herbert Anderton, David Scott, Robert Billingham Herod – Frank Mullings
Synopsis	Two acts, five scenes: Israel during the Roman Era. An abridged version of the pageant, telling the story of the nativity of Christ from the Annunciation to the flight into Egypt.

Unlike Boughton's other operas, *Bethlehem* (premiered on the same day as Lehmann's *Everyman*) was designed for Glastonbury, with its limited stage facilities and amateur participants, and, perhaps ironically, this resulted in fewer performances than *The Immortal Hour*. The large cast and episodic narrative also set the work apart. Originally congregational carols separated the episodes, similar in function to the chorales in Bach's Passions, but these were later replaced by fully worked out choral settings. Several traditional melodies were used and much of the remaining music employs a similar style, with the exception of that for Herod's court which sometimes lapses into clichéd orientalisms. The *Musical Times* praised the work, saying 'Thank Heaven, Boughton can write a tune and is

---

[14] A run of 216 performances commenced on 13 October 1922, easily surpassing *Ivanhoe*; a second run of 160 performances soon followed; see Hurd, pp. 146–51.

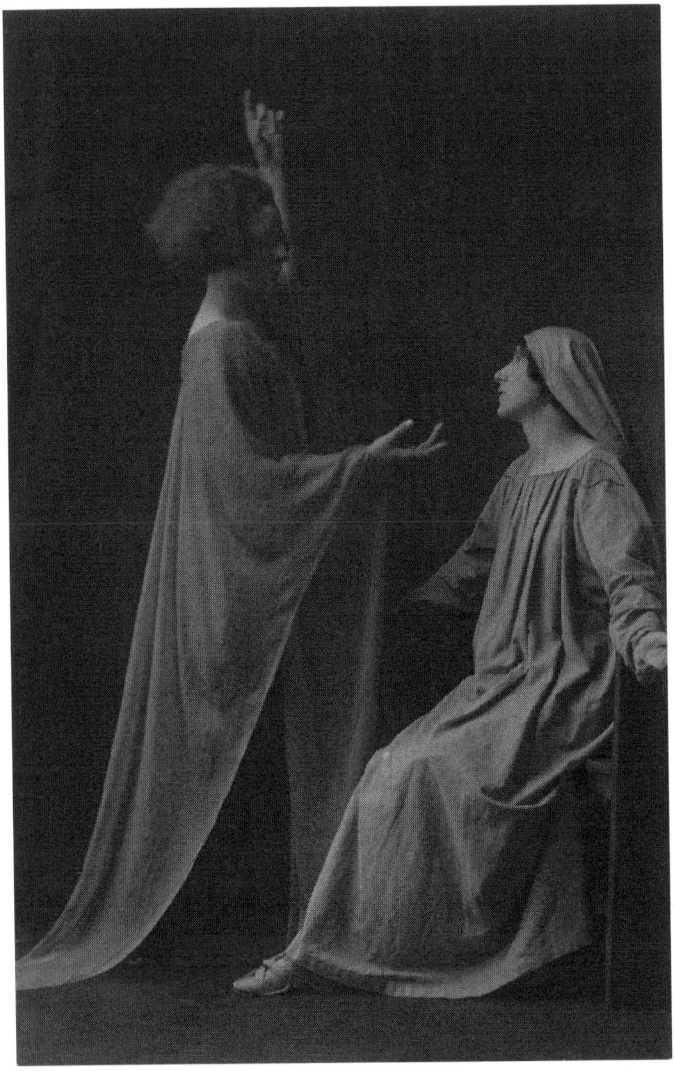

Figure 6.1 Dorothy Silk as Mary and, possibly, either Leonora Allen or Kathleen Beer as Gabriel in Boughton's *Bethlehem*, Glastonbury New Year Festival, January 1921

not afraid of letting us see that he can!'[15] Despite attractive and skilfully wrought music, *Bethlehem* was not taken up by professional companies, but became popular for a time with amateur societies.

15 *MT*, 1 February 1916, p. 94.

The Round Table

Libretto	Reginald Buckley and Composer
Premiere	14 August 1916, Assembly Rooms, Glastonbury, Somerset
Sources	Autograph score: BL, Add MSS 50964–5
Principal Cast	Merlin – Percy Heming Arthur – Frederic Austin Guenevere – Irene Lemon Lancelot – Percy Snowden
Synopsis	Three acts: Britain, fifth to seventh centuries. Merlin lodges a sword in a stone and Arthur retrieves it. Merlin tells Arthur that kingship is his destiny; he must marry Guenevere, lover of Lancelot, to unite the knights, of whom Lancelot is the most powerful. At the Pentecostal feast Guenevere laments losing Lancelot but urges him to support Arthur's search for the Holy Grail. Although unenthusiastic, Lancelot and the other knights agree.

The Round Table was the second in a cycle of five Arthurian music-dramas Boughton planned with Reginald Buckley. The first, *The Birth of Arthur*, completed in 1909, was intended for the 1914 Glastonbury Festival but, for practical reasons, *The Immortal Hour* was substituted. Extracts from *Arthur* were heard in 1914 and 1915, but Boughton's conception of music-drama was evolving and he decided not to revise *Arthur* (performed complete in 1920), but to work on *The Round Table*, extensively modifying Buckley's libretto in the process. Despite the usual basic Glastonbury scenery and only a piano as accompaniment, the work was quite well received at its first performance. Colles stated that 'there is much beautiful and suggestive music',[16] but both he and *The Times* criticised the book as too episodic, and reserved their greatest praise for the final act which 'gives strong contrast of character – Guenevere, torn between love and loyalty … [and] Lancelot, burning with devotion to the Queen and … almost a contempt for Arthur's idealism'.[17] Although revived at Glastonbury in the 1920s, the work was not taken up more widely and remains unpublished.

Bunning, Herbert (1863–1937)

La Princesse Osra

Libretto	Maurice Bérenger after Anthony Hope, 'The Happiness of Stephen the Smith', in *The Heart of Princess Osra*
Premiere	14 July 1902, Covent Garden, London (Grand Opera Syndicate)

16 *MT*, 1 September 1916, pp. 399–400.

17 *The Times*, 16 August 1916, p. 9.

Source	Vocal Score: Enoch & Sons (London, 1902)
Principal Cast	Osra – Mary Garden Stephane – Adolphe Maréchal Prince Henri – Paul Séveilhac King Henri – Pol Plançon Fou do Roi (Jester) – Charles Gilibert
Synopsis	Three acts: medieval Ruritania. King Henri orders Stephane, a smith, to marry Countess Hilda to punish her for loving Prince Henri. Stephane secretly loves Osra and refuses Hilda. Stephane reveals his feelings to Osra; initially she ridicules him but her attitude gradually changes. Stephane helps Prince Henri and Hilda elope; the King, convinced of Stephane's involvement, stabs him; Osra tells him that she will marry him and he dies contented.

Bunning was Music Director at the Lyric and Prince of Wales Theatres in the 1890s and chiefly a composer of lighter music. The single performance of *La Princesse Osra* generated mainly negative reaction; the *Musical Standard* described the love music as 'tame and spiritless', and declared that the 'writing for the voices is ineffective'.[18] *The Times* advised Bunning to try light opera as his gifts were 'lyrical rather than dramatic'[19] but the *Monthly Musical Record* could not concede even this, stating that 'the music lacks life, melodic distinction, and sincere emotion'.[20] The book and libretto (written and set in French) are also problematic; in Act I the characters barely engage with each other but declaim a series a long monologues. Bunning had studied with Massenet and critics agreed that his music reflected this; although incorporating leitmotifs, the number structure is reinforced by conservative tonal language.

Butler, Thomas (Whitwell) O'Brien (1861–1915)

Muirgheis

Libretto	Nora Hopper Chesson
Premiere	7 December 1903, Theatre Royal, Dublin (Amateur)
Source	Vocal Score: Breitkopf & Härtel (London, 1910)
Principal cast	Diarmuid – A.M. Tyrrell Donn of the Sand Hills – Mr J. O'Byrne Maire – Lilly O'Dempsey Muirgheis – May MacCallum

[18] *MS*, 9 July 1902, p. 37.

[19] *The Times*, 15 July 1902, p. 7.

[20] *MMR*, 1 August 1902, p. 154.

Synopsis	Three acts: Ireland 'at the dawn of Christianity'. Muirgheis and Maire both love Diarmuid, a neighbouring chieftain; Diarmuid favours Muirgheis. Maire asks the fairy king Donn to take Muirgheis to his realm and, at her wedding, she disappears. Diarmuid does not transfer his affections and Maire asks Donn to return Muirgheis, knowing that she must sacrifice herself in payment. Muirgheis returns with no memory; this is restored by the tears she sheds on seeing Maire's dead body.

Butler studied with Stanford briefly at the Royal College in the late 1890s. *Muirgheis* is incorrectly cited as the first opera with an Irish libretto; Chesson wrote in English and an Irish translation was made by Tadhg Ó Donnchadha for the published score.[21] Butler endeavoured to create an Irish sound-world largely by writing pastiches of traditional music but with mixed results. The premiere suffered from poor diction (of the English text) and no printed libretto for the audience to follow. The *Weekly Irish Times* gave the work a poor review:

> One would fain encourage Irish art, but it must be confessed that *Muirgheis* does not possess the elements of popularity. We do not think that it is more characteristically Irish than Stanford's *Shamus O'Brien* ... Mr O'Brien Butler has not yet attained the art of writing a good opera. His vocal music contained one or two pleasing melodies and choruses. But in general his vocal writing is monotonous.[22]

Butler was a victim of the German attack on the liner *Lusitania* in 1915.

Capes, John Moore (Rev) (d. 1889)

The Druid

Libretto	Composer
Premiere	15 February 1879, St George's Hall, London
Sources	Vocal score: publisher unknown, c. 1879
Principal cast	Cadwallon – Isidore De Lara Mona – Elène Webster Ghilda – Ellen Marchant Flavian – Mr Seligmann

[21] For further information see Joseph Ryan, 'Opera in Ireland before 1925', in Gareth Cox and Axel Klein (eds) *Irish Music in the Twentieth Century (Irish Musical Studies 7)* (Dublin, 2003), pp. 39–55 (pp. 51–2); Axel Klein, 'Stage Irish, or the National in Irish Opera, 1780–1925, *Opera Quarterly*, 21 (2005), pp. 27–67; Axel Klein, 'Celtic Legends in Irish opera 1900–1930', *Harvard Celtic Colloquium*, 24/25 (2004–5), pp. 40–53 (pp. 44–6).

[22] *Weekly Irish Times*, 12 December 1903, p. 2.

Synopsis	Three acts: North Wales, second century CE. Cadwallon, a Celtic druid, leads a revolt against the Romans and captures the centurion Flavian, a Christian convert. The Celts plan to sacrifice Flavian and Cadwallon's daughter Mona but both escape; the Celts blind Cadwallon and exile him and his other daughter, Ghilda. Captured by the Romans, Mona and Ghilda, who has also converted to Christianity, refuse to worship Apollo, and are both executed; Flavian tells Cadwallon that their deaths were not in vain.

Although advertised as an opera, the only traced performance was at a concert with piano accompaniment. Practically the piece is a cantata; although the score includes stage directions, the characters barely interact in a succession of arias, choruses and occasional spoken lines. Musically the work is uninspired and occasionally technically incompetent. The *Era* remarked that 'the reverend composer's talent ... does not, we think, lie in the direction of dramatic writing'.[23]

Cellier, Alfred (1844–91)

The Masque of Pandora

Libretto	Bolton Rowe, pseudonym of B.C. Stephenson, after Longfellow's eponymous version of the Greek myth
Premiere	10 January 1881, Boston Theatre, Boston MA
Sources	Libretto: Houghton, Mifflin (Boston, 1881)
Synopsis	Three acts, four scenes: mythical Greece. Zeus creates the first woman and names her Pandora. She is taken from Olympus by Hermes to Prometheus and then Epimetheus. Left alone, Pandora opens a box and incurs the gods' wrath. As the sun rises, however, Pandora and Epimetheus resolve to start their lives anew.

Cellier's only grand opera pre-dates his musical comedies and was written while touring the United States with the D'Oyly Carte troupe. The music is untraced; one review described it is 'sweet and interesting' but unlikely to 'create much enthusiasm';[24] it has not been performed in Britain.

---

23 *Era*, 23 February 1879, p. 5. See also *Graphic*, 22 February, p. 179; *PMG*, 21 February, p. 12.

24 *Orchestra*, 1 March 1881, p. 230. See also *MS*, 12 March, p. 174.

Clutsam, George (1866–1951)

A Summer Night

Libretto	Clutsam, after Margaret of Navarre's *Heptameron*
Premiere	23 July 1910, London, His Majesty's Theatre (Beecham)
Sources	Vocal Score: Chappell (London, 1910)
Cast	Lisa – Beatrice la Palme Toni – Walter Hyde Niccolo – Harry Dearth Facio – Lewis Cairns James
Synopsis	One act: Facio and Niccolo wager that Facio can persuade Lisa, his servant, to meet him for a tryst. Lisa agrees, but understands the plot and tells Lucretia, Facio's wife, and Toni, her betrothed. Lucretia takes Lisa's place but does not realise Niccolo has taken that of Facio. The deceptions are revealed; Lucretia and Facio make up, Lisa and Toni remain united, and Niccolo forgoes future mischief.

An Australian, Clutsam settled in London 1890. He became music critic of the *Observer* in 1908, and composed in most musical genres.[25] Although subtitled an 'opera comique', Clutsam aspired to something musically more complex than this implies and produced a score of considerable complexity and sophistication which aimed to support a natural flow of action and reflect the characters' motives and moods. While the music is not especially original, it is well-wrought and often very effective, with an easy flow of attractive melody. Clutsam was well versed in contemporaneous trends in opera, and employed flexible formal structures, and a tonal palette comparable to Elgar's in its sophistication. Reviewers also praised the orchestration. The main weakness is that the musical ambition hampers easy comprehension of the farcical aspects of the plot; more than one reviewer suggested that spoken dialogue was necessary to understand the intricacies of the action.[26] Nevertheless, this is a deft work, comparable to Smyth's *The Boatswain's Mate*. Despite positive reviews Beecham gave *A Summer Night* only one performance.

King Harlequin (König Harlekin)

Libretto	Rudolph Lothar, from his eponymous play
Premiere	8 November 1912, Kürfürstenoper, Berlin
Source	Vocal score: Chappell (London, 1911)

[25] For more biographical information see Philip Scowcroft, *British Light Music* (London: Thames, 1997), pp. 33–4.

[26] For representative reviews see *Observer*, 24 July 1910, p. 9; *MT*, 1 September, p. 595; *SR*, 30 July, pp. 138–9; *Era*, 30 July, p. 11.

Synopsis	Four acts: a fictional medieval kingdom. Prince Bohemund, corrupt and immoral, returns home as his father, the King, dies. Bohemund is accompanied by a troupe of Italian mummers, among whom is Harlequin, who is virtually Bohemund's double. Both enamoured of Columbine, they fight over her; Harlequin kills Bohemund, takes his place and is proclaimed king; only the dowager Queen realises the truth. Harlequin rules well; Tancred, Bohemund's uncle, fails to corrupt him. At a comedy played by the mummers, the disillusioned Harlequin covertly reveals his true identity to Columbine and they flee. Tancred takes his place as king.

King Harlequin was Clutsam's most ambitious operatic score and the book facilitated a display of both serious and lighter styles. Influenced by Wagner, Humperdinck and Richard Strauss, the writing is sophisticated, including complex contrapuntal textures, but is also restless, especially in Act I, in which Clutsam's predilection for seventh and ninth chords at times becomes obsessive. The contrasts between lighter and more serious moods are sometimes jarring; as in Smyth's *Fantasio*, the music often weighs down the humorous aspects of the story. Nevertheless, Clutsam demonstrated serious intent and skill. Although successfully performed in Berlin,[27] the work has never been performed in Britain.

Cockle, George

The Castle of Como

Libretto	Charles Searle, after Bulwer-Lytton's *The Lady of Lyons*
Premiere	2 October 1889, Opera Comique, London
Source	Libretto: D. Allen (London, 1889)
Principal cast	Pauline – Rosina Isidor Claude Melnotte – Mr Cadwaladr Beauseant – Leo Stormont Widow Melnotte – Amy Martin
Synopsis	See Cowen's *Pauline* (below), which is based on the same source.

Cockle, a wealthy amateur, spared no expense in producing his opera, including planning for a six-month run, but it was withdrawn within a month. The music is untraced. The extensive reviews were variable; a comment that the music 'never rises above praiseworthy mediocrity' is representative.[28]

---

27 *MT*, 1 December 1912, p. 804.

28 *Era*, 5 October 1889, p. 9. See also *PMG*, 3 October, p. 6; *Standard*, same date, p. 5; *MP*, 4 October, p. 5; *Graphic*, 5 October, p. 419.

Cole, James Parry (1836–?)

A Romance of the Harem

Libretto	Arthur Sketchley, pseudonym of George Rose.
Premiere	28 April 1887, Kilburn Town Hall, London
Sources	Vocal score: publisher unknown, undated
Principal cast	Lulu Pasha – R. Lansmere Osman – Rowland Guy Zuleika – Lillian Shelbourne Leila – Susanna Cole
Synopsis	Two acts. Osman, believed killed in battle by Lulu Pasha, covertly returns to his wife, Leila. Pasha plans to dispose of his wife Zuleike and take Leila for himself. After an operetta-like plot in which various characters hide in vases and overhear each other, Pasha and his henchman Mallalabad are exposed and disgraced; Osman and Leila are free to live together again.

Cole's opera recalls the mid-century approach of Balfe and Wallace, with self-contained, simply structured and regularly phrased numbers, but connected by secco recitative; the harmonic language is equally old-fashioned. Rose (1817–82) was known as a witty writer and the *Era* suggested that a comic adaptation would have produced a better result; the music was referred to as containing some 'graceful passages' but also 'commonplace'.[29] Cole also composed light comic operas, including *The Golden Wedding* (1885),[30] and *The Black Count* (1890).[31]

Collinge, Frederick C.

Grace Darrell

Libretto	Raymond James
Premiere	12 September 1896, Leinster Hall, Dublin (Carl Rosa)
Principal cast	Grace Darrell – Bessie Macdonald Dorothy – Louise Kirkby Lunn Charles II – William Paul Gideon Grimthorpe – Arthur Winckworth Sir Gilbert Darrell – Robert Cunningham

29 *Era*, 4 June 1887, p. 16.

30 *MP*, 9 March 1885, p. 2.

31 *MS*, 2 August 1890, p. 102.

Synopsis	One act: England, 1651. At Darrell Grange a disguised Charles II is almost caught by Parliamentarians but, thanks to the ingenuity of Grace, Dorothy and Gilbert, all four escape to France, leaving the Roundhead Grimthorpe wounded.

Nothing is known of Collinge other than that he was a local composer; both the libretto and music are untraced. *Grace Darrell* was well received at its only performance: '[the vocal music is] very melodious and, as regards the orchestration, it is replete with rich harmony, although possibly a slight tendency towards an excess of melodramatic music might be traced.'[32]

Corder, Frederick (1852–1932)

Nordisa

Libretto	Composer, after the French melodrama *Les Bergères Des Alpes*
Premiere	26 January 1887, Royal Court Theatre, Liverpool (Carl Rosa)
Source	Vocal Score: Forsyth Brothers (Manchester, 1887)
Principal Cast	Count Oscar Lydal – Edward Scovel Lieutenant Frederick Hansen – James Sauvage Minna – Georgina Burns Andreas Brand – Max Eugene Nordisa – Julia Gaylord
Synopsis	Three acts: Norway, mid-eighteenth century. Minna and Frederick are in love but, as Baroness Nymark's daughter, she is betrothed to Oscar; he prefers Brand's daughter Nordisa. As Nordisa guards the mountain cattle, she and Oscar declare their love but are isolated by an avalanche. Several months later Oscar returns home and agrees to marry Minna; as they finalise arrangements, Nordisa arrives, followed by Brand, who has a deathbed confession from Minna's nurse: Minna and Nordisa were swapped at birth. As Oscar was betrothed to the baroness's daughter his engagement is to Nordisa, leaving Frederick to marry Minna.

Nordisa was not Corder's first opera: extracts of his *Le Mort D'Arthur* were performed in concert in 1879; he also composed operettas in the early 1880s.[33] Although known as a Wagnerian – Corder and his wife translated several of Wagner's libretti – the book of *Nordisa* was, in Corder's words, 'written on old-fashioned lines rather than according to modern models … As regards the music the composer has attempted nothing unusual unless the endeavour to please the general public rather than to educate or astonish them may be so considered'.

[32] *FJ*, 14 September 1896, p. 4; see also *Era*, 19 September, p. 11.

[33] See *DN*, 10 February 1879, p. 2; *Graphic*, 15 February, p. 155; Kurt Gänzl, *British Musical Theatre* (London and Basingstoke, 1986 (vol. 1).

Corder's motivations are unknown; possibly either he or Rosa were conscious of the failures of Stanford and Mackenzie's earlier quasi-Wagnerian operas. Consequently, Corder's score builds on the mid-century models of Balfe and Wallace; the contrived story,[34] which unfortunately recalls *HMS Pinafore*, is conveyed through a libretto written entirely in rhyming couplets. The music is always technically competent but rarely inspired; in attempting to evoke Norwegian dance music Corder, like Grieg, over-used open-fifth drones.

The work's reception was curious: its premiere in Liverpool garnered generally good reviews. The *Musical Standard* praised the libretto as 'a vast improvement' on Rosa's other commissions, and predicted that 'the work will live and become popular'.[35] When *Nordisa* was performed in London, however, it was widely criticised. *The Times* questioned Corder's motives,[36] as did the *Athenaeum*, stating that Corder had 'in some instances sacrificed his art for the sake of popularity'.[37] Corder himself was allegedly unhappy with the change in press reaction,[38] but the damage was done. At the end of Rosa's London season the *Musical World* commented, 'the less said of *Nordisa* the better',[39] and the work was rapidly dropped.

Cowen, Frederic (1852–1935)

Pauline

Libretto	Henry Hersee, after Bulwer-Lytton's play *The Lady of Lyons*
Premiere	22 November 1876, Lyceum Theatre, London (Carl Rosa)
Source	Vocal score: Boosey (London, ?1876)
Principal cast	Pauline Deschapelles – Julia Gaylord Claude Melnotte – Charles Santley Beauseant – F.H. Celli Glavis – James Turner

[34] Cowen believed that Corder was forced by Rosa to include the avalanche to show off a new staging effect; see Frederic Cowen, *My Art and My Friends* (London, 1913), pp. 242–3. At the first London performance the avalanche 'gave great delight to a great part of the audience although it covered another part with dust' (*SR*, 7 May 1887, p. 655).

[35] *MS*, 12 February 1887, pp. 100–101; see also *Academy*, 5 February, pp. 770–71; *MT*, 1 February, p. 100.

[36] *The Times*, 6 May 1887, p. 13.

[37] *Athenaeum*, 14 May 1887, pp. 648–9 (p. 649). A selection of reviews is quoted in *MW*, 14 May, pp. 376–9.

[38] *MW*, 21 May 1887, p. 393.

[39] *MW*, 11 June 1887, p. 457.

Synopsis	Four acts: France, 1790s. Claude loves Pauline but she rejects him as he is a gardener's son; she has previously also rejected Beauseant and Glavis. They plot revenge; Claude disguises himself as a prince and successfully woos Pauline. They are married but Claude's deception is exposed and she again rejects him. Claude leaves and joins the army. Beauseant's renewed advances lead Pauline to realise her true feelings and she welcomes Claude's subsequent return.

Cowen's first opera was the first work commissioned by Rosa.[40] *Pauline* was traditionally conceived, employing spoken dialogue and separate musical numbers. Although competently written with some attractive numbers and a clear interest in orchestral detail, *Pauline* is also uneven; Cowen struggled to create tension in the confrontational sections and was not always helped by Hersee's libretto (which incorporated many of Bulwer-Lytton's original lines that contrast in style with Hersee's contribution).

The work attracted much critical attention. The casting of Claude as a baritone, driven by the need to use Charles Santley effectively, attracted some adverse comment,[41] and Hersee's libretto also attracted mixed reviews: for the *Athenaeum* it resembled too much 'the ballad opera of the Bunn school',[42] but the *Academy* deemed it 'much above the average'.[43] Cowen's score likewise received varied comments. The *Academy*'s view was representative: 'Where the composer has written up to his own standard he has been mostly very successful; the shortcomings are chiefly noticeable where he seems to have written for popularity and not for art'.[44] Acknowledging the work's conventional style, the *Morning Post* declared that 'if Mr Cowen is not the "coming man" in English opera, he is at any rate a very good *locum tenens*'.[45] Overall, however, the work did not garner public support and was dropped from Rosa's repertory after one season.[46]

Thorgrim

Libretto	Joseph Bennett, after 'Viglund the Fair' in Magnusson and Morris's *Three Northern Love Stories*
Premiere	22 April 1890, Theatre Royal, Drury Lane, London (Carl Rosa)

---

40 For his own account of events, see Cowen, pp. 237–42.

41 Cowen cited this as the main reason for the work's failure, along with Hersee's libretto (Cowen, p. 240).

42 *Athenaeum*, 25 November 1876, p. 696.

43 *Academy*, 2 December 1876, p. 553.

44 Ibid.

45 *MP*, 23 November 1876, p. 6.

46 Rosa asked Cowen to rewrite the opera for a tenor lead but Cowen gave up the commission; Rosa threatened to prosecute but, although the issue was resolved, they did not work together again for over a decade (Cowen, p. 242).

Source:	Vocal Score: Novello (London, undated)
Principal cast	King Harald – F.H. Celli Eric – Max Eugene Helgi – Leslie Crotty Thorgrim – Barton McGuckin Arnora – Mlle Tremelli Olof Sunbeam – Zelie de Lussan
Synopsis	Four acts: Norway, tenth century. Half-brothers Thorgrim and Helgi fall out when Harald shows favour to Thorgrim. To restore peace, Thorgrim leaves with Harald. At court, Thorgrim and Helgi's betrothed, Olof, fall in love; Olof's father refuses Thorgrim's request to marry her, and Thorgrim leaves Harald's service. The lovers meet but are discovered by Helgi and his mother Arnora. Believing that he is destined always to be beaten by Thorgrim, Helgi refuses to fight him. At Helgi and Olof's wedding, Thorgrim intervenes; during a skirmish, the lovers escape.

After breaking with Rosa over *Pauline*, Cowen abandoned opera composition until their relationship recovered. Rosa commissioned *Thorgrim* from Cowen having already received Bennett's libretto.[47] Rosa's death delayed the premiere but Augustus Harris honoured the commitment to Cowen, resulting in the Drury Lane production. Cowen's style had matured; although still resolutely tonal and number-based, *Thorgrim* has a wider harmonic palette and more flexible approach to structure. The incorporation of reminiscence motifs led contemporaneous critics to conclude that *Thorgrim* was strongly Wagnerian, a view reinforced by the book and the prominence of the orchestra. In reality these aspects are mainly superficial; set pieces, connected by sections of accompanied recitative abound, and chromatic inner parts and some unexpected modulations do not disguise the regular periodisation and closed tonal planning.

The premiere of *Thorgrim* was attended by the Prince and Princess of Wales and other royalty and viewed as a major event. Reception was generally positive but with reservations. Although Bennett's prose was welcomed, several journals criticised the unsympathetic nature of the characters. The *Era* praised the drama and characterisation in the score, but conceded that while 'Mr Cowen's work will gain much credit from high-class musicians … [it] is not likely to please or attract the public';[48] the *Morning Post*, however, reached the opposite conclusion and forecast a good future for the work.[49] The *Musical Standard* also praised the work but tellingly referred to a score 'replete with scholastic devices' in which, however

---

47 For his own account, see Cowen, pp. 242–6. Part of his chronology is inaccurate: if, as Cowen claimed, Rosa wanted his staged avalanche incorporated into *Thorgrim*, negotiations must have taken place in 1886 at the latest since the device was instead used in Corder's *Nordisa* in early 1887 (see above).

48 *Era*, 26 April 1890, p. 8.

49 *MP*, 23 April 1890, p. 7.

'we expected a greater flow of melody'.[50] Despite a well-produced premiere and a good reception, *Thorgrim* was soon dropped. Cowen himself could not explain its failure, concluding only that it must have lacked 'that indefinable *something* which attracts the public'.[51]

Signa

Libretto	Gilbert A'Beckett and H. Rudall, after Marie Louise Ramé's eponymous novel (published under pseudonym Ouida); revisions by Frederick Weatherly
Premiere	12 November 1893, Teatro dal Verme, Milan 30 June 1894, Covent Garden, London (Royal Opera)
Source:	Vocal Score: E. Ascherberg (London, 1894)
Principal cast (London)	Signa – Ben Davies Bruno – Sig. Ancona Sartorio – Sig. Castelmary Gemma – Mlle Nuovina
Synopsis	Originally four acts, compressed to three for Milan, further reduced to two for London. Final synopsis: Italy, late nineteenth century.[52] Signa, an amateur singer, is invited to Naples by the impresario Sartorio, despite the protests of Signa's uncle, Bruno. Tempted by the dancer Gemma, whom he loves, Signa decides to leave. In Naples Gemma leaves Signa for a Duke, and Signa's career collapses. Bruno fails to persuade Signa to return home; he accuses Gemma of being a wanton and stabs her. When Signa discovers that she is dead, he stabs himself.

The composition and production history of *Signa* is complex. Originally intended for Carte's Royal English Opera, that institution's collapse before *Signa* was finished forced Cowen to look elsewhere. Seeing no other opportunities for a London premiere he decided, for unknown reasons, to try Italy. Projected productions at Genoa and Florence fell through but the work was accepted by Sonzogno in Milan. After two performances the two men fell out and *Signa* was withdrawn but was taken up by Harris, who gave a revised, shortened version at Covent Garden.[53]

---

50 *MS*, 26 April 1890, p. 385. See also *The Times*, 23 April, p. 10; *Standard*, same date, p. 5; *MT*, 1 May, pp. 277–9.

51 Cowen p. 245.

52 For a summary of the original book see *MT*, 1 January 1893, pp. 20–21, and of the three act version, *MT*, 1 December, pp. 726–7.

53 For his own account, see Cowen, pp. 246–62; brief reports in *MT* confirm his summary regarding projected productions in Italy (see 1 November 1892, p. 682; 1 February 1893, p. 85; 1 March, p. 148; 1 May, p. 276). Cowen and Sonzogno exchanged letters describing their dispute in *The Times* (23 November 1893, p. 8, and 24 November, p. 11).

Unfortunately this condensation undermined the lead characters: Signa appeared weak and irresolute, while Gemma was transformed from the libertine of Ouida's novel into a selfish girl. Neither are sympathetic and, in Cowen's words 'the plot moved so fast that the motives of the characters … became a stone wall impossible to see through' while the music sounded like a patchwork of randomly connected passages.[54] Cowen's musical style remained fundamentally the same in both *Thorgrim* and *Signa*, but the latter better suited his lyrical gifts and penchant for delicate orchestration, and contains several diegetic songs and dances.

Critical reception was mixed: of the Milan production, the *Musical Times* stated that 'Cowen's peculiar gifts have found completer and more distinctive expression than in any of his previous works … [it is] a genuinely beautiful work of art',[55] while *The Times*'s review of the London performance was also mainly favourable.[56] The *Musical Standard* was critical, however, declaring that *Signa* was neither 'an emphatic success', nor 'a work of great merit', while allowing that the compression of the work cannot have helped.[57] Although the work was given four performances at Covent Garden, it was neither revived nor taken up by other companies.

Harold

Libretto	Sir Edward Malet, revised by Frederick Weatherly
Premiere	8 June 1895, Covent Garden, London (Royal Opera)
Source:	Vocal Score: Joseph Williams (London, 1895)
Principal cast	(King) Harold – Philip Brozel William, Duke of Normandy – David Bispham Alfnoth and Archbishop Stigand – William Dever Edith – Emma Albani Princess Adela – Louise Meisslinger
Synopsis	Four acts: England and Normandy, 1065–66. Harold, outlawed by King Edward, falls in love with Edith, Alfnoth's daughter. He swears loyalty to William to evade arrest by Siward. In Bayeux, Harold longs to return to Edith; when Edward's death is confirmed, Harold realises that he has betrayed his country. He travels to London; Stigand absolves Harold of his oath to William and encourages him to take the throne, as does Edith, now a nun. Harold is killed at Hastings; Edith recovers his body and William is proclaimed king.

Although *Signa* was not a great success, Harris commissioned another opera from Cowen. The choice of Edward Malet, a diplomat with no theatrical experience as librettist, is mystifying; his book is unwieldy, comprising a series

54 Cowen, p. 261. In the revised version the Duke is reduced to just two lines early in Act II; Sartorio appears only in Act I.

55 *MT*, 1 December 1893, pp. 726–7 (p. 727).

56 *The Times*, 2 July 1894, p. 8.

57 *MS*, 7 July 1894, p. 4.

of largely unconnected episodes, and requiring a large cast. The scenario does, however, contain opportunities for set pieces and diegetic items, which clearly appealed to Cowen.[58] Structurally, Cowen took the same approach as in his two previous operas. He found it difficult, however, to create dramatic tension in the active sections, and the set pieces are the most successful.

Harold was the first work in decades produced in English during a Covent Garden grand season. Critical reaction was mainly positive; the *Musical Times* declared that 'the melodies are direct and English in character, the vocal parts are effectively laid out for the voices, and the instrumentation is throughout masterly'.[59] *The Times* noted 'a distinct advance in the handling of dramatic scenes' although the score was 'a little wanting in actual beauty'.[60] Nevertheless, *Harold* was discarded after one season. Cowen claimed that Harris told him that 'he had received a letter from one of his influential lady patrons to the effect that she and her friends did not go to Covent Garden to hear English opera, and that if he [Harris] intended to continue that sort of thing, they would have to give up subscribing'.[61] Cowen composed no further operas and concentrated his efforts on other genres.

Davis, John David (1867–1942)

The Zaporogues

Libretto	E. Lawrence Levy, after Gogol's *Taras Bulba*
Source	Vocal Score: Publisher unknown, undated
Premiere	7 May 1895, Theatre Royal, Birmingham (Birmingham Amateur Grand Opera Company)
Principal cast	Zephé – Mrs Trevarthen Reige – Miss J.L. Gell Galaudovitch – Joseph Chambers Ostap – F. Sampson André – Percy Taunton Taras Bulba – A. Mancus

---

[58] For his own account, see Cowen, pp. 262–6, which also includes an anecdotal summary of Harris's working methods.

[59] *MT*, 1 July 1895, p. 453.

[60] *The Times*, 10 June 1895, p. 8. See also *Athenaeum*, 15 June, p. 779; *MN*, same date, pp. 558–9; *MS*, same date, pp. 467–9 (all positive). A sceptical review appeared in *SR*, same date, pp. 786–7.

[61] Cowen, p. 266.

Synopsis	One act: Eastern Europe, sixteenth century. Cossacks besiege the city of Duobno; it is relieved by André, son of the Cossack leader Taras Bulba; André has changed sides after falling in love with a local girl, Zephé. Bulba and his soldiers (the Zaporogues) confront André and Bulba kills him.

Davis studied in Frankfurt and Brussels, and taught at the Midland Institute, Birmingham, and the Guildhall School. He composed in a variety of genres but this is his only known opera.[62] *The Stage* praised the performance and stated that 'the music is very appropriate'.[63]

De Lara, Isidore (1858–1935)[64]

De Lara and Stanford were the most prolific British composers of operas in this period. De Lara's long-standing relationship, possibly intimate, with Princess Alice of Monaco, secured several performances at Monte Carlo and almost certainly helped De Lara elsewhere.[65] He lived in Monaco for over 20 years, only returning to England in 1915; consequently his work made relatively little impression in Britain, with only *Messaline* enjoying a measure of popularity. An inveterate Francophile, De Lara was strongly influenced by such composers as Bizet, Massenet and Saint-Saëns, but his work was often unfocused and consequently uneven. A singer himself, he believed in vocal primacy, albeit supported by delicate and often intricate orchestral accompaniments, but he rarely delivered the essential concomitant, a strong melody, and lacked the self-discipline needed to conceive of his scores as integrated and unified wholes.

The Light of Asia

Libretto	William Beatty Kingston, based on the poem by Sir Edwin Arnold
Premiere	11 June 1892, Covent Garden, London (Royal Opera)
Sources	Vocal Score: B. Moccata & Co (London, 1891) Autograph Score: BL, Music Miscellaneous Deposit 1996/17

62 For further biographical information see James Brown and Stephen Stratton, *British Musical Biography* (Birmingham, 1897), p. 119.

63 *Stage*, 9 May 1895, p. 9. At the time of writing the only traced vocal score, at the British Library, was inaccessible due to asbestos contamination.

64 For De Lara's own account see his autobiography *Many Tales of Many Cities* (London, 1928); his assertions are often contradicted in other sources.

65 De Lara started as a singer; he composed at least one operetta in the 1880s (*The Royal Word,* 1883); 'Isidore de Solla' (possibly a pseudonym) was also active at this time (see Gänzl, *British Musical Theatre*, vol. 1).

Principal cast	Siddârtha – Jean Lassalle Yasôdhará – Emma Eames
Synopsis	Prologue and three acts: Buddha is reincarnated as Siddârtha, an Indian prince. By his father's will, Siddârtha lives with his wife in an isolated palace. After some years he leaves this haven to learn the full extent of human nature. Following trials and tests he achieves Nirvana and peace settles upon the world.

De Lara's first serious opera was conceived as a cantata but Victor Maurel allegedly suggested that it would make an effective stage work.[66] Harris took it up; De Lara made revisions and acquired an Italian version of the libretto, despite Kingston's objections.[67] The opera was deemed unsuccessful by critics as it was insufficiently dramatic.[68] Reviews were negative: *The Times* referred to 'a total want of continuity or unity of style',[69] the *Monthly Musical Record* to a work that was 'immature and crude' although it allowed that 'there is decided promise of better things'.[70] In addition to lacking dramatic impetus and incident, thin, static textures predominate, emphasising the absence of action. De Lara's francophilia is obvious; vocal pre-eminence is combined with a straightforward tonal language imbued with enharmonic modulations and shifts. Cast as a traditional number opera, De Lara showed little ability to create a sustained line of thought and most numbers are short; overall the work lacks coherence and direction.

Amy Robsart

Libretto	Augustus Harris and Paul Milliet, after Walter Scott's *Kenilworth*
Premiere	23 July 1893, Covent Garden, London (Royal Opera)
Sources	Vocal Score: Paris (Choudens, 1894)
Principal cast	Amy Robsart – Emma Calvé Elizabeth I – Mme Armand Earl of Leicester – Albert Alvarez Varney – Jean Lassalle

66 De Lara, pp. 85–8.

67 De Lara portrayed himself as an innocent victim in this episode, overwhelmed by Harris and Maurel, and afraid of opposing them for fear of making enemies at Covent Garden.

68 See, for example, *Speaker*, 18 June 1892, p. 736.

69 *The Times*, 13 June 1892, p. 11.

70 *MMR*, 1 July 1892, p. 154.

Synopsis	Three acts: England, 1570s. Amy wants to make her covert marriage to Leicester public; he refuses as he is, unknown to Amy, being courted by Elizabeth. Enlightened by Varney, Leicester's squire, Amy travels to Kenilworth and partially explains her situation to Elizabeth. Leicester is about to confess the truth but, realising that this would lead to his execution, Amy fabricates insanity. She retires to Cumnor Hall where Varney, determined to see Leicester become King and to be ennobled himself, contrives an 'accident' in which Amy falls to her death.

De Lara claimed that Harris felt guilty about *The Light of Asia* and commissioned *Amy Robsart* by way of compensation. Harris chose the subject but engaged Milliet as the opera could not be produced at Covent Garden in English. The score of *Amy Robsart* contains greater textural variety; the work again is very sectionalised but its primary weakness is uninspired melodic writing, an obvious failing in a transparent voice-dominated style. Unusually, press reviews concluded that the libretto was superior to the music and the scenario contains much dramatic incident. *The Times* declared that 'the melodies, if such they can be called, are a little less incoherent than before; now and then a "figure" of an accompaniment is carried on through several strains … in this music there is neither colour nor character of any kind whatever'.[71] Other writers were less hostile but still critical: Shedlock stated that De Lara's 'intentions are good, but he at present lacks the power to carry them out successfully … [he] must try and shake off the influence of contemporary writers'.[72] The reception was almost certainly coloured by a perception that social connections had eased De Lara's passage; Stanford's *Veiled Prophet*, performed three days later was more favourably received.[73]

Moïna[74]

Libretto	Louis Gallet, after a scenario by the composer
Premiere	14 March 1897, Salle Garnier, Monte Carlo
Sources	Vocal Score: Choudens (Paris, 1896)

71 *The Times*, 21 July 1893, p. 8. For a more positive review see *MN*, 29 July, p. 108.

72 *Academy*, 29 July 1893, p. 98. See also *MS*, same date, pp. 89–90.

73 *Amy Robsart* was also performed at Monte Carlo, Florence, Lyons and St Petersburg (De Lara, p. 109).

74 For further information on the production of De Lara's operas in Monaco see T.J. Walsh, *Monte Carlo Opera 1879–1909* (Dublin, 1975).

Synopsis	Two acts: County Cork during the 1798 Rebellion. Lionel, an English captain, is in love with Moïna, but she loves Patrice, an Irish rebel. Patrice and Moïna are cornered in a church but Lionel will not permit gunfire in a sacred place and Patrice escapes. He is subsequently captured; Moïna initially agrees to grant a favour to Lionel if he releases Patrice but stabs Lionel instead and sends his body into the bay on a boat. The boat's lamp alerts the approaching French fleet, which turns back. The lovers are discovered by the English and shot.

The first of De Lara's operas to be premiered at Monte Carlo, the story of *Moïna* has a remarkable affinity with Stanford's contemporaneous *Shamus O'Brien*. But while Stanford's comic opera makes both heroes and villains of the Irish, and mere fools of the English, in De Lara's tragic scenario the Irish are valiant rebels and the English irredeemable oppressors. Otherwise the works are entirely different: in *Moïna* De Lara maintained his established style but demonstrated a greater knowledge of Wagner; attempts at Irish 'local colour' are refracted through this Franco-German prism. Earlier weaknesses remain apparent, in particular an inability to maintain momentum as the music is constantly interrupted by tempo changes and pauses. Reviews in the British press, although mainly brief, were fairly positive: John Runciman, admitting a soft spot for De Lara's music, asserted that it contained 'the best passages Mr De Lara has ever written'.[75] For unknown reasons the work was not produced in Britain, although the scenario cannot have helped its prospects.

Messaline

Libretto	Armand Silvestre and Eugène Morand
Premiere	21 March 1899, Salle Garnier, Monte Carlo 13 July 1899, Covent Garden, London (Grand Opera Syndicate)
Source	Vocal Score: Choudens (Paris, 1899)
Principal cast (London)	Messaline – Mme Héglon (also at Monte Carlo) Hélion – Albert Alvarez Harès – M Renaud
Synopsis	Four acts, Rome, first century CE. Messaline, the Roman Empress, seduces Harès; when he later sees her seducing his brother, Hélion, Messaline has Harès thrown into the river. Harès survives and confronts his brother and former lover. Hélion, believing he is being attacked, kills Harès; remorseful he leaps into the circus arena, where the lions await him.

[75] *SR*, 20 March 1897, pp. 288–90 (p. 289). See also *MS*, 20 March, p. 185; *MT*, 1 April, p. 265; *MMR*, same date, pp. 75–6.

Messaline was De Lara's most popular opera; in addition to productions in Monte Carlo and London, it was performed across Europe.[76] In Monaco, Runciman gave another positive review, asserting that '*Messaline* is not only Mr De Lara's best work, but by far the strongest and most effective opera written for some years ... Nothing in the attempts of our other English composers compares ... with its dramatic intensity and simplicity and naked strength'.[77] In London, the work divided critics; Messaline's voracious sexuality was controversial with the *Outlook* referring to 'an effective, if unpleasant book'[78] and the *Musical Times* claiming that the libretto 'can only appeal to admirers of the *décadent* school ... music allied to an ignoble and sordid subject, if true to its illustrative purpose, must lack nobility and those qualities which distinguish truly great art works'.[79] Edward Baughan freely admitted his preference for 'the solid Wagner style', and believed that the score 'is not passionate enough ... it is too sentimental and cloyingly sweet'.[80] Runciman modified his previously effusive position but still proclaimed *Messaline* 'a singularly fine and powerful work'.[81] Musically, the opera constitutes an advance upon *Moïna*; reminiscence motifs, though unsubtly used, give a greater sense of overall coherence, and there are more extended passages, although the work is still fragmented in many places. De Lara's harmonic language also advanced, including more exotic chromatic side steps and seventh chords, but rhythmically it remained diffuse and often lacking in impetus.

Sanga

Libretto	Eugène Morand and Paul Choudens
Premiere	21 February 1906, Théâtre de l'opéra, Nice
Sources	Vocal score, Choudens (Paris, ?1906)
Synopsis	Four acts: French alps, early twentieth century. Jean, son of Vigord, is in love with one of their farm hands, Sanga, but Vigord wants Jean to marry Lena. Sanga prays for an avalanche to destroy the village; it arrives as Jean and Lena marry in the church. The snow rapidly melts, causing a flood; Vigord and Lena are drowned. Sanga uses a boat to rescue Jean but they decide instead to die together and are swept away by the waters.

Like *Moïna*, *Sanga* was not performed in Britain. At Nice the work 'was very favourably received',[82] but in Paris (Opéra Comique, 9 December 1908) the

[76] For his own production list, see De Lara, p. 141.

[77] *SR*, 1 April 1899, pp. 394–6; for other positive reviews see *Dome*, 1 July, pp. 76–80; *MMR*, 1 May, p. 102.

[78] *Outlook*, 15 July 1899, p. 772.

[79] *MT*, 1 August 1899, pp. 535–6 (p. 535).

[80] *MS*, 22 July 1899, pp. 52–3 (p. 53).

[81] *SR*, 22 July 1899, pp. 100–101 (p. 101).

[82] *MT*, 1 April 1906, p. 270.

reception was more equivocal: De Lara cited B.W. Findon's review which claimed that 'a house crowded from floor to ceiling was moved to generous and spontaneous applause,'[83] but the *Musical Standard* reported the 'indifferent success' of a work that 'proved more ambitious than powerful or original'.[84] De Lara's score exhibits the same musical strengths, weaknesses and stylistic features as *Messaline*, allowing for the slighter and more anodyne story, but does not advance upon them.

Soléa

Libretto	Isidore De Lara and Jean Richepin
Premiere	19 December 1907, Stadttheater, Cologne
Sources	Vocal score: Choudens (Paris, 1907)
Synopsis	Four acts: Rhodes, 1522. The island, a stronghold of the Knights Hospitaller, is invaded by the Ottoman Suleiman the Magnificent. In a final attempt to defeat Suleiman, the lovers Lioncel and Soléa secrete themselves in a powder store in the depths of the citadel and blow themselves up.

Soléa was commissioned by Otto Lohse following the successful production of *Messaline* at Cologne, although De Lara had conceived the scenario in 1902.[85] The premiere attracted little attention in Britain and *Soléa* has never been performed in the British Isles. Although De Lara's music was wrought in the same manner as *Messaline* and *Sanga*, aspects of the scenario clearly inspired him: the music in the opening market scene is both intricate and tuneful although it remains essentially derivative; the Spanish characters Chiquita and Romabombas afforded De Lara the opportunity to indulge in some *Carmen*-like excursions, including the inevitable Habañera, but this is well-managed and developed over an extended period, indicating again De Lara's growing interest in unifying his scores. The inclusion of several diegetic dances facilitates a greater degree of rhythmic vitality than in De Lara's other operas.

Les Trois Masques

Libretto	Colautti, after Charles Méré's eponymous play
Premiere	24 February 1911, Grand Théâtre, Marseilles
Sources	Vocal score: Choudens (Paris, 1911) Orchestral score: L'Auteur (Paris, 1912)

83 *Morning Advertiser*, quoted in De Lara, p. 203.

84 *MS*, 19 December 1908, p. 395.

85 De Lara, p. 187.

Synopsis	Four acts: Corsica, early nineteenth century. Paolo loves Viola, daughter of Vescotelli. She falls pregnant with Paolo's child; Vescotelli demands that they marry, but Paolo's father, Prati della Corba, refuses his permission. Vescotelli declares a vendetta. During Carnival the lovers disguise themselves as Pierrot and Columbine; Vescotelli's three sons, also disguised, bring him home. Apparently too drunk to stand, it transpires that Pierrot has been stabbed; the vendetta is fulfilled.

Les Trois Masques contains curiously less local colour than either *Soléa* or *Naïl* although a quasi-Gypsy style (again founded in part on *Carmen*) appears in parts of the score. De Lara's musical style was by now stable and the approach in *Les Trois Masques* is consistent with the preceding operas; the full score shows De Lara's skills as an orchestrator and the opulence and variety in his sound-world often covers up weak themes and fragmented structures. The premiere of the opera attracted little interest in the British press; according to De Lara, the opera was performed in Paris in 1913 and he negotiated performances in several other cities in 1914 but the outbreak of war prevented them.[86]

Naïl

Libretto	Jules Bois
Premiere	21 April 1912, Theatre Lyrique de la Gaîté, Paris 18 July 1919, Covent Garden, London (Beecham Opera Company)
Sources	Vocal score, Paris (Choudens, 1911)
Principal cast (London)	Naïl – Rosina Buckman Hadyar – Frank Mullings The Emir – Percy Heming
Synopsis	Three acts: Algerian desert, late nineteenth century. Naïl loves the rebel Hadyar. At a local café Naïl dances for the customers; the Emir, a puppet ruler installed by the French, tries to seduce her but fails. Hadyar accuses him of selling out; as they fight the café is surrounded by soldiers and the lovers escape. At an oasis, the Emir captures Hadyar and crucifies him. Rather than be abducted, Naïl drinks poison and falls dead at Hadyar's feet.

Naïl originated in 1905 at a request from Emma Calvé, who had sung in other De Lara operas, for an 'Arabian' role. She secured a commission for De Lara from the Opéra Comique in Paris, an unheard-of honour as only French composers were invited to write for the Paris houses. Calvé withdrew, however, on her marriage, and the first performance of the opera was delayed.[87] As with his other post-1900 operas, the premiere of *Naïl* was barely noticed by the British press, but his return

86 De Lara, p. 211.

87 For a fuller account, see De Lara, pp. 188–92.

to England in 1915 and his war-time work as a concert promoter re-established him in the British consciousness. *Naïl* was the first opera by De Lara to be seen in Britain since the 1901 revival of *Messaline* at Covent Garden. *The Times*'s review of Beecham's performance was nonetheless equivocal, stating that 'it is not exactly English opera' and described De Lara's attempts at local colour as 'doing frankly weird things with drums and harp and harmonica notes'.[88] The exoticism draws magpie-like on the lexicon established by Ravel, Debussy, Saint-Saëns, Borodin and Rimsky-Korsakov, employing arabesques, augmented seconds and triads, ostinato rhythms, modal inflections and mixtures, and the whole tone scale, which, although not ineffective, was hardly original.

Delius, Frederick (1862–1934)

Koanga

Libretto	Charles Keary, after George Cable's *Grandissimes*
Premiere	30 March 1904, Stadttheater, Elberfeldt A partial concert performance was given on 30 May 1899 at St James's Hall, London
Sources	Vocal Score: Boosey & Hawkes (Winthrop Rogers) (London, 1935) Autograph Score: Jacksonville University, Florida
Synopsis	Three acts; Louisiana, mid-eighteenth century. Acting as narrator, Uncle Joe tells the story of Palmyra, a slave serving as Clotilda's maid, who is pursued by Simon Perez, her master Martinez's overseer. When a new slave, Koanga, is brought to the plantation, Palmyra realises that he is a prince and Voodoo priest. Martinez orders her to manipulate Koanga into co-operating with him and declares that Palmyra and Koanga will be married. Before the wedding Clotilda confesses that Palmyra is her illegitimate half-sister and Perez tries to abduct her. Koanga kills Perez and is condemned to death; Palmrya stabs herself.

Only two of Delius's operas were performed publicly before 1918.[89] Having spent much time overseas, he was little-known in Britain and, due to its distinctive style, pre-war performances of his music often generated puzzlement. The extracts of *Koanga* heard in 1899, despite a poor performance, drew genuine admiration: the *Musical Standard* described the music as 'most remarkable' and 'full of life and colour [which] with all its picturesqueness is massively emotional'.[90] The first staged performance, however, was barely noticed by the British press.

88 *The Times*, 19 July 1919, p. 12.

89 *Irmelin*, *The Magic Fountain* and *Margot la Rouge* were not performed publicly until 1953, 1977 and 1983 respectively.

90 *MS*, 3 June 1899, p. 338.

Romeo und Juliet auf dem Dorfe / A Village Romeo and Juliet

Libretto	Composer, after Gottfried Keller's eponymous novella (German translation by Jelka Delius)
Premiere	21 February 1907, Komische Oper, Berlin 22 February 1910, Covent Garden, London (Beecham)
Source	Vocal Score: Verlag Harmonie (Berlin, 1910) Full Score: Boosey & Hawkes (London, c. 1985)
Principal cast (London)	Sali – Walter Hyde Vreli – Ruth Vincent Dark Fiddler – Robert Maitland
Synopsis	Six scenes: Childhood friends Sali and Vreli fall in love but know their fathers will oppose the match due to a dispute over a piece of land belonging to the Dark Fiddler. When Vreli and Sali are caught together by Vreli's father Marti, Sali hits him; Marti later loses his sanity. Vreli and Sali leave their village but cannot find contentment. Finally they set sail on a barge, watched by the Dark Fiddler; Sali sinks the barge and he and Vreli drown.

The German premiere of *A Village Romeo and Juliet* also attracted little attention in Britain but Beecham's production exposed Delius to more scrutiny. His work was overshadowed, however, by the first British performance of a Strauss opera (*Elektra*) in the same season. Critical reaction was equivocal, noting an absence of dramatic action and the tableau-like structure (similar criticisms had previously been levelled at *Ivanhoe* and *Eugene Onegin*). John Runciman recognised 'many fine passages such as the skirling of the Black Fiddler … and, most beautiful of all, the closing scene',[91] but predicted that they were destined to become concert items.

D'Erlanger, Frederic (1868–1943)

Inès Mendo (produced under the pseudonym Frederic Regnal)

Libretto	P. Decourcelle and A. Liorat, after Prosper Merimée's eponymous play
Premiere	10 July 1897, Covent Garden, London (Grand Opera Syndicate)
Source	Vocal Score: Privately printed, 1897; copy at BL.
Principal cast	Don Salvador de Mendoza – Albert Alvarez Duke of Mendoza – Marcel Journet Inès Mendo – Mme Saville Juan Mendo – M Renaud

91 *SR*, 12 March 1910, p. 327.

Synopsis	Three acts, four scenes: Galicia, 1640. Salvador, the Duke's son, and Inès are in love. Juan, Inès's father, reluctantly consents to their marriage as he secretly holds a hereditary position as public executioner. When Salvador kills a man who serenades Inès he is condemned to death. Before the execution he marries Inès; Juan cannot bring himself to execute Salvador and stabs himself instead, just as the Duke arrives with a royal pardon.

Born in France, D'Erlanger moved to England as a child; he was naturalised in 1886. He was primarily a businessman but also an enthusiastic musician and was a Director of the Grand Opera Syndicate for many years.[92] *Inès Mendo* was D'Erlanger's second stage work (an earlier comic opera, *Jehan de Saintré*, was performed at Aix-les-Bains and Hamburg in 1894). Notwithstanding his connection to Covent Garden, *Inès Mendo* was well received by both audience and critics: the *Athenaeum* stated that 'if Mr Regnal is an amateur, he understands how to compose as few amateurs have done in the history of the art', although it noted an over-reliance on contemporaneous French style.[93] The *Academy* referred to a 'decidedly clever work' and a 'dramatic instinct … [which] if not strong is always appropriate' and forecast popularity.[94] The *Musical Times* also highlighted the derivative musical style but acknowledged D'Erlanger's technical skill.[95] These are appropriate judgements: the composer was influenced by Gounod, Massenet and Bizet and, while the music is superficial and overly dependent on a limited number of devices, it is also technically accomplished, and has a stronger melodic sense than many other works of the same period.

Tess

Libretto	Luigi Illica after Thomas Hardy's *Tess of the D'Urbervilles*
Premiere	10 April 1906, Teatro San Carlo, Naples 14 July 1909, Covent Garden, London (Grand Opera Syndicate)
Source:	Vocal Score: Ricordi (London, ?1909)
Principal cast (London)	Tess – Emmy Destinn Angel Clare – Mr R. Martin Alec – Mario Sammarco Jack – Charles Gilibert Joan – Mme Lejeune Aby – Mlle de Lys

---

92 For further biographical information, see D'Erlanger's obituary in *The Times* (26 April 1943, p. 6).

93 *Athenaeum*, 17 July 1897, p. 106.

94 *Academy*, 17 July 1897, p. 58. See also *MN*, same date, p. 55.

95 *MT*, 1 August 1897, pp. 532–3.

Synopsis	Four acts: Wessex, 1870s. Tess, a poor farmer's daughter, and Angel Clare fall in love. On discovering that her family is related to the rich D'Urbervilles, Tess seeks their help. Alec D'Urberville seduces her; a child is born but dies soon afterwards. Tess and Clare marry, but on their wedding night he discovers the details of Tess's past; Tess commits suicide.

Tess was the first opera to be based on a work of Thomas Hardy, whom D'Erlanger had approached in 1902 to secure his consent for an adaptation.[96] The premiere at the Teatro San Carlo (whose company gave autumn opera seasons at Covent Garden 1904 to 1907) was disrupted by a serious eruption of Mount Vesuvius; *Tess* was subsequently given at Milan (1908), Chemnitz and Budapest (1911), revived at Covent Garden (1910), and broadcast by the BBC (22 February 1929). The score, which employs a standard number-based structure with superimposed reminiscence motifs, is extremely fluent and melodic; tonal language is conventional but always elegant with mediant relationships, augmented triads and modal inflections used effectively but their repetition and a lack of rhythmic impetus are weaknesses. D'Erlanger's facility as a melodist explains the work's good reception; while never approaching either Bizet or Puccini in inspiration, the music is always accessible, untaxing, and strongly Italianate in style.

The choice of subject was a brave one: Hardy was a highly regarded novelist and *Tess* well-known. Although commentators regretted the loss of characters, details and nuances in Illica's adaptation, they recognised a successful adaptation and effective libretto. Regarding the music the consensus was that D'Erlanger had surpassed *Inès Mendo*, but, despite charm and technical skill, it lacked a strongly individual style.[97] While D'Erlanger's connection to Covent Garden was well-known, his work was viewed as worthy of production on its own merits.

Noël

Libretto	P. and J. Ferrier
Premiere	28 December 1910, Opéra Comique, Paris
Source:	Vocal Score: Ricordi (Paris, 1912)
Synopsis	Two acts: France, early twentieth century. Madeline, who years before abandoned her lover Jacques, returns, on Christmas Eve, with a baby. She abandons it in a church nativity scene. The priest discovers the child; Madeleine is found freezing on the streets. At a hospital Jacques forgives her and she dies; Jacques and his wife Blanche agree to raise the child, Noël, as their own.

D'Erlanger's final opera is similar in style to his previous works. The slight and sentimental story suited his lyrical facility, as did the lack of dramatic incident. The

[96] For a fuller account, see Desmond Hawkins, *The Tess Opera* (Taunton, 1984).

[97] See *The Times*, 15 July 1909, p. 13; *Athenaeum*, 17 July, p. 79; *MT*, 1 August, p. 533.

work was not performed in Britain and the Paris performances attracted attention in the British press. D'Erlanger believed that the Catholic imagery rendered *Noël* unsuitable for performance in Britain.[98]

Drysdale, Learmont (1866–1909)

The Red Spider

Libretto	S. Baring Gould, after his eponymous novel
Premiere	25 July 1898, Marina Theatre, Lowestoft
Source	Libretto: J. Tamblyn (London, 1898) Autograph Score: NLS, MS 3199
Principal cast	Honor Luxmore – Miss Carr Shaw Mrs Veale – Jessie Browning Lawyer Langford – Leslie Walker Larry Langford – Frank Pemberton Charles Luxmore – Vernon Cowper
Synopsis	Three acts; Devon, 1760. Honor (the 'Red Spider') is heir to a fortune but the documents proving her entitlement are lost. She is the sweetheart of Larry Langford, but is also desired by his father. A plot by Mrs Veale to secure the lawyer for herself by disgracing Honor's brother Charles initially backfires but eventually results in the desired happy ending: Honor and Larry are free to marry, while Mrs Veale secures the lawyer, who then produces the missing papers that secure Honor's wealth.

Scottish composer Drysdale's only performed opera is a 'romantic-comic' work; its premiere was well received and a 20-week provincial tour followed. One review complained that 'the comic aspect is for the most part conspicuous by its absence, and the music … savours rather of grand opera',[99] but another stated that it included the 'prettiest tunes and rhythms imaginable' although 'his music, like the libretto, is lacking in dramatic strength'.[100] Drysdale completed other light operas and one grand opera, *Fionn and Tera*, announced by Oscar Hammerstein in 1912, but not produced.[101]

---

98 *Bookman*, 1 September 1933, p. 306.

99 *Bury and Norwich Post*, 9 August 1898, p. 6.

100 *MN*, 22 October 1898, p. 360, of the performances in Liverpool. See also *Era*, 30 July, p. 9.

101 See also Janey Drysdale, *Biography of Learmont Drysdale with marginal notes*, at BL, shelfmark X.439/3073.

Dyer, Arthur Edwin (1843–1902)

The Lady of Bayonne

Libretto	William McGowan, after Gilbert Parker's *Baron of Beaugard*
Premiere	9 February 1897, Opera House, Cheltenham
Principal Cast	Lisette – Vera Vanderleur Cartouche – D'Arcy de Ferras Count Raymond of Bayonne – H.C. Portaway Susanne – Mrs G.B. Ferguson Léon – Herbert Taylor
Synopsis	One act; France, early 1700s. Lisette reluctantly marries Cartouche but is in love with the absent Raymond. Raymond returns and annuls the marriage. Cartouche curses Raymond for his intervention; to avenge himself Cartouche destabilizes a wooden bridge. As Raymond and Lisette walk across, it collapses and they both die. Cartouche is killed by Léon, Lisette's father.

The music is untraced. Reviews described the opera as ambitious and effective although the absence of a chorus contributed to a lack of spectacle. Unusually for a provincial premiere, it was reviewed in *The Times*, which deemed the music 'scholarly without being pedantic'.[102] Dyer, who held an Oxford D.Mus., and McGowan were both employed at Cheltenham College.[103]

Edwards, Julian (1855–1910)

Victorian

Libretto	J. Anderson, after Longfellow's *The Spanish Student*
Premiere	6 April 1883, Theatre Royal, Sheffield
Sources	Vocal Score: Hutchings and Romer (London) (undated)
Principal Cast	Victorian – Mr R. Hollings Hypolito – Lucy Franklein Count Di Lara – Albert McGuckin Preciosa – Philippine Siedle Bartolome – James Sauvage

---

[102] *The Times*, 10 February 1897, p. 9. Some leitmotifs are given in *Minim*, 1 March, pp. 152–3.

[103] An obituary of Dyer is in *Organist and Choirmaster*, 1 May 1902, p. 112.

Synopsis	Four acts; Madrid. Preciosa, a gypsy dancer, is enamoured of Victorian. He has rivals, however, in Bartolome and Di Lara; the latter convinces Victorian that Preciosa has been unfaithful and Victorian leaves her. Di Lara is stabbed by Bartolome. When Victorian discovers Di Lara's lie he seeks out Preciosa, who forgives him; Bartolome attempts to murder Victorian, but is foiled by Hypolito, who shoots Bartolome.

A Mancunian, Edwards established a reputation in the 1870s as an operetta composer; *Victorian* was his first serious stage work.[104] Preciosa bears a passing resemblance to Carmen, and Edwards's score occasionally exhibits Bizet's influence, but is fundamentally an old-fashioned number opera, with a tonal language and phrase structure reminiscent of pre-1850 Italian opera; occasionally the music is barely technically competent. Reviews were mixed: regarding the premiere the *Era* was quite generous, describing it as 'a far better opera than the average', some numbers as 'charmingly pretty', though 'some are too reminiscent of other composers'.[105] The same journal savaged the Covent Garden production (19 January 1884), however, saying that Edwards was 'utterly destitute of the ability to write dramatic music', and dismissing the libretto as 'awful trash'.[106]

King Rene's Daughter

Libretto	Stanislaus Stange, after Henrik Hertz's eponymous play
Premiere	22 November 1893, Herrmann's Theatre, New York
Sources	Vocal Score: John Church Company (Cincinatti, New York and Chicago, 1893)
Synopsis	One act. Provence, mid-fifteenth century. Iolanthe, unaware of her blindness, is seen by Tristan, who falls in love with her. He explains to Iolanthe that she is blind and she is cured by the Moor, Ebn Jahia. Tristan renounces a childhood betrothal in favour of Iolanthe, only to discover that she is King René's daughter, to whom he has been pledged all along.

Edwards emigrated to the United States in 1888 and focused on musical comedy; some of these works also appeared in Britain. He retained an interest in grand opera and wrote at least two such works in America, but they were not produced in Britain.[107] *King René's Daughter* is a more ambitious and mature work

---

[104] For further information on Edwards's musical comedy works see Kurt Gänzl, *The Encyclopaedia of the Musical Theatre* (New York, 1994) 2 vols, vol 1, pp. 400–401.

[105] *Era*, 14 April 1883, p. 8.

[106] *Era*, 26 January 1884, p. 6.

[107] Although termed a 'romantic opera', the musical style and structure of *Brian Boru* (Broadway Theatre, New York, 19 October 1896) are those of operetta; when Stanford's *Shamus O'Brien* opened at the same theatre a few weeks later (5 January 1897); the *New*

than *Victorian*; characterised by a surer technique and a desire for the music to reflect dramatic and emotional developments more directly, the work employs reminiscence motifs, a more varied number-based structure and a harmonic language which, although always securely rooted, is not lacking in adventure or interest; the vocal score also implies some ambitious orchestral textures. The *New York Times* criticised a lack of strong melodies and expressive passages but did not, unfairly, recognise the work's strengths.[108]

The Patriot

Libretto	Stanislaus Stange
Premiere	23 November 1908, Fifth Avenue Theatre, New York
Source	Vocal Score: Witmark & Sons (New York, 1907)
Synopsis	One act; Valley Forge, Pennsylvania, 1777. George Washington takes shelter at Manheim's farm during a storm; the pro-English farmer and his allies plot to murder Washington as he sleeps, but he swaps rooms with Manheim's daughter Marian and she is stabbed instead.

The Patriot is brief and modest, lacking the musical ambition and scope of *King René's Daughter*; the more rigid number-based structure of operetta dominates and the musical language is old-fashioned for the time of composition. The work's integrity is not aided by the incredibility of the story. Despite these weaknesses, the work 'launched successfully'.[109]

Esposito, Michele (1855–1929)

The Post Bag

Libretto	Alfred Graves
Premiere	27 January 1902, St George's Hall, London (two piano accompaniment) 14 March 1902, Gaiety Theatre, Dublin (orchestral accompaniment)
Source	Vocal Score: Boosey (London and New York, 1902)
Cast	Kitty O'Hea – Evangeline Florence Phelim – Joseph O'Mara Seaghan – Denis O'Sullivan

York Times tellingly commented, 'The only disappointment … will be for those who expect to see and hear one of our unhappily familiar breed of "comic operas"' (6 January 1897).

108 *New York Times*, 23 November 1893.

109 *New York Times*, 23 November 1908.

Synopsis	One act; contemporary Ireland. Kitty receives a letter from her absent fiancé Brian but cannot read it as it is in Irish. Phelim and Seaghan, both enamoured of Kitty, separately translate the letter but their versions differ widely. Their ulterior motives are exposed; as Kitty notices some English writing on the envelope Brian's horn is heard in the distance.

A Neapolitan married to a Russian, Esposito settled permanently in Dublin in 1882 and devoted himself to promoting art music in Ireland.[110] He embraced Irish musical culture and both of his operas are both based on Irish themes. Although entitled an 'operetta', Esposito did not mean to imply that *The Post Bag* was a musical comedy. While there are humorous elements in the story the music runs continuously, creating an interesting hybrid work. Anticipating Holst's *At the Boar's Head* (1924), Esposito used Irish folksongs, or pastiche imitations, and the music flows rapidly and vivaciously. The tonal language is conventional but well-handled and contains some interesting devices such as an extended passage based on a flattened seventh pedal but, comprising entirely short self-contained numbers and no recitative or spoken dialogue, the work lacks overall coherence. Graves's libretto is Anglo-Irish in its outlook, with a dig at the Irish language revival and its promoters, the Gaelic League. Conceived perhaps more as a *pièce d'occasion*, the work was nevertheless well received.[111]

The Tinker and the Fairy

Libretto	Douglas Hyde, after his own eponymous Irish play
Premiere	29 March 1910, Theatre Royal, Dublin (Dublin Amateur Operatic Society)
Source	Vocal Score: Breitkopf & Härtel (London, ?1910)
Principal cast	Fairy – Nettie Edwards Youth – Thomas Collins Tinker – John Browner
Synopsis	One act: The Fairy has been condemned by her Queen to a mortal life unless she is kissed by a man on her dying day. The Youth refuses her request as she is old and ugly. She appeals successfully to the Tinker, and regains her beauty and youth. As they kiss again, fairy music is heard; initially indecisive, she chooses to return to the fairy realm, leaving the Tinker lamenting his loss.

Esposito's musicianship is readily apparent in this Märchenoper; Hyde's unaffected and well-structured libretto is skilfully set and the music includes leitmotifs, some elegant songs, dramatically appropriate music, and a harmonic language which utilises Wagnerian tonal flexibility and elements characteristic of Irish folksong

110 For further information see Jeremy Dibble, *Michele Esposito* (Dublin, 2010).

111 *MT*, 1 April 1902, p. 259.

to contrast the fairy and mortal realms. The *Irish Times* stated that, 'Dr Esposito's musical setting is just what is required. He has not made it so elaborate as to get out of proportion with the subject, and, quite appropriately, the music is pleasant rather than deep,'[112] but its sole amateur performance in Dublin generated little press coverage other than in Irish newspapers. The *Irish Times*'s comments notwithstanding, *The Tinker and the Fairy* is still one of the most effective operas produced in this period and has been undeservedly neglected.

Farjeon, Harry (1878–1948)

Floretta

Libretto	Eleanor Farjeon, after a story by Heinrich Zschökke
Premiere	17 July 1899, St George's Hall, London
Source	Libretto: Henderson and Spalding (London, 1899)
Principal Cast	Prince Henry of Béarn – R. Whitworth Mitton Lagaucherie – Ernest Torrence Lubin – Philip Suckling Floretta – Ethel Wood Countess d'Ayelle – Julia Franks
Synopsis	Two acts; south-west France, 1566. Henry and Floretta, a gardener's daughter, are in love, provoking the jealousy of Lubin, another gardener. Henry is sent away by Lagaucherie, his tutor, but the lovers pledge to be faithful. A year later Henry returns, enamoured of the Countess d'Ayelle. On seeing Floretta his old feelings reawaken, but she realises they are transitory. Lubin renews his suit, but Floretta drowns herself. Henry finds her body.

Farjeon was a student and later teacher at the Royal Academy.[113] His only opera was a student work; in later life he focused on piano music. The music of *Floretta* is untraced; the book suggests a clear number-based structure, possibly with spoken dialogue. Although concise, the libretto suffers from the drawbacks typical of the time in its cumbersome and faux-archaic use of language. The *Musical News* commended a 'gift of graceful melody and a lively imagination' and also noted that 'considerable skill is shown in handling the orchestra'.[114] The *Monthly Musical Record* stated that the music was 'full of promise, and for a youthful student the wealth of melody was remarkable', but dismissed the book and argued that next time Farjeon should 'obtain a more dramatic subject'.[115]

112 *IT*, 30 March 1910, p. 7; see also *MT*, 1 May, p. 322.

113 For additional biographical information see Scowcroft, p. 116.

114 *MN*, 22 July 1899, p. 84.

115 *MMR*, 1 August 1899, p. 178.

Farmer, John (1835–1901)

Cinderella

Libretto	Henry S. Leigh, after the traditional folktale
Premiere	23 November 1883, Harrow School, Harrow (concert)* 17 May 1885, Albany Hall, Kingston-on-Thames (staged)
Source	Vocal score: publisher unknown (Harrow) (?1882)
Principal cast (staged performance)	Prince Mirabel – G.A. Colvill Malatesta (his tutor) – A.E. Twiss Baron Pomposo – A. Barrett Cinderella – José Sherrington Priscilla and Tabitha (the 'ugly sisters') – Miss Bruce; Miss Bradley Fairy Queen – Miss Farmer
Synopsis	Four acts; As in the folktale with minor amendments.

*Other concert performances were given at St James's Hall (2 May 1884; see *Academy*, 10 May 1884, p. 340) and Glasgow City Hall (28 February 1885; see *MT*, 1 April 1885, p. 212). A rumoured production by Carl Rosa did not take place (*MS*, 15 December 1883, p. 369).

Farmer was music master at Harrow when *Cinderella* was written. The opera comprises a highly conventional number-based structure, influenced by lighter musical styles, including that of Sullivan. Although tuneful and well-wrought (the *Musical World* stated that 'the themes are melodious and the scoring musicianly'[116]), the work is repetitive and conventional.

Fox, George

Robert Macaire

Libretto	Composer, after the French melodrama *L'auberge des Adrets*
Premiere	20 September 1887, Crystal Palace, London
Principal cast	Clementine – Mathilde Bauermeister Germeuil – Douglas Cox Marie – Lucy Franklein Robert Macaire – George Fox Jacques Strop – J.G. Taylor Charles – Herbert Sims Reeves

[116] *MW*, 1 December 1883, p. 755.

Synopsis	Two acts: L'auberge des Adrets, near Grenoble. Clementine and Charles, a foundling, are to be married. The escaped criminal Macaire takes a room at the inn; the next morning Germeuil, Clementine's father, is found murdered. Marie is suspected, but Macaire recognises her as the wife he deserted years before; Charles is their son. Macaire confesses to Germeuil's murder, and is shot as he attempts to escape.

Little is known of Fox; he sang with various touring companies and contributed music to a number of light and comic stage works.[117] The music of *Robert Macaire* is lost. Reviews described the music resembling that of Balfe and Wallace, with superimposed reminiscence motifs. During a short provincial tour, critics referred to 'graceful songs and pleasing combinations for the chorus',[118] 'music of the old fashioned style' and a libretto which might 'have excited envy in the breast of the poet Bunn though, we should imagine, in no other'.[119]

The Corsican Brothers

Libretto	Charles Bradberry, after Dion Boucicault's eponymous play
Premiere	25 September 1888, Crystal Palace, London
Principal cast	Fabian and Louis de Franchi – George Fox Emilie de Lesparre – Mathilde Bauermeister Chateau Renaud – Bernard Lane Montgiron – Douglas Cox Clara – Clara Leslie
Synopsis	Corsica and Paris, early nineteenth century. Brothers Fabian and Louis can perceive each others' thoughts and feelings. They have fallen in love with Emilie; Fabian gives her up to Louis, who follows her to Paris to find that she is married; her husband, Montgiron, impressed by Louis's honesty in admitting his love, entrusts her to Louis while he is away. Emilie is pursued by Renaud; offended, Louis challenges him and is killed. Fabian sees a vision of Louis's death; he kills Renaud.

The music of Fox's second opera is also lost; it incorporated recitative (an ill-judged decision according to newspaper critics), but was otherwise similar in style to *Robert Macaire*. The first performance was very poor; of the music the *Daily*

[117] See Brown and Stratton, p. 151, and references in Kurt Gänzl, *British Musical Theatre* (London and Basingstoke, 1986), vol. 1.

[118] *Era*, 24 September 1887, p. 14; see also *Stage*, 23 September, p. 16.

[119] *Reynolds's Newspaper*, 12 February 1888, p. 8, of the performances at the Standard Theatre, Shoreditch. See also *Liverpool Mercury*, 16 November, p. 8, and Gänzl, *British Musical Theatre*, vol. 1, pp. 333–4.

News commented that 'Mr Fox is at his best where he is least ambitious',[120] while the *Era* judged it less successful than *Robert Macaire*.[121]

Nydia

Libretto	Composer, after Edward Bulwer-Lytton's *The Last Days of Pompeii*
Premiere	10 May 1892, Crystal Palace, London
Source	Vocal score: Hutchings and Romer (London, 1892)
Principal cast	Glaucus – Derward Lely Arbaces – Henry Pyatt Ione – Giulius Valda Nydia – Mlle de Rideau
Synopsis	Five acts, ten scenes; Pompeii, 79 CE. Nydia, a blind slave, loves the noble Glaucus but he loves Ione, who reciprocates, despite attempts by the priest Arbaces to defame him. Glaucus strikes Arbaces and is condemned to death. When he is to be thrown to the lions, Vesuvius erupts. Nydia, Ione and Glaucus escape to a boat but Arbaces is killed; seeing Glaucus and Ione happy together, Nydia throws herself overboard.

Fox's most ambitious opera is a sprawling affair (containing several sub-principal roles and episodes omitted from the synopsis) which closely follows Lytton's original and incorporates several sections of his dialogue. Fox again employed a rigid number-based structure, Bizet, Meyerbeer and early Verdi being the preferred models (Nydia's reminiscence motif is similar to the 'Fate' theme in *Carmen*). Individual numbers are clearly structured and the harmonic language is unadventurous and predictable. *The Times* stated that *Nydia* contained 'little that is either very original or very charming, [but] is not without a certain amount of dramatic fitness',[122] while the *Era* recommended a substantial reduction in length and in the number of scenes.[123] A single performance was given by Harris at Drury Lane on 23 July 1892.

Frewin, Tom Harrison (1865–1938)

The Gay Lothario

Libretto	Composer
Premiere	4 January 1916, Grand Opera House, Middlesbrough (Harrison Frewin Company)

120 *DN*, 26 September 1888, p. 6. See also *Graphic*, 29 September, p. 342.

121 *Era*, 29 September 1888, p. 13.

122 *The Times*, 16 May 1892, p. 13. See also *MT*, 1 June 1892, p. 360.

123 *Era*, 14 May 1892, p. 10.

Principal Cast	Camilla – Raymonde Amy Leonela – Ruth Wynne Ancelmo – Kingsley Lark Lothario – John Clark
Synopsis	One act: Ancelmo, Camilla's husband, challenges Lothario to woo her in order to test her fidelity; he is successful. Aided by the maid Leonela, the lovers elope; Ancelmo commits suicide.

Although Frewin was primarily a conductor, he also composed; some short salon pieces and an overture were published. The music of this opera is lost; the *Stage* stated that 'the libretto is very interesting, and the music both well scored and replete with melody'.[124] Despite being produced by his own company, no further performances of the opera have been traced.

Gatty, Nicholas (1874–1946)

Greysteel

Libretto	Reginald Gatty, after the Icelandic saga 'Gisli and the Soursop' as translated by George Dasent
Premiere	1 March 1906, Theatre Royal, Sheffield (Moody-Manners Opera Company as part of Sheffield University Opera Week)
Sources	Libretto: Leng & Co (Sheffield, 1906) Scena: Cary & Co (London, 1915)
Principal cast	Ingiborga – Enriquetta Crichton Ari – Hendrik Van Lachtertrop Gisli – Charles Carter Kol – Marshall Vincent Bjorn the Black – George Nielson
Synopsis	One act: Kol, a serf, laments that Ari will not fight the outlaw Bjorn, with Greysteel, Kol's dwarf-forged sword. Gisli, Ari's brother, loves Ari's wife, Ingiborga. When Ari is killed by Bjorn, Gisli swears vengeance; Kol offers him Greysteel, with which Gisli kills Bjorn. Gisli and Ingiborga come together and Kol gains his freedom.

Gatty was born near Sheffield and educated at Cambridge and the Royal College. The music of *Greysteel* is untraced, apart from the scena in which Ingiborga laments Ari; this recalls Siegfried's funeral march, and Wagner's influence was noted by the *Era*, which commented that Gatty 'has treated the theme well. The orchestration is effective, and the frequent use of the brass and woodwind instruments is especially appropriate to a subject dealing with passion and fighting.'[125] The libretto is burdened by archaic language but avoids clichéd rhyming schemes. *Greysteel* was

[124] *Stage*, 13 January 1916, p. 23.

[125] *Era*, 10 March 1906, p. 19. A qualified review is in *MS*, 10 March, p. 149.

expanded to two acts and performed at Sadler's Wells in 1938. The largely new first act was reviewed more positively than the original music.[126]

Duke or Devil?

Libretto	Ivor Gatty
Premiere	16 December 1909, Gaiety Theatre, Manchester (Moody-Manners Opera Company)
Sources	Vocal Score: Novello & Co (London, 1912)
Principal cast	Duke of Bologna – Charles Moorhouse Pietro – Seth Hughes Priest – Charles Magrath Vincenzo – Mr R. Matthews Bianca – Raymonde Amy
Synopsis	One act: The long-absent Duke returns to Bologna but is mistaken by the townspeople for the Devil. The Duke is condemned to death; Bianca argues for leniency and is condemned as a witch; Pietro, her sweetheart, pleads for her and is also condemned. Vincenzo, a gentleman in waiting, persuades the townspeople that the Duke is not the Devil; Pietro and Bianca are reprieved while the Duke leaves, vowing not to return.

Gatty's second opera aspires to a lighter tone than *Greysteel*; the incidents in the book are viewed as farcical rather than melodramatic. The score does not always reflect this, however, and is sometimes over-earnest. The *Musical Times* optimistically declared Gatty to be 'the Elgar of … British serious music-drama' and 'one of the most gifted of native operatic composers'.[127] Although lacking the implied distinctive style, the music is well-wrought and dramatically aware, via good pacing and the use of distinctive textures for different characters; the town watchmens' 'framing scenes' at the beginning and end, are particularly effective. Gatty maintained an interest in opera through the rest of his career; three more works were performed after the Great War: *Prince Ferelon* (1919); *The Tempest* (1920); and *King Alfred and the Cakes* (1930).

Hervey, Arthur (1855–1922)

Ilona

Libretto	Mrs Arthur Hervey
Premiere	12 May 1914, Royal Court Theatre, London

[126] *Stage*, 31 March 1938, p. 10.

[127] *MT*, 1 January 1910, p. 25.

Principal cast	Ilona – Bettina Freeman Thérèse – Miss di Temple Van Loo – Ivor Walters Lucian – Julian Henry
Synopsis	One act: Holland, seventeenth century. Van Loo, a famous Dutch artist, paints the portrait of Thérèse, a famous actress, who recites impassioned passages from her latest play during the sitting. Ilona, Van Loo's wife, overhears the recitation and mistakes her husband's motives. His assistant Lucian persuades Ilona to elope. Just before they leave, the two men fight; Van Loo is wounded but tells Ilona the truth before he dies.

Hervey was best-known in his lifetime as a writer on music and was music critic of the *Morning Post* (1892–1908). He also composed steadily, and several works, mainly orchestral, were premiered in the Edwardian decade. A one-act comic opera, *The Fairy Post-Box*, was given at the Royal Court Theatre on 21 May 1885.[128] The music of *Ilona* is lost, but was praised in the *Musical Times*: 'To this fast-moving story, Mr Hervey has supplied a delightful score. He presents an extraordinary amount of variety in a short time … For the wife, there is good dramatic writing in the best modern Italian style, and for the actress passages of lyric charm unquestionably French … The instrumentation is masterly, its touch firm, and its point always appropriate'.[129]

Holbrooke, Josef (1878–1958)

Pierrot and Pierrette

Libretto	W.E. Grogan
Premiere	11 November 1909, His Majesty's Theatre, London
Source	Vocal Score: Orchestral Publishing Company (London, 1909)
Principal cast	Pierrot – Albert Archdeacon Pierrette – Esta D'Arod Nurse – Katherine Jones Stranger – Leon de Sousa
Synopsis	Two acts: an 'old world garden'. Pierrot and Pierrette live contentedly in their isolated garden, looked after by the Nurse. A Stranger convinces Pierrot to leave with promises of excitement outside. Pierette misses him and rejects the advances of the Stranger. When Pierrot returns, dissipated and disillusioned, she welcomes him back.

Holbrooke's first opera is scored for a small orchestra (including concertinas), and employs light melody-led textures in a flexible number structure with coherence

[128] For further information see his obituary in *MT*, 1 April 1922, p. 277.

[129] *MT*, 1 June 1914, p. 392. See also *Stage*, 14 May, p. 24.

provided by reminiscence motifs. A predilection for waltz-like textures creates a lighter mood but the harmonic language, although tonally secure, is flexible and sophisticated. Critical reception was generally complimentary; *Cremona* described the opera as 'a charming little work',[130] while the *Musical Times* stated that 'Mr Holbrooke's music in opera is just as good as it is in anything else',[131] although it perceived a disjunction between the inconsequential story and overly serious music. After minor revisions, the work was re-published as *The Stranger*.

The Children of Don

Libretto	T.E. Ellis, pseudonym of Lord Howard de Walden, after sections of the *Mabinogion*
Premiere	15 June 1912, London Opera House, London (Oscar Hammerstein)
Sources	Vocal Score: Miles & Co (London, 1912)
Principal cast	The Children of Don, by different fathers: Gwydion – Alan Turner Govannion – Andrew Shanks Goewin – Jeanne Jomelli Gwion – Frederick Blamey Elan – Augusta Doria Math – Henry Weldon
Synopsis	Three acts: Ancient Britain. The stolen magic cauldron of King Arawn is installed in a temple overseen by the High Priest Math, who makes Gwydion its guardian. Elan, who has recently given birth to a son, Dylan, fathered by Lyd, the Sea-King, proposes marriage to Gwydion, but he rejects her. Govannion tries to seduce Goewin, a priestess, but fails. Math chides Gwydion for failing to protect Goewin, and transforms Gwydion and Govannion into wolves. They kill Goewin. Returned to human form, Gwydion suggests Elan takes Goewin's place as a priestess, but Math refuses when he learns of Dylan. Gwydion kills Math; Govannion throws Dylan into the sea but, being Lyd's son, he comes to no harm. Unknown to Elan, Gwydion rescues and adopts him.

The Children of Don and *Dylan* form the first two parts of the trilogy, *The Cauldron of Annwn*, based on sections of the medieval Welsh stories, the *Mabinogion*; the final part, *Bronwen*, was produced at Huddersfield (Carl Rosa Company, 1 February 1929). *Dylan* was composed first, but the operas were performed in order. *The Children of Don* was given by Oscar Hammerstein, almost certainly in order to secure De Walden's support for the London Opera House.

Holbrooke's reputation for expansive scores requiring massive resources was reinforced by *The Children of Don*. The work is one of the most fluidly structured, contrapuntally involved, dissonant and tonally restless scores produced by a

[130] *Cremona*, 1 December 1909, pp. 159–60 (p. 160).

[131] *MT*, 1 December 1909, p. 795; see also *The Times*, 12 November, p. 13.

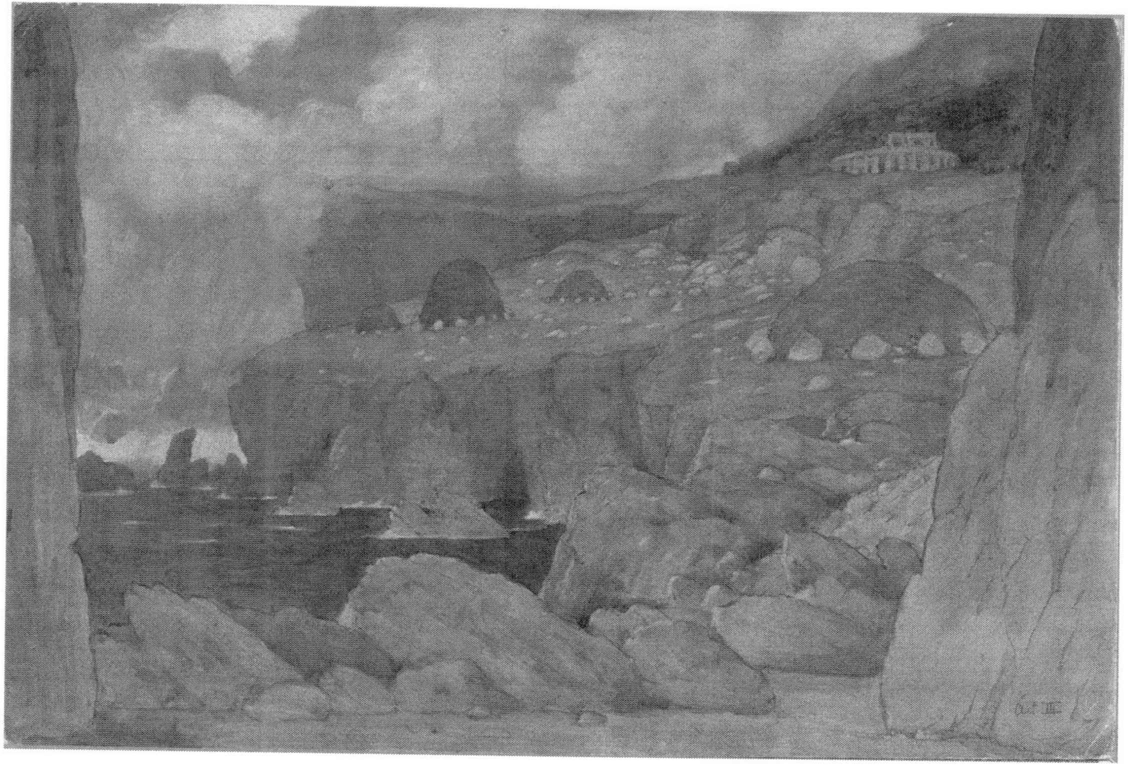

Figure 6.2 Scene design for *The Children of Don* (Act III) by Sidney Syme

British composer before 1914.[132] In combination with the convoluted book, which is overburdened with characters, almost unremittingly gloomy, and comprises prolix and complex language, the work was almost guaranteed to fail. Most critics were hostile – the *Musical Standard* railed: 'The subject is quite out of touch with the thought of the twentieth century. We want human beings on the stage – and no magic!' and concluded that the music was 'dry, bitter, mechanical, often meaningless and intensely unattractive'.[133] Herman Klein, a supporter of both Hammerstein and Holbrooke, admitted the work's failure, and criticised the libretto's 'feeble characterisation and faulty construction' but argued that the score was 'a marvel of ingenuity', and urged Holbrooke to consider the singers more sympathetically.[134] John Runciman, typically contrary, stated that 'It contains a great deal of the most magnificent music ever written by an Englishman … it is [also] as horribly monotonous an opera as I ever patiently endured to the end'.[135]

Dylan, Son of the Wave

Libretto	T.E. Ellis, after sections of the *Mabinogion*
Premiere	4 July 1914, Theatre Royal, Drury Lane, London (Thomas Beecham)
Source	Vocal Score: Novello & Co (London, 1910)
Principal cast	Dylan – Frederic Austin Govannion – Robert Radford Gwydion – Robert Maitland Gwyddno – Frank Mullings Elan – Doris Woodall Lyd, the Sea-King – Edmund Burke Seithenin – Frederick Ranalow
Synopsis	Three acts: Ancient Britain, 20 years after *The Children of Don*. Elan is a guest in the coastal castle of Gwyddno, a vassal of Gwydion. She does not recognise Dylan when he appears before her as a minstrel. Gwydion reveals the truth but at the sea shore Govannion kills Dylan. Govannion takes refuge with Seithenin as Lyd vows to avenge himself for Govannion's attempted murder of Dylan (see *The Children of Don*). His first attempt fails; Govannion returns to Gwyddno's castle but the sea overwhelms Govannion before he can enter.

Dylan was originally conceived as an independent work and de Walden's book is consequently simpler and more effective as it does not include excessive amounts of expository material. Problems remain: the language is prolix and the

[132] For a discussion of the opera, with particular reference to the treatment of leitmotifs, see Anne-Marie Forbes, 'Josef Holbrooke's *Cauldron of Annwn* and metempsychosis in music', *Musicology Australia*, 27 (1994) pp. 43–59.

[133] *MS*, 22 June 1912, pp. 383–4 (p. 383).

[134] *MT*, 1 July 1912, pp. 450–51 (p. 451).

[135] *SR*, 22 June 1912, pp. 775–76 (p. 775). See also *Academy*, same date, p. 773.

plot consistently strenuous with only the bucolic Seithenin providing some relief, alongside a more extensively employed chorus. Holbrooke's musical style in both works is similar. Helped by a better production, *Dylan* was received more positively than *The Children of Don*, but critics identified similar strengths and weaknesses. The *Musical Times* argued that 'there is a future for [Holbrooke] if he can apply his talent to a really dramatically written book', using this as justification for 'unequal' music which contained 'longeurs that are oppressive' but also 'reveals more power than any other dramatic music we have heard by this composer'.[136] The *Athenaeum* commented that 'at the present day [Wagner's] influence ought to have become faint'.[137] *Bronwen*, which contains different characters, was completed in 1920, and, by the time of its premiere, the debts to Wagner appeared even more anachronistic. Changing tastes, and the works' manifest weaknesses and extravagant production demands sidelined the trilogy permanently.[138]

Holst, Gustav (1867–1934)

Sāvitri

Libretto	Composer, after an episode in the *Mahābhārata*
Premiere	5 December 1916, London, Wellington Hall (London School of Opera)
Sources	Vocal Score and Full Score: J Curwen & Sons (London, 1923) Autograph score: Bodleian Library, University of Oxford, MS Don.c.3.
Cast	Satyavān – George Pawlo Sāvitri – Mabel Corran Death – Harrison Cook

136 *MT*, 1 August 1914, p. 539, which also mentions the innovative use of a cinematograph to illustrate the flight of water fowl in Act III. See also *Academy*, 18 July, pp. 85–6.

137 *Athenaeum*, 11 July 1914, p. 58; see also *SR*, 26 July, pp. 106–7.

138 Holbrooke composed two other operas before 1918. *Varenka* (*c*. 1907) is lost; the ballet-opera *The Enchanter* (1914) is frequently stated to have been performed in Chicago in spring 1915 but no performance has been traced. Holbrooke did travel to the United States in August 1915 intending to supervise a production in which Anna Pavlova took the leading role, but he was involved in a car accident which led to its postponement (and, apparently, eventual cancellation). See Keith Money, *Anna Pavlova: Her Life and Art* (New York, 1982), pp. 211–27; Quaintance Eaton, *The Boston Opera Company* (New York, 1965), pp. 271–7; *MT*, 1 July 1915, pp. 401–2; 1 September, p. 561.

Synopsis	One act: Sāvitri hears the voice of Death, who has come to take her husband, Satyavān. He dismisses her fears and Death takes him. Sāvitri asks Death to take her too, but he instead grants her a boon. She asks for a complete life; Death accedes and Sāvitri tells him that this means life with Satyavān. Outwitted, Death brings Satyavān back to life and leaves.

Holst maintained a life-long interest in dramatic music but *Sāvitri*, composed in 1908–09 was the only serious work performed before 1918.[139] One of the most distinctive and individual British operas of this period, the sparse musical language of *Sāvitri* is highly evocative although its slender textures can only sustain a work of its 30-minute duration. Holst's previous attempts encompassed an eclectic variety of styles (continued after *Sāvitri*); here the transparent and minimal means, unconventional orchestral requirements and simple story are well matched in an evocative and accessible work.[140] At the time of its premiere *Sāvitri* attracted little press attention but *Era* was very complimentary: 'its originality is certainly a challenge to the accepted school of opera … he has treated [the *Mahābhārata*] in a dignified and beautiful way'.[141]

Klein, Manuel (1876–1919)

Bow Sing

Libretto	Carroll Fleming from a theme suggested by Arthur Voegtlin
Premiere	24 February 1911, Ladbroke Hall, London (copyright performance)
Source	Vocal score: Witmark & Sons (New York, 1911)
Principal cast	Bow Sing – Ethel Royale Eric D'Arcy – Orlando Barnett
Synopsis	One act; three scenes: Hong Kong, early twentieth century. Bow Sing, a tea house worker, looks for her 'master', D'Arcy. When he arrives, he tells her that their relationship must end because he is leaving China. As he later boards his ship Bow tries to see him once more but a guard stops her. She watches the ship sail and sinks to the ground in despair.

139 The works preceding *Sāvitri* are: *Lansdown Castle* (operetta in two acts, amateur performance at Cheltenham, 7 February 1893); *The Revoke* (1895, one act, privately played through at the Royal College); *Sita* (three acts, 1900–06, a long Wagnerian work on an Indian story, highly commended in the Ricordi Opera Competition won by Edward Naylor's *Angelus* (see below); unperformed); *The Youth's Choice* (1902, one act, unperformed).

140 For further commentary and analysis see Michael Short, *Gustav Holst: The Man and His Music* (Oxford, 1990).

141 *Era*, 20 December 1916, p. 8.

Klein, a brother of Herman, emigrated to the United States in the 1890s.[142] As with Julian Edwards, his output was dominated by music for Broadway. *Bow Sing* is a curious hybrid: the musical language is simple and reminiscent of musical comedy in texture, and employs a strict number-based structure, yet runs continuously (without spoken dialogue), setting a melancholy romantic story with affinities to *Madama Butterfly*. Although there is little dramatic tension, individual numbers are well-crafted and largely free of attempts to create a pseudo-Oriental sound-world.

Knox, David (?1877/78–1933)

Giuliana

Libretto	Composer, translated from E. Golisciani's Italian version.
Premiere	19 November 1913, Opera House, Cheltenham (Moody-Manners Company)
Principal cast	Paolo – Frank Christian Count Daniele – Flintoft Moore Lorenzo – Hubert Dunkerley Marta – Olive Westwood Giuliana – Susanna Salvani
Synopsis	Daniele convinces Marta, his former mistress, to persuade Giuliana, a grave-digger's daughter, to yield to his advances; in return, he will marry Marta. Daniele's seduction succeeds; when Giuliana realises that he will not marry her, she confesses to her brother Paolo, who shoots Daniele.

'David Knox' is probably a pseudonym for Eustace Blois, Managing Director of the Covent Garden Opera Syndicate from 1928 to 1933.[143] The music of the opera is untraced. A lukewarm review in the *Stage* complained that the 'dramatic element is too slender' and that the music contained 'many happy little suggestions of good things which mostly seem to fizzle out', but the work had 'clarity, and in places decided power'.[144] The musical style was deemed old-fashioned, pre-dating both Wagner and Puccini.

142 For further biographical information see Gänzl, *Encyclopaedia*, vol. 1, p. 782.

143 Blois's obituary in *The Times* (18 May 1933, p. 16) states that an unnamed opera by him was in the repertory of the Moody-Manners Company, of which he was a member, and this is the only work traced which might fit the circumstances; see also John Lucas, *Thomas Beecham: An Obsession with Music* (Woodbridge, 2008), p. 191.

144 *Stage*, 27 November 1913, p. 31; see also *MT* (1 December, p. 807). Performances in Hanley were announced (*Stage*, 11 December, p. 5) but no others have been traced.

Lehmann, Liza (1862–1918)

Everyman

Libretto	A reduced version of the traditional English morality play
Premiere	28 December, 1915, Shaftesbury Theatre, London (Beecham & Courtneidge)
Source	Vocal Score: Blythe (London, 1916) [only traced copy in BBC Music Library]
Principal cast	Everyman – Edith Clegg Good Deeds – Miriam Licette Death – Frederic Austin Knowledge – Maude Murray Fellowship – Alfred Heather Riches – Frederick Ranalow Messenger – Herbert Langley Beauty – Eda Bennie Discretion – Ethel Toms Five Wits – Denis Byndon-Ayers Strength – Arthur Wynn Priest's Voice – Herbert Langley
Synopsis	As in the traditional play: Everyman is informed by Death that it is time to face judgement; in his final hours Everyman meets various 'characters', but only Good Deeds stays with him to the end, when he dies and is welcomed to heaven.

Lehmann composed two light stage works (*Sergeant Brue* (1904) and *The Vicar of Wakefield* (1906)) but *Everyman* was her only serious stage work. Lehmann claimed that several production difficulties hampered the work and she believed that producing a serious work at Christmas in war time was a misjudgement.[145] Reviews were mixed; the *Stage* praised both music and production,[146] and the *Musical Standard* declared that '*Everyman* is a splendid argument for opera in English … her handling of the inflections in the recitatives was a revelation.'[147] *The Times*, however, deemed it 'discreetly solemn' and lacking in variety,[148] while the *Era* stated: 'If the object of setting drama to music is to intensify the emotions which underlie the words, [and] to supply what is beyond the power of speech to express, it must be questioned whether Miss Liza Lehmann has succeeded in accomplishing her task'.[149] Lehmann believed herself that Beecham would have been more supportive had he seen *Everyman* on stage; he did not revive it.

145 See Liza Lehmann, *The Life of Liza Lehmann by Herself* (London, 1919), pp. 199–205.

146 *Stage*, 30 December 1915, p. 24.

147 *MS*, 8 January 1916, p. 31.

148 *The Times*, 29 December 1915, p. 11.

149 *Era*, 5 January 1916, p. 14.

Löhr, Hermann (1871–1943)

Sarenna

Libretto	Avon Marsh
Premiere	7 September 1907, Lyric Theatre, London (Moody-Manners Company)
Sources	Vocal score: Chappell & Co. (London, 1907)
Principal Cast	Michael Heard – Lewis James Will Hendon – Joseph O'Mara Ruth Hendon – Miss Penrose Hardinge Sarenna – Kate Anderson
Synopsis	One act: An English village, *c.* 1810. Will Hendon has returned from war, accompanied by Sarenna, a Spanish gypsy. Ruth, his sister, cautions him: Michael Heard, the village sexton, wants to avenge himself for the suicide of his daughter, whom Hendon seduced years previously. When Hendon later abandons Sarenna, she betrays him to Heard, who kills him.

Hermann Löhr achieved modest success composing popular songs; *Sarenna* is his only known opera. While the scenario recalls *Cavalleria Rusticana*, Löhr's music is eclectic: the drinking choruses are rumbustious glees, many others sections are derived from contemporaneous verismo scores, while Sarenna's first song is – somehow inevitably – a reworking of Carmen's 'Habañera'. Although the score is derivative and conventionally structured and, in the words of the *Musical Times*, 'is obvious and direct in expression, subtleties and complexities being studiously avoided',[150] the music in *Sarenna* is the product of an able composer: the firmly tonal harmonic language is controlled effectively with plenty of colourful inflections, and there is a strong melodic and dramatic flow. The opera was produced in a double bill with Gatty's *Greysteel*; Manners does not appear to have given it again.

Lyon, James (1872–1949)

Storm Wrack

Libretto	T. Barlow
Premiere	15 February 1918, Shakespeare Theatre, Liverpool (Phillips Opera Company)

[150] *MT*, 1 October 1907, p. 672. A more qualified review appeared in *Stage*, 12 September, p. 17.

Principal cast	Margot – Florence Morden René – Gwynne Davies Pierre – Lewis James
Synopsis	René, a fisherman, is in love with his partner Pierre's wife, Margot; neglected by Pierre, Margot has drifted into the affair. Pierre overhears René urging Margot to elope and challenges him. Pierre is about to kill René when a signal is heard indicating a ship in distress; both men leave for the rescue effort while Margot realises that Pierre still loves her.

An autodidact, Lyon held a variety of teaching and organists' positions. The music of *Storm Wrack* is untraced. The *Stage* commented that, 'he has a strong sense of the tonal colour, and his music uplifted, strengthened and supported the dramatic action in a most satisfactory manner. He uses one theme frequently and with good effect, but his music generally lacks continuity and homogeneity. It was too restless and disconnected to be wholly satisfactory.'[151] The Phillips Company was taken over by the Rosa later in 1918 and *Storm Wrack* discarded from its repertory.

MacAlpin, Colin (1870–1942)

King Arthur

Libretto	Composer
Premiere	5 November 1897, Temperance Hall, Leicester (concert performance) 6 July 1903, Royalty Theatre, London (first known staged performance)
Source:	Vocal Score: Bosworth & Co (London, ?1897)
Principal cast	Arthur – H. Piercy Guinevere – Medora Henson Lancelot – Andrew Black Modred – A. Page
Synopsis	Three acts; Post-Roman Britain. Guinevere is escorted to Camelot by Lancelot to marry Arthur. Modred suspects that Guinevere and Lancelot are lovers but she denies it; they are later discovered together and Lancelot kills Modred. Guinevere flees to a nunnery, where Arthur tells her to purify herself through faith.

Leicester-born MacAlpin's first opera includes spirited music but also an over-reliance on set pieces, especially extended choruses; there is little character delineation or development. Modred, for example, has only a few seconds' sight

[151] *Stage*, 21 February 1918, p. 17. See also *Liverpool Echo*, 16 February, p. 4.

of Guinevere and Lancelot before concluding that they are lovers. MacAlpin was infatuated by the more conservative elements of Wagner, often recalling parts of *Lohengrin* and *Die Meistersinger* but, although the harmonic language shows some sophistication, MacAlpin was rarely able to break away from regular periodisation and interesting ideas become relentless in structure and repetition. The *Daily Telegraph* asserted that the work would succeed better as a cantata.[152] Regarding the first staged performance, the *Musical Standard* was quite positive: although 'the listener was not surprised by any novelty in the music', it praised 'several climaxes of real power, because they were climaxes, not mere musical explosions'.[153]

The Cross and the Crescent

Libretto	John Davidson, after François Coppée's *Pour la Couronne*
Premiere	17 September 1903, Covent Garden, London (Moody-Manners)
Principal cast	Prince Michael Brancomir – William Dever Constantine Brancomir – Joseph O'Mara Ibrahim – Charles Magrath Bazilide – Toni Seiter Militza – Fanny Moody
Synopsis	Four acts, five scenes: Bulgaria, fifteenth century. Michael, a successful Christian warrior, is persuaded by Bazilide, his wife, and Ibrahim, a Turkish agent, that he should become the puppet King of Bulgaria. Constantine, Michael's son, and a slave-girl he has saved, Militza, frustrate the plan. Constantine kills Michael and alerts the Christians to an imminent Turkish attack. The Turks win; Constantine is blamed because he deprived the Christians of their best warrior. In order to free Constantine from taunting, Militza stabs him and then herself.

MacAlpin's second opera won a competition for new British work run by Charles Manners; MacAlpin received £250, and 10 per cent of all production profits. The latter cannot have amounted to much as the opera does not appear to have been performed more than once. The music is untraced. Despite a strong cast, the premiere was imperfect; reviews were moderate and repeated many criticisms levelled at *King Arthur*. The *Musical Times* recognised MacAlpin's talent and aspiration, but also his inexperience.[154] A less charitable review in the *Monthly Musical Record* accused MacAlpin of being 'hypnotised by Wagner. He remembers all the mannerisms of the great master and many of the themes,' but nevertheless allowed that 'there is much of promise in the work'.[155]

---

152 Quoted in *Leicester Mercury*, 13 November 1897, p. 6.

153 *MS*, 11 July 1903, p. 20.

154 *MT*, 1 October 1903, p. 673.

155 *MMR*, 1 October 1903, p. 195.

The Vow

Libretto	James Blackhall, after the story of Jephtha, in Judges, Old Testament
Premiere	15 May 1915, Theatre Royal, Nottingham (Moody-Manners)
Principal cast	Caleb – Seth Hughes Jaaron – Charles Moorhouse Watchman – Hubert Dunkerley Manoi – Kitty Brownless
Synopsis	One act: Manoi awaits the return of her father Jaaron from battle. He is preceded by Caleb, who wants to warn Manoi that Jaaron has sworn to sacrifice the first person who greets him on his return in thanks for victory. Manoi refuses to hear him and is the first person to greet Jaaron. Jaaron believes he must fulfil his promise; Manoi agrees. As the curtain falls the sacrifice is imminent.

A third opera by MacAlpin, *Ingomar*, was proposed for production by Charles Manners in 1909, but his scheme was aborted (see Chapter 3). The music for both *Ingomar* and *The Vow* are untraced. According to reviews *The Vow* was, like *The Cross and the Crescent*, structurally indebted to Wagner; 'there are no set numbers, the voice parts being solely concerned with the development of the story, and while there are no "tunes", there is melody of a strong, fibrous order'.[156] The *Musical Standard* was generous: 'as the opera only lasts forty minutes and is for the most part strenuous and quick-moving, it is no little to his credit that [MacAlpin] has achieved several pages of great emotional beauty. The song which Caleb sings just previous to the entrance of Jaaron is a veritable gem, while the final section proves that the composer can rise to great emotional heights when his librettist allows him'.[157] The Moody-Manners suspended operations a year later; *The Vow* was not taken up by any other companies.

MacCunn, Hamish (1868–1916)

Jeanie Deans

Libretto	Joseph Bennett, after Walter Scott's *The Heart of Midlothian*
Premiere	15 December 1894, Lyceum Theatre, Edinburgh (Carl Rosa)
Source:	Vocal Score: Mathias & Strickland (London, 1894)

156 *Stage*, 20 May 1915, p. 22.
157 *MS*, 29 May 1915, p. 417.

Principal cast	Jeanie Deans – Marie Duma Effie Deans – Alice Esty Staunton – E.C. Hedmondt David Deans – Alec Marsh Dumbiedykes – L. Pringle Madge Wildfire – Louise Meisslinger
Synopsis	Four acts: Edinburgh and Richmond, 1730s. Jeanie's sister Effie is wrongfully arrested for murdering her child. Effie's lover, Staunton, wants Jeanie to secure Effie's release by perjuring herself but she refuses. Staunton eludes the police with the help of Madge Wildfire; with a mob, he storms the prison but Effie refuses to leave. Jeanie agrees to petition the king and, helped by Dumbiedykes, travels to Richmond. She secures pardons for Effie and Staunton and returns in time to free Effie from the gallows.

MacCunn had previously made a reputation with his overture *The Land of the Mountain and Flood* (1887) and *Jeanie Deans* was similarly celebrated as possessing an overtly Scottish character. While the structure is largely conventional (primarily number-based with some substantial sections of arioso and accompanied recitative), MacCunn's melodic and harmonic approach is quite individual, incorporating some diegetic pastiche folk songs (sung by Madge in Acts II and IV and Dumbiedykes in Act III), and a predilection for augmented triads, deft enharmonic shifts, modal inflections (flattened sevenths and supertonics), pentatonicism, and some complex chromatic harmonies over pedal points. The scene at Richmond contrasts with those in Scotland through the use of the minuet from Handel's 'Water Music'. Bennett's compression of Scott's novel is generally successful and allows for some light relief within the serious plot; the lack of a conventional pair of lovers helps rather than hinders.

The work was generally well received but the Rosa's absence from London made it hard for the opera to gain a national reputation and attention shifted to *Diarmid*, which MacCunn was already planning when *Jeanie Deans* was premiered. The *Monthly Musical Record* referred to a lyrical element 'more prominent than is usual than with the composer',[158] but MacCunn's more adventurous writing drew some criticism; the *Musical Times* highlighted melos that 'is at times rather unquiet and even ungainly in its harmonic progressions'[159] and the *Musical News* argued that 'there is wanting in the music spontaneity and a naturalness of expression, the composer striving too much after originality'.[160]

158 *MMR*, 1 December 1894, pp. 276–7 (p. 276).

159 *MT*, 1 December 1894, pp. 816–17 (p. 816).

160 *MN*, 24 November 1894, p. 442.

Diarmid

Libretto	John Campbell, Marquess of Lorne (later Duke of Argyll), after (another) John Campbell's *Popular Tales of the West Highlands*
Premiere	23 October 1897, Covent Garden, London (Carl Rosa)
Sources	Vocal Score: Boosey & Co (London, 1897) Autograph score: University of Glasgow, MS MacCunn 27
Principal cast	Diarmid – Philip Brozel Fionn – Mr Maggi Eragon – Charles Tilbury Grania – Marie Duma Eila – Louise Kirkby Lunn Freya – Agnes Janson
Synopsis	Four acts: Ancient Scotia. Diarmid, a warrior, is made invulnerable by the gods, except for the soles of his feet, and the goddess Freya makes him irresistible to all women. Grania, King Fionn's wife, and their daughter Eila fall in love with Diarmid, who reciprocates the attentions of Grania. Diarmid defeats the Norse invaders led by Eragon but Fionn is determined to avenge himself and induces Diarmid to walk on the poisonous bristles of a wild boar; Diarmid succumbs as Fionn withholds the antidote. Grania dies of grief.

Diarmid attracted far more scrutiny than *Jeanie Deans*, mainly due to the novelty of its librettist being a son-in-law of Queen Victoria. The book is flawed: the poisonous boar is a bizarre agent of death, and an incongruous chorus of goblins and elves appears in Act III; the prose is verbose and contrived. The music is often vigorous and rhythmically vital, building up sustained momentum in places, but its restlessness, and the overuse of chromatic scales, mediant shifts, and ostinati are often oppressive; it is less obviously 'Scottish' than *Jeanie Deans*. Critical reaction was mixed: appraisals of the libretto varied from the complimentary ('very dextrously handled … [and] marked by conspicuous literary ability'[161]) to the disparaging ('the plot … would be entirely incomprehensible without a previous description of it, so fragmentary and episodical is the book'[162]). Regarding the music, a greater consensus prevailed, the *Daily News* referring to an 'immense advance upon his previous opera',[163] and the *Era* stating that 'Mr MacCunn has treated the story in a very dramatic manner, but has not discarded the attraction of a graceful melody'.[164] *Diarmid* did not survive long in the Rosa's repertory; MacCunn subsequently focused on other genres and on his conducting career. A musical comedy, *Prue*, was started in 1904 but abandoned, and a second

161 *MP*, 25 October 1897, p. 6.

162 *DN*, 25 October 1897, p. 6.

163 Ibid.

164 *Era*, 16 October 1897, p. 19.

collaboration with Argyll, *The Breast of Light*, was unfinished at MacCunn's premature death.[165]

MacKenzie, Alexander (1847–1935)

Colomba

Libretto	Francis Hueffer, after Prosper Merimée's eponymous novel
Premiere	9 April 1883, Theatre Royal, Drury Lane, London (Carl Rosa)
Sources	Vocal Score: Novello, Ewer & Co (London, 1883) Autograph Score: RAM, MS 1106 (sketches at MS 1290A)
Principal cast	Count de Nevers – Henry Pope Orso della Rebbia – Barton McGuckin Giuseppe Barracini – William Ludwig Colomba – Alwina Valleria Lydia – Mlle Baldi Chilina – Clara Perry
Synopsis	Four acts: Corsica, 1816. Nevers, his daughter Lydia, and Orso, return to Corsica after the Napoleonic wars. Orso learns from his sister Colomba that their father has been murdered by Barracini; Colomba wants revenge. When conclusive evidence against Barracini emerges Orso challenges him. Orso is duplicitously wounded by Barracini's brother Antonio, and kills both men in self-defence. A detachment of soldiers sent to arrest Orso fire accidentally at Colomba and Chilina. Nevers, convinced of Orso's innocence, ends the battle, but Colomba dies of her wounds.

Expectations of *Colomba* were high: although Thomas's *Esmeralda* was premiered in the same season, Mackenzie's score was known to embrace the 'advanced' compositional techniques of Wagner, and overshadowed its Francophile contemporary.[166] Hueffer was also known as a committed Wagnerian. For its time and place, Mackenzie's score was extremely ambitious and the first British opera performed in London to reject completely the mid-century style of Balfe and Wallace. Voluminous press coverage was partly influenced by Hueffer's contribution, which divided critics evenly: William Beatty Kingston called it 'little short of a marvel',[167] while T.L. Southgate wrote that 'Dr Hüffer possesses little poetic feeling'.[168] Of the music, critics were mainly positive, regarding *Colomba* as

[165] University of Glasgow, MSS MacCunn 30 and 31, and 17 respectively.

[166] An extended article outlining the work's musical structure appeared in *MT*, 1 April 1883, pp. 215–18; this was not a disinterested gesture as Novello published both the journal and the vocal score.

[167] *Theatre*, 1 May 1883, pp. 287–94 (p. 291).

[168] *MS*, 21 April 1883, pp. 247–9 (p. 249).

a significant achievement which presaged great things for the future; the *Academy* stated, 'Mr Mackenzie has originality and shows dramatic power. The Colomba music throughout the piece is of the highest interest',[169] while the *Monthly Musical Record* opined that, 'it may be questioned whether ever a first opera was written which evidenced so much aplomb, so high a degree of completeness and "go"'.[170] Although contemporaneous reaction invariably mentioned Wagner, *Colomba*'s indebtedness is limited: the similarities are more superficial, including continuous music, extensive use of arioso, a prominent orchestra, reminiscence motifs, and an absence of Italianate vocalisation, but *Colomba* also includes easily discernible separate numbers in distinct forms, diegetic items, and consistently secure tonal foundations. The work was retained in the company's repertory until 1885 after which it was superseded by *The Troubadour*; it was also produced in Germany, including Hamburg and Darmstadt.[171] It was revived by the Royal Academy in 1909 and in a revised version by the Royal College in 1912.[172]

The Troubadour

Libretto	Francis Hueffer
Premiere	8 June 1886, Theatre Royal, Drury Lane, London (Carl Rosa)
Sources	Vocal Score: Novello, Ewer & Co (London, 1886) Autograph Score: RAM, MS 1107
Principal cast	Count Raimon – Leslie Crotty Margarida – Alwina Valleria Azalais – Marian Burton Count Robert – Barrington Foote Guilem de Cabestanh – Barton McGuckin
Synopsis	Four acts: Provence, medieval period. Margarida, wife of Raimon, and the troubadour Guilem are in love. At a banquet Guilem sings passionately to Margarida but, as her sister Azalais stands next to her, his motives are unclear. While hunting, Raimon confronts Guilem; Margarida is about to confess when Azalais intervenes and declares that Guilem is her lover. Raimon and Count Robert, Azalais's betrothed, plot to undermine Guilem. Robert challenges him; during their fight Margarida intervenes, inadvertently giving herself away. Robert arranges for Guilem to be killed; Margarida commits suicide.

Rosa commissioned a second opera from Mackenzie who again asked Hueffer for a libretto.[173] Hueffer, recently appointed editor of the *Musical World*, included

[169] *Academy*, 14 April 1883, p. 266.

[170] *MMR*, 1 May 1883, pp. 106–8 (p. 107).

[171] For Mackenzie's own account of the work see *A Musician's Narrative* (London, 1927), pp. 110–13 and 118–20.

[172] See *MT*, 1 December 1912, p. 785.

[173] For his own account, see Mackenzie, pp. 142–4.

substantial advanced coverage in the journal and secured similarly generous publicity from sympathetic colleagues.[174] This puffery may have backfired as the work was received far more equivocally than *Colomba*. Hueffer's libretto was criticised, this time more for its subject matter ('somewhat unsavoury'[175] and 'repulsive and dull'[176]) than its literary quality, while Mackenzie's score, regarded as an advance on *Colomba*, nevertheless provoked a mixed reaction.[177] *The Troubadour* is undoubtedly more complex: the tonality, rhythm and phase structures are more restless and unpredictable, and the arioso much more flexible and prevalent, although there are several distinct numbers. This complexity comes at the expense of accessibility and a sense of tautness: in the Act III love duet for example, the music wanders aimlessly and lacks a cogent climax. The work was rapidly dropped, not even featuring in Rosa's 1886–87 provincial tour.[178]

The Cricket on the Hearth

Libretto	Julian Sturgis, after Charles Dickens's eponymous novella
Premiere	6 June 1914, Royal Academy of Music, London
Sources	Vocal Score, Bosworth and Co, (London, 1901) Autograph Libretto: RAM, MS 1249
Principal cast	The original production used two casts: John Peerybingle – Robert Pitt/Cecil Simms Dot Peerybingle – Lily Fairney/May Purcell Caleb Plummer – Raymond Ellis/Ernest Butcher Bertha Plummer – Nellie Evans/Louise Brooks Edward Plummer – Gerald Harris/Willie Michael Tackleton – Mr Fancourt/Leonard Hubbard May Fielding – Winifred Burnand (both casts) The Cricket-Fairy – Miss Tomes/Gwenny Roberts
Synopsis	Three acts: England, mid-nineteenth century. John and Dot, guarded by the Cricket-Fairy, take in a disguised Edward Plummer, long-lost son of Caleb. At a celebration of the forthcoming marriage of Caleb's employer Tackleton to May, Edward's former fiancée, Edward privately confesses his identity to Dot. Tackleton, seeing them together, insinuates to John that Dot is being unfaithful. John wants to shoot Edward but is stopped by the Cricket-Fairy. Edward reveals his identity and is reunited with May. Tackleton gracefully accepts the situation.

---

174 *MT*, 1 June 1886, pp. 317–22.

175 *MS*, 31 July 1886, pp. 72–3 (p. 73).

176 *MoM*, 1 July 1886, p. 63.

177 See ibid., and *Academy*, 12 June 1886, pp. 423–4 (p. 424); *SR*, same date, pp. 810–11; *Era*, same date, p. 15.

178 Mackenzie wrote that he realised the work was doomed at the end of the Drury Lane dress rehearsal (Mackenzie, p. 144).

Mackenzie composed no more serious operas after the failure of *The Troubadour*. In 1888 he was appointed Director of the Royal Academy which limited the time he could devote to writing.[179] *The Cricket on the Hearth* was completed in 1902 but not performed due to the contemporaneous appearance in Britain of Goldmark's eponymous work. Like *Shamus O'Brien*, it draws on the mid-century tradition and is a straightforward number opera with spoken dialogue; most musical items are reflective character pieces and do not advance the drama. Also like Stanford, however, Mackenzie aspired to a higher level of musical sophistication than that of musical comedy, and was largely successful; transparent periodisation and forms predominate, as does diatonic harmony, but the variations of accompaniment, and careful use of harmonic and melodic inflections, raise the opera well above standard musical comedies. Francis Barrett was effusive: 'To find that Sir Alexander could command a light and fanciful style was no surprise ... he has surpassed himself by the skill with which he is grave and gay in turn, brings tears to our eyes or laughter to our lips'.[180] The unlucky timing of the premiere and the work's intermediate nature almost certainly militated against its becoming established.

Maclean, Alick (1872–1936)[181]

Petruccio

Libretto	'Sheridan Ross', pseudonym of the composer's sister
Premiere	29 June 1895, Covent Garden, London (Royal Opera)
Source:	Vocal Score: Willcocks & Co (London, ?1895)
Cast	Mother – Edith Miller Elvira – Fanny Moody Giovanni – William Dever Rubino – John Child Petruccio – Charles Manners

[179] Mackenzie contemplated an opera based on Coppée's *Le Luthier de Cremone* in the mid 1890s but abandoned it (Mackenzie, p. 143); he also composed two operettas, *His Majesty* (produced by D'Oyly Carte at the Savoy Theatre, 20 February 1897) and *The Knights of the Road* (Palace Theatre, 27 February 1905).

[180] *MT*, 1 July 1914, p. 460.

[181] For additional biographical information, see Scowcroft, p. 130.

Synopsis	One act: Mexico, late nineteenth century. Before the curtain: Rubino and Elvira eloped after which he accidentally killed her father; Elvira and her mother emigrate from Italy to a new life in Mexico. On stage: Elvira and Petruccio, a Creole, have just married. Returning home, Elvira is amazed Rubino, who begs her to elope again. Rubino is seen by Elvira's mother and brother, Giovanni. The two men fight and Rubino is killed. Elvira breaks away from Petruccio and collapses on Rubino's body.

Petruccio was the first of Maclean's operas to be performed, and won the prize of £100 in a competition sponsored by Charles Manners and Fanny Moody for a one-act opera without chorus. The plot draws on recently fashionable 'verismo' works. Petruccio is not only an outsider, but also outside the action. He 'introduces' the opera (like Uncle Joe in *Koanga*) and the incidents are portrayed as memories. Maclean was strongly influenced by Verdi, Mascagni and Leoncavallo; he aimed at a continuous musico-dramatic flow although some 'set' numbers are easily discernible, as are character motifs. A predilection for diminished sevenths at climactic moments and added ninths and elevenths pay diminishing returns as the work progresses. The *Musical Times* stated that Maclean 'has talent, and in due course he should develop individuality';[182] *The Times* more pointedly observed, 'that there exist no fewer than 42 [other competition entries] of inferior merit ... may well appal even the most sanguine believer in British art'.[183] The *Era*, however, forecast that 'Mr Maclean will eventually strike out a path for himself, and become a prominent and successful composer'.[184]

Quentin Durward / The King's Prize

Libretto	Sheridan Ross, after Walter Scott's *Quentin Durward*
Premiere	29 April 1904, Royalty Theatre, London (London Music School)
Source:	Vocal Score (*Quentin Durward*): Edwin Ascherberg (London, 1894) Libretto (*The King's Prize*): W.T. Haydock (London, 1904)
Principal cast	Quentin Durward – Percy Bates Louis XI of France – Arthur Durand Charles, Duke of Burgundy – R. Jecks Crèvecoeur – Edwin Webster William de la Marck – A[lbert?] Kennedy Isabelle, Countess of Croye – Daisy Campbell Lady Hameline – Blanche Newcombe

182 *MT*, 1 August 1895, p. 526.

183 *The Times*, 1 July 1895, p. 8.

184 *Era*, 6 July 1895, p. 9.

Synopsis	(*The King's Prize*) Three acts: France, fifteenth century. Quentin, a Scottish soldier in Louis's service, is ordered to protect Isabelle and her mother, who are hiding from Charles and his vassal Crèvecoeur, whom Isabelle is reluctantly to marry. Crèvecoeur demands Isabelle's return; Louis refuses and Crèvecoeur renounces Burgundy's loyalty to France. The outlaw de la Marck also seeks Isabelle; when Quentin captures him his reward, suggested by Isabelle and agreed by Louis and Charles, is Isabelle's hand.

Maclean composed the first version of this opera as *Quentin Durward* when barely 20; this was not performed, and was substantially rewritten as *The King's Prize*. The music of the revised version is untraced; the plot is different after the first part of Act I. Maclean may have reused music but it would have required extensive rewriting. In both versions the scenarios are unwieldy; Ross followed Scott's original closely and although minor characters and incidents were eliminated in the second version, the book remains convoluted. The libretto and music employ a traditional format with several set pieces and diegetic numbers; Maclean preferred modern Italian composers to Wagner as models. The *Musical Times* was quite generous, stating that 'Mr Maclean succeeds in interesting his audience by means of a fluent melodiousness, rhythmic variety and charm, and clever characterisation'.[185] Maclean later revised the opera again, reducing it to one act of 90 minutes, and restored the original title of *Quentin Durward*; this version was produced by the Rosa Company (13 January 1920, Theatre Royal, Newcastle-upon-Tyne).[186]

Die Liebesgeige / The Hunchback of Cremona

Based on the play *Le Luthier de Cremone* by François Coppée, with a libretto by his sister 'Sheridan Ross' this opera was performed at Mainz on 15 April 1906.[187] Its premiere attracted little attention in the British press and the work was not performed in the United Kingdom. The music is untraced.

Maître Seiler / Die Waldidylle

Libretto	Sheridan Ross, after Erckmann & Chatrian's *Tales of the Rhineland*
Premiere	20 August 1909, Lyric Theatre, London (Moody-Manners)
Principal cast	Maître Seiler – Lewis James Lotte – Raymonde Amy Wilhelm – Seth Hughes Yeri – Charles McGrath

185 *MT*, 1 June 1904, p. 398.

186 Reviewed in *Stage*, 15 January 1920, p. 19.

187 *MS*, 21 April 1906, p. 251.

Synopsis	One act: Maître Seiler, a middle-aged judge, visits his friend Yeri, and is attracted to Yeri's daughter, Lotte. She is friendly towards Seiler, hoping to secure a job for her sweetheart Wilhelm. Seiler initially misinterprets her behaviour, but on learning the truth from Wilhelm accepts his lot, gives Wilhelm the job he seeks, and persuades the previously unwilling Yeri to allow Wilhelm and Lotte to marry.

The music is untraced. Reviews agree on the light story and light musical treatment of *Maître Seiler* and found the opera pleasing if not original: the *Musical Times* was positive, declaring that 'Mr Maclean has an uncommon power as a writer for the stage … he has provided [the story] with a musical setting of much tender charm and of sincerity and depth of feeling'. George Clutsam was damning: 'It almost seems that Mr Maclean has deliberately endeavoured to bring his musical inspiration down to the lowest level … It is only fair to Mr Maclean to state that his attempt at being utterly obvious met with success, and that he had gauged the intelligence of his audience with some surety'.[188] Despite the predominantly positive reaction to the work, the Moody-Manners Company did not retain it in its repertory.

McSwiney, Paul (1856–89)

Amergen!

Libretto	Composer
Premiere	23 February 1881, Theatre Royal, Cork
Source	Libretto: P.F. Murphy & Co (Cork, 1881)
Principal cast	Conaire Mor – W. M'Cormac Amergen – F. Sylvanni Calmar – J.D. Fitzgerald Cathal – F. O'Keeffe Adela – Bessie Craig
Synopsis	Prologue and two acts: Ireland, ninth or tenth century. Amergen, a young poet, wishes to be 'king for a day'. Conaire Mor, the king, in disguise, arranges for Amergen to be drugged and conveyed to the palace. Amergen falls in love with Adela, Mor's daughter, but Mor disapproves. When the Vikings are heard approaching, Mor, Amergen, Calmar and Cathal all leave to fight. The Vikings are defeated, due to the heroism of an unnamed soldier. Mor declares that the hero can name his reward. Amergen steps forward and claims Adela as his prize.

McSwiney was raised in Cork but emigrated to New York shortly after the premiere of *Amergen!*, and died there, aged 33. The music is untraced; the libretto outlines a conventional number-based structure and a variety of rhyming poetic

188 Quoted in *MS*, 28 August 1909, pp. 131–2.

forms. The opera was very well received; McSwiney managed every aspect of its production. That the only professional singer in the cast, Bessie Craig, had recently appeared in Cork as Josephine in *HMS Pinafore* may, in combination with the form of the libretto, imply something about the nature of McSwiney's music. The *Era* and *Musical Times* both published positive reviews of the production but without giving substantive comment on the music.[189]

Maddison, Adela (1862–1929)[190]

Der Talisman

Libretto	Composer, after the eponymous play by Ludwig Fulda
Premiere	19 November 1910, Opera House, Leipzig
Synopsis	Fulda's play is an elaborated version of 'The Emperor's New Clothes' by Hans Christian Andersen.

Adela Maddison's took four years to compose her only known opera; the music is lost. *The Times* and the *Era* both gave positive accounts of the work and its reception in Leipzig. Of the music, the latter noted, 'The traces of the influence of the modern French school are frequently apparent, and this is not a disadvantage, but rather the contrary … [I]ts chief strength lies in the instrumentation, which contains an abundance of light and shade of dramatic power and delicate sparkling humour such as few modern operas can show. There are no 'tunes' yet the effect of the music in its entirety is exceedingly melodious … The German criticisms are wonderfully gracious to the work of a foreigner and a woman to boot'.[191] As Maddison was a friend and possibly also a lover of Gabriel Fauré, the French influence is unsurprising. Despite its success, the opera was not performed in the United Kingdom; Maddison's being domiciled overseas and domestic circumstances may have worked against her.

Mallandaine, John Elliott (1841–86)

Celia, the Gypsy Girl

Libretto	Elliott Galer

[189] *Era*, 5 March 1881, p. 14; *MT*, 1 May, p. 247.

[190] For biographical information see Sophie Fuller, *The Pandora Guide to Women Composers* (London, 1994), pp. 203–6.

[191] *Era*, 26 November 1910, p. 17; see also *The Times*, 21 November, p. 12.

Premiere	20 October 1879, Royal Opera House, Leicester
Principal cast	Captain Seaton – Elliott Galer Celia – Carina Clelland Lord Belmore – Charles Horsman Ronald – Mrs Elliott Galer
Synopsis	Three acts; England, seventeenth century. Belmore's daughter Celia is lost in a forest and adopted by gypsies; she forms a sibling-like bond with Ronald. Fifteen years later, Seaton, travelling to see Belmore, stumbles on the gypsy camp, and is drawn to Celia. He proposes marriage and is accepted. At Belmore Castle, in a series of dreams, Celia's true identity is revealed to Seaton; Belmore and Seaton return to the camp and father and daughter are reunited.

Mallandaine composed at least two operas before *Celia*.[192] In 1879 he was working as Musical Director at the Royal Princess's Theatre, London, but emigrated to the United States in 1881. Galer was lessee of Leicester's Opera House and the premiere of *Celia* was given for his benefit. The music is untraced; reviews in local newspapers are generally complimentary and imply that the work was cast on mid-century lines with spoken dialogue and ballad-like musical numbers. The libretto was described as 'unequal' but 'considerably above the average standard of such compositions', while of Mallandaine's music it was stated 'if [he] is unable to rival the grandest effects of the great masters of operatic harmony, he has at all events succeeded in producing much that cannot fail to please and delight'.[193] No subsequent performances have been traced.

Miles, Philip Napier (1865–1935)

Westward Ho!

Libretto	E.F. Benson, after Charles Kingsley's eponymous novel
Premiere	4 December 1913, Lyceum Theatre, London (London Academy of Music)
Principal cast	Rose – Hope Charteris Amyas – Philip Brandreth Frank – W. Ellis Guzman – Raymond Ellis Eustace – William Waite

[192] *Countess Rosa* (1864) and *The Two Orphans* (1874) are mentioned in Brown and Stratton, p. 269, as are comic operas.

[193] *Leicester Daily Mercury*, 21 October 1879, quoted in *Era*, 26 October, p. 9.

Synopsis	Prologue, three acts, and epilogue. Selected episodes from the novel are used: Frank initiates the Brotherhood of the Rose which Amyas and his friends join, but Eustace rejects. Guzman, a Spaniard, makes love to Rose, spurring Amyas's jealousy and a long-running feud. Rose is later found in a Spanish prison and rejects the advances of Eustace; Frank is found in the same prison. Amyas and Richard Grenville chase Guzman across the Bristol Channel, but Guzman's ship is wrecked and he is blinded by a lightning strike.

Miles was a wealthy Bristolian and amateur musician who studied in Dresden and with Hubert Parry.[194] *Westward Ho!* is the only one of his six operas performed before 1918.[195] *The Times*, noting a lacklustre performance, stated that the audience needed a thorough knowledge of Kingsley's novel to make sense of the episodes extracted from it, and added that Miles, 'has produced delightful music where the opportunities were of the simple lyrical kind … [but] There is much, especially in the first act, which is merely suave, much dialogue moves too slowly, many places where the stage is kept at a standstill while the orchestra has something to say'.[196] No subsequent performances have been traced.

Moore, Harold

The Magic Fountain

Libretto	J.R.J. Johnston
Premiere	1 February 1894, St George's Hall, London
Source	Libretto: Publisher unknown (?London, ?1892) [copy in BL]
Principal cast	Elsie – Margaret Nutter Ruth – Magdaline Lockie Rudolph – Philip Brozel Wizard of the Fountain – Frank Wilson

[194] He was also a supporter of Boughton and facilitated performances of several of his operas in the 1920s; see Hurd, pp. 123–32.

[195] *Fireflies* and *Markheim* were performed in Bristol in October 1924, in a week of opera organised by Miles, which included Vaughan Williams's *The Shepherds of the Delectable Mountains* and Falla's *El retablo de Maestro Pedro* (*MT*, 1 November 1924, pp. 1031–2).

[196] *The Times*, 5 December 1913, p. 11.

Synopsis	Prologue and three acts: By a fountain, time unspecified. Elsie and Rudolph part when he is called to his ship. The Wizard, seeking vengeance on Elsie's mother Ruth, who spurned him and remained faithful to her husband, creates a vision in which Elsie sees Rudolph being unfaithful. The Wizard offers revenge; Elsie pledges to abjure all lovers as payment. When Rudolph returns, Elsie rejects him. Ruth curses the Wizard and encourages Elsie to take Rudolph back. The Wizard's power forces Elsie to stab Rudolph; Ruth and Elsie lament their fate and the Wizard rejoices.

Virtually nothing is known of Harold Moore.[197] He was a student at the Royal Academy when this opera was produced; the music is untraced. The *Monthly Musical Record* described the scenario as 'unpleasant' while the score contained 'some good and graceful passages and well-balanced phrases' but also stated that Moore 'has not yet acquired the art of dramatic expression'.[198] The *Musical News* noted the seemingly disparate influences of Mendelssohn, Wagner, Mascagni and Leoncavallo.[199]

Naylor, Edward (1867–1934)

The Angelus

Libretto	Wilfrid Thornley
Premiere	27 January 1909, Covent Garden, London (Grand Opera Syndicate)
Sources	Vocal Score
Principal cast	Abbot Tunstall – Robert Radford Brother Francis – Francis Maclennan Beatrice – Florence Easton Catherine – Edith Clegg Death – Edna Thornton Sylvia – Cicely Gleeson-White

[197] A sacred cantata, *The Darkest Hour* (1908), gained some recognition, but no other works attracted attention.

[198] *MMR*, 1 March 1894, p. 65.

[199] *MN*, 10 February 1894, p. 124.

Synopsis — Prologue and four acts: time and place unspecified. Tunstall commissions Francis to find a herb, the elixir of which confers immortality. Death warns Tunstall not to frustrate God's will. On his journey, Francis meets Beatrice, Queen of the Revels; she chooses Francis as her consort for the day. Francis renounces his vocation but still wants to acquire the herb. Following Tunstall's instructions, Francis finds the herb in a temple and takes it, despite the warnings of Sylvia, a nymph. Francis returns to Beatrice; Death appears, takes Beatrice, and forces Francis to drink the elixir, condemning him to miserable immortality.

Naylor had studied with Stanford at the Royal College and was for many years organist of Emmanuel College, Cambridge. *The Angelus* won a competition launched in 1905 by the publisher Ricordi; it was lavishly produced as part of Richter's second 'English Ring' season at Covent Garden and was consequently the subject of heightened expectations.[200] The opera was indifferently received, however, with critics unable to agree on its style. *The Times* stated that the composer was 'well versed in the operatic conventions of the times,'[201] but Arthur Poyser argued that '[he] knows nothing … of Bizet, Verdi or Wagner … [He] ignores the achievements of his immediate predecessors and sets us down in an atmosphere of mid-Victorian oratorio,'[202] and described the accompaniment in Beatrice's Act IV 'Spinning Song' as being 'heavy-footed enough to suggest a lyric about the suburban trains on the South Eastern Railway'. The *Musical Times* stated that 'the treatment not infrequently verges on the commonplace' but acknowledged that 'it contains some excellent music … Dr Naylor possesses considerable dramatic power'.[203]

Naylor's music exemplifies the clichéd view of British composers being unable to shake off anthem and oratorio; in the lighter passages, for example when Beatrice is introduced as Queen of the Revels, there is some engaging, if safe music, but in darker sections, such as Tunstall's opening monologue, the work becomes turgid. The set pieces are most successful but Naylor struggled to create musically contrasted characters. Thornley's libretto is verbose, and overloaded with roles and incidents. *The Angelus* was revived by the Rosa Company at Covent Garden in 1921 but, in the words of *The Times*, 'it cannot be said that the impression conveyed last night was any more favourable than the original one'.[204]

---

[200] Full details of the competition are given in *MS*, 21 January 1905, p. 37. Twenty-nine entries were received and judged anonymously by Tito Ricordi, Percy Pitt, Stanford, and Joseph Bennett (*MT*, 1 February 1908, pp. 93–94). Stanford and Harry Higgins, of the Grand Opera Syndicate, exchanged a series of heated letters in *The Times* regarding the production of the work, Stanford alleging a lack of Syndicate support (see 19 December 1908, p. 13; 21 December, p. 11; 25 December, p. 11; 29 December, p. 8; 30 December, p. 9; and 7 January 1909, p. 9).

[201] *The Times*, 29 January 1909, p. 10.

[202] *MS*, 6 February 1909, pp. 84–5.

[203] *MT*, 1 March 1909, pp. 176–7.

[204] *The Times*, 2 December 1921, p. 8.

Nicholls, Frederick (1871–?)

A Prodigal Son

Libretto	Edward Noddall Willett
Premiere	18 March 1896, Domestic Mission Hall, Liverpool (Amateur production)
Sources	Libretto: Lee & Nightingale (Liverpool, ?1896)
Principal cast	Syra – Annie Nelson Otharl – Dora Nazeby Rosarian – F. Barlow Gamon – Woodville Francis Zandoris – Fred Owens
Synopsis	Rosarian, a frustrated writer, returns to his homeland, followed by his wife and daughter, Syra and Otharl. At his childhood house Rosarian meets Zandorian, his father, and Gamon, his brother, who embrace and reject him respectively. Gamon has become a miser but when Rosarian sings of the beauty of flowers, Gamon softens, and the family members are brought together.

Little is known of Nicholls, who gained some recognition between the wars as a composer of light music. The music is untraced; press coverage was sparse, but reviews quite complimentary.[205] No later performances have been traced.

O'Donnell, Bertram Walton (1887–1939)

The Demon's Bride

Libretto	Emma Lomax
Premiere	22 May 1909, Royal Academy of Music, London

O'Donnell established a highly regarded career as a military musician between the wars, most notably as conductor of the BBC Military Band from 1927 to 1937.[206] The one-act *Demon's Bride* dates from his student years at the Royal Academy (where he later taught). A tantalising review in *Cremona* states that it depicts the 'yearning of Elsie, who acts in subservient slavery to a band of smugglers, for a little freedom, which is accomplished only by her marrying the demon. The music is clever, dramatic, and humorous by turn, full of colour,

---

205 See *MN*, 28 March 1896, p. 302; *Era*, 21 March, p. 13.

206 For further biographical information see Scowcroft, pp. 73–5.

while the instrumentation is rich at times and curiously consistent with the subject throughout. More should be heard of this'.[207]

O'Dwyer, Robert (1862–1949)

Eithne

Libretto	Thomas O'Kelly
Premiere	2 August 1909, Round Room, Rotunda, Dublin (semi-staged, amateur) 16 May 1910, Gaiety Theatre, Dublin (professional)
Sources	Vocal Score: Cramer and Wood (Dublin and New York, 1910) Autograph Score: NLI, MS MU-vb-31
Principal cast (Gaiety production)	High King of Ireland – William Dever Ceart – Joseph O'Mara King of Tir-na-n-Og – O'Carroll Reynolds Nuala – Lillian Matthews Eithne – Evelyn Duffy
Synopsis	Two acts, four scenes: Ireland before the Anglo-Norman invasions. Ceart is elected Tanist (heir-apparent) to the High King of Ireland. He is opposed by his two step-brothers but peace is restored by Nuala, Ceart's foster-mother and banished Queen of the fairy realm of Tir-na-n-Og. Later, the High King, Ceart, and the court see Eithne, the spellbound Princess of Tir-na-n-Og. In the fairy realm, aided by a magic sword and ring, Ceart overcomes the King of Tir-na-n-Og, releases Eithne, and restores Nuala to her repentant husband. Ceart and Eithne return to earth. The High King has died; Ceart's succession is proclaimed and he marries Eithne.

In the view of the *Irish Times*, *Eithne* was 'likely to prove memorable in the annals of the day of Gaelic renaissance, for it marks the production of the first genuine Irish opera – native opera in the old tongue of Eire. It opens an entirely new epoque, and it unfolds prospects of Ireland once again being a musical nation'.[208] Unlike Butler's *Muirgheis*, *Eithne* was conceived in Irish and is musically a much more ambitious work.[209] Although commended for its patriotic intent, the work was received somewhat equivocally; local critics acknowledged O'Dwyer's attempt to incorporate the 'modes and cadences of Irish music',[210] but

[207] *Cremona*, 1 July 1909, p. 92. The work is also mentioned in Frederick Corder, *A History of the Royal Academy of Music 1822–1922* (London, 1922), p. 91.

[208] *IT*, 3 August 1909, p. 6.

[209] For more information see: Ryan, 'Opera in Ireland'; Klein, 'Stage Irish'; Klein, 'Celtic Legends'.

[210] *IT*, 17 May 1910, p. 5.

were conscious of external influences, although for the *Irish Times* these were the Wagner of *Tannhäuser* and *Lohengrin*, while for the *Freeman's Journal* the music contained 'reminiscences of Verdi and of the good old Italian method'.[211] O'Dwyer's score contains elements of all three: regularly phrased melodies predominate, as does a strongly voice-dominated texture; in terms of creating a representation of the magical Other, Esposito was more successful in *The Tinker and the Fairy*. Harmonically O'Dwyer's music shows little advance on *Shamus O'Brien*, although in sections of dramatic tension, for example the confrontation between Ceart and the Spirit, a more fluid tonal language appears. Commentators were nevertheless impressed by the work's assurance and hoped that O'Dwyer would compose more. They were to be disappointed; he spent most of his subsequent career as an academic, being appointed Professor of Irish Music at University College, Dublin, in 1914.

Old, John (1827–92)

Herne

Libretto	Edward Oxenford
Premiere	14 December 1887, Town Hall, Reading
Sources	Vocal Score: Stanley, Lucas and Weber (London, ?1879)
Synopsis	Three acts: Windsor Castle and Forest, mid-1530s. Lord l'Estrange celebrates his impending marriage to Constance, ward of Henry VIII when the horn of Herne the Hunter is heard outside. When Constance, Henry and Anne Boleyn join the festivities, Herne appears and carries Constance off to his glade in the forest. He makes advances to her but she rebuffs him; Henry's soldiers surround the glade and Constance is released. The royal party return to the castle and the couple are married in the chapel.

Old studied with Loder and Goss at the Royal Academy. *Herne* comprises separate numbers but without spoken dialogue; Oxenford's scenario is slight, anticlimactic and employs constant rhyming couplets. Old's music is competent and often tuneful with occasionally adventurous, but also amateurish, harmonic excursions (for example in l'Estrange's recounting of the legend of Herne in Act I); more often it is regressive and lapses into persistent four-bar phrases. The music and the drama are sometimes mismatched, for example in the Act I finale in which a terrified Constance is spirited away by Herne to the accompaniment of a galop. No detailed press reviews of *Herne* have been traced.

[211] *FJ*, 3 August 1909, p. 2.

Parry, Joseph (1841–1903)

Blodwen

Libretto	Mynyddog, pseudonym of Richard Davies, English translation by David Rowlands
Premiere	21 May 1878, Temperance Hall, Aberystwyth 15 June 1878, Alexandra Palace, London (concert performances)
Sources	Vocal Score: J. Parry and Sons (Aberystwyth, 1878)
Synopsis	Three acts: Wales, late fourteenth century. At a celebration of Ellen and Arthur's wedding at Maelor Castle, Howell and Blodwen fall in love. Plantagenet troops arrive demanding the castle's surrender. The bard Iolo foresees tragedy; Howell and Arthur leave to fight as the English approach. Although the English are defeated, Arthur is mortally wounded and Howell captured. When Blodwen visits him in Chester gaol news is brought of the English king's death and an amnesty for Welsh prisoners.

Born in Merthyr Tydfil, Parry emigrated to Pennsylvania with his family aged 13 but returned to Britain in his late twenties and was taught by Sterndale Bennett before being appointed Professor of Music in 1873 at the newly founded University College Wales. A prolific composer and ardent promoter of Welsh language and culture, Parry was very popular in Wales and its diaspora but his music made little impact elsewhere.

After the first performance at Aberystwyth, the specially formed Welsh Representative Choir gave *Blodwen* in several towns, including Bristol, Newport, Cardiff, Swansea and Aberdare.[212] The opera was lauded in Wales as the first setting in Welsh of a Welsh story. Popular at Eisteddfodau, Parry claimed that, by 1896, over 500 performances had been given around the world but the first staged performance has not been traced.[213] *Blodwen* is a highly conventional work: its 41 brief numbers are all self-contained but there is no spoken dialogue; Parry's harmonic language is that of Schubert and Mendelssohn, and easy lyrical melodies and regular periodisation dominate.

212 For reviews of the Aberystwyth and London performances see *WM*, 24 May 1878, p. 4; *MS*, 22 June, p. 384.

213 The performance cited in *OperaGrove* (Swansea, 20 June 1878) was a concert (Stanley Sadie (ed.), *The New Grove Dictionary of Opera* (4 vols, London, 1992), vol. 4, p. 890); a semi-staged performance was given in Aberdare in late December 1879 (*WM*, 31 December 1879, p. 4) but four years later *MS* reported that a fully-staged professional performance had yet to take place (21 July 1883, p. 38).

Arianwen

Libretto	D. Rowlands
Premiere	5 June 1890, Theatre Royal, Cardiff
Sources	Chorus parts: Snell & Sons (Swansea, 1931); the remainder of the music is untraced Autograph score: NLW, MS 9297E (part only) Libretto: [no publisher] (?1890) [copy in NLW]
Principal cast	Arianwen – Maggie Davies Peggi Wyllt – Hannah Jones Walter Mostyn – Maldwyn Humphries Twm Shon Twm – David Hughes Morgan Jones – John Walters
Synopsis	Three acts: Wales, late eighteenth century. Twm wants his daughter Arianwen to marry rich Morgan Jones but she is in love with Walter, a fisherman. When Walter is endangered at sea Arianwen risks her life to save him, in contrast to Morgan's cowardice. Twm rejects Morgan in favour of Walter, who is proved by Peggi to be the heir to a large estate.

Before *Arianwen*, Parry's second opera, *Virginia*, was given a private performance with piano and harmonium accompaniment (12 July 1883, Theatre Royal, Swansea) but no professional performances have been traced; the music is untraced.[214] *Arianwen* was described as 'lighter in vein than *Blodwen*',[215] and incorporated spoken dialogue and comedic elements. The Cardiff performances caused some controversy in religious circles on moral grounds.[216] A specially formed company took *Arianwen* on tour in Wales and gave 50 performances by the end of August 1890.[217]

Sylvia

Libretto	Mendelssohn Parry
Premiere	12 August 1895, Theatre Royal, Cardiff
Principal cast	Thurston – Franklin Clive Osmund – Hannah Jones Severus – Meurig James Arthur – Maldwyn Humphries Stella – Rosa Montague Sylvia – Louise van Dalle

214 See *WM*, 13 July 1883, p. 3.

215 *WM*, 6 June 1890, p. 3.

216 See *PMG*, 16 June 1890, p. 6; *WM*, 18 June, p. 2; 23 June, p. 6.

217 *WM*, 5 September 1890, p. 4.

Synopsis	Three acts: Salisbury Plain during the Roman occupation. At Stonehenge, Arthur, a shepherd, falls asleep. Fairies appear; Stella, their Queen, explains their fate should they be seen, embraced or kissed by a mortal. Arthur wakes and sees the fairy Sylvia; she becomes mortal. They embrace, and Sylvia is instantly enamoured. Arthur, his brother Osmund, the druid Thurston and Sylvia travel to the Roman camp at Old Sarum; the governor, Severus, insults Sylvia and she stabs him. Thurston tells her that she will be executed. As Arthur and Sylvia kiss she 'dies' and returns to the fairy realm.

Parry's fourth opera was his first with a non-Welsh theme (*The Maid of Cefn-Ydfa* was composed earlier; see below). The music is untraced. Although more ambitious in scope than either *Blodwen* or *Arianwen*, the *Western Mail* stated that 'this has not prevented the composer from introducing music of a light and airy character … [and it is] full of bright and sparkling melodies'.[218] Despite a triumphant reception in Cardiff, the work attracted virtually no attention in the national or musical press.

The Maid of Cefn-Ydfa

Libretto	Joseph Bennett, after a traditional story
Premiere	15 December 1902, Grand Theatre, Cardiff (Moody-Manners Company)
Sources	Libretto: proof copy in NLW (?1902)
Principal cast	Ann Thomas – Fanny Moody Will Hopkin – Joseph O'Mara Anthony Maddocks – Charles Manners Mrs Thomas – Enriquetta Crichton Kate – Lily Moody Robert Jenkins – George Fox
Synopsis	Three acts and an epilogue: Wales, early eighteenth century. Will, a bard, and Ann are in love, but her mother disapproves, preferring the solicitor Anthony Maddocks. Mrs Thomas, Anthony, and the maid, Kate, hope to humiliate Will by persuading the virtuoso Robert Jenkins to sing against him at the Eisteddfod but Will wins nevertheless. Ann is imprisoned at home by her mother; realising that she is dying of a broken heart, Kate brings Will to see her, but it is too late.

Parry's third opera was composed in 1890;[219] the music is untraced. Parry stated that he had 'endeavoured to speak in the Mozartian and Beethoven language of rhythm, harmony and melody',[220] suggesting a continuation of his established style. The *Musical Times* noted the inclusion of spoken dialogue and the use of

[218] *WM*, 13 August 1895, p. 6.

[219] *WM*, 5 September 1890, p. 4.

[220] *Stage*, 18 December 1902, p. 18.

traditional melodies but 'by harmonising ... [them] in modern manner ... he has lost a means of effective contrast'.[221] Parry died less than two months later; at least three more stage works were left unperformed (*King Arthur*, *His Worship the Mayor*, and *Y ferch o'r Scer* (*The Lady of Sker*)).[222]

Pelissier, W. Harvey (?1872–?)

Connla of the Golden Hair

Libretto	Composer, after the version of the traditional story in Joseph Jacobs's *Celtic Fairy Tales*
Premiere	19 May 1903, Antient Concert Rooms, Dublin (concert performance)
Source	Vocal Score: Curwen & Son (London, 1903)
Synopsis	Two acts: Ireland, CE 150. Connla, son of Conn, King of Erin, hears the seductive voice of the Queen of Moy-Mell; she tries to lure him away to her fairy realm but is foiled by the druid, Coran. The fairies later appear again, hypnotising all but Connla, who agrees to go with the Queen. The others reawaken and mourn Connla's leaving.

Pelissier's work won the cantata prize at the 1903 Feis Ceoil but it seems certain that a staged performance was his preferred option although none has been traced. Pelissier employed an extensive system of reminiscence motifs to create coherence in otherwise very sectionalised music; a table of all 17 is supplied in the vocal score and deemed essential for an 'absolute comprehension of the dramatic intention of the work'. The music contains no attempts to incorporate traditional Irish elements and Pelissier's harmonic language is derived from early Wagner and Weber. Reviews were negative; the *Musical Standard* stated that, 'the two great climaxes are most dramatic, though hardly pleasant ... [and] the music is most difficult and ungrateful to sing or to hear ... there are whole pages one does not wish ever to hear again', but added, by way of compensation, that 'the work shows undoubted promise'.[223]

---

[221] *MT*, 1 January 1903, p. 31.

[222] Parry considered *King Arthur*, written on Wagnerian lines, his best and most ambitious work. This would be a significant departure from his earlier operas in style and construction; see *WM*, 12 March 1897, p. 7, which also includes a plot synopsis. The music is untraced. A fourth work, *Ceridwen*, performed at the Liverpool Eisteddfod in 1900, is 'a dramatic cantata or one act opera' according to the published vocal score.

[223] *MS*, 30 May 1903, p. 343–4. The *Weekly Irish Times* concluded that the work would fail on stage as it did not 'possess sufficient of dramatic interest to hold the attention of an audience' (23 May, p. 23).

Philpot, Stephen Rowland (1870–1950)

Dante and Beatrice

Libretto	Joseph Forster and William Miller, after Dante
Premiere	25 November 1889, Gresham Hall, Brixton, London (concert performance) 7 June 1918, Shaftesbury Theatre, London (Carl Rosa)
Sources	Vocal Score: Mathias and Strickland (London, 1893)
Principal cast (Rosa production)	Dante – Albert Bond Giotto – Frank Clarke Cavalcante – Frederick Clendon Corso – George Gorst Beatrice – Beatrice Miranda
Synopsis	Three acts or scenes: Florence, 1290. Dante is secretly in love with Beatrice; his friends, Giotto and Cavalcante are convinced that Beatrice reciprocates but is also tongue-tied. Dante quarrels with Corso over Beatrice and they fight; Dante wins but spares Corso, and is congratulated for his chivalry. Dante and Beatrice confess their love at Beatrices's birthday celebrations, but she later becomes ill and dies, leaving Dante in despair.

Philpot studied at the Royal Academy with George Macfarren and completed *Dante and Beatrice* before he was 20. Despite early precocity, he never established a substantive reputation. The 1889 concert performance received little press coverage: Philpot was born in Brixton and the event was clearly designed to support a young local composer; brief press reviews were lukewarm.[224] The Rosa Company presented the opera (possibly revised since publication) as a new work in 1918 and initially gave an abridged version.[225] The work remained in the company's repertory, later in the full version, until at least 1920, when it was given at Covent Garden. Of the 1918 performance the *Musical Standard* said that 'the music is throughout romantic and tuneful but never reminiscent … his opera is a splendid addition to our music'.[226] The *Musical Times* was more qualified, criticising the structure of the libretto and tellingly noting that 'it is to the composer's credit that knowing his limitations he does not strain to be "modern"'.[227] The published score, issued when Philpot was 23, is remarkably ambitious, but the composer over-extended himself: it contains some clumsy modulations and, in an attempt

---

224 See *MW*, 30 November 1889, pp. 856–7; *PMG*, 26 November, p. 6; *MS*, 7 December, p. 498.

225 For further information on the acceptance of the opera, and biographical details, see *Deseret News* (Salt Lake City, Utah), 15 June 1918, p. 3.

226 *MS*, 22 June 1918, p. 317.

227 *MT*, 1 July 1918, pp. 324–5. Other reviews are at *Era*, 12 June, p. 13; *Stage*, 10 June 1920, p. 14; 23 September, p. 16; *MT*, 1 October, pp. 690–91; *The Times*, 18 December, p. 8.

to respond minutely to the text, frequent changes of tempo and texture result in a lack of coherence, while the diegetic dance numbers veer towards a clichéd and incongruous lighter style.

Zelica

Libretto	Unknown, after 'The Veiled Prophet' from Thomas Moore's *Lalla Rookh*
Premiere	17 December 1890, Gresham Hall, Brixton, London; 8 December 1891, Prince's Hall, London; (concert performances)
Principal cast	Zelica – Anna Williams Azim – Ben Davies Mokanna – Dan Price
Synopsis	Two acts: Persia, eighth century. Azim, a follower of the veiled prophet, Mokanna, looks for his love, Zelica; she believes he is dead. The lovers see each other and Mokanna confesses to Zelica that he is an impostor. Azim consequently joins the Caliph's army besieging Mokanna's castle. Mokanna realises he is defeated; he gives Zelica his cloak and veil and stabs himself. When Azim re-enters the castle, he mistakes the veiled Zelica for Mokanna and stabs her.

Based on the same story as Stanford's *Veiled Prophet* (not heard in Britain until 1893), the music of Philpot's second opera, composed, like *Dante and Beatrice*, before he was 20, is untraced. The concert performances were not successful: the *Musical Standard*, which had commended *Dante and Beatrice*, criticised the book, observing that, 'we are sorry that a young composer not altogether destitute of a thin veil of melody, should have worked upon words so poor and silly, that not even the musical genius of a Gounod could make them successful,'[228] while the *Era* stated that 'at present, his wings are not sufficiently strong to soar so high as grand opera … [which] requires the dramatic as well as the musical faculty'.[229]

La Gitana

Libretto	Leslie Morton
Premiere	22 November 1895, Theatre Royal, South Shields 19 March 1896, Elephant and Castle Theatre, London (both Valentine Smith)
Principal cast	Calla Kena – Bella Rosa Isabella – E. von Ravensberg Riaz – T.H. Wood Giacomo – Valentine Smith

228 *MS*, 27 December 1890, p. 522.

229 *Era*, 12 December 1891, p. 7.

Synopsis	Two acts: Rural Castille, 1750. Calla Kenna, an itinerant fortune teller, has been cast aside by Giacomo in favour of Isabella; Calla has taken up with Riaz but remains bitter. Seeking guidance, Giacomo and Isabella visit the fortune teller but Isabella enters her cavern alone. Calla drugs Isabella and covers her body with a cloth. An anxious Giacomo enters and Calla, unrecognised, induces him to plunge a knife into the cloth-covered mound. Calla tries to escape but is accidentally stopped by Riaz; Giacomo stabs Calla in revenge.

The music of Philpot's third opera (the first to be staged) is untraced; it was better received than his two previous attempts, the *Era* commenting that 'the music is dramatic in style and displays considerable artistic conception. There are several bright, catchy airs, [and] the choruses, though intricate, have much to recommend them'.[230] The *Musical News* less flatteringly noted that the music was 'tuneful, but teeming with reminiscences from operas by Bizet, Mascagni, Gounod, Offenbach etc.'.[231] *La Gitana* was given by James Turner in 1898 and 1904.[232]

Nigel

Libretto	Percy Pinkerton
Premiere	25 January 1907, Grand Theatre, Birmingham (abridged) 14 February 1908, Brixton Theatre, London (complete) (both James Turner)
Sources:	Unpublished manuscript material, Carl Rosa Archive, Liverpool Central Library.
Principal cast (Brixton)	Margery – Jessie Dennis Nigel – Charles Le Sueur Geoffrey – George Ridding Winifred – Christine Gomez
Synopsis	Three acts: England during the Civil War. Nigel, a Cavalier, and Winifred, the sister of the Roundhead, Geoffrey, are in love. Nigel is captured but Geoffrey promises to release him if he gives up Winifred and all his lands, and emigrates. Nigel refuses but is later freed from prison by Winifred and Margery, a village girl. Margery hides Nigel in a barn; he is discovered by Geoffrey but a Cavalier Captain appears and kills Geoffrey, enabling Nigel and Winifred to be together.

No reviews have been traced of the first performance. In reviewing the complete performance at Brixton, the *Stage* dismissed the libretto as uninteresting and sketchy, but praised the music as 'tuneful, engaging, and invariably pleasing

230 *Era*, 30 November 1895, p. 13. See also *Stage*, 28 November, p. 14; *Era*, 21 March, 1896, p. 11.

231 *MN*, 14 December 1895, p. 511.

232 See *Era*, 5 March 1898, p. 10; *Stage*, 11 February 1904, p. 13.

music'.[233] Philpot does not appear to have composed any more operas; his career was brought full circle by the Carl Rosa Company's production of *Dante and Beatrice* in 1918 (see above).

Price, Addison

The Nuns of Ardboe

Premiere	3 May 1918, Shakespeare Theatre, Liverpool (H.B. Phillips Opera Company)

Virtually nothing is known about this work or its composer; the music is untraced. Gordon Williams states that the opera had already been given in France and Belgium, but any performances attracted no comment in the British musical press.[234] The *Musical Times* mentions the first performance in Liverpool *en passant*, merely commenting that Price's music 'has a welcome lyrical quality as well as dramatic suggestiveness and orchestral colour'.[235] The Phillips troupe was taken over by the Rosa Company within a few months and Price's opera was not taken up by the merged enterprise.

Pritchard, C.E.

Kunacepa

Libretto	Leconte de Lisle (French), translated by A.W. Jordan
Premiere	9 June 1903, Queen's Hall, London (concert performance)
Source	Vocal Score: Novello & Co (London, 1903)
Synopsis	Four acts: Kingdom of Oudh, India, 400 BCE. The Rajah has neglected to make a human sacrifice and must forfeit an innocent man in atonement. The Brahmin and his wife refuse to give up their eldest and youngest sons and Kunacepa, the middle son, realises that he must die instead. The King of Vultures tells Kunacepa and Santa, his beloved, to seek guidance from Vicvamitra. He tells Kunacepa to follow the sacrificial ritual but also to recite a hymn to Indra. When Kunacepa does this a horse appears to take his place; the lovers are saved.

233 *Stage*, 20 February 1908, p. 19.

234 See Gordon Williams, *British Theatre in the Great War: A Re-evaluation* (London, 2003), p. 283.

235 *MT*, 1 June 1918, p. 279.

Although only given a concert performance, stage directions in the vocal score and an extensive ballet at the beginning of Act IV imply that Pritchard intended the work to be staged. According to reviews of *Kunacepa*, Prichard studied at the Paris Conservatoire with Franck and Massenet; no further biographical information has been traced. Critical reaction was negative; the *Musical Standard* described the opera as 'a weak pot-pourri of Wagner, Massenet etc. etc.'.[236] Stage directions and ballet music notwithstanding, the libretto structure leans towards that of a cantata, with little interaction between the characters. Despite the exotic subject, Pritchard's musical language is resolutely European: the sacrificial march resembles Siegfried's in *Götterdämmerung*, while there are frequent passages of tonal stasis.

Raybould, Clarence (1886–1972)

The Sumida River

Libretto	Marie Stopes, after a Japanese Noh Play
Premiere	15 August 1916, Glastonbury (Glastonbury Music Festival)
Principal cast	Ferryman – Percy Heming Mother – Irene Lemon
Synopsis	One act: A mother searching for a lost child crosses the Sumida River by ferry; as the ferryman talks to her, she realises that her child is in fact dead. When they reach the opposite bank, they kneel in front of Buddha, who grants the mother a vision of her child.

Born in Birmingham, Raybould may have first come into contact with Boughton via Granville Bantock; he appeared on several occasions as a pianist at the Glastonbury Festivals. Although later known as a conductor, Raybould produced a small amount of music. *The Sumida River*, which anticipates Britten's interest in Japanese Noh by 50 years, was his only opera. Unfortunately the music is untraced and it was somewhat overshadowed by the premiere on the previous day of Boughton's *Round Table*. *The Times* gave a positive review: 'Mr Raybould's music ... is full of a beautiful melody which never wholly defines itself, but yet has a very real appeal. We have spoken of him before as the skilful pianist who takes the place of the orchestra; it is delightful to find that he is also a composer of real imagination and remarkable sensitiveness'.[237] The work was revived at Glastonbury in 1919 and broadcast by the BBC on 25 September 1937.

---

236 *MS*, 13 June 1903, p. 376–77; see also *The Times*, 10 June 1903, p. 12; *Stage*, 11 June, p. 15.

237 *The Times*, 17 August 1916, p. 3; see also *Western Daily Press*, 22 August, p. 4; *Stage*, 14 December, p. 24;

Rendle, Lily

The Traitress

Libretto	Norman Ingall
Premiere	4 March 1914, Arts Centre, Mortimer Street, London
Principal cast	Beatrice – Hilda Miles Helen – Gladys Palmer Richard – Harry Edmonds Will Hood – Norman Ingall
Synopsis	Two acts: Helen is in love with Richard, but he is betrothed to her sister Beatrice. Will Hood conspires with Helen to lure Beatrice away, but Richard pursues them. Richard and Beatrice are reunited; Will and Richard fight; when Helen, remorseful, intervenes, Will falls over a cliff and is killed. Richard and Beatrice forgive her.

Nothing is known of the composer and the music is untraced. The *Stage*'s review was moderate: '*The Traitress* makes rather poor opera. Neither the author nor the composer show any sign of scorning the beaten track … Miss Rendle has applied music that, while appropriate, never rises to any great height'.[238]

Rôze, Raymond (1875–1920)

Joan of Arc

Libretto	Composer
Premiere	1 November 1913, Covent Garden, London
Source	Vocal score: Metzler & Co (London, 1909)
Principal cast	Joan of Arc – Lilian Granfelt Durand – Furness Williams Charles VII – Henry Rabke Philip, Duke of Burgundy – Charles Mott
Synopsis	Prologue, three acts, and seven tableaux: France, early fifteenth century. Joan receives a sword from her uncle, Durand, which she takes as a message from God. She visits Charles and explains that she is destined to fight for France and to conduct him to Reims for his coronation. At Orléans, Joan defeats Philip of Burgundy and persuades him to return to Charles's side; Charles is crowned but Philip betrays him again. Joan fights on at Compiègne but is captured, tried, and burnt at the stake.

[238] *Stage*, 12 March 1914, p. 28.

Rôze was the son of soprano Marie, a long-standing member of the Rosa Company. Educated at the Brussels Conservatoire, Rôze later worked for Herbert Beerbohm Tree and Henry Irving at the Lyceum and Her Majesty's Theatres. *Joan of Arc* is a sprawling work: a huge cast is required yet, by representing most of the dramatic incidents via *tableaux vivants*, Rôze failed to create an effective scenario, although there are many opportunities for spectacle. Rôze's music is no more effective: while tuneful, it is unoriginal, and relies on the overuse of a small number of harmonic devices such as mediant modulations. The vocal writing is often technically faulty; leitmotifs serve to bring some sense of unity. Many reviewers were positive and the work was well produced: *The Stage* remarked that 'suave and engaging phrases abound throughout the work, which … bear unmistakably the imprint of Gounod and Wagner … The amalgam … is fairly interesting and pleasing almost throughout'.[239] *The Times* was more critical, stating that the music 'often seemed entirely disconnected from the action on the stage … [the] clinging to solid blocks of harmony … and the inability to make the harmony progress on a logical tonal basis, are the two main causes why the music does not live'.[240]

Selby, Thomas Leeson (1827–?)

Adela

Libretto	J.H. Browne
Premiere	8 February 1888, Mechanics' Institute, Nottingham; repeated 7, 8, and 9 June, Theatre Royal, Nottingham
Source	Vocal Score: Johnson (Nottingham, ?1872)[241]
Principal cast	James V of Scotland – E.H. Johnson Redhall – M.H. Chadbourne Earl of Ashkirk – Arthur Johnson Sir Roland Vipont – J. Lambert Madgalen – Poppie Lymn Lady Adela – Mrs Whitehill Lady Sybil Douglas – Fannie Lymn

---

[239] *Stage*, 6 November 1913, p. 32; see also *MT*, 1 December, p. 806; *Academy*, 22 November, p. 664.

[240] *The Times*, 3 November 1913, p. 12.

[241] The vocal score is undated, but the British Library copy is date-stamped 1872. Brown and Stratton incorrectly attributed this opera to Bertram Luard Selby (p. 365).

Synopsis	Three acts: Edinburgh, 1537. At a reception for James and his new wife Magdalen, Adela, sister of the banished Ashkirk, is accused of sorcery as the Queen faints when Adela kisses her hand. Adela is imprisoned by her unwanted suitor Redhall but, with the help of Ashkirk's betrothed, Sybil, she escapes. She is recaptured and put on trial. Adela's betrothed, Roland, slays Redhall in a duel, and secures pardons for Adela and Ashkirk from James, enabling both couples to marry.

Little is known of Selby, who made a slight impact as a composer of glees;[242] *Adela* is his only known opera. The *Era* stated that 'for the music, we have nothing but the highest commendation … [Selby's] numbers are rich with melody, admirably in keeping with the situations, while the orchestration is especially skilful, full, and musician-like'.[243] The score, composed some years earlier, is fluent and well written, but old-fashioned, recalling by turns Rossini, Mozart, Balfe and Hérold. Within this framework, however, Selby showed skill in creating longer structures, and some originality: in the D minor sonata-form overture, for example, the second subject is presented in E, and the first subject recapitulation in A minor.

Skinner, Florence Marian (Mrs Stuart Stresa)

La Regina di Scozia

Libretto	Composer
Premiere	14 July 1883, Folies Dramatiques, London
Sources	Vocal Score: Florence and Rome (no publisher, 1883)
Principal cast	Maria, Queen of Scots – Talia Lue David Rizzio – Cecilia Boasso Earl of Bothwell – Ernesto Faletti John Knox – Aldighieri Aristide
Synopsis	Three acts: Scotland, 1566–67. Set at various locations, the opera recounts events in Mary's life: her relationship with her secretary, Rizzio, and his murder; her subsequent relationship with Bothwell; his flight, and her forced abdication.

242 See *MS*, 8 December 1894, p. 455.

243 *Era*, 11 February 1888, p. 9; See also *Era*, 9 June, p. 17; *Stage*, 15 June, p. 12.

Little is known of Skinner.[244] Reviews of *La Regina di Scozia* were excoriating: the *Athenaeum* stated that 'a more crude and amateurish production has rarely been placed before the public. To criticise it in detail would be a complete waste of space'.[245] The work, which has an Italian libretto, is a poor pastiche of the Italian style of 50 years earlier; while there are some attractive melodies, the music lacks harmonic interest, textural variety and dramatic awareness.

Smyth, Ethel (1858–1944)

Fantasio[246]

Libretto	Composer, after Alfred de Musset's eponymous play
Premiere	24 May 1898, Weimar
Sources	Vocal Score: C.G. Röder (Leipzig, 1899) Manuscript material: BL, Add MSS 45934–7
Synopsis	Three acts. Fantasio, a young student, disguises himself as a jester in order to gain access to Princess Danila, who is to be married to the pompous Duke of Croatia. Fantasio's antics provoke Danila's doubt and she cancels the wedding while also showing increasing interest in Fantasio. The Duke threatens revenge but, when Fantasio challenges him to a duel, he renounces Danila rather than fight.

Passionately interested in opera, Smyth was one of this period's most successful exponents, gaining good reviews for all three operas seen in Britain before 1918. Her first opera, *Fantasio*, was written in German, in which she was practically fluent, and was entered into a Munich-based competition; Smyth touted it round several German theatres before it was accepted at Weimar. The performance attracted little attention in the British press. The revival, at Karlsruhe in February 1901, brought more coverage but the work was not taken up by any British companies. Smyth's score contains much intricate detail and shows skill and some inspiration but its serious endeavour often mismatches the comedy of the story; *The Times* dismissed the latter as 'fantastic almost to incoherence'.[247]

---

[244] See Brown and Stratton, p. 376; a comic opera, *La Suocera* (*The Mother-in-Law*) was produced at Naples (*MS*, 11 August 1877, p. 84).

[245] *Athenaeum*, 21 July 1883, p. 90; see also *MP*, 16 July, p. 2; *Standard*, 16 July, p. 2.

[246] For a detailed examination of Smyth's first three operas and quotation of many significant but unpublished letters, see Rachel Gibbon, *The Early Operas of Dame Ethel Smyth (1858–1944): Geneses, Performance, Structure* (unpublished PhD dissertation, University of Manchester, 2005). For Smyth's own account of her first three operas see Ethel Smyth, *What Happened Next* (London: Longman, Green & Co, 1940).

[247] *The Times*, 15 February 1901, p. 13; see also *MS*, 23 February, pp. 117–18.

Der Wald

Libretto	Composer
Premiere	9 April 1902, Königliches Opern, Berlin 18 July 1902, Covent Garden, London (Grand Opera Syndicate)
Sources	Vocal Score: Schott & Co (London, 1902) Autograph score: BL, Add MSS 49538
Principal cast (London)	Duke Rudolf – David Bispham Iolanthe – Olive Fremstad Heinrich – Herr Pennarini Röschen – Frau Lohse Pedlar – Robert Blass
Synopsis	Prologue and one act: a forest, time unspecified. Röschen and Heinrich are soon to marry. When Iolanthe, Rudolf's sadistic mistress, sees Heinrich she commands him to enter her service but he refuses. Rudolf and his soldiers catch a Pedlar; they dangle him down a well and find a dead deer Heinrich and Röschen hid earlier. Iolanthe decides to spare Heinrich if he enters her service, but he again refuses. Iolanthe's soldiers kill Heinrich; Röschen collapses lifeless on his body.

Der Wald was produced in both England and Germany much more readily than *Fantasio*. The Berlin performances were well received but not without incident as anti-British sentiment was elevated due to the Boer War. The London performances, although almost derailed (see Chapter 3), were also successful and overshadowed Bunning's *La Princesse Osra*, premiered four days earlier. The *Musical Standard* was positive, chiding Smyth only for being influenced too much by Wagner at a time when he could be viewed as *passé*.[248] *The Times*, however, stated, '*Der Wald* is not a great opera. Nor is Miss Smyth a great composer, though she is probably the leader of her sex', but acknowledged 'a power of musical expression and a sense of dramatic fitness that deserve cultivation'.[249]

Smyth's score shows a definite advance on *Fantasio*; the music and the book are appropriately matched and a greater variety of moods and textures presented. Although the work is Germanic and especially Wagnerian, the music is nevertheless attractive and dramatically effective. This is especially true in the passages for Heinrich, Röschen and the villagers; Rudolf, a humiliated coward, and the sadistic Iolanthe are not so vivid, but still have character. The wood-nymphs' opening and closing tableaux successfully portray a contrasted magical world.[250]

[248] *MS*, 26 July 1902, pp. 54–5; see also *Athenaeum*, same date, p. 134.

[249] *The Times*, 19 July 1902, p. 8.

[250] For further discussion see Elizabeth Kertesz, 'The Germanness of English Music: Reflections on the Critical Reception of Ethel Smyth's *Der Wald*' in Brenton Broadstock (ed.) *Aflame with Music: 100 Years of Music at University of Melbourne* (Melbourne,

The Wreckers / Strandrecht / Les Naufrageurs

Libretto	Harry Brewster (in French); later translated into German and English
Premiere	11 November 1906, Leipzig 22 June 1909, His Majesty's Theatre, London (Beecham)
Sources	Universal Edition (London and Vienna, 1916) Autograph score: BL, Add MSS 45939–41 Additional manuscript material: BL, Add MSS 68893–901
Principal cast (London)	Pascoe – Arthur Winckworth Thirza – Mme De Vere Sapio Mark – John Coates Avis – Elizabeth Amsden Lawrence – Lewis James
Synopsis	Three acts: Cornwall, mid-eighteenth century. The villagers' ability to wreck ships is hampered by someone secretly lighting warning beacons. Avis accuses Pascoe but the culprit is Mark, who is in love with Pascoe's wife, Thirza. Mark and Thirza decide to leave the village after lighting one more beacon. They are seen by Pascoe who collapses in shock nearby. At an impromptu court the villagers believe they have the evidence to condemn Pascoe but Thirza and Mark return and confess; the villagers chain the lovers in a tidal cave in which they drown.

The Wreckers was well received in both Germany and Britain and is now regarded as Smyth's most successful opera. The Leipzig performances were reported favourably in the British press;[251] following a failed attempt to secure production at Covent Garden, the work was given a partial concert performance in London (Queen's Hall, 30 May 1908[252]), and finally staged a year later.[253] This performance was received variably; a highly complimentary review in *The Times* referred in qualified terms only to the melodramas and some of the orchestration,[254] and the *Musical Standard* termed it 'very decent stuff indeed',[255] but Filson Young's review exemplifies the additional challenges Smyth faced: 'the

Australia, 1996), pp. 79–86; Aidan Thomson, 'Decadence in the forest: Smyth's *Der Wald* in its critical context' in Cornelia Bartsch, Rebecca Grotjahn and Melanie Unseld (eds), *Felsensprengerin, Brückenbauerin, Wegbereiterin: die Komponistin Ethel Smyth* (2 vols, Munich: Allitera Verlag, 2010), vol. 2, pp. 218–49.

251 See *Athenaeum*, 17 November 1906, p. 627; *MT*, 1 December, p. 830.

252 For reviews see *MS*, 6 June 1908, pp. 353–4; *Athenaeum*, same date, p. 706; *Cremona*, 1 June, pp. 63–4.

253 For further commentary see Kathleen Abromeit, 'Ethel Smyth, *The Wreckers*, and Sir Thomas Beecham', *Musical Quarterly*, 73 (1989), pp. 196–211.

254 *The Times*, 23 June 1909, p. 10.

255 *MS*, 26 June 1909, pp. 403–4 (p. 404).

A NEW OPERA BY AN ENGLISHWOMAN.

Drawn by H. C. Seppings Wright.

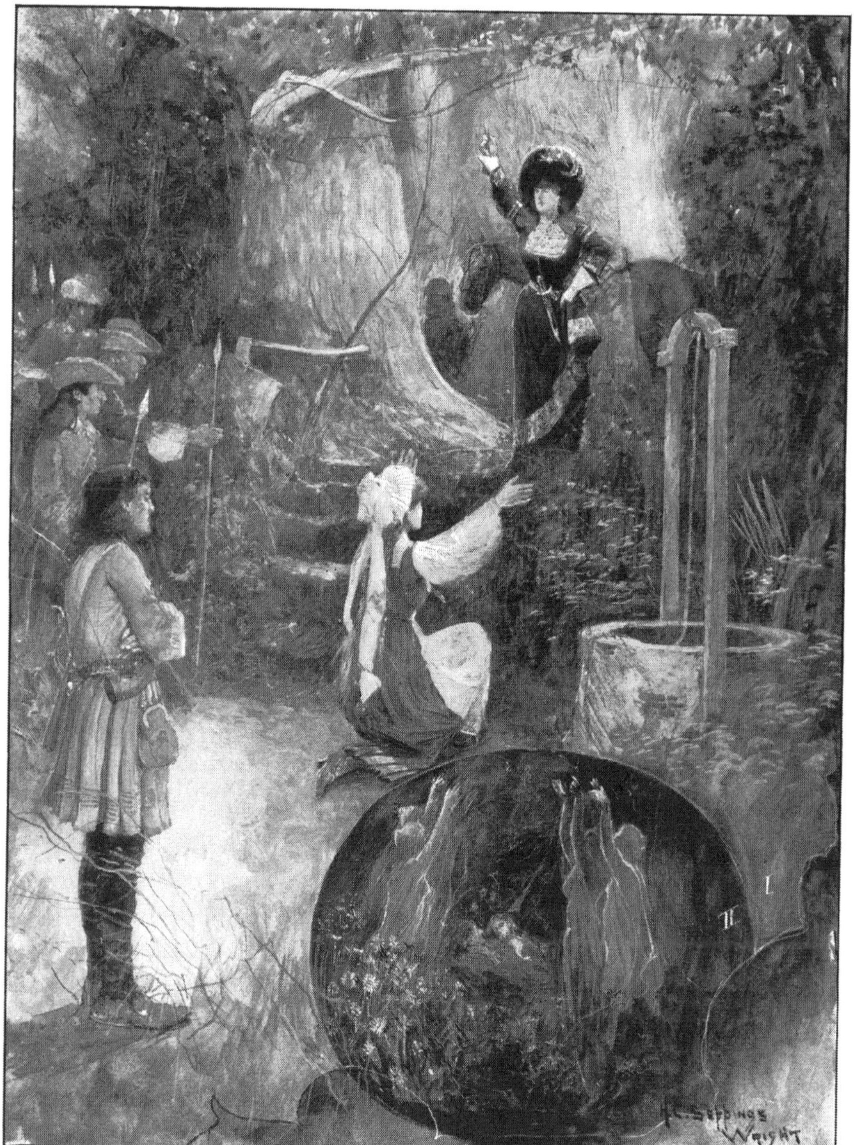

1. Iolanthe Pronouncing Heinrich's Doom. 2. Spirits of the Wood.

SCENES FROM "DER WALD," PRODUCED AT COVENT GARDEN ON JULY 18.

The opera, written and composed by Miss E. M. Smyth, symbolises the transience of human passion as contrasted with the quiet endurance of nature. The work opens and closes with a vision of forest nymphs sacrificing to Pan, and across the dream is flung a fierce, brief drama of human love and hate.

Figure 6.3 'Scenes from *Der Wald*, produced at Covent Garden on July 18' (*Illustrated London News*, 26 July 1902)

music is wonderfully well written, and often shows a largeness of conception and constructive power that are rare among modern composers … [but] there is a lack of tenderness in this music which is continually disappointing … I am convinced in my own mind that part of the aridity and unkindness and sometimes excessive masculinity of the music is due to the fact that Miss Smyth is a woman and not a man'.[256] Beecham included the work in his 1910 season but it was overshadowed by the performances of *Elektra* (see Chapter 3).

While Smyth's score is uneven, it contains much very impressive music; the vivid musical representation of the sea precedes Britten's *Peter Grimes* by almost 40 years. The musical structure is dynamic, incorporating both diegetic numbers (especially choruses) but also flexible arioso and extended solos and duets. The influence of Wagner is still obvious, but is moderated and moulded into a more individual style which also incorporates folksong-like melodies, the English hymn tradition, and strong orchestral colour. Smyth's tonal language remained that of the late nineteenth century but is both expressive and carefully planned.

The Boatswain's Mate

Libretto	Composer, after the eponymous story by W.W. Jacobs
Premiere	28 January, 1916, London, Shaftesbury Theatre (Beecham)
Sources	Vocal Score: Forsyth Brothers (London and Manchester, ?1915) Autograph score: BL, Add MSS 45942–3
Principal cast	Harry Benn – Courtice Pounds Ned Travers – Frederick Ranalow Mrs Waters – Rosina Buckman Policeman – Arthur Wynn
Synopsis	One act, two scenes: England, early twentieth century. Harry, a boatswain, hopes to persuade the widow Mrs Waters to marry him; he pays Ned to fabricate a break-in at Mrs Waters's pub. Before Harry can 'rescue' her, she outwits both men; she pretends to kill Ned which drives Harry to confess his plot to a policeman. Ned is revealed alive and well; Harry leaves humiliated, and Ned and Mrs Waters start a gentle courtship.

In her fourth opera Smyth turned to modern comedy. Jacobs's story was adjusted to bring Mrs Waters and her triumph over Benn to the fore; Smyth's feminism is thus readily apparent, emphasised by the quotation from her *March of the Women* in the overture. A number opera with sprightly and unaffected dialogue, *The Boatswain's Mate* contains much engaging material, including pastiche English folksongs, but also more flexible sections which advance the plot and incorporate some adventurous musical language (seventh and ninth chords, modal inflections and mixtures, metrical dissonances). In the diegetic numbers deft reharmonisations

256 *SR*, 26 June 1909, pp. 810–11 (p. 811).

maintain interest, and Smyth showed a neat sense of irony by employing a waltz when Mrs Waters tells a shocked Benn to dispose of Travers's body.

Of the British operas premiered in Beecham's 1915–16 season, *The Boatswain's Mate* was the most successful and the only one to be revived subsequently. The *Era* commented, 'Dr Smyth has once more asserted herself as a composer of power and originality. The main impression given by her music is that of an abounding restless vitality'.[257] Two further comic operas, *Fête Galante* and *Entente Cordiale* were produced in 1923 and 1926 respectively.

Somerville, Reginald (1867–1948)

The Prentice Pillar

Libretto	Guy Eden, after the eighteenth-century legend of the Apprentice Pillar in Rosslyn Chapel
Premiere	24 September 1897, London, Her Majesty's Theatre (Hedmondt Opera Company)
Sources	Vocal Score: Novello & Co (London, 1899)
Principal cast	Vincenzo – Arthur Winckworth Brunone – Holmer Lind Alan – William Paull Lisetta – Attalie Claire
Synopsis	One act: Rosslyn Chapel, near Edinburgh, fifteenth century. Vincenzo, a sculptor, lies ill so Alan, his apprentice, completes a pillar for him. Alan is in love with Vincenzo's daughter Lisetta, provoking the jealousy of Brunone, another apprentice. When Vincenzo arrives, Brunone exposes the lovers; Vincenzo stabs Alan and Lisetta collapses in shock. The completed pillar is then revealed and Vincenzo sees that he has killed a worthy successor.

The Prentice Pillar is an apprentice work: Somerville found effective modulations difficult, often relying on sequential patterns to avoid tonal stasis, and was over-reliant on regular periodisation, leading at times to monotony. The final action of the opera (Alan's stabbing, Lisetta's collapse, and the exposure of the pillar) are all accomplished in a mere 20 bars. The *Standard* detected French, Italian and Wagnerian influences in the music, and declared that Somerville's themes lacked 'freshness'; it did, however, allow that 'this may come, for he is evidently a skilled musician, and writes with much taste'.[258] The *Athenaeum* was less positive, stating that Somerville 'showed no originality whatever in his score,

[257] *Era*, 2 February 1916, p. 11.

[258] *Standard*, 25 September 1897, p. 3.

though it is carefully written'.[259] The opera was revived by the National Grand Opera Company on its 1899 tour, alongside *The Three Musketeers*.[260]

The Three Musketeers

Libretto	Herbert Whitney, after the eponymous novel by Dumas
Premiere	24 March 1899, Royal Court Theatre, Liverpool (National Grand Opera Company)
Principal cast	Louis XIII – Henry Beaumont Duke of Buckingham – Alec Marsh Cardinal Richelieu – Whitney Tew Rochefort – C.F. Cooke Athos – William Llewellyn Porthos – Robert Cunningham Aramis – Haigh Jackson D'Artagnan – Roland Cunningham Anne of Austria – Maria Titiens Constance – Bertha Cooke
Synopsis	A highly condensed version of the novel.

The music of *The Three Musketeers* is untraced; it was not well received and some reviewers argued that the work was not an opera but a play with incidental music. Whitney's scenario was criticised for overly condensing the novel while retaining too many characters; Somerville's music was dismissed in the *Musical Standard* as 'not of a very high order',[261] while the *Era* stated that 'it cannot be fairly said that Mr Somerville comes up to the expectations of those who desire the advancement of art in England'.[262] Somerville was not entirely deterred and composed a comic opera in the Savoy tradition (*The Mountaineers*, 1909) and two further serious operas, (*Antoine* (Carl Rosa, 1919) and *David Garrick* (Carl Rosa, 1920)).

Stanford, Charles Villiers (1852–1924)[263]

The Veiled Prophet of Khorassan

Libretto	William Barclay Squire, after Thomas Moore's *Lalla Rookh*

[259] *Athenaeum*, 2 October 1897, p. 461; see also *Era*, 2 October, p. 11; *MP*, 25 September, p. 5.

[260] See *Era*, 11 March 1899, p. 9.

[261] *MS*, 15 April 1899, p. 237.

[262] *Era*, 1 April 1899, p. 11; see also *Glasgow Herald*, 30 March, p. 7.

[263] For more detailed discussed see Paul Rodmell, *Charles Villiers Stanford* (Aldershot, 2002); Jeremy Dibble, *Charles Villiers Stanford: Man and Musician* (Oxford, 2002).

Premiere	6 February 1881, Hoftheater, Hannover British: 26 July 1893, Covent Garden, London (Royal Opera)
Sources	Vocal Scores: Bote & Bock (Berlin, 1881); Boosey & Co (London, 1893) Autograph Score: RCM, MS 4164.
Principal cast (London)	Caliph – Sig. de Vaschetti Mokanna – Mario Ancona Zelica – Lillian Nordica Azim – Sig. Viguar Fatima – Lucille Hill
Synopsis	Three acts: Persia, eighth century. Azim, the lost lover of Zelica, is to lead the veiled prophet Mokanna's forces against the Caliph. When Zelica sees him, she tells him that Mokanna is false; he urges her to flee with him, but she will still not break her oath of loyalty. Azim switches to the Caliph's side. Mokanna loses the battle but manages to retain his followers' trust. They feast but Mokanna has poisoned the wine; as they die Mokanna removes his veil. The Caliph's army is heard approaching; Mokanna escapes and commits suicide. The lovers are reunited.

Alongside De Lara, Stanford was the most consistently active opera composer in this period, returning to the genre throughout his career. In addition to the works performed before 1918 he completed three others, and embarked upon another two.[264] Despite this activity, Stanford enjoyed little sustained success, due to weaknesses in individual works and the unpropitious circumstances which affected all composers.

Stanford's first opera shows some maturity. While mainly a number-based work, it also incorporates some more flexible arioso passages and pre-Wagnerian reminiscence motifs. The harmonic language is fundamentally that of Schumann but includes attempts at exoticism via modality (most notably in the song 'There's a bower of Roses'). Despite a fairly successful premiere at Hannover,[265] it was 12 years before *The Veiled Prophet* was performed in Britain; Stanford revised the score for the Covent Garden performance, which was given in Italian. Critical reception was again variable: the *Era* stated that 'there is a dryness and want of

[264] *Lorenza* (1894) and *Christopher Patch* (1897) have never been performed; *The Travelling Companion*, completed in 1916, was not seen on stage until 1924. Stanford and Gilbert A'Beckett planned a third collaboration, based on Tennyson's play *Beckett* in 1883–84, but no music was composed; *The Miner of Falun* (1889) was abandoned after one act was completed (see Chapter 2).

[265] The British press emphasised Stanford's achievement in securing an overseas premiere, and selectively quoted German reviews (for example, '[Stanford] evinces the possession of the really extraordinary talent for dramatic composition' (*Neue Berliner Musikzeitung* quoted in *Athenaeum*, 19 February 1881, p. 273). For his own account see Charles Stanford, *Pages from an Unwritten Diary* (London, 1914), pp. 189–93.

charm in many portions of the score' while acknowledging that the opera was 'the work of an earnest, competent and highly cultured musician'.[266] The *Musical Standard* deemed it 'little more than an oratorio transferred to the stage',[267] but the *Academy* was more positive, allowing that 'in spite of its weaknesses, Dr Stanford's opera is really clever and interesting'.[268]

Savonarola[269]

Libretto	Gilbert A'Beckett
Premiere	18 April 1884, Stadttheater, Hamburg British: 9 July 1884, Covent Garden, London (German Opera Season)
Sources	Vocal Score: C.G. Röder (Leipzig, ?1884) Autograph Score: RCM, MSS 4160 and 4161
Principal cast (London)	Savonarola – [Albert?] Stritt Clarice/Francesca – Fräulein Schaernack Rucello – Herr Scheidemantal Sebastiano – Herr Kaps
Synopsis	Prologue (Ferrara, 1475) and three acts (Florence, 1498). Savonarola and Clarice are in love but she is betrothed to Rucello; Savonarola decides to become a monk. In Florence, Rucello has raised Clarice's daughter Francesca; Savonarola rules the city. Rucello and Francesca plot to overthrow Savonarola; Sebastiano tries to dissuade her. Francesca is captured; Savonarola realises that she is Clarice's daughter but the people force him to imprison her. Rucello frees Francesca, who changes sides; a mob kills Sebastiano and takes Savonarola prisoner; he is burnt at the stake and Francesca dies as she sees a vision of heaven.

Savonarola was unsuccessful, suffering from a poor book, lacklustre music, excessively heightened expectations and an inadequate British premiere. While affording plenty of opportunities for spectacle (processions of monks, angry crowds, brawls, the 'bonfire of the vanities') the personal drama is contrived and ineffective. Stanford's second and third operas reflect his interest in Wagner; in *Savonarola* a more chromatic tonal language is adopted but is overly reliant on sequences, and diminished and augmented chords. The British press emphasised positive German reviews, raising expectations unrealistically.[270] The London

---

266 *Era*, 29 July 1893, p. 13; see also *Theatre*, 1 September 1893, pp. 174–6.

267 *MS*, 29 July 1893, p. 90.

268 *Academy*, 29 July 1893, p. 98.

269 For a detailed account Paul Rodmell, 'A Tale of Two Operas: Stanford's *Savonarola* and *The Canterbury Pilgrims* from Gestation to Production', *Music and Letters*, 78 (1997), pp. 77–91. For his own account see Stanford, pp. 244–6.

270 *Era* quoted the *Hamburger Nachrichten*: '[*Savonarola*] surpasses all novelties of the kind which we have witnessed in Hamburg for a long time back' (26 April 1884, p. 7);

production was beset by problems, resulting in a poor premiere. Critical reaction was hostile: Hueffer wrote of 'the almost total absence of any dramatic qualities properly so-called'[271] and Kingston deemed the book 'dull [and] stilted' but not 'so crushingly tiresome as the music fitted to it'.[272] Stanford himself 'scarcely recognised the opera I had seen at Hamburg a few weeks before'.[273] Like Mackenzie in *Colomba* and *The Troubadour*, Stanford over-extended himself: neither the book nor the music is sufficiently robust to create a successful work.

The Canterbury Pilgrims

Libretto	Gilbert A'Beckett
Premiere	28 April 1884, Theatre Royal, Drury Lane, London (Carl Rosa)
Sources	Vocal Score: Boosey & Co (London, 1884) Autograph Score: RCM, MS 4232
Principal cast	Cicely Blount – Clara Perry Geoffrey Blount – G.H. Snazelle Hubert Lovel – Ben Davies Sir Christopher Synge – William Ludwig Dame Margery Synge – Marian Burton Hal o'the Chepe – Barrington Foote
Synopsis	Three acts: England, late fourteenth century. Hubert and Cicely are in love, but her father Geoffrey disapproves and sends her to Canterbury. Christopher, who has taken a fancy to Cicely, plots to abduct her, aided by Hal. Hubert and Margery, Christopher's wife, both discover the plot and work to frustrate it. After much confusion, Hubert finds himself on trial with Christopher as judge, but Hubert exposes Christopher and is backed by Margery and Cicely. Hubert is released and Geoffrey consents to his marrying Cicely.

Stanford's second collaboration with A'Beckett was commissioned by Rosa, composed immediately after *Savonarola*, and produced just 10 days later. The lighter story was handled more successfully by both parties although the libretto is overly wordy and replete with faux-archaic English, while Stanford's interest in Wagner results in some leaden treatment of the story's humour, some of which parallels situations in *Die Meistersinger*. Reminiscence motifs are better integrated than previously into music containing extended sections of irregularly periodised arioso; Stanford employed 'Sumer is icumen in' to emphasise the work's English *locus*. Critical reaction was qualified; Kingston, who later condemned *Savonarola*, praised the book as 'the best operatic libretto of this or any other day', while

see also *MS*, 26 April, p. 269.

271 *The Times*, 11 July 1884, p. 4.

272 *Theatre*, 1 August 1884, p. 79; see also *MW*, 12 July, p. 431; *SR*, 19 July, p. 79. More positive reviews are in *Academy*, 12 July 1884, p. 36; *MS*, 19 July, pp. 19–20.

273 Stanford, p. 245.

noting that the music 'abounds in "continuous melody" of an extremely attractive and interesting character, but it is conspicuously lacking in the sort of tunes that listeners will carry away with them'.[274] The *Musical Times* praised the comic scenes but stated that 'the love music is cold'.[275] Rosa dropped the opera after one season.

Shamus O'Brien

Libretto	George Jessop, after Joseph Sheridan Le Fanu's eponymous poem
Premiere	2 February 1896, Opera Comique Theatre, London (Shamus O'Brien Opera Company)
Sources	Vocal Score: Boosey & Co (London, 1896) Autograph Score: BL, MS Loan 84.II.42
Principal cast	Shamus O'Brien – Denis O'Sullivan Norah O'Brien – Louise Kirkby Lunn Kitty O'Toole – Maggie Davis Father O'Flynn – Charles Magrath Mike Murphy – Joseph O'Mara Captain Trevor – W.H. Stephens
Synopsis	Two acts, three scenes: County Cork, Ireland, 1798. Shamus, a rebel, is sought by British soldiers. His wife, Norah, correctly worries that Mike, who is in love with her, will betray him. Her sister, Kitty, flirts with Captain Trevor; a disguised Shamus leads Trevor and his soldiers away and loses them but, helped by Mike, they catch Shamus. The banshee is heard, foretelling a death; as Shamus is led to the scaffold O'Flynn frees him. Mike tries to stop Shamus; the soldiers shoot but hit Mike and Shamus escapes.

Stanford's most successful opera descends from the mid-century works of Balfe and Wallace, with a story containing humour, romance and melodrama; it employs spoken dialogue rather than continuous music. *Shamus O'Brien* was produced in a 'run' by a specially formed company rather than one of the 'grand opera' troupes, followed by long provincial and American tours. It was Stanford's only opera to enjoy occasional revivals during his lifetime although he himself banned performances from about 1912.[276] The scenario and libretto draw upon the 'Stage Irish' tradition

274 *Theatre*, 1 May 1884, p. 250. A month later, however, Kingston referred to it as 'singularly tedious' (*Theatre*, 1 June, p. 306).

275 *MT*, 1 June 1884, pp. 333–4; see also *The Times*, 29 April, p. 8; *Era*, 3 May, p. 11; *MMR*, 1 June, p. 139.

276 For further commentary on the historical and political background see Michael Murphy, 'Nation, Race and Empire in Stanford's Irish Works: Music in the Discourse of British Imperialist Culture' in Richard Pine (ed.), *Music in Ireland 1848–1998* (Cork, 1999), pp. 46–55; Jean Marie Hoover, 'Constructing Ireland: Culture and Politics in Stanford's *Shamus O'Brien*', in Jeremy Dibble and Bennett Zon (eds), *Nineteenth-Century British Music Studies*, Volume 2 (Aldershot: 2002), pp. 126–36; David Cooper, 'Stanford and

soon to be surpassed by the Irish Literary Revival of Yeats, Synge and Gregory; nevertheless Stanford's music was highly regarded and Irish audiences enjoyed the work when it was revived in Dublin in 1924. The opera is more simply constructed than Stanford's previous operas, employing a clear number-based format; it still exhibits sophistication, however, with careful orchestration, a flexible approach to standard forms and phrase lengths, and some good handling of dramatic tension. Much of the score is a well-informed pastiche of Irish folk music as Stanford knew it. Critical reaction was very positive; the *Musical Times* called the work 'a little masterpiece'[277] while the *Theatre* paid Stanford the backhanded compliment that he had 'condescended to be absolutely tuneful'.[278]

Much Ado About Nothing

Libretto	Julian Sturgis, after Shakespeare
Premiere	30 May 1901, Covent Garden, London (Grand Opera Syndicate)
Sources	Vocal Score: Boosey & Co (London, 1901) Autograph score: RCM, MS 4165.
Principal cast	Claudio – John Coates Hero – Suzanne Adams Beatrice – Marie Brema Benedick – David Bispham Don John – Lawrence Rea
Synopsis	Four acts: Sicily, thirteenth century. A condensed version of the play; Dogberry and Verges appear only at the beginning of the last act.

In an unusual move, *Much Ado About Nothing* was produced, in English, by the Grand Opera Syndicate. Sturgis, who had previously worked with Goring Thomas and Sullivan, supplied a libretto which is, for the greater part, a reduced version of the play and contains much of the original dialogue. Set pieces imbue the work with a traditional feel but Stanford also incorporated some true leitmotifs. Many passages are very effective although the verbal sparring of Beatrice and Benedick does not always succeed. Critical reaction was quite positive: *The Times* stated that 'the action is carried on with very great skill in a flowing and really vocal style'[279] while the *Athenaeum* asserted that the 'varied moods are so appropriate [and] the contrasts so striking',[280] but also believed that the music lacked soul and

LeFanu's *Shamus O'Brien*: Protestant Constructions of Irish Nationalism in Late Victorian England' in Rachel Cowgill, David Cooper and Clive Brown (eds), *Art and Ideology in European Opera* (Woodbridge, 2010), pp. 85–102.

277 *MT*, 1 April 1896, p. 240.

278 *Theatre*, 1 April 1896, p. 224.

279 *The Times*, 31 May 1901, p. 4.

280 *Athenaeum*, 8 June 1901, p. 733. See also *MT*, 1 July 1901, p. 388. Runciman was negative, deeming the work 'the least original thing Dr Stanford has written' (*SR*, 8 June, p. 735).

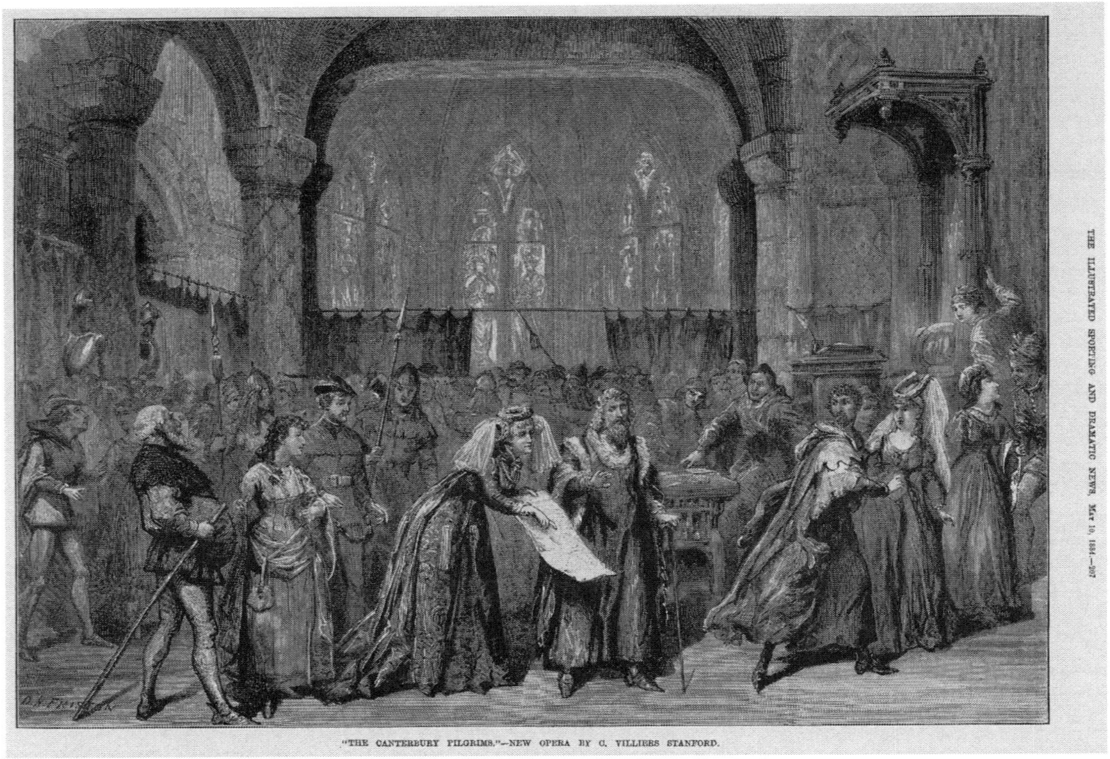

Figure 6.4 '*The Canterbury Pilgrims*: New opera by Dr C Villiers Stanford', *Illustrated Sporting and Dramatic News*, 10 May 1884

was overly indebted to other composers. The opera was taken up by the Moody-Manners Company for one season and also performed in Leipzig in 1902.

The Critic

Libretto	Lewis Cairns James after Sheridan's eponymous play
Premiere	14 January 1916, Shaftesbury Theatre, London (Beecham & Courtneidge)
Sources	Vocal Score: Boosey & Co (London, 1915) Autograph Score: RCM, MS 4153.
Principal cast	Tilburina – Caroline Hatchard Don Whiskerandos – Frank Mullings Sir Walter Raleigh – Percy Heming Sir Christopher Hatton – Sydney Russell
Synopsis	Two acts: Tilbury Fort, late sixteenth century, framed by England, late eighteenth century. Sneer, the critic, has come to watch a rehearsal of Puff and Dangle's latest opera *The Spanish Armada*, set at Tilbury Fort. The plot is nonsensical, and the 'opera' incorporates both real and fictional characters, whose actions and motivations are unexplained; it ends with a grand pageant showing the rivers of England and a triumphant Walter Raleigh defeating the Spanish.

Stanford composed *The Critic* in summer 1915; Sheridan's play was both escapist in its farcical humour but also topical as Puff's 'play within a play' has the approach of the Spanish Armada as a backdrop. In concept, *The Critic* is a distinctive work although there are obvious parallels with Strauss's *Ariadne auf Naxos*: *The Spanish Armada* contains no coherent plot, and sends up theatrical conventions and characters. James confined himself to reducing Sheridan's work and adapting it to transform Puff's play into an opera. Stanford matched this with parodies of operatic styles, references to other works, and 'mistakes' in the orchestral parts, all of which highlight Dangle's inadequacy as a composer. Unable to judge the work by conventional values, reviewers were mainly happy to accept *The Critic* as a somewhat cerebral piece of light relief in war-time. The *Musical Times* deemed it 'a delightful and amusing entertainment'[281] and the *Stage* 'brilliantly successful'.[282] Runciman, however, argued that 'most of the music is neither good nor bad; it serves'.[283] Despite the positive reception Beecham only retained the work in his repertory for one season.

[281] *MT*, 1 February 1916, p. 95.

[282] *Stage*, 20 January 1916, p. 22.

[283] *SR*, 29 January 1916, pp. 106–7.

Stanislaus, Frederick (1844–91)

The Lancashire Witches

Libretto	R.T. Gunton, after William Harrison Ainsworth's eponymous novel
Premiere	20 October 1879, Theatre Royal, Manchester
Sources	Vocal Score: [publisher unnamed], (London, ?1880)
Principal cast	Alizon – Edith St. John Mother Demdyke – Mrs R. Power Sir Ralph Ashton – Furneaux Cook Richard Ashton – H. Hallam Master Hopkins – G. Leitch King James I – Richard Temple Alice Nutter – Alice Cook
Synopsis	Two acts: Pendle, Lancashire, early seventeenth century. Alizon and Richard are in love, but Ashton's father Ralph opposes the match as it is rumoured that Alizon's grandmother, Demdyke, is a witch. Hopkins, a witchfinder, and James, disguised, arrive in the village. James is drawn to Alice. On Pendle Hill the witches enact their rituals, witnessed by Richard, Alizon, James and Alice. Hopkins and his soldiers arrive and capture everyone except Alice. She reveals James's true identity. James releases Richard and Alizon, who is revealed to be Alice's daughter stolen by Demdyke many years previously. The lovers are free to marry.

Stanislaus was an experienced music director and was employed at the Theatre Royal, Manchester, until shortly before this opera was produced.[284] The *Era* described the libretto as 'cleverly and gracefully written' and the music as 'of a high class, yet popular'.[285] The *Musical Standard* was also complimentary, its critic remarking, 'I am afraid that it is too good for the million of this present time'.[286] Stanislaus's score shows a high level of competence and some inspiration within a traditional number-based framework; the constant rhyming couplets of the libretto are oppressive, despite the composer's attempts to obscure them in recitatives. Despite scoring a local success, Stanislaus is not known to have composed any other operas.

---

[284] For further biographical information see Brown and Stratton, p. 390, and Gänzl, *British Musical Theatre*, vol. 2, p. 1360.

[285] *Era*, 26 October 1879, p. 6.

[286] *MS*, 8 November 1879, p. 290. See also *Athenaeum*, 1 November, p. 571.

Sullivan, Arthur Seymour (1842–1900)

Ivanhoe[287]

Libretto	Julian Sturgis, after Walter Scott's eponymous novel
Premiere	31 January 1891, Royal English Opera House, London
Sources	Vocal Score: Chappell & Co (London, 1891) Full Score: Amber Ring (London, ?2008)
Principal cast	Rebecca – Margaret McIntyre Ivanhoe – Ben Davies King Richard – Norman Salmond Cedric – Frangcon Davies Rowena – Esther Palliser
Synopsis	Three acts, nine scenes: England, late twelfth century. A selection of episodes from the novel, focusing on Ivanhoe, his father Cedric, Rowena, with whom Ivanhoe is in love, and the Jews, Isaac and Rebecca. Many other characters appear including Robin of Locksley, Friar Tuck, Prince John, and the Knights Templar.

For many years Sullivan was urged to produce an opera which demonstrated an intent more serious than that of his collaborations with Gilbert. Although *The Yeomen of the Guard* (1888) was more sombre than previous Savoy Operas, it was still perceived as a part of that oeuvre; it did, however, provide Sullivan with a stepping stone towards *Ivanhoe*. No other British opera of this period had such heightened expectations placed upon it. Great things were expected of Sullivan, and Carte built a new theatre with the expectation that *Ivanhoe* would inaugurate a new age in English opera. Despite a successful premiere and the longest run of performances achieved by any British grand opera, within two years, *Ivanhoe* was regarded as a failure and was rarely revived.[288] Although initial reviews over-praised *Ivanhoe*, which is an uneven and problematic work, Carte's misguided management was more responsible for later perceptions than the work itself.

Sturgis, a relative tyro, faced a considerable challenge. Critics generally agreed that he had successfully condensed Scott's complex story ('cleverly arranged'[289] and even 'an improvement on the novel'[290]), but the scenario assumed previous knowledge and led later to perceptions of a series of unconnected *tableaux*, exacerbated by the decision to preserve popular minor characters.

---

[287] For detailed discussion see: Arthur Jacobs, *Arthur Sullivan: A Victorian Musician* (Oxford, 1984), pp. 306–30; Jeff Dailey, *Sir Arthur Sullivan's Grand Opera* Ivanhoe (Lewiston (New York), 2008).

[288] A condensed version was produced by the Rosa Company in 1894–95; Beecham revived *Ivanhoe* in 1910; it was also produced in Berlin in 1895.

[289] *MoM*, 1 March 1898, pp. 43–4 (p. 43).

[290] *MS*, 7 February 1898, p. 105.

Sullivan aimed at greater musical flexibility than previously while retaining vocal primacy and in part succeeded. Some numbers, such as Rebecca's 'Is there no way of safety?' (Act II) include subtle harmonic changes and chromatic inflections but its major key apotheosis ('Spirit who movest') lapses into cliché, leaving the impression that Sullivan could not discard his earlier self. Similarly, Sullivan often reverted to regularly periodised paragraphs and rhythmic patterns while failing to produce flexible arioso. The result is an overly sectionalised score which lacks longer cohesive structures. Beecham's 1910 revival afforded an opportunity for more detached assessment. Reflecting a consensus, the *Athenaeum*, while allowing that Sullivan's music was 'spontaneous', concluded that *Ivanhoe* seemed old-fashioned even for its own time, although it acknowledged that while 'Sullivan did not succeed in writing an epoch-making work, no British composer has since achieved that feat'.[291]

The Beauty Stone

Libretto	Arthur W. Pinero and J. Comyns Carr
Premiere	28 May 1898, Savoy Theatre, London
Sources	Vocal Score: Chappell & Co (London, 1898) Autograph Score: Bodleian Library, Oxford University
Principal cast	Philip, Lord of Mirlemont – George Devoll Simon Limal – Henry Lytton The Devil – Walter Passmore Laine – Ruth Vincent Saida – Pauline Joran
Synopsis	Three acts, seven scenes: Flanders, early fifteenth century. The Devil, in disguise, plays a mischievous game with a magical 'beauty stone' which transforms its holder. The stone is successively possessed by Laine, who attracts the attention of Philip; her father Simon; and Saida, former love of Philip. When Philip later returns blinded after a battle, he again courts Laine, unable to see her original unsightly appearance. Saida, frustrated at her failure, discards the stone; the Devil picks it up and leaves, annoyed that his game was not more amusing. Philip announces that he will marry Laine.

In *The Beauty Stone* Sullivan and his librettists aimed at creating a work halfway between *Ivanhoe* and the earlier 'Savoy Operas', closer in approach to *The Yeomen of the Guard* and the mid-century operas of Balfe and Wallace. Although expectations were not as high as with *Ivanhoe*, the collaboration between Sullivan, Carr and Pinero was highly regarded and this, together with certain miscalculations (the piece was not typical light Savoy Theatre fare) undermined

[291] *Athenaeum*, 12 March 1910, p. 317; see also *MS*, same date, p. 163; *The Times*, 9 March, p. 12; *MG*, 9 March, p. 9.

The Beauty Stone.[292] The complex and convoluted story (which relies, ironically, on a version of the 'lozenge' plot Sullivan despised) resulted in an unwieldy work. Despite opening to many favourable reviews,[293] the mismatch between audience and work led to an early closure. A reduced version was produced by the Rosa Company in 1901–02 but was no more successful and was abandoned.

Musically the work is a hybrid: in places 'Savoy Sullivan' is readily apparent (for example, the Act I chorus of Beauty Contest competitors), whereas in others a more tonally fluid language is employed (Simon and Joan's Act I duet), but Sullivan rarely managed to escape regular phrasing and enclosed structures in the manner that Stanford did in *Shamus O'Brien*, a work of similar sentiment and aspiration.

Thomas, Arthur Goring (1850–92)

Esmeralda

Libretto	T. Marzials and Alberto Randegger after Victor Hugo's *The Hunchback of Notre Dame*
Premiere	26 March 1883, Theatre Royal, Drury Lane, London (Carl Rosa)
Sources	Vocal Score: Boosey & Co (London, 1883) Drafts and sketches of revisions for the 1890 revival: BL, Add MS 36739
Principal cast	Esmeralda – Georgina Burns Phoebus – Barton McGuckin Claude Frollo – William Ludwig Quasimodo – Leslie Crotty
Synopsis	Four acts: Paris, late fifteenth century. Quasimodo and Frollo, a monk enamoured of Esmeralda, abduct her; she is rescued by Phoebus, with whom she falls in love. At Esmeralda's house, Quasimodo stabs Phoebus; Quasimodo escapes and Frollo accuses Esmeralda of Phoebus's murder. Frollo later promises to secure Esmeralda's release from prison if she accepts him, but she refuses. Phoebus, who, it transpires, was only wounded, declares Esmeralda's innocence. Frollo attempts to stab Phoebus again but Quasimodo gets in the way and is stabbed instead. Frollo is seized and the lovers are reunited.

Trained at the Royal Academy and the Paris Conservatoire, Thomas produced the most successful of the Rosa commissions of the 1880s.[294] Unlike Stanford

292 In a newspaper interview Carr tried to direct expectations away from light comedy; see *PMG*, 9 May 1898, p. 11.

293 See, for example, *MN*, 4 June 1898, p. 550; *MT*, 1 July, p. 472; *Lute*, same date, pp. 717–18. An excoriating review appeared in *Academy*, 4 June, p. 611.

294 A juvenile opera, *Don Braggadocio*, was left unfinished; *The Light of the Harem* was part-performed privately at the Royal Academy in 1879.

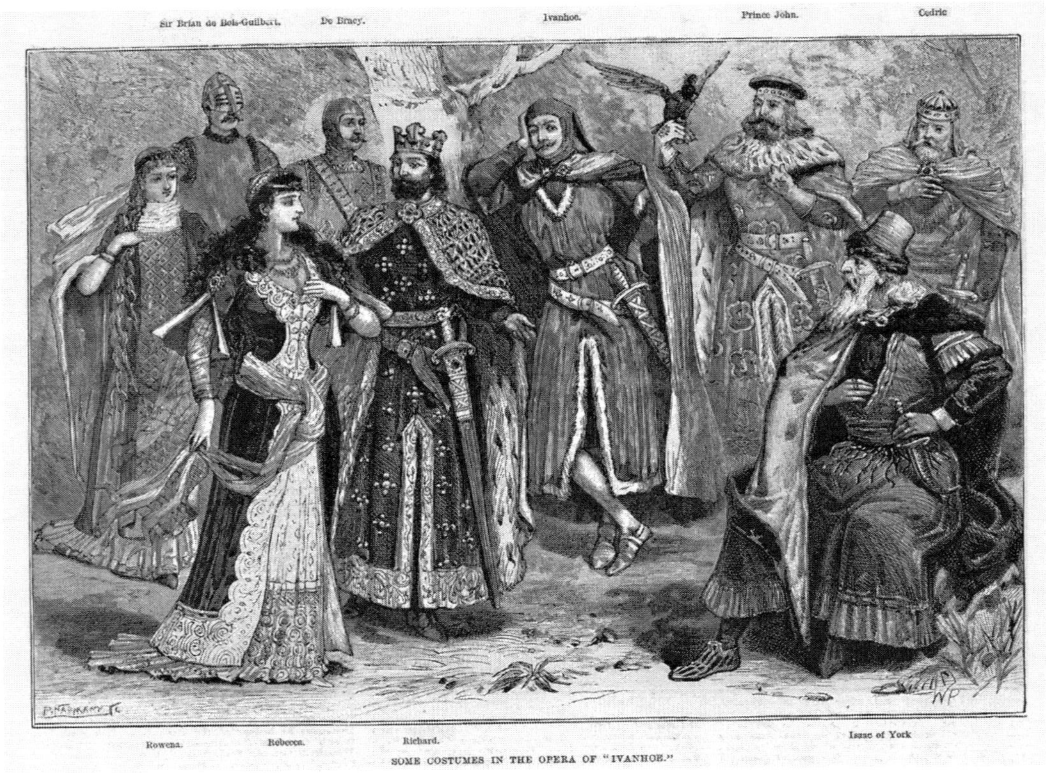

Figure 6.5 'Some costumes in the opera of *Ivanhoe*' (*Illustrated London News*, 31 January 1891

and Mackenzie, he looked primarily to France for inspiration. Critics, mindful of Rosa's endeavours, were complimentary: the *Athenaeum* referred to 'a work higher in aim, and to a certain extent in accomplishment, than any previous opera by an English composer'[295] and the *Musical Standard* called it a 'really picturesque work, containing many good things and well deserving a lasting success'.[296]

The influence of composers such as Ambroise Thomas and Gounod is shown in light textures, lyrical lines and delicate orchestration, while from Wagner Thomas took a desire to create a more flexible formal structure which responded more immediately to the libretto, and, to a very limited extent, reminiscence themes. *Esmeralda* was popular in the provinces in the 1880s and also performed overseas. For the 1890 revival at Covent Garden Thomas made many revisions; at the end Phoebus dies of his earlier wound and Esmeralda commits suicide.[297] Subsequent performances were infrequent, and when the Rosa Company revived the opera in 1908 the *Musical Standard* dismissed the 'inept and utterly fatuous libretto' and stated that Thomas's 'limitations in such affairs as emotional intensity and depth of conviction are manifest on every hand'.[298]

Nadeshda

Libretto	Julian Sturgis
Premiere	16 April 1885, Theatre Royal, Drury Lane, London (Carl Rosa)
Source	Vocal Score: Boosey (London, 1885)
Principal cast	Nadeshda – Alwina Valleria Princess Natalia – Josephine Yorke Prince Voldemar – Barton McGuckin Prince Ivan – Leslie Crotty Ostap – W.H. Burgon
Synopsis	Four acts: near Moscow, 1760. Rival siblings Ivan and Voldemar are both captivated by the serf Nadeshda. In order to placate Ivan, Voldemar offers him a gift of his choice, and he chooses Nadeshda. Frustrated, Voldemar frees her so that she cannot be the prize; Ivan vows revenge. Voldemar and Nadeshda fall in love, irking Ivan and the serf Ostap, who also loves Nadeshda. When Natalia, Voldemar's mother, learns of the situation, she disowns him. Ivan, meanwhile, tries to seduce Nadeshda; Ostap stabs him. Remorseful, Ostap stabs himself, and Ivan dies in his mother's arms. Natalia asks Voldemar and Nadeshda for forgiveness.

295 *Athenaeum*, 31 March 1883, pp. 417–18 (p. 417).

296 *MS*, 31 March 1883, pp. 190–91 (p. 190); see also *MN*, same date, pp. 192–3; *MT*, 1 April, pp. 191–2.

297 Although Hugo's novel ends in tragedy, Thomas's abandoning of the opera's original happy ending was criticised (see *MS*, 19 July 1890, p. 44; *MT*, 1 August, p. 473).

298 *MS*, 11 January 1908, p. 21.

Nadeshda incorporates developments of the techniques Thomas used in *Esmeralda*. There is no real Russian *tinta* in the music; 'local colour' is contained in such devices as insistent dance rhythms, modal inflections and mixtures. The predominant influence is that of France but the English glee style is apparent in some of the choruses. Critical reception was generally positive; there was a consensus that Thomas had made a 'marked advance'[299] since *Esmeralda*. Although felt to be uneven, especially in the later acts, Kingston referred to a 'great, real, and legitimate success'.[300] The *Musical Standard* was the main detractor, detecting, in turns, too much Wagner, Auber, and Meyerbeer.[301] Sturgis's first libretto was also well received but after the long first performance substantial cuts were made leading to 'briskness being felt where at first a lagging sensation qualified the listener's pleasure'.[302] Despite these improvements the work did not hold the stage and was dropped from the Rosa's repertory after 1886. Nevertheless, Rosa commissioned a third work, this time for his short-lived light opera company, but Thomas committed suicide before the work was finished. Sydney Waddington completed *The Golden Web* and the Rosa's grand opera troupe produced it in 1893 (15 February, Liverpool).

Thomas, Vincent (1873–1940)

Eos and Gwevril

Premiere	18 April 1902, St George's Hall, London (London & Westminster Bank Orchestral Society)

Virtually nothing is known of Vincent Thomas; like fellow countryman Joseph Parry, he was especially interested in Welsh subjects. The performance of three operas before 1918 suggests ambition but his works were not taken up more widely. The music of *Eos and Gwevril* is untraced; the one substantive review contains no plot scenario and implies that the music was mainly conventional (referring to a 'too symmetrical, melodious type of vocal music') but commends 'a decided power of thematic invention' and the orchestral writing: 'a continuous commentary on the drama in the modern style'.[303]

299 *Academy*, 25 April 1885, p. 301.

300 *Theatre*, 1 May 1885, pp. 244–7 (p. 246).

301 *MS*, 25 April 1885, pp. 255–6.

302 *MW*, 2 May 1885, p. 274.

303 *MS*, 26 April 1902, p. 261. Thomas was employed by the London & Westminster Bank when the opera was premiered.

Gwenevere

Libretto	Ernest Rhys
Premiere	13 November 1905, Coronet Theatre, Notting Hill, London
Sources	Libretto: J M Dent (London, 1905)
Principal cast	Gwenevere – Aurélie Révy Morgan le Fay – Kathleen Maureen Arthur – Edward Iles Lancelot – Robert Cunningham Mordred – Frederick Ranalow Merlin – Whitney Tew
Synopsis	Three acts: Merlin brings Gwenevere to Camelot, where she marries Arthur, despite the opposition of Morgan and Mordred. Gwenevere is attracted to Lancelot, and when meeting in secret they are seen by Mordred, who betrays them; Merlin foresees doom. Arthur is wounded in battle; before he dies he forgives Lancelot and Gwenevere, who have both joined monastic orders. Arthur's body is taken to Avalon.

Thomas's second opera, the music of which is also untraced, was produced professionally, and attracted more attention than *Eos and Gwevril*. It was apparently conceived in the same vein as its predecessor, with the orchestra acting as a commentator on the stage action. Reviews were consistent, criticising a book lacking in dramatic incident and a score which suffered as a consequence: the *Musical Times* argued that Thomas 'would seem to have been paralysed by the strong lyrical element in Mr Rhys's book'.[304]

Enid

Libretto	Ernest Rhys
Premiere	24 November 1908, Court Theatre, London
Sources	Vocal score: Boosey & Co. (London, 1913)
Principal cast	Prince Geraint – Gwynne Davies Earl Doorm – Ian MacRobert Enid – Laura Evans

[304] *MT*, 1 December 1905, p. 809; see also *Era*, 18 November, p. 6; *Stage*, 16 November, p. 16.

Synopsis	Two acts: Doorm and Geraint are sworn enemies and the situation is exacerbated when Geraint prevents Doorm from marrying Enid. They settle their differences in a tournament in Cardiff; Geraint wins. Enid and Geraint grow close but he misunderstands her concern for Doorm and removes her from Cardiff. They are attacked by bandits and are brought back to the town, Geraint apparently dead. When Geraint hears Doorm once more declaring his love for Enid, he awakes and kills Doorm. The lovers are reconciled.

Thomas's third opera attracted still more attention despite an imperfect performance. The *Stage* referred to an 'especial talent for free and flowing melody,[305] while *The Times* declared *Enid* 'undoubtedly an improvement on its predecessor'.[306] There are structural faults: several incidents are reported rather than seen (the tournament, for example, takes place offstage while the audience sees Enid watching from her bedroom window) and Thomas remained wedded to a rather inflexible number-based structure and conventional tonal language, aside from occasional modal inflections. Thomas and Rhys produced a third Arthurian work, a two-act masque entitled *The Quest for the Grail* (Hampstead Conservatoire, 1914),[307] but Thomas subsequently focused on musical direction. A fourth opera, *A Tale of Alsatia*, was, however, scheduled for production in 1925 and *Enid* was broadcast by the BBC on 12 June 1937.[308]

Tolkien, Frederick

Adela

Libretto	Composer
Premiere	14 April 1897, Wigan, Court Theatre (Neilson Opera Company)
Source	Vocal Score: Ascherberg (London, 1895)[309]
Principal cast	Guillermo – Frank Reid Ricardo – Somers Grime Helena – Marie Alexander Adela – Marie Elster

305 *Stage*, 26 November 1908, p. 20

306 *The Times*, 25 November 1908, p. 14.

307 See *Stage*, 15 January 1914, p. 25.

308 See *Stage*, 5 February 1925, p. 13, and 10 June 1937, p. 8, respectively.

309 The only traced copy is substantially incomplete (BL, shelfmark G.937.p.(1.)).

Synopsis	Three acts; Seville, eighteenth century. Guillermo and Ricardo are both enamoured of Adela; both she and Helena are in love with Guillermo. Ricardo and Helena plot to imprison Guillermo by accusing him of theft; they succeed, but Helena, terminally ill, later confesses her falsehood. She dies; Guillermo is imprisoned and Ricardo released. Guillermo escapes but is unable to prevent Adela and Ricardo's marriage; Guillermo stabs himself.

Virtually nothing is known of Tolkien. *Adela* was allegedly taken up by Harris but his death prevented its production in London.[310] Tolkien's score is ambitious, and its structure influenced by Wagner and late Verdi, with some clearly delineated numbers but a predominance of free arioso passages; these are not always successful and the work lacks direction. Although securely tonal, there are some interesting harmonic devices but also some inept modulations. The *Stage* stated that 'the greater part of the music is, without doubt, excellent, but the libretto is feeble and commonplace'.[311] No further performances have been traced. Tolkien wrote at least two other operas before 1918: *For Love* (published 1898) does not appear to have been performed, and *Lola Descartes* (published 1912) was given by the O'Mara Company at Leeds in 1922.

Walter, Ida

Florian

Libretto	D. Latham and Grace Latham, after Margaret Roberts's *Scheiden thut Weh*
Premiere	14 July 1886, Novelty Theatre, London
Principal Cast	Florian – Ben Davies Crescenz – Miss Griswold
Synopsis	Four acts: medieval Germany. Florian has been appointed chief of the Wolfsdorf town musicians and has fallen in love with Crescenz, an innkeeper's daughter. While Florian is at a banquet, Crescenz takes food and drink to his musicians but they have contracted plague. Crescenz returns, infected, and collapses and dies in Florian's arms.

Ida Walter was a student at the Royal Academy and niece of John Walter, proprietor of *The Times*. The music is untraced and Walter is not known to have written any other stage works. Reviews, possibly condescending due to the composer's gender and social connections, were ambivalent. The *Graphic* stated

[310] Partial biographical information is given in a newspaper cutting attached to the vocal score of *Adela* (see previous note); this states that he was an autodidact, lived in Eastbourne, and pursued a career in business.

[311] *Stage*, 22 April 1897, p. 9; see also *Era*, 24 April, p. 11.

that Walter possessed 'the gift of melody, and the still rarer and more estimable virtue of unpretentious simplicity',[312] but the book was ridiculed in the *Era* as being 'almost destitute of dramatic qualities'.[313]

Webber, Amherst (1867–1946)

Fiorella

Libretto	Victorien Sardou and G.B. Ghensi
Premiere	7 June 1905, Waldorf Theatre, London
Source	Vocal Score: Enoch & Co (Paris, 1905)
Principal Cast	Fiorella – Mme de Cisneros Zerbina – Mlle Ferraris Don Agostino – Antonio Pini-Corsi Gattinara – Sig. Angelini-Fornari Cordiani – Sig. Pezzutti
Synopsis	One act: Venice, sixteenth century. Fiorella loves Cordiani, but her guardian Agostino bans her from seeing him as he has lost a fortune gambling. Zerbina, Fiorella's maid, enables a clandestine meeting between the lovers. She accidentally allows Gattinara, a brigand, to evade capture as he passes through the door Zerbina has left open for Cordiani. When Gattinara discovers that Cordiani lost his money to one of Gattinara's less scrupulous associates, he restores it. Agostino's opposition to Cordiani is removed and the lovers are free to marry.

Webber studied at Oxford, Dresden and Paris, and worked at Covent Garden.[314] *Fiorella* was originally intended for performance in Jean de Reszke's private theatre in Paris[315] but de Reszke allowed it to be performed in an opera season mounted to inaugurate the Waldorf Theatre. Webber was strongly influenced by Bizet and Massenet and the score is quite well-paced and constructed; the music flows quickly and fluently. Webber stated that 'the piece is rather on the lines of the old classical comic opera, and the music is in the same style … It had to be in proportion to the sentiment of the piece, which was, of course, light and humorous'.[316] The texture is driven by elegant vocal melody, but not at the expense of supporting texture: *The Times* commented that 'the orchestra is always going on

312 *Graphic*, 17 July 1886, p. 59.

313 *Era*, 17 July 1886, p. 12; see also *DN*, 16 July, p. 6.

314 He co-founded the Webber-Douglas School of Singing in 1926; this merged with the Central School of Speech and Drama in 2005.

315 *MS*, 17 June 1905, p. 378.

316 Ibid.

with fascinating little developments of figures'.[317] Although conceived as a *pièce d'occasion*, and somewhat derivative and deliberately un-innovative, *Fiorella* is an elegant piece and the music serves the drama well.

Table 6.1 Operas premiered in Britain and Ireland 1875–1918 in chronological order

Year	Composer	Opera
1876	Cowen	*Pauline*
1878	Parry	*Blodwen*
1879	Capes	*The Druid*
	Mallandaine	*Celia, the Gypsy Girl*
	Stanislaus	*The Lancashire Witches*
1881	Cellier	*The Masque of Pandora*
	Stanford	*The Veiled Prophet*
	McSwiney	*Amergen!*
1883	Thomas, A G	*Esmeralda*
	Edwards	*Victorian*
	Mackenzie	*Colomba*
	Skinner	*La Regina di Scozia*
	Farmer	*Cinderella*
1884	Stanford	*Savonarola*
	Stanford	*The Canterbury Pilgrims*
1885	Thomas, A G	*Nadeshda*
1886	MacKenzie	*The Troubadour*
	Walter	*Florian*
1887	Corder	*Nordisa*
	Cole	*A Romance of the Harem*
	Fox	*Robert Macaire*
	Old	*Herne*
1888	Selby	*Adela*
	Fox	*The Corsican Brothers*
1889	Cockle	*The Castle of Como*
	Philpot	*Dante and Beatrice*

[317] *The Times*, 8 June 1905, p. 10; see also *MT*, 1 July 1905, p. 476.

Year	Composer	Opera
1890	Cowen	*Thorgrim*
	Parry	*Arianwen*
	Philpot	*Zelica*
1891	Sullivan	*Ivanhoe*
1892	Fox	*Nydia*
	De Lara	*The Light of Asia*
	Bantock	*Caedmar*
1893	De Lara	*Amy Robsart*
	Cowen	*Signa*
	Edwards	*King René's Daughter*
1894	Moore	*The Magic Fountain*
	MacCunn	*Jeanie Deans*
1895	Davis	*The Zaporogues*
	Cowen	*Harold*
	Maclean	*Petruccio*
	Parry	*Sylvia*
	Philpot	*La Gitana*
1896	Stanford	*Shamus O'Brien*
	Collinge	*Grace Darrell*
	Nicholls	*A Prodigal Son*
1897	De Lara	*Moïna*
	Tolkien	*Adela*
	D'Erlanger	*Inès Mendo*
	Somerville	*The Prentice Pillar*
	MacCunn	*Diarmid*
	MacAlpin	*King Arthur*
1898	Smyth	*Fantasio*
	Sullivan	*The Beauty Stone*
	Drysdale	*The Red Spider*
1899	De Lara	*Messaline*
	Somerville	*The Three Musketeers*
	Farjeon	*Floretta*
1901	Stanford	*Much Ado About Nothing*
1902	Esposito	*The Post Bag*

Year	Composer	Opera
	Smyth	*Der Wald*
	Thomas, V	*Eos and Gwevril*
	Bunning	*La Princesse Osra*
	Parry	*The Maid of Cefn-Ydfa*
1903	Pelissier	*Connla of the Golden Hair*
	Pritchard	*Kunacepa*
	MacAlpin	*The Cross and the Crescent*
	Butler	*Muirgheis*
1904	Delius	*Koanga*
	Maclean	*The King's Prize*
1905	Webber	*Fiorella*
	Thomas, V	*Gwenevere*
1906	De Lara	*Sanga*
	Gatty	*Greysteel*
	D'Erlanger	*Tess*
	Maclean	*Die Liebesgeige*
	Smyth	*The Wreckers*
1907	Philpot	*Nigel*
	Delius	*Romeo und Juliet auf dem Dorfe*
	Löhr	*Sarenna*
	De Lara	*Soléa*
1908	Edwards	*The Patriot*
	Thomas, V	*Enid*
1909	Naylor	*The Angelus*
	O'Donnell	*The Demon's Bride*
	Holbrooke	*Pierrot and Pierette*
	Gatty	*Duke or Devil?*
1910	Esposito	*The Tinker and the Fairy*
	O'Dwyer	*Eithne*
	Clutsam	*A Summer Night*
	Maddison	*Der Talisman*
	D'Erlanger	*Noël*
1911	De Lara	*Les Trois Masques*
	Klein	*Bow Sing*

Year	Composer	Opera
1912	De Lara	*Naïl*
	Holbrooke	*The Children of Don*
	Clutsam	*King Harlequin*
1913	Rôze	*Joan of Arc*
	Knox	*Giuliana*
	Miles	*Westward Ho!*
1914	Rendle	*The Traitress*
	Hervey	*Ilona*
	Mackenzie	*The Cricket on the Hearth*
	Holbrooke	*Dylan, Son of the Wave*
	Boughton	*The Immortal Hour*
1915	MacAlpin	*The Vow*
	Bainton	*Oithona*
	Boughton	*Bethlehem*
	Lehmann	*Everyman*
1916	Frewin	*The Gay Lothario*
	Barkworth	*Romeo and Juliet*
	Stanford	*The Critic*
	Smyth	*The Boatswain's Mate*
	Boughton	*The Round Table*
	Raybould	*The Sumida River*
	Holst	*Sāvitri*
1918	Lyon	*Storm Wrack*
	Price	*The Nuns of Ardboe*

Chapter 7

Epilogue: Opera in the British Isles in 1918

At the signing of the armistice in 1918 the operatic culture of the British Isles was, to a large extent, little changed from 40 years earlier. It would be wrong to infer from this that the United Kingdom had experienced 40 years of stasis but, in terms of organisational structures, public engagement with the genre, and composer achievement, there had been little radical change or development; rather, 'progress' had been incremental and reactive rather than pro-active. Those involved had, for the greater part, been carried along by wider tides of change – social, economic, and musical – rather than shaping them themselves. When there were moments of transformative pressure from within, there was neither the collective consensus or support nor the presence of sufficiently charismatic and indomitable individuals to make substantial or irrevocable changes.

In respect of opera performances, the West End of London saw the greatest fluidity throughout this period with instances both of extreme brilliance and total disaster. After decades of elite internationalism, the war years witnessed a change in provision that was welcomed by many commentators: opera in English finally dominated the West End, while Covent Garden's exclusive and cosmopolitan approach was in abeyance. Thomas Beecham's seasons in particular were taken as proof that the London audience would, after a little cajoling through force of circumstance to get them through the theatre doors, embrace opera in the vernacular if it was well produced. Commentators at least hoped that this finally heralded the end of international seasons led by expensive star singers playing to a socially exclusive audience which, in turn, both dominated and undermined the rest of the nation's operatic culture. They were to be disappointed: the war years turned out to be an incremental shift rather than the fundamental change many had anticipated. In 1919 Beecham rejoined a reactivated Grand Opera Syndicate for a traditional early summer season at Covent Garden. Although for some years subsequently things failed to run smoothly and new enterprises, most notably the British National Opera Company, endeavoured further to embed vernacular opera in the West End, the aspiration to hold the traditional, international season based on the model managed by Harris 30 years earlier proved resilient and, although the 1920s and '30s proved to be years of instability and further change, this preference remained deeply ingrained. Conversely, touring companies still found the West End a challenging environment in which to operate and were cautious about venturing there. In essence, therefore, the situation in the West End in 1918 was not dissimilar to that of 1875: the organisational structures and business models remained fundamentally the same and, consequently, development was slow and change marginal. The fundamental ethos, that the West End reacted to developments in Europe rather than trying to lead them, remained dominant throughout.

Beyond central London, the war had not turned into the calamity for the touring companies that many had feared. Although they endured many difficulties, most obviously the increasing shortage of male performers, the troupes proved remarkably resilient, supported by a public that in many instances embraced entertainment more fully than it had in peace-time. While the Moody-Manners Company was a high-profile casualty of the war, most touring companies carried on, allowing for various mergers and reorganisations, as they had done previously. In 1918, touring troupes were almost as active as they had been five years previously. The approach they adapted, however, was one of continuity and stability. The organisational structures, provision and consumption of opera in the provinces – in all senses: location and frequency of visits, repertory, performance standards, and attendances – remained essentially the same in 1920 as in 1890. It was in the years immediately preceding the war that the touring troupes reached their zenith both in size and scope. In the post-war period, the advent of radio broadcasts and the rapidly increasing popularity of cinema started to erode the support networks the companies had built up over decades and maintained even through the war.

In terms of repertory, British opera companies remained largely reactive and inclined to follow dominant continental trends. It was still largely the case that operas were only performed in Britain after they had been successful elsewhere. Although the West End repertory of the Edwardian years included works which brought entirely new sound-worlds to London, such as Debussy's *Pelléas et Mélisande* and Strauss's *Salome*, the business model did not encourage daring innovation. As in the case of opera during the Great War, perhaps the greatest amount of courage can be attributed to Thomas and Joseph Beecham, who promoted Russian opera (and ballet) in the early 1910s, but even this was not an original act, singers such as Chaliapin having appeared in Europeans opera houses and in New York before arriving in London. Similarly, the production of Strauss's operas, for all the controversy and interest they generated, followed rather than led European culture. Such events do, however, demonstrate that the companies operating in the West End had become less conservative in their outlook, and were prepared to embrace new continental works far more readily than had previously been the case: operas by Puccini, Strauss and others appeared in London within two or three years of their continental premieres, compared to the far longer lapses that frequently occurred during the 1870s and '80s. While one might speculate that such performances were driven by a desire to be seen to be fashionable rather than by profound cultural and intellectual engagement (the production by the Grand Opera Syndicate of *Parsifal* in spring 1914 just about as early as was legally and practically possible is one event that suggests this), the appearance of so many new operas, coupled with rising production standards, undoubtedly meant that London retained its status as one of Europe's leading operatic centres. Outside London the repertory remained confined and largely static, the high profile but transient activities of such men as Beecham, Quinlan and Denhof apart. For provincial audience members – who formed the overwhelming majority of the nation's opera-goers – a one-week visit by a touring company in 1918 would include as many works that they would have seen in 1875 as new ones, and the operas added to the core repertory, such as *Carmen*, *Cavalleria Rusticana* and *Madama Butterfly*, were clear continuations of the musical styles to which audiences were accustomed. Although Wagner too had been taken up by many touring companies from the 1890s onwards, it was the early Wagner of *Tannhäuser* and *Lohengrin*, rather than the later Wagner of *Tristan und Isolde* or even *Die Meistersinger*. In short, the touring companies' organisational and financial structures, and much of the provincial audience's relatively infrequent exposure to opera encouraged practical and ideological caution and a preference for the familiar; only on a few occasions did more radical departures succeed, such as in Beecham's performances of Russian operas in Manchester and elsewhere during the war years.

That further change was not achieved was principally attributable to a static business model. Throughout the country, opera continued to be organised on a purely commercial basis and it remained a high-risk venture. Occasionally individual companies achieved a lucrative success but, for much the greater part, existence was precarious and a 'safety first' mentality inevitably dominated. At Covent Garden, where the Grand Opera Syndicate did consistently good business, returns for investors appear to have been prioritised over artistic innovation, unless there was sufficient pressure from well-connected subscribers to act otherwise – but while this led, for example, to the rapid arrival of Puccini's operas in London, the undoubted hostility of the same people to almost all native composers ensured that British music was virtually excluded from Covent Garden throughout the Syndicate's tenure. For those parties seeking a more dynamic and adventurous model of opera production, particularly in respect of native works, the foundation of a national opera house became a both a fundamental and emblematic means of achieving it. The objectives and potential benefits laid down for such an institution were wholly unrealistic but were also, in any case, irrelevant, as there was never a substantive likelihood that a national opera house would be established, due to a consistently unsympathetic political environment. Lobbying for its foundation came primarily from a small London-based professional elite that never succeeded in building up a larger support base or in winning the intellectual argument in favour of the financial support necessary to run such an enterprise. Neither did the advocates of a national opera (nor the campaigners working to establish a national theatre) manage to overcome the perception that the performing arts and, especially, those that were theatre-based, were more about entertainment than edification or improvement, even though these last aspects had been the justification in some municipalities for modest support of concerts and organ recitals, and had also been widely accepted in respect of museums, art galleries and libraries. Despite persistent campaigning, public financial support for the performing arts was only established on a permanent peacetime basis by the foundation of the Arts Council of Great Britain in 1946. The equivalent organisation in the Republic of Ireland was established in 1951.

For British composers too, the environment remained challenging. Although the number of new works premiered, as listed in Chapter 6, is far from insignificant, and greater than most subsequent commentators have acknowledged, it can hardly be deemed a cohesive corpus, still less a tradition. Disincentives to opera composition were powerful: financial rewards for such massive undertakings were slight at best and wholly unpredictable. An unknown number of works never reached the stage and many that did were performed only once or twice before being discarded. Opportunities in other genres were greater in number and more promising in outlook; the lack of change in organisational structures within British opera throughout this period constantly reinforced that basic truism. The perception that opera composition was more trouble than it was worth was reinforced in all manner of ways. The music colleges, for example, did not promote opera within their curricula. The Royal Academy was more progressive than the Royal College, as the performance of several student works noted in Chapter 6 shows, but still unsystematic. Stanford, despite his personal enthusiasm for the genre, appears never to have incorporated composing for the stage into his teaching at the Royal College, while composition teaching in the universities remained fundamentally focused on producing sacred choral music. The basic hostility of Covent Garden to native composers was also a disincentive, especially as there were no other regular fora in central London for the performance of new works. While the Rosa and Moody-Manners troupes in particular premiered several British operas, their inability to retain them in their repertories for extended periods, together with long absences from central London, did not provide composers with the encouragement needed for sustained production of new works. In this sense, the presence of a national opera house, even though it could not possibly have satiated the demand for new productions that certainly would have been placed upon it, might have encouraged British composers to more persistent efforts through which individuals' techniques could have developed, and enabled more systematic learning through appraising the works of others and exchanging ideas. It is unsurprising therefore that, in the absence of opportunities, most composers chose to focus on other genres. A small number, who had steadily cultivated international connections, looked overseas for alternative production opportunities but this was a minority activity and never feasible for most British composers.

As discussed in Chapter 5, it was not just a lack of opportunity that hampered the composition of new operas. The lack of an established form and style, and the absence of a critical consensus as to how a representative British opera might look and sound, persistently handicapped aspiring composers. The rejection of the mid-century English Romantic tradition of Balfe, Wallace and Benedict, on the grounds that it was too sentimental, vapid, and unambitious, reinforced by its apparent adoption as a model by the emerging light opera genre, removed the only approach that might be viewed as indigenous. In the absence of a widely accepted replacement, British operas composed after 1875 exhibited a diffuse and essentially derivative range of styles, forms and methods, none of which inspired a strong enough sense that first-night critics and audiences had seen something that was both distinctive and likely to prove popular. There was neither a sufficient level of compositional activity, nor a strong enough sense of shared purpose to achieve this consensus. This is not to say that no worthy operas were produced: several works were characterised by interesting and impressive music, credible drama, and overall cohesion. In practical terms, however, the challenges presented by opera production have always made it the most difficult musical genre in which to stage revivals of neglected works, especially those which were not acclaimed at the time.

The story of opera in Britain between 1875 and 1918 is one of mixed fortunes. On the positive side, more people had more opportunities to see opera than at any time previously and, almost certainly, than at any time since; the United Kingdom was certainly not 'das Land ohne Oper'. The West End maintained at least one internationally recognised opera house throughout the period which, especially after 1887, played a large repertory of works and employed many of the leading performers of the time while, outside central London, touring companies travelled around the country bringing performances within the reach of the majority of people who lived in or near towns of significant size. That these performance networks endured in a challenging commercial environment suggests that theatre-goers maintained a persistent interest in the genre. On the negative side, performance standards were often indifferent, and repertory restricted; the lack of adequate supporting structures hampered the establishment of a canon of contemporaneous works as composers found it difficult to get their works on stage and to keep them there, as did a fundamentally reactive approach to repertory. Despite frequent aspirations otherwise, Britain's operatic culture remained indebted to activities in mainland Europe but the nation's producers and consumers also became increasingly conscious of this fact. In this period, therefore, fundamental change may have been only gradual, but the interest in opera was never abandoned, and its presence in the national conscience raised. The structures established in the late nineteenth century continued in use for many years after 1918, just as the ideological and aesthetic issues raised in the Victorian years continued to be debated. Their individual and combined impacts continue to be felt a century later.

Bibliography

Autograph and Archival Sources

Autograph manuscripts of operas are given in the relevant entries in Chapter 6.
Correspondence of Rutland Boughton: BL, Add MSS 52364–6.
Archive of Brett and L'Estrange (solicitors): Public Records Office Northern Ireland (Belfast), deposit D1326/25/3.
Archive of the Carl Rosa Opera Company: Liverpool Central Library.
Diaries of Frederick Gye: ROHA.
Papers of Hamish MacCunn: Glasgow University Library.
Archive of the Moody-Manners Opera Company: Glasgow City Archives.
Correspondence of Percy Pitt: BL, Egerton MSS 3301–06.
Archive of the Theatre Royal, Huddersfield: WYAS, B/HTR.

Published Sources

British Opera in Retrospect (London: British Music Society, 1985)
The English Opera Association (Limited) (London: [publisher unknown] 1864/5?).
The History of the Theatre Royal, Dublin (Dublin: [publisher unknown], 1870).
Minutes of the Metropolitan Board of Works January–June 1877 (London: Judd & Co., 1877).
Minutes of the Metropolitan Board of Works July–December 1882 (London: Judd & Co., 1882).
Select Committee on Theatres and Places of Entertainment with proceedings, minutes of evidence, appendix and index, British Parliamentary Papers Report, 1892 (reprinted Shannon: Irish University Press, 1970).
Select Committee on Theatrical Licences and Regulations with proceedings, minutes of evidence, appendix and index, British Parliamentary Papers Report, 1866 (reprinted Shannon: Irish University Press, 1970).
Abromeit, Kathleen, 'Ethel Smyth, *The Wreckers*, and Sir Thomas Beecham', *Musical Quarterly*, 78 (1989), 196–211.
Albani, Emma, *Forty Years of Song* (London: Mills & Boon, 1911).
Arditi, Luigi, *My Reminiscences* (London: Skeffington, 1896).
Aspden, Suzanne, 'Ballads and Britons: Imagined Community and the Continuity of "English Opera"', *Journal of the Royal Musical Association*, 122 (1997), 24–51.
Baker, J. Percy, 'Sir Alexander Mackenzie and his work at the Royal Academy of Music, London', *Musical Quarterly*, 13 (1927), 14–28.

Bax, Arnold, *Farewell My Youth* (London: Longmans & Co., 1943).
Beale, Thomas Willert, *The Light of Other Days Seen Through the Wrong End of an Opera Glass*, (London: Bentley, 1890).
Beecham, Thomas, *A Mingled Chime* (London: Hutchinson & Co., 1944).
Bennett, Joseph, *Forty Years of Music* (London: Methuen & Co., 1908).
Benson, E.F., *As we were: a Victorian peep-show* (London: Longmans, Green & Co, 1930).
Biddlecombe, George, *English Opera from 1834 to 1864 with particular reference to the works of Michael Balfe* (New York: Garland, 1994).
Bispham, David, *A Quaker Singer's Recollections* (New York: Macmillan, 1920).
Blackwell, Michael, *Theatre Royal Norwich: the first 250 years* ([UK]: Connaught, 2007)
Bledsoe, R.T., *Henry Fothergill Chorley: Victorian Journalist* (Aldershot: Ashgate, 1998).
Boosey, William, *Fifty Years of Music* (London: Ernest Benn, 1931).
Booth, Michael R., *Theatre in the Victorian Age* (Cambridge: Cambridge University Press, 1991).
Boughton, Rutland, *Music Drama of the Future* (London: William Reeves, 1911).
Brown, James, and Stratton, Stephen, *British Musical Biography* (Birmingham: S.S. Stratton 1897; reprinted New York: Da Capo Press, 1971).
Bunn, Alfred, *The Stage: both before and behind the curtain* (3 vols, London: Richard Bentley, 1840).
Caird, William, 'A Plea for National and Municipal Theatres', *Westminster Review*, 179 (1913), 562–74.
Cavanagh, John, *British Theatre: A Bibliography 1901–85* (Mottisfont, Hants.: Motley Press, 1989).
Chadwick, Stanley, *Theatre Royal: The Romance of the Huddersfield Stage* (Huddersfield: The Advertiser Press, 1941).
Chamier, Jacques Daniel, *Percy Pitt of Covent Garden and the BBC* (London: Edward Arnold, 1938).
Chapman, Raymond, *The Sense of the Past in Victorian Literature* (London: Croom Helm, 1986).
Clericus, M.A. [alias for Rev Richard Hibbs], *Remarks on the Italian Opera in Edinburgh with reference to Dr Guthrie's proposal* (Edinburgh: W P Guthrie, 1854).
Colles, Henry, and Cruft, John, *Royal College of Music: A Centenary Record 1883–1983* (London: Royal College of Music, 1982).
Corder, Frederick, *A History of the Royal Academy of Music 1822–1922* (London, 1922).
Courtneidge, Robert, *I Was an Actor Once* (London: Hutchinson, 1930).
Cowden, Robert, *Concert and Opera singers: A Bibliography of Bibliographical Research Materials* (Westport, CT: Greenwood Press, 1985).
Cowgill, Rachel and Holman, Peter (eds), *Music in the British Provinces 1690–1914* (Aldershot: Ashgate, 2007).

Cowgill, Rachel, Cooper, David, and Brown, Clive (eds), *Art and Ideology in European Opera* (Woodbridge: Boydell, 2010).
Cowgill, Rachel and Poriss, Hilary (eds), *The Arts of the Prima Donna in the Long Nineteenth Century* (Oxford: Oxford University Press, 2012).
Cowen, Frederic, *My Art and My Friends* (London: Edward Arnold, 1913).
Cox, Gareth, and Klein, Axel (eds), *Irish Music in the Twentieth Century (Irish Musical Studies 7)* (Dublin: Four Courts, 2003).
Crowest, Frederick, 'English Opera *in nubibus*', *National Review*, 12 (1888), 185–201.
Cunningham, John E., *Theatre Royal: The History of the Theatre Royal, Birmingham* (Oxford: George Ronald, 1950).
Dailey, Jeff S., *Sir Arthur Sullivan's Grand Opera* Ivanhoe *and its Theatrical and Musical Precursors* (New York: Edwin Mellen Press, 2008).
Damrosch, Walter, *My Musical Life* (New York: Charles Scribner, 1923).
Davis, Tracy C., *The Economics of the British Stage 1880–1914* (Cambridge: Cambridge University Press, 2000).
De Lara, Isidore, *Many Tales of Many Cities* (London: Hutchinson & Co., 1928).
Dent Edward, ed. Hugh Taylor, *Selected Essays* (Cambridge: Cambridge University Press, 1979).
Dibble, Jeremy, *C. Hubert H. Parry: His Life and Music* (Oxford: Oxford University Press, 1992).
Dibble, Jeremy, and Zon, Bennett (eds), *Nineteenth-Century British Music Studies*, Volume 2 (Aldershot: Ashgate, 2002).
Dibble, Jeremy, *Charles Villiers Stanford: Man and Musician* (Oxford: Oxford University Press, 2002).
Dibble, Jeremy, *Michele Esposito* (Dublin: Field Day, 2010).
Dideriksen, Gabrielle, and Ringel, Matthew, 'Frederick Gye and "The dreadful business of opera management"', *Nineteenth Century Music*, 19 (1995–96), 3–30.
Dunhill, Thomas, 'Charles Villiers Stanford: Some Aspects of his Work and Influence', *Proceedings of the Royal Musical Association*, 42 (1927), 41–65.
Eames, Emma, *Some Memories and Reflections* (New York: Appleton & Co., 1927).
Eaton, Quaintance, *The Boston Opera Company* (New York: Appleton Century, 1965).
Eden, David, and Saremba, Meinhard, *The Cambridge Companion to Gilbert and Sullivan* (Cambridge: Cambridge University Press, 2009).
Edwards, Owain Tudor, *Joseph Parry 1841–1903* (Cardiff: Gwasg Prifysgol Cymru, 1970).
Evans, Hilary, and Evans, Mary, *The Party that lasted 100 days: The Late Victorian Season; A Social Study* (London: Macdonald and Jane's, 1976).
Fifield, Christopher, *True Artist and True Friend: a Biography of Hans Richter* (Oxford: Clarendon Press 1993).
Fitzgerald, Percy, *A World Behind the Scenes* (London: Chatto & Windus, 1881).

Forbes, Anne-Marie, 'Celticism in British Opera 1878–1938', *Music Review*, 47 (1986–87), 176–83.

Forbes, Anne-Marie, 'Josef Holbrooke's *Cauldron of Annwn* and metempsychosis in music', *Musicology Australia*, 17 (1994), 43–59.

Foreman, Lewis, *From Parry to Britten: British Music in Letters 1900–45* (London: Batsford, 1987).

Forsyth, Cecil, *Music and Nationalism: A study of English Opera* (London: MacMillan, 1911).

Foulkes, Richard, *Church and Stage in Victorian England* (Cambridge: Cambridge University Press, 1997).

Fuller, Sophie, *The Pandora Guide to Women Composers: Britain and the United States, 1629–present* (London: Pandora, 1994).

Galloway, William J., *The Operatic Problem* (London: Long, 1902).

Galloway, William J., *Musical England* (London: Christophers, 1910).

Gänzl, Kurt, *British Musical Theatre* (2 vols, London and Basingstoke: Macmillan, 1986).

Gänzl, Kurt, *The Encyclopaedia of the Musical Theatre* (New York: Schirmer 1994).

Gatens, William, 'John Ruskin and Music', *Victorian Studies*, 30 (1986), 77–97.

Gilbert, Susie, *Opera for Everybody* (London: Faber and Faber, 2009).

Glover, James, *Jimmy Glover, His Book* (London: Methuen & Co., 1911).

Goddard, Joseph, *The Rise and Development of Opera* (London: William Reeves, 1911).

Godwin, George, *On the desirability of obtaining a National Theatre not wholly controlled by the prevailing public taste* (London: Wyman & Sons, 1878).

Goossens, Eugene, *Overtures and Beginners: A Musical Autobiography* (London: Methuen & Co., 1951).

Graves, Perceval, 'The Moody-Manners Partnership', *Opera*, 9 (1958), 558–64.

Greene, Harry Plunket, *Charles Villiers Stanford* (London: Edward Arnold & Co., 1935).

Gruneisen, Charles, 'The Opera Season of 1870', *Era Almanack 1871*, 16–22.

Gyger, Alison, *Opera for the Antipodes: Opera in Australia 1881–1939* (Sydney: Currency and Pellinor, 1990).

Hadden, J. Cuthbert, 'The Question of Subsidised Opera', *Gentlemen's Magazine*, 298 (1905), 295–304.

Hall-Witt, Jennifer, *Fashionable acts: Opera and elite culture in London 1780–1880* (Durham, NH, and London: University of New Hampshire Press, 2007).

Harcourt, Bosworth, *Theatre Royal, Chronicles of an old playhouse* (Norwich: Norfolk New Company, 1903).

Harris, Augustus, 'The Opera in England: Some Notes and Reminiscences', *New Review*, 9 (1893), 257–67 and 343–52.

Hauger, George, 'Stanford's Early Operas', *Opera*, 35 (1984), 724–9.

Hauger, George, 'Cowen and English Opera', *Opera*, 29 (1978), 863–8.

Hauk, Minnie [Baroness de Wartegg], *Memories of a Singer* (London: A.M. Philpot, 1925).

Haweis, Hugh R., *Music and Morals* (London: [no publisher], 1871).

Hawkins, Desmond, *The Tess Opera* (Taunton: Thomas Hardy Society (Monograph No. 3), 1984).

Hodgart, Matthew, and Bauerle, Ruth, *Joyce's Grand Operoar: Opera in* Finnegan's Wake (Urbana, IL: University of Illinois Press, 1997).

Howells, Herbert, 'Address to the Royal Musical Association on the Centenary of Stanford's Birth', *Proceedings of the Royal Musical Association*, 80 (1952–53), 19–31.

Howes, Frank, *The English Musical Renaissance* (London: Secker & Warburg, 1966).

Hueffer, Francis, 'The chances of English opera', *Macmillan's Magazine*, 40 (1879), 57–65.

Hueffer, Francis, *Half a Century of Music in England 1837–1887: Essays Towards a History* (London: Chapman & Hall, 1889).

Hughes, Gervase, *Sidelights on a century of music 1825–1924* (London: Macdonald & Co., 1969).

Hughes, Meirion, *The English Musical Renaissance and the Press 1850–1914: Watchmen of Music* (Aldershot: Ashgate, 2002).

Hurd, Michael, *Rutland Boughton and the Glastonbury Festivals*, (New York: Oxford University Press, 1993).

Hurst, P.G., *The Age of Jean de Reszke (Forty Years of Opera 1874–1914)* (London: Christopher Johnson, 1958).

Hutchinson, John, *The Dynamics of Cultural Nationalism* (London: Allen & Unwin, 1987).

Hutton, Arthur, 'A National Opera House', *Contemporary Review*, 68 (1895), 58–64.

Hynes, Samuel, *A War Imagined – The First World War and English Culture* (London: Pimlico, 1990).

Jacobs, Arthur, *Arthur Sullivan: A Victorian Musician* (Oxford: Oxford University Press, 1984).

Kertesz, Elizabeth, 'The Germanness of English Music: Reflections on the Critical Reception of Ethel Smyth's *Der Wald*' in Brenton Broadstock (ed.) *Aflame with Music: 100 Years of Music at University of Melbourne* (Melbourne, Australia: University of Melbourne, 1996).

Kingston, William Beatty, *Music and Manners: Personal Reminiscences and Sketches of Character* (2 vols, London: Chapman & Hall, 1887).

Klein, Axel, 'Stage Irish, or the National in Irish Opera, 1780–1925', *Opera Quarterly*, 21 (2005), 27–67.

Klein, Axel, 'Celtic Legends in Irish opera 1900–1930', *Harvard Celtic Colloquium*, 24/25 (2004–05), 40–53.

Klein, Herman, *Musical Notes 1888* (London and New York: Novello, Ewer & Co, 1889).

Klein, Herman, *Thirty Years of Musical Life in London 1870–1900* (London: Heinemann, 1903).
Klein, Herman, *The reign of Patti*, (London: Fisher Unwin, 1920).
Klein, Herman, *Musicians and Mummers* (London: Cassell & Co., 1925).
Klein, Herman, *The Golden Age of Opera*, (London: Routledge & Sons, 1933).
Klein, John W., 'Tragic forgotten pioneer: Arthur Goring Thomas', *Music Review*, 36 (1975), 180–86.
Knowles, Sebastian G.D. (ed.), *Bronze by Gold: The Music of Joyce* (New York: Garland, 1999).
Lamb, Andrew, '*Ivanhoe* and the Royal English Opera', *Musical Times*, 104 (1973), 475–8.
Ledbetter, Gordon, *The Great Irish Tenor: John McCormack* (Dublin: Town House, 2003).
Lehmann, Lilli (trans. Alice Seligmann), *My Path Through Life* (London: G.P. Putnam's Sons, 1914).
Lehmann, Liza, *The Life of Liza Lehmann by Herself* (London: Fisher Unwin, 1919).
Leiser, Clara, *Jean de Reszke and the Great Days of Opera*, (London: Gerard Howe, 1933).
Levey, R.M., *Annals of the Theatre Royal, Dublin* (Dublin: Joseph Dollard, 1880).
Levy, Lawrence, *Birmingham Theatrical Reminiscences* (Birmingham: J.G. Hammond, 1922).
Lowe, George, *Josef Holbrooke and his Work* (London: Kegan Paul, Trench & Trubner, 1920).
Lowerson, John, *Amateur Operatics: A social and cultural history* (Manchester: Manchester University Press, 2005).
Lubbeck, Percy, and Benson, Arthur, 'Julian Sturgis', *Monthly Review*, 16 (1904), 111–24.
Lucas, John, *Thomas Beecham: An Obsession with Music* (Woodbridge: Boydell Press, 2008).
McCann, Wesley, *H.B. Phillips Impresario: The Man who Brought McCormack, Kreisler and Robeson to Derry* (Belfast: Belfast Society in association with the Ulster Historical Foundation, 2001).
Mackenzie, Alexander, 'The Aspects and Prospects of Music in England', *Quarterly Musical Review*, 3 (February 1887), 38–50.
Mackenzie, Alexander, *A Musician's Narrative* (London: Cassell & Co, 1927).
Maclean, Charles, 'Sullivan as a National Style Builder', *Proceedings of the Musical Association*, 28 (1901–02), 89–104.
Macqueen-Pope, W.J., *Theatre Royal, Drury Lane* (London: W.H. Allen, 1945).
Maitland, John Fuller, 'Wanted – An Opera', *Nineteenth Century*, 43 (1898), 977–84.
Maitland, John Fuller, *Grove's Dictionary of Music and Musicians* (5 vols, 2nd ed., London: Macmillan & Co., 1902).

Maitland, John Fuller, *English Music in the Nineteenth Century* (London: Grant Richards, 1902).

Maitland, John Fuller, 'Music versus the Opera', *Nineteenth Century and After*, 51 (1902), 112–22.

Maitland, John Fuller, *A Doorkeeper of Music* (London: John Murray, 1929).

Maitland, John Fuller, *The Music of Parry and Stanford* (Cambridge: W. Heffer & Sons, 1934).

Mapleson, James H., *The Mapleson Memoirs 1848–1888* (2 vols, London: Remington, 1888).

Marwick, Arthur, *The Deluge: British Society and the First World War*, (Basingstoke: Macmillan, 1991).

Maynard, Walter [alias of Thomas Willert Beale], *The Entertaining Impresario* (London: Bradbury, Evans & Co., 1867).

Mensiaux, Marie de, *Trebelli: A Biographical Sketch and Reminiscences of Her Life* (London: Henry Potter, 1890).

Mitchell, Jerome, *The Walter Scott Operas* (Birmingham, AL: University of Alabama Press, 1977).

Mitchell, Jerome, *More Scott Operas* (Lanham, MD: University Press of America, 1996).

Money, Keith, *Anna Pavlova: Her Life and Art* (New York: Knopf, 1982).

Neilson, Francis, *My Life in Two Worlds* (Appleton, WI: C.C. Nelson, 1952–53).

Norris, Christopher, *Music and the Politics of Culture* (London: Lawrence & Wishart, 1989).

Northouse, Cameron, *Twentieth-Century Opera in England and the United States* (Boston: G.K. Hall, 1976).

Parry, Hubert, *Style in Musical Art* (London: Macmillan, 1911).

Pater, Walter, *The Renaissance: Studies in art and poetry* (2nd ed., London: Macmillan & Co., 1888).

Pemberton, Edgar, *The Theatre Royal, Birmingham, 1774–1901* (Birmingham: [no publisher], 1901).

Pine, Richard (ed.), *Music in Ireland 1848–1998* (Cork: The Mercier Press, 1999).

Pirie, Peter, *The English Musical Renaissance* (London: Gollancz, 1979).

Planché, J.R., *Suggestions for establishing an English art theatre* (London: Wyman, 1879).

Potterton, Robert, 'Joseph O'Mara', *North Munster Antiquarian Journal*, 1990 (23), 83–95.

Reid, C., *The Music Monster: A Biography of James William Davison, Music Critic of* The Times *of London* (London: Quartet, 1984).

Rémo, Félix, trans. A.J. Robertson, *Music in the Land of Fogs* (London: Kent and Co., 1887).

Rhodes, R. Crompton, *The Theatre Royal, Birmingham* (Birmingham: Moody Brothers, 1924).

Riviere, Jules, *My Musical Life and Recollections* (London: Sampson Low, Marston, 1893).

Roberts, Peter, *The Old Vic Story: A Nation's Theatre 1818–1976* (London: W.H. Allen, 1976).

Rodmell, Paul, 'A Tale of Two Operas: Stanford's *Savonarola* and *The Canterbury Pilgrims* from Gestation to Production', *Music and Letters*, 78 (1997), 77–91.

Rodmell, Paul, *Charles Villiers Stanford* (Aldershot: Ashgate 2002).

Rodmell, Paul, '"The Italians are Coming": Opera in mid-Victorian Dublin', in Rachel Cowgill and Julian Rushton (eds), *Europe, Empire and Spectacle in Nineteenth Century British Music* (Aldershot: Ashgate 2006).

Rodmell, Paul (ed.), *Music and Institutions in Nineteenth-Century Britain* (Aldershot: Ashgate, 2012).

Rosa, Carl, 'English Opera', *Murray's Magazine*, 1 (1887), 460–70.

Rosenthal, Harold, *Two Centuries of Opera at Covent Garden* (London: Putnam, 1958).

Rosenthal, Harold, 'The Carl Rosa Story', *Opera*, 18 (1967), 272–8; 460–64; 547–50; 719–26.

Rowell, George, *The Old Vic Theatre: A History* (Cambridge: Cambridge University Press 1993).

Rutherford, Susan, *The Prima Donna and Opera* (Cambridge: Cambridge University Press, 2006).

Sachs, Edwin O., and Woodrow, Ernest A.E., *Modern Opera Houses and Theatres* (3 vols, London: B.T. Batsford, 1896–98).

Santley, Charles, *Reminiscences of My Life* (London: Pitman & Sons, 1909).

Scott, Hugh Arthur, 'Against a Subsidised Opera', *Nineteenth Century and After*, 55 (1904), 752–64.

Scowcroft, Philip, *British Light Music* (London: Thames, 1997).

Shaw, George Bernard, *Music in London 1890–94* (3 vols, New York: Vienna House, 1973).

Shaw, George Bernard, *London Music in 1888–89 as heard by Corno di Bassetto* (New York: Vienna House, 1973).

Sheehan, Vincent, *The Amazing Oscar Hammerstein* (New York: Simon & Schuster, 1956).

Sheldon, A.J., *Notes on Rutland Boughton's* The Immortal Hour (Birmingham: Cornish Brothers, 1922).

Sheppard, F.H.W. (gen. ed.), *Survey of London: Volume XXXV. The Theatre Royal, Drury Lane and the Royal Opera House Covent Garden* (London: Athlone Press, 1970).

Short, Michael, *Gustav Holst: The Man and His Music* (New York: Oxford University Press, 1990).

Smyth, Ethel, *What Happened Next* (London: Longmans & Co, 1940).

Stanford, Charles, *Pages from an Unwritten Diary* (London: Edward Arnold, 1914)

Stanford, Charles Villiers, *Studies and Memories* (London: Archibald Constable, 1908).

Stockdale, Freddie, *Emperors of Song: Three Great Impresarios* (London: J. Murray, 1998).

Stradling, Robert, and Hughes, Merion, *The British Musical Renaissance: Construction and Deconstruction* (2nd ed., Manchester: Manchester University Press, 2001).

Taylor, George, *Players and Performance in the Victorian Theatre* (Manchester & New York: Manchester University Press, 1989).

Temperley, Nicholas (ed.), *Music in Britain: The Romantic Age 1800–1914* (London: Athlone Press, 1981).

Temperley, Nicholas (ed.), *The Lost Chord: Essays on Victorian Music* (Bloomington, IN: Indiana University Press, 1989).

Tetrazzini, Luisa, *My Life of Song* (London: Cassel & Co., 1921).

Thomson, Aidan, 'Decadence in the forest: Smyth's *Der Wald* in its critical context', in Cornelia Bartsch, Rebecca Grotjahn and Melanie Unseld (eds), *Felsensprengerin, Brückenbauerin, Wegbereiterin: die Komponistin Ethel Smyth* (2 vols, Munich: Allitera Verlag, 2010).

Timms, Susie, *Mapleson: Victorian Opera Impresario* ([no location]: Bezazzy, 2007).

Verney, Frederick, 'A Municipal Concert Hall for London', *Nineteenth Century and After*, 58 (1905), 561–69.

Wagstaff, John, *André Messager: A Bio-Bibliography* (New York: Greenwood Press, 1991).

Walsh, T.J., *Monte Carlo Opera 1879–1909* (Dublin: Gill & MacMillan, 1975).

Ward, John, 'Carl Rosa come to Town: the Opera Season of 1873', *Manchester Sounds*, 5 (2004–05), 5–27.

Watson, Alfred E.T., *A Sporting and Dramatic Career* (London: MacMillan, 1918).

White, Eric Walter, *A register of first performances of English operas and semi-operas: From the 16th century to 1980* (London: Society for Theatre Research, 1980).

White, Eric Walter, *A History of English Opera* (London: Faber, 1983).

Williams, Gordon, *British Theatre in the Great War: A re-evaluation* (London: Continuum, 2003).

Wood, Henry, *My Life of Music* (London: Victor Gollancz, 1938).

Zon, Bennett (ed.), *Nineteenth-Century British Music Studies, Volume 1* (Aldershot: Ashgate, 1999).

Index